ENGLISH AS LANGUAGE

Backgrounds, Development, Usage

CHARLTON LAIRD
ROBERT M. GORRELL
University of Nevada

HARBRACE SOURCEBOOKS

Harcourt, Brace & World, Inc.
New York · Burlingame

Library of Congress Catalog Card Number: 61-9886

Printed in the United States of America

[b·6·61]

ON THE COVER: *A diagram of the letter "A," as an electronic computor changes it into a form it can "understand" and use.*

ACKNOWLEDGMENTS

The editors wish to thank the following for their permission to reproduce material in this book.

American Dialect Society: The selection from David W. Maurer, "The Argot of the Racetrack," *PADS* (Publications of the American Dialect Society), No. 16 (November, 1951). Used by permission of the American Dialect Society. The selection from Herbert Hughes, "A Word List from Louisiana," *PADS*, No. 15 (April, 1951). Used by permission of the American Dialect Society. The selection from Harold B. Allen, "Minor Dialect Areas of the Upper Midwest," *PADS*, No. 30 (November, 1958). Used by permission of the American Dialect Society. The selection from Albert H. Marckwardt, "Principal and Subsidiary Dialect Areas . . . ," *PADS*, No. 27 (April, 1957). Used by permission of the American Dialect Society. The selection from Norman D. Hinton, "The Language of Jazz Musicians," *PADS*, No. 30 (November, 1958). Used by permission of the American Dialect Society.

American Name Society: The selection from Thomas Pyles, "Bible Belt Onomastics or Some Curiosities of Anti-Pedobaptist Nomenclature," *Names*, VII (June, 1959). Used by permission of the American Name Society.

Appleton-Century-Crofts, Inc.: The selection from *Facts about Current English Usage*, by Albert H. Marckwardt and Fred G. Walcott. Copyright, 1938, The National Council of Teachers of English. Material in the selection by Sterling A. Leonard originally published in *Current English Usage*. Used by permission of Appleton-Century-Crofts, Inc. The selection from *A History of the English Language*, by Albert C. Baugh. Second edition copyright © 1957, Appleton-Century-Crofts, Inc. Reprinted by permission of the publishers.

Brandt & Brandt: The selection from C. E. Montague, *A Hind Let Loose*, Doubleday and Company, 1924. Used by permission of Brandt & Brandt.

Thomas Y. Crowell Company: The selection from *Dictionary of American Slang*, compiled by Harold Wentworth and Stuart Berg Flexner. Copyright, 1960, by Thomas Y. Crowell Company, New York, publishers.

The John Day Company, Inc.: The selection from *Grammar Without Tears* by Hugh Sykes Davies, 1953, by permission of The John Day Company, Inc., publisher, and The Bodley Head, Ltd.

E. P. Dutton & Co., Inc.: The selection from Luigi Pirandello, "Six Characters in Search of an Author," in *Naked Masks*, ed. by Eric Bentley, Dutton Everyman Paperbacks, 1952. Used by permission of E. P. Dutton & Co., Inc.

Educational Forum: The selection from Bertrand Evans, "Grammar and Writing," *Educational Forum*, XXIII (January, 1959). Used by permission of *The Educational Forum*.

Fortune: The selection from Suzanne K. Langer, "The Lord of Creation," *Fortune* (January, 1944). Courtesy of Fortune Magazine.

Harcourt, Brace and Company, Inc.: Selection from *Language* by Edward Sapir, copyright, 1921, by Harcourt, Brace and Company, Inc.; copyright, 1949, by Jean V. Sapir. Reprinted by permission of the publishers. The selection from *Babbitt* by Sinclair Lewis, copyright, 1922, by Harcourt, Brace and Company, Inc.; copyright, 1950, by Sinclair Lewis. Reprinted by permission of Harcourt, Brace and Company, Inc.

Harper & Brothers: The selection from *The Bible: A New Translation* by James Moffatt.

Copyright, 1922, 1935 and 1950 by Harper & Brothers. Used by permission of the publishers. The selection from Paul Roberts, *Understanding English*, Harper & Brothers, 1958. Used by permission of the publishers.

Alfred A. Knopf, Inc.: The selection from Sir Ernest Gower, *Plain Words: Their ABC*, Alfred A. Knopf, 1955. Used by permission of the publishers and Lord Conesford.

Methuen and Co., Ltd.: The selection from C. L. Wrenn, *The English Language*, Methuen and Co., 1949. Used by permission of the publishers.

National Council of Teachers of English: The selection from James Sledd, "Grammar or Gramarye?" *English Journal*, XLIX (1960). Used by permission of the National Council of Teachers of English. The selection from John S. Kenyon, "Cultural Levels and Functional Varieties of English," *College English*, X (October, 1948). Used by permission of the National Council of Teachers of English.

Thomas Nelson & Sons: The selection from the Revised Standard Version of the *Bible*. Copyright 1946 and 1952 by the Division of Christian Education of the National Council of Churches and used by permission.

The New Yorker: The selection from James Thurber, "The Weaver and the Worm." Reprinted by permission; © 1956 The New Yorker Magazine, Inc.

The New York *Times:* The selection from J. C. Furnas, "Speaking of Books," New York *Times Book Review* (February 28, 1960). Used by permission of The New York *Times* and the author. The selection from H. Glueck Croce, New York *Times Magazine* (November 29, 1959). Used by permission of The New York *Times*. The selection from an interview with W. Somerset Maugham, in "Topics of the *Times*," New York *Times* (February 4, 1960). Used by permission of The New York *Times*. A selection from a news story, "Heat Put on English," New York *Times* (August 11, 1959). Used by permission of The New York *Times*. A selection from a news story, "U.S. Aide Creates 'Resilrig' English," New York *Times* (November 15, 1959). Used by permission of The New York *Times* and Reuters.

Oxford University Press: The selections from W. H. Fowler, *A Dictionary of Modern English Usage*, Clarendon Press, 1926. Used by permission of the Oxford University Press, N. Y., and the Clarendon Press.

Penguin Books, Ltd.: The selection from Simeon Potter, *Our Language*, Penguin Books, 1950. Used by permission of the publishers.

Philosophical Library: The selection from A. S. Diamond, *History and Origin of Language*, Philosophical Society, 1959. Used by permission of the Philosophical Library.

Prentice-Hall, Inc.: The selection from Stuart Robertson and Frederic G. Cassidy, *Development of Modern English*, 2nd ed. © 1954, Prentice-Hall, Inc., Englewood Cliffs, N. J. Used by permission of the publishers.

The Reporter: "*For Who the Bell Tolls*," from "The Reporter's Notes," December 27, 1956; "Letter to the Editor" by Ellsworth Barnard, from *The Reporter*, January 24, 1957. Reprinted by permission of *The Reporter*.

Paul R. Reynolds & Son: Selection from "Is French Knockouté?" by Joseph Wechsberg, New York *Times Magazine*, June 28, 1959. Used by permission of The New York *Times*, Paul R. Reynolds & Son, 599 Fifth Avenue, New York 17, N. Y., and the author.

The Ronald Press Company: The selection from J. N. Hook and E. G. Mathews, *Modern American Grammar and Usage*. Copyright 1956, The Ronald Press. Used by permission of the publishers.

University of Chicago Press: The selection from Mitford M. Mathews, *A Dictionary of Americanisms on Historical Principles*. Copyright, 1959, by the University of Chicago. Used by permission of the publishers.

University of Michigan Press: The selection from Hans Kurath, *A Word Geography of the Eastern United States*, University of Michigan Press, 1949. Used by permission of the publishers.

The World Publishing Company: The entry for *horse* from *Webster's New World Dictionary of the American Language*, College Edition, copyright 1960 by The World Publishing Company. Used by permission of The World Publishing Company. The selection from Charlton Laird, *The Miracle of Language*, The World Publishing Company, 1953. Used by permission of the publishers. The selection from David B. Guralnik, *The Making of a Dictionary*, The World Publishing Company, 1953. Used by permission of the publishers.

Contents

Introduction

This book brings together selected materials with which the student can grow in his use of language by growing in his knowledge of the way language works, by discovering its workings for himself. It is not intended mainly as a collection of readings, however valuable such collections may be. Roughly, the book falls into three parts: (1) a sequence of informative articles to encourage the student to develop a modern understanding of language and to suggest the multiplicity of modern language study through one procedure, linguistic geography; (2) a body of materials for the study of English from about the year 1000 to today; for the early material editorial apparatus has been supplied which should make even Old English relatively easy; the material offers a spread in time and in dialect distribution, and wherever feasible discussions of language have been used so that the student can observe at once growth in the language and growth in the study of language; (3) a selection of modern controversial discussions of usage, chosen because usage occasions excitement and because even beginning students can do original work in it, whereas they cannot work readily on disputed etymologies. Lack of space precluded contrasting views on other approaches to language. The English language has been used exclusively, partly because it is the native tongue north of the Rio Grande and partly because when one studies language he must study it on the basis of an individual language. This book is about English as language; we hope that the student will progress as rapidly as possible from the study of his native tongue to an awareness of the nature of language itself.

Neither by our selection nor by our comments have we attempted to judge the wisdom, reliability, or accuracy of various writers. Obviously, many of the early selections seem absurd in the light of knowledge revealed in the writings of later scholars. Webster's views on the origins of language or Harris's descriptions of "universal" grammar are interesting, even amusing, historically, but they depend often on misinformation and unjustified preconceptions. We have not consistently pointed out what seem to us inadequacies in such statements, for one purpose of the book is to give the student practice in evaluating evidence; by comparing early statements with the selections from modern scholars, and by relying on his own observations, he can usually judge the reliability of a comment. On questions about which modern writers disagree we have avoided taking sides, although our attitudes may be evident from time to time in the comments or in the nature of our choices.

The study suggestions have various purposes. At the end of each main section are suggestions of two sorts. The first is intended to stimulate study and discussion of major issues in language, the second to provide specific topics which individuals or panels may investigate and report upon or which the teacher may use to assign brief papers. Inevitably, these two lists are not mutually exclusive. Suggestions for longer papers appear at the end; these, again, are of two sorts. Some can be used if the instructor wishes to control all materials and to require fairly long papers which can be written from the book itself; others will send the student to the library to supplement the materials which he has already canvassed in his text.

So that they can serve as sources for such subjects as the history of spelling and punctuation, the selections have been reproduced as nearly in their original form as seemed feasible. When anything has been modernized, the changes are noticed in the headnote introducing the selection. Early transcriptions of Old English have been rendered in modern type, a few obvious typographical errors in modern articles have been corrected, and footnotes have sometimes been expanded into standard forms; but in general the texts reproduce the originals. Omissions are indicated by the standard ellipses (. . .). Footnotes in the selections retain their original numbers; sometimes, therefore, because of omissions, numbers are not consecutive. Translations are provided for passages that a modern reader cannot easily understand.

Whenever possible, we have attempted to provide machinery so that reference can be made to the original printing of the text from which each selection is taken. The headnotes for each selection include information about the edition of the work which provided copy for the selection, and within the text, between slant bars, the end of each page is recorded. Thus, a footnote to a quotation from the selection from Sheridan could read

> Thomas Sheridan, *A General Dictionary of the English Language* (Dublin, 1784), p. viii.

This indicates that the material occurs before the indicated /viii/, which marks the end of page viii of the original. Scrupulous practice would require reference to the present text also, since the student presumably has not consulted the original. If full bibliographical details for this volume have been given in an earlier footnote, the following would suffice:

> Thomas Sheridan, *A General Dictionary of the English Language* (Dublin, 1784), p. viii; in Laird and Gorrell, p. 159.

In some of the older books, pages are not numbered; for these reference is made to signature marks (for example, *A2*, or *A2ᵛ*, for the verso of page A2). If the page is not identified in any way, we have supplied the apparent pagination within brackets. No pages are indicated for quotations from alphabetically arranged vocabularies in dictionaries, since reference can be made directly to the entry:

> William Kenrick, *A New English Dictionary of the English Language* (London, 1773), under *horse*.

Charlton Laird
Robert M. Gorrell

January 3, 1961

I. A LANGUAGE MISCELLANY

One of the most obvious testimonials to the importance of language is the extent and the variety of comments about it. Hundreds of people, whether serious students of language or not, have had things to say about language — praising it, trying to explain it, observing its peculiarities. Following are random observations that in one way or another concern language.

Language is the highest and most amazing achievement of the symbolistic human mind. The power it bestows is almost inestimable, for without it anything properly called "thought" is impossible. The birth of language is the dawn of humanity. The line between man and beast — between the highest ape and the lowest savage — is the language line. Whether the primitive Neanderthal man was anthropoid or human depends less on his cranial capacity, his upright posture, or even his use of tools and fire, than on one issue we shall probably never be able to settle — whether or not he spoke. — Susanne K. Langer, "The Lord of Creation," *Fortune*, January, 1944.

Language, as well as the faculty of speech, was the immediate gift of God. — Noah Webster, *American Dictionary*, 1828.

In his whole life man achieves nothing so great and so wonderful as what he achieved when he learnt to talk. — Ascribed to "a Danish philosopher" in Otto Jespersen, *Language*, 1922.

Most people, asked if they can think without speech, would probably answer, "Yes, but it is not easy for me to do so. Still I know it can be done." Language is but a garment! But what if language is not so much a garment as a prepared road or groove? It is, indeed, in the highest degree likely that language is an instrument originally put to uses lower than the conceptual plane and that thought arises as a refined interpretation of its content. The product grows, in other words, with the instrument, and thought may be no more conceivable, in its genesis and daily practice, without speech than is mathematical reasoning practicable without the lever of an appropriate mathematical symbolism. — Edward Sapir, *Language*, 1921.

Language, in its most important and characteristic aspect, is the reverse of what it is generally supposed to be. Instead of consisting of a bundle of labels which name the thing to which they are attached, it rather consists of labels which obtain their meaning from the things to which they are attached; and these things, like all else in the world, are forever changing, and with them changes the meaning of the labels. — A. S. Diamond, *The History and Origin of Language*, 1959.

Language is the armory of the human mind; and at once contains the trophies of its past, and the weapons of its future conquests. — Samuel Taylor Coleridge, *Biographia Literaria*, 1817.

A man is worth as many men as he knows languages. — Ascribed to Charles V, Holy Roman Emperor, 1500-1558.

Language is ever needing to be recalled, minted, and issued anew. — Archbishop Richard C. Trench, *Parables*, 1877.

O harsh lips! I now hear all around me such words as *common, vices, envy, malice;* even *virtue, study, justice, pity, mercy, compassion, profit, commodity, colour, grace, favor, acceptance.* But whither, I pray in all the world, have you banished those words which our forefathers used for these new-fangled ones? Are our words to be exiled like our citizens? Is the new barbaric invasion to extirpate the English tongue? — Alexander Gill, *Logonomia Anglica*, 1619.

English, which when the Anglo-Saxons first conquered England in the fifth and sixth centuries was almost a "pure" or unmixed language — which could make new words for new ideas from its own compounded elements and had hardly any foreign words — has become the most "mixed" of languages, having received throughout its history all kinds of foreign elements with ease and assimilated them all to its own character. — C. L. Wrenn, *The English Language*, 1949.

Custom is the most certain mistress of language, as the public stamp makes the current money. — Ben Jonson, *Grammar*, 1640.

Hamburger, a humble immigrant meat that came to this country from Germany and soared to fame on a bun, has lately been causing a stir among the French, who have always snubbed it as parvenu. As part of a drive against high food prices, the National Confederation of French Butchery is now urging people to buy fewer fancy cuts of beef and try those of lesser status, chopped and sold as "viande hachée" (also known as hamburger, pronounced "om-bour-*zhay*"). — Grace H. Glueck, the New York *Times Magazine*, November 29, 1959.

I have an idea that in two or three hundred years English will be the universal language spoken all over the world. Of course, it won't be the English we speak now; it will probably be even more strange than the language of Chaucer is to us now, but it will be founded on the language of today. — W. Somerset Maugham, interview on the eve of his eighty-sixth birthday (quoted in the New York *Times*, February 4, 1960).

Our Children are not Witches, that they should guess to Read Right by the Letter, . . . and the Masters are no very great Conjurers, to perceive nothing; what contradictions they make 'em swallow.

First then dayes, that is da — yes, why should not yes spell yes at the end, as well as at the beginning of a word: Again, why might we not spell dayes thus, daise as well as praise, and spell praises, prayes [*sic*], da — i — se: I see day, why not se, see, as well as he, h —? And why not dase, dayes, and phrayes, phrase, or phraise, phrase, and daze, dayes; and why not daze, or dase, daisey, or daisy, hei, daisy: how can Ladies be blam'd for Writing bad English, when Scholars spell no better? — G. W. [John White?], *Magazines, Or, Animadversions on the English Spelling,* 1703.

A member of *L'Office du Vocabulaire Français* claims they do not seek to ostracize foreign words but merely to regulate their entry. "The object is to guard against words that are used through ignorance and snobbishness when adequate French equivalents are available." As an example of an "adequate French equivalent" he quotes *homme d'affaires* instead of "business man." (He was not sure whether a French business woman would like to be called *une femme d'affaires,* especially if she has one.) . . . The O. V. F. took several polls (some incorrigibles call them "gall*ups*"), querying people in various walks of life about whether certain indispensable English words ("sex appeal"?) should be adopted and in what form, and whether certain English words ("strip tease"?) should be Frenchified, and in what way. — Joseph Wechsberg, the New York *Times Magazine,* June 28, 1959.

Spanish is the language for lovers, Italian for singers, French for diplomats, German for horses, and English for geese. — Spanish proverb.

When the American Ambassador tells us, in some degree at least seriously, that better English is spoken in America than in England, it is really a little too much. . . . The Americans are rich. They are, or seem to be, confident of themselves. They excel at the business of games. They make things "hum." But it is absurd to pretend they speak good English. Their English, and their spelling of English . . . are most unpleasant. Their twang is sometimes so. — *Saturday Review* (London), December 13, 1913.

The first white cherry blossoms flickered down a gully and robins clamoured.

Babbitt . . . driving a good motor . . . stopped . . . to have the petrol tank filled.

The familiar rite fortified him; the sight of the tall red-iron petrol-pump, the hollow-tile and terra-cotta garage, the window full of the most agreeable accessories—shiny casings, sparking-plugs with immaculate porcelain jackets, tyre-chains of gold and silver.

[Later] he shouted at a respectable-looking man who was waiting for a tramway car, "Have a lift? . . . it's a fellow's duty to share the good things of this world with his neighbours. . . ."

Babbitt fell into a great silence and devoted himself to the game of beating tramway cars to the corner: a spurt, a tail-chase, nervous speeding between the huge yellow side of the tram and the jagged row of parked motors, shooting past just as the tram stopped . . . past groceries and laundries and chemist shops. . . . Hoardings with crimson goddesses nine feet tall advertising cinema films. . . . Then the business centre, the thickening darting traffic, the crammed trams unloading, and high doorways of marble and polished granite. — Sinclair Lewis, *Babbitt*, London, Panther edition, 1959.

They put the king's English to death so charmingly. — Edward G. G. Howard, *Rattlin' the Reefer*, 1836.

The Patent Office has discovered that the English language is too complex and ambiguous to be understood by modern computers. So it is creating a new vocabulary with sounds which if alien to the human ear, will fit well on a magnetic tape.

The new language is called "ruly English" in contrast to everyday "unruly English." . . . [The new vocabulary deals] with the problem of indicating differences in degree between two qualifying words such as resilience and rigidity. The "ruly" word for that is "resilrig," which serves as a root for various prefixes. A somewhat rigid object would be "sli (slightly) resilrig" while a very flexible one would be "sub (substantially) resilrig."

In the same manner "adornblem" (from adorn and blemish) refers to a pleasing or displeasing visual appearance. Its modifiers are again "sli (slightly) adornblem," or displeasing to the eye, and "mat (materially) adornblem," which would refer to something rather attractive. — Special dispatch to the New York *Times*, November 16, 1958.

An anonymous writer in the august London *Times Literary Supplement* is unhappy about the British edition of a recent American translation from the French of "Portrait of a Man Unknown" by Nathalie Sarraute. The sore point is not the quality of the novel or the faithfulness of the rendering but the "Americanisms" in the text, including "even the American spelling." Surmising that the book was reproduced "By some sort of photo-lithographic process from the American edition," this cultivated viewer-with-alarm goes on:

"By reason of relative costs we are likely to see more of this. It is the kind of thing about which people get cross." — New York *Times Book Review*, February 28, 1960.

A purist today took issue with British use of "meaningless prepositions in the American manner."

F. E. Bailey, in a letter to the *Daily Telegraph*, complained about a story headed "Facing up to the heat."

He declared that since World War II British newspapers had been spattered with such phrases and the result "is murder for an English child learning its own language."

Mr. Bailey, the purist, declared:

"One does not meet up with one's girl friend, one meets her.

"One does not sit in on a committee, one sits on it.

"One does not test out a car, one tests it.

"Nor does one try out a horse, or a recipe, one tries them." — Reuters dispatch from London, August 10, 1959.

Have you shuddered as I have at the appearance of the pleonastic "like"? E.g., "You like take a bus up Seventh Avenue," or "You turn left at the corner like." Is this American, or is there a Cockney echo in it like? — Unpublished correspondence.

In order to illustrate the progress (or whatever it is) of our language I am compiling a brochure on bottlenecks. I shall accordingly be grateful for any significant additions to these examples from recent journalism:

1. "The biggest bottleneck in housing," meaning the worst, most constricting, and presumably narrowest bottleneck.

2. "Bottlenecks must be ironed out" (leading article in the daily press).

3. "Bottlenecks ahead" and "Bottleneck in bottles" (recent headlines).

4. "The economy of the Ruhr is bound to move within a vicious circle of interdependent bottlenecks."

5. "What is planned is actually a series of bottlenecks. The most drastic bottleneck is that of machine tools."

6. "One bottleneck . . . which is particularly far-reaching and decisive."

[In a later publication.] Before leaving my Hon. Friend, I must thank him for adding his delightful "overriding bottleneck" to my celebrated collection of bottlenecks. Hitherto, my favourites were the "drastic bottleneck," the "vicious circle of interdependent bottlenecks," and, perhaps the best of the whole collection, the "worldwide bottleneck." — Henry Strauss, quoted in Sir Ernest Gowers, *Plain Words: Their A B C*, 1954.

A weaver watched in wide-eyed wonder a silkworm spinning its cocoon in a white mulberry tree.

"Where do you get that stuff?" asked the admiring weaver.

"Do you want to make something out of it?" inquired the silkworm, eagerly.

Then the weaver and the silkworm went their separate ways, for each thought the other had insulted him. We live, man and worm, in a time when almost everything can mean almost anything, for this is the age of gobbledygook, double-talk, and gudda.

Moral: A word to the wise is not sufficient if it doesn't make any sense. — James Thurber, "The Weaver and the Worm," *New Yorker*, August 11, 1956.

THE FATHER. But don't you see that the whole trouble lies here. In words, words. Each one of us has within him a whole world of things, each man of us his own special world. And how can we ever come to an understanding if I put in the words I utter the sense and value of things as I see them; while you who listen to me must inevitably translate them according to the conception of things each one of you has within himself. We think we understand each other, but we never really do. — Luigi Pirandello, *Six Characters in Search of an Author*, 1921.

But with Dick it had passed as a thing of course that in chaff and in politics words were used not as themselves but as something less, as you might use cricket-bats for lighting fires, or train sweet-peas up fly-rods. Not till now had he seen, with eyes fully open, the rite of splashing solemnly about in a vocabulary, for splashing's sake, the preference for just jingling, for the sound they made, the bunch of keys that, rightly turned in the locks, were inlets to gardens by rivers in Bagdad. And the strangest thing of all was connoisseurship in the practice; to a man like his uncle there were, it would seem, a better and a worse in the trade of making words stand for nothing; there were qualities of nullity, degrees of skill in keeping mind and heart blank; the void was not all one, nor zero a level. — C. E. Montague, *A Hind Let Loose*, 1924.

VIOLA. They that dally nicely with words may quickly make them wanton.

CLOWN. I would, therefore, my sister had had no name, sir.

VIOLA. Why, man?

CLOWN. Why, sir, her name's a word; and to dally with that word might make my sister wanton. But indeed words are very rascals since bonds disgraced them.

VIOLA. Thy reason, man?

CLOWN. Troth, sir, I can yield you none without words; and words are grown so false, I am loath to prove reason with them.

— William Shakespeare, *Twelfth Night*, III, i, 17-29.

Subjects for Discussion

1. Some of the preceding observations appear to be the result of prolonged thought or study and deep conviction; others are relatively trivial, even petulant or bad tempered. Which of the observations would you put in which class? Are there some that you would put in still another class?

2. In the British edition of Lewis's *Babbitt*, a work which enjoys a world reputation as an accurate picture of a segment of American life in the period after the first World War, the spellings of words, and even some words themselves, have been changed from American to British idiom. Which words in the quoted passage can you identify as being not American usage? Is British writing printed in the United States with British or American spelling? Can you give examples? What would be the reaction in England and America to printing British classics in American idiom? For example, what would be the reaction to making Gabriel Oak, the shepherd in Thomas Hardy's *Far from the Madding Crowd*, talk like a Montana sheepherder?

3. Can you find in these quotations evidence that language and society are or are not interdependent?

4. Various observers have various attitudes toward language. Some of the writers quoted here seem to be thinking of language as an important human characteristic. Others seem to think of it as the private possession of a restricted group of people. Cite two examples of each of these attitudes. Describe other attitudes toward language which seem to you to be behind some of the statements.

5. What basic differences in attitudes toward language are apparent in the statements of Alexander Gill and C. L. Wrenn?

6. What attitudes toward the relative merits of British and American English are revealed in the comments?

II. LANGUAGE AS IT WORKS

Alexander Pope long ago reminded us that the proper study of mankind is man. He might have added that language, man's greatest invention, is also unusually worthy of study. The more we learn about language the more we understand that it is not only the means of our communication and the instrument with which we have preserved our civilization, but that it is also the instrument with which, more than any other, our brains work. With the development of a sense of symbol and creativity — with language — man became human. When we study language we are studying one of the mighty forces that have made man what he is and may yet help to make him something better.

Man has not always studied language, and when he did study it, he often had little sound basis on which to work. Man has been using language for tens of thousands of years, probably for hundreds of thousands. During most of this time he presumably did not think much about language or even talk about it, any more than he talked about learning to walk or to focus his eyes; he just used language, and went on building it, mainly unconsciously. When man did start to study language, to find out what it is and how it works, he knew so little about it that he made unreliable assumptions which did much to vitiate what might otherwise have been good work. For example, he assumed that God gave man perfected language as a single gift, that language readily becomes corrupted but that man can keep it "pure" or return it to an earlier purity, that to have a good language man should "fix" it in the sense of determining an absolute form for it, and that once he has it fixed he should enforce rules so that it will not change. Western Europeans — and correspondingly, Americans — assumed that all languages would be essentially like western European languages.

All these assumptions now seem to us erroneous, not to say silly. Languages have been changing and growing, and not mainly decaying, for the thousands of years for which we have linguistic records — and these records antedate October 4, 4004 B.C., when Bishop Butler supposed God gave man language. If God ever gave man language as a single gift, apparently the gift needed a good bit of tinkering before it would work adequately for a sophisticated culture; we can infer that it had been growing for tens of thousands of years prior to the period for which we have direct evidence.

Nor is the notion that language should be purified any longer plausible. What does "pure" mean? Pure what? Purified of what? If "pure" means unchanged, uninfluenced by any other language, or uniform, no such language exists. Even if we could purify a language we should not know how to begin; we should not know what to do to it to make it pure. All the great languages are hodgepodges; in fact, one might plausibly infer the greater the hodgepodge the greater the language. At the very least, purity would seem not to be the ultimate virtue in language; "purity," apparently, has usually meant what I speak as against what you speak, or sometimes the language of the "best" people. The trouble is that the "best" people do not always speak the best language, if by "best" in language we mean the clearest, the most vigorous, the most precise, or the most inspired.

What of the third assumption, that a language can be fixed with rules? No language ever has been; presumably no language ever will be. In the seventeenth and eighteenth centuries the great French Academy, assuming that the French language was at that time perfect and could only decline if left to its own devices, prepared a monumental dictionary to "fix" it just as it was. The dictionary required the extended labors of many learned men; it has great value as a study of French at a certain point in its growth, but it failed almost completely of its supposed purpose. The French language, like all languages, went gaily on its way, changing in ways that the French Academy had never anticipated. If it was affected at all by the dictionary and the Academy's rules, we do not know how. As for the fourth assumption, that all languages are like western European languages, few assertions could be more fantastically wrong, although even today many well-read people accept the assumption without ever phrasing it. Some languages are so foreign to speech like English, French, and Latin that they do not rely mainly on words or sentences as speakers of English define these terms.

If, then, we can not purify language, or keep it from changing, or refine it into what we may assume it should be, what can we do? At least we can attempt to find out what it is and how it works. We shall not help language or ourselves if we accept false assumptions, and we may not be able to discover reliable answers to all our questions. But an understanding of language seems to promote the use of language, both as a means of thinking and expressing the results of our thinking, and as a means of approaching the thinking that others have done.

If we are to study language, what information do we need in order to start? We cannot hope to absorb modern knowledge about language; only an expert who spends many years at the job can do that. But we should be able to assemble a few fundamental principles and enough selected data to see how these principles reveal language. The following are certainly among these principles:

1. All languages seem to have been always changing; presumably they have always changed, are changing now, and will continue to change in spite of anything we or anyone else can do to stop them.

2. When language changes it does so in accordance with tendencies having a considerable degree of regularity, tendencies which may conflict, but which can be described psychologically, sociologically, and linguistically.

3. Language seems to have grown notably by language families and by dialects within languages. Back of the changes incident to this growth stands the ideolect, the individual's way of speaking, which will differ at least slightly from the ideolect of every other speaker.

4. Insofar as we know, language is made and preserved by people using it, and only by people using it, although this use may be considerably altered by people who think, talk, and write about language.

5. Written language is very important, and has been particularly important in the last few decades, but language as we know it has always had an oral basis and it will probably continue to be essentially oral.

To these statements about language we might add one observation: scholars have now built up a great body of information about language that would seem to be reliable, along with remarkable techniques for studying it. This second section of the book is intended to summarize some of the most important knowledge requisite to any study of language and to suggest some of the newer linguistic techniques.

1.   J. N. HOOK AND E. G. MATHEWS

The Families of Languages

Relationships among languages are as complicated as those among human families; discovering and describing kinships has been a fascinating and important work of the scholars of language. The following outline of some major relationships is from J. N. Hook and E. G. Mathews, *Modern American Grammar and Usage* (New York, 1956).

Although we may never be able to say precisely how language began, we know that men speak diverse tongues, we know of some languages that have become extinct, and we may suppose that the number of extinct languages exceeds the number of modern languages in possibly as great a ratio as dead human beings exceed live ones. According to a study made in 1939 by Louis H. Gray, 2796 languages, exclusive of dialects, are spoken in the twentieth century. There is reason to believe that tens of thousands of languages have become extinct, often leaving no visible trace.

Living languages fall into groups called families. The usual estimate is that approximately two hundred such families exist, although the number may be shown to be smaller if study of the so-called primitive languages reveals some now unknown relationships.

Only on a prolonged world tour would an American traveler be likely to encounter representatives of many of these families: one family, the Indo-European, he would find again and again. If he flew to the Far East he would encounter Indo-Chinese in China, Thailand, Burma, and Tibet (although the family relationship between Chinese-Siamese and Burmese-Tibetan is not definitely known); Indo-Chinese and Indo-European languages are spoken by more persons than are any others. Mongolian is not Chinese; it appears to be more closely related to Turkish and Finnish. Some of the languages of central

Asia are hardly known to the outside world. In Japan /11/ the traveler would find another language, very different from Chinese, and in Korea he would hear speech that may possibly be related to Japanese; in northern Japan he would find Ainu, apparently not related to Japanese. In India he would encounter Indo-European, although he most certainly would not recognize in Hindi, Bengali, Singhalese, and other languages anything related to his own; still different would be the Dravidian languages of southern India, which belong to another family. Oceania speaks primarily Malayo-Polynesian, but Dutch, French, English, and other Indo-European languages would be found side by side with the native tongues. Australia to the American would appear an English-speaking country, but in the hinterlands he would discover complex primitive languages.

If our traveler headed westward across the Indian Ocean to Africa, he would find representatives of more families of languages, including various Negro, Negrito, Sudanic tongues, and in North Africa languages such as Berber, Hebrew, and Ethiopic. Crossing the Mediterranean, he would discover many varieties of Indo-European; except for the Basques, Finns, Hungarians, and Turks, nearly all Europeans speak an Indo-European language. Crossing the Atlantic to the Americas, the traveler would still find Indo-European in the ascendancy, but if he were curious about the native languages of North American and South American Indians, he would find them not only distinct from Indo-European but also from one another. Some linguists estimate that there are as many as 150 existing Indian languages in North America, in possibly as many as 50 families.

Attempts, not entirely satisfactory, have been made to point out the distinctive traits of the most important families of language. Indo-European, the only family with which most Americans are familiar, was originally highly inflected, although some modern Indo-European languages, notably English, have lost many inflections. The term "inflectional" implies /12/ that many words change their forms to indicate their syntactic relationships with other words. Thus English *the girl runs*, in the plural becomes *the girls run;* Latin *puella amat* (the girl loves) shows inflectional change in *puellam amat* ([someone] loves the girl). French uses a variety of endings for the word *courir* (run) to show differences in person or time. English *long* employs the forms *longer* and *longest* to show degrees of comparison, and German has similar forms in *lang, länger, längst.* In some Indo-European languages other modifications are made to indicate what grammarians call case, gender, mood, and voice. The various modifying elements may occur within a word or at either the beginning or the end.

The "agglutinative" languages are somewhat like the inflectional, and occasionally overlap, but make still more extensive use of prefixes and suffixes, each of which is likely to carry as distinct a meaning as a separate "word." Examples of the agglutinative languages are Finnish, Hungarian, Turkish, and to some extent Japanese.

Some nineteenth and twentieth century grammarians have also referred to the "incorporating" languages, represented by many Amerindian tongues, which virtually obliterate the distinction between word and sentence by incorporating in a single word a rather complex thought, such as "I chased the buffalo over the hill." Jespersen said, "Primitive linguistic units must have been much more complicated in point of meaning, as well as much longer in point of sound, than those with which we are most familiar." Many of those linguistic units we should probably classify as words.

At the far extreme from the incorporating languages are the "isolating," of which the Indo-Chinese tongues are the major ones. Chinese depends upon word order and upon separate modifying words to secure the effects that inflection provides in Indo-European; in addition, in spoken Chinese, variations in tone are more important in conveying meaning than /13/ they are in most other languages. English, interestingly enough, through its centuries of losing inflections, has almost become an isolating language. French provides another example of a tendency away from inflection; although derived from Latin, French is not nearly so highly inflected as is Latin, and many inflectional endings that remain in French spelling are not revealed in pronunciation.

The distinctions between families of languages are not firm boundary lines. Just as two human families may share certain characteristics, so may two families of languages. Characteristics of inflectional languages may overlap those of the isolating; for instance, English now depends almost as much upon word order as does Chinese. Or inflectional languages may overlap the agglutinative, as in such an ordinary English word as *unlovable*, which adds a prefix and a suffix to the root word to convey the meaning "not capable of being loved." Inflectional languages may even overlap the incorporating; in Latin, for instance, one word may express the sentence idea, "I had been walking." The descriptions of family characteristics, then, are only rough and general, subject to exceptions.

Of greatest interest to Americans is the Indo-European family, for English is one member of one group within that family. The generally recognized Indo-European groups are Indo-Iranian, Balto-Slavic, Hellenic, Italic, Celtic, Armenian, Albanian, and Teutonic (Germanic).

Important members of the Indo-Iranian group are Kashmiri, Bengali, Hindi, Panjabi, Singhalese, Romany, Afghan, Persian, Kurdish, and certain extinct languages such as Sanskrit, Prakrit, and Avestan. (An extinct language may have living descendants, but is not itself spoken or written today, except possibly by certain scholars.) Balto-Slavic includes Bulgarian, Serbo-Croatian, Slovenian, Russian, White Russian, Ukrainian, Czechoslovak, Sorbian, Polish, Lithuanian, and /14/ Lettish. Hellenic is Greek, including the extinct Ionic, Attic, Doric, and Aeolic, as well as Modern Greek. Italic consists of the extinct Oscan, Umbrian, Sabellian, and Latin, and the living descendants of Latin: chiefly French, Spanish, Portuguese, Italian, and Romanian. Celtic includes Welsh, Breton, Irish, Gaelic, Manx, and the extinct Gaulish and Cornish. Hittite and Tocharian are extinct languages, evidently Indo-European, but too little is known of them to place them with much accuracy.

The Teutonic or Germanic group is subdivided as follows:

East: Gothic (now extinct)

North: Old Norse (extinct), Icelandic, Swedish, Danish, Norwegian

West (High): Old High German (extinct), Bavarian (extinct), Middle High German (extinct), German

West (Low): Old Saxon (extinct), Low German (Plattdeutsch), Dutch, Flemish, Frisian, Old English (extinct), Middle English (extinct), English

Linguists who have made intensive studies of Indo-European languages explain their common characteristics in this way: Before the dawn of writing a rather homogeneous group of people lived perhaps in the part of Russia formerly identified as Lithuania (or maybe in the Crimea) and perhaps were spread through much of northern and central Europe. They spoke a highly inflected language of which we have no direct documentary evidence because they did not read and write. As the centuries passed, these people extended their influence through travel and conquest, penetrating eventually as far as the subcontinent that we call India. They intermarried with people speaking other languages, and they made their homes in most of Europe and in large parts of Asia. Because of intermarriage, because of scanty communication, and because of a seemingly inevitable tendency for languages in different regions to become more and more disparate, the one original language became a number of languages. They still retained inflection as a common characteristic, and they still kept, often in altered /15/ form, many of the words in the original vocabulary. As long ago as the eighteenth century, Sir William Jones noted the similarities among Indo-European languages; in 1867 W. D. Whitney pointed out such parallels as these:

English	Lithuanian	Celtic	Latin	Greek	Persian	Sanskrit
three	tri	tri	tres	treis	thri	tri
seven	septyni	secht	septem	hepta	hapta	sapta
me	manen	me	me	me	me	me
mother	moter	mathair	mater	meter	matar	matar
brother	brolis	brathair	frater	phrater		bhratar
night	naktis		noctis	nuktos		nakta

When the descendants of primitive Indo-European became highly diversified languages, those people who had settled in India could no longer converse with their fellows who had settled in France or in Russia. Soon they lost all memory of a common linguistic heritage. Not until comparative grammarians of the nineteenth century studied painstakingly a host of languages did the common elements become apparent.

Each group of languages within the family acquired its own characteristics. It is impossible to describe here the peculiarities of the other linguistic groups, but five distinctive features of the Teutonic group may be briefly noted.

In Teutonic languages the accent became fixed upon the root syllable of a word. Thus *love* in its various forms is pronounced *lov'able, lov'ing, be-*

lov'ed, un love'ly. In contrast Latin *a'mo* (I love) is accented on the first syllable, but *a mā'mus* (we love) is accented on the second. If you are familiar with Greek or with Latin or any of its descendants, you can think of other examples, to be contrasted with the fixed accents of most English or German words. Not every Teutonic word possesses stability of accent, but enough do for us to consider this quality a characteristic of the group.

A second characteristic is that Teutonic languages tend to use auxiliaries, or helpers, with basic verbs to indicate various /16/ tenses, voices, and moods, but the other Indo-European languages usually employ single verb forms. English *I was calling* is equivalent to Latin *vocābam; I shall call, vocābō; I shall be called, vocābor; I shall have called, vocāvèrō;* (if) *I were called, vocārer*. Latin does employ some auxiliary verbs in the passive voice, and its descendants sometimes employ them in the active as well (*e.g.* French *j' étais venu = I had come,* and Spanish *yo habré enseñado = I shall have taught*). But in general the verb forms in Teutonic are simpler than the others, once one has learned the significance and the order of auxiliaries. Much of the simplicity is attributed to the use of the auxiliaries, and some to the loss of complex voice, number, and tense forms.

The Teutonic verb differs from other Indo-European verbs in its formation of the past tense. Typically the Teutonic past tense is formed by the addition of *-ed* (*-te* in German) to the basic verb form. In other languages more drastic changes are necessary, as in the Latin use of the endings *-bam, -bās, -bat, -bāmus, -bātis, -bant*. In English the past tense of *play* is *played* for all three persons and for both singular and plural. German is a little less simple, with the forms *spielte, spieltest, spielte, spielten, spieltet, spielten*. The Teutonic verbs that employ an *-ed* or a *-t* or a *-te* in the past are usually called "weak" or "regular"; a second group, containing such verbs as *sing* and *write*, are the "strong" or "irregular" verbs. This twofold classification is certainly not to the advantage of Teutonic languages (the modern English strong verbs, for instance, cause endless difficulty), but it is nevertheless definitely easier for a nonnative to learn than are the manifold conjugations that exist in the Italic and most other Indo-European languages.

A fourth characteristic of Teutonic no longer exists in English, although it formerly did. This is a double declension of adjectives. German still retains this useless feature, which complicates still further an already complicated pattern. In brief, the principle is that an adjective preceding a noun takes a "strong" ending which shows case, number, and gender, unless /17/ the adjective follows a word like *der* which already does the same work. After a word like *der* the adjectival ending is "weak." But if the adjective follows a word equivalent to English *to be*, it takes no ending at all. So we have *ein kleiner Bruder* (a little brother), *der kleine Bruder* (the little brother), *Mein Bruder ist klein* (My brother is little). The Scandinavian languages and Dutch possess a similar declension of adjectives.

Finally, Teutonic differs from other Indo-European languages in that early Teutonic underwent a shifting of consonants that did not take place elsewhere, even though different shifts occurred in other languages. Although the Danish Rasmus Rask probably discovered this shift, its description is customarily called "Grimm's Law" because Jacob Grimm first made it generally known. A simplified explanation of the Rask-Grimm discovery is this: An unknown number of centuries ago, in Teutonic, the Indo-European *bh*, *dh*, and *gh* became *b*, *d*, and *g* respectively; in words already pronounced with *b*, *d*, and *g* these sounds shifted to *p*, *t*, and *k*; *p*, *t*, and *k* changed to *f*, *th*, and *h*. Knowing this principle, we can often see previously unsuspected relationships between English words and, say, Latin. For example, consider the Latin *piscis*. Latin underwent no shift, but in Teutonic *p* changed to *f*. Thus Latin *piscis*, Old Norse *fiskr*, Old English *fisc*, and German *Fisch* are essentially the same. Latin *pecu* (money) is the equivalent of Old English *feoh* (Modern English *fee*), in which we have *f* instead of *p*, *h* instead of *c*. English *tooth* may be seen as a cousin to Sanskrit *dant-* (Latin *dent-*, Greek *odont-*). The similarities in these words you can spot rather easily by noting how Grimm's Law applies: *tu, thou; tres, three; cord-, heart; corn-, horn; can-, hound*.

Within the Teutonic group English is most closely related to Frisian, a language spoken by a few hundred thousand inhabitants of the Netherlands and the North Sea coastal islands, and now considerably overlaid with Dutch. Dutch itself, the variant of Dutch spoken in parts of Belgium and called Flem- /18/ ish, and the Low German spoken in the "lowlands" of northern Germany are also near relatives of English.

High German, which is the literary German taught in schools, belongs in the West Teutonic group with English, Dutch, Low German, and their variants. It is less closely related to English than the other languages are because the Angles, Saxons, and Jutes who settled England were from northern Germany, not the southern part which is the home of High German. The differences between English and High German seem greater than they really are, however, because of a consonant shift that occurred in High German but not in English, Dutch, or Low German. The German word *tief* does not resemble its English synonym *deep*, but when one learns that in High German a shift occurred from *d* to *t* and another from *p* to *f*, he sees that the two words are basically the same. *Ding* and *thing*, *dies* and *this*, *kalt* and *cold*, *Katze* and *cat*, *Pfeffer* and *pepper*, *Grabe* and *grave* are among the rather large number of pairs of words that would today be virtually the same had the High German consonant shift not occurred. In this shift the sound that remained as *d* in English became *t* in German; *t* became *z, tz*, or *s; th* became *d* (an interesting parallel appears in the speech of certain Americans who say *dis* and *dat* instead of *this* and *that*); *p* usually became *pf or f*; *v* often became *b*; and *k* sometimes became *ch*. Knowing of this shift, an American studying German may rather quickly add a large number of words to those in which no shift is involved but which he already recognizes as the equivalent of English: *Maus, mouse; Fleisch, flesh; Flunder, flounder; Eis, ice; Schweinefett, lard* (*swine fat*); and hundreds of others. /19/

2. PAUL ROBERTS

A Brief History of English

Professor Paul Roberts has specialized in applications of the modern study of language to the teaching of English, both abroad in Italy and Egypt, and through textbooks published in this country. The following selection is taken from *Understanding English* (New York, 1958). In the portion of the chapter not here reprinted, Roberts sketches the historical background of the origin of English. He points out that the Romans had occupied the island of Britain from about 43 A.D. to sometime in the fourth century, civilizing and later Christianizing the more amenable of the Celts who were then living there, particularly in the less mountainous areas of the island. When the Romans withdrew because of troubles on the Continent which threatened Rome, peoples from the northern coast of Europe speaking various dialects of Low West Germanic moved in, the Angles to the east and north, the Saxons to the south and west, and Jutes in the southeast corner. They were pagans, and compared with the Romans relatively unsophisticated people, hunters, fishers, and simple farmers. During some two centuries after about 400 A.D. they overcame the Celts, battled with one another to establish little kingdoms, were formally converted to Christianity, and established some relationships with the Irish Celts to the west and the Continental peoples to the east and south. By the late seventh century they had learned to read and write enough to record their language, which we call Anglo-Saxon or Old English. These peoples, along with the Celts they had subdued, continued to form the basic population of the island, although in the late ninth century it was overrun by Danes and Norwegians, commonly known as Norsemen, and in 1066 it was overcome by another body of northerners who had adopted Frankish culture and were known as Normans. From changes associated with these and later developments, English is usually divided into the following chronological periods: Old English, from the beginnings to about 1100; Middle English, 1100 to 1500; Modern English, 1500 to today. Modern English is often divided into Early Modern English, 1500 to 1700; Late Modern English, after 1700.

We may now have an example of Old English. The favorite illustration is the Lord's Prayer, since it needs no translation. This has come to us in several different versions. Here is one:

Fæder ure þu ðe eart on heofonum si þin nama gehalgod. Tobecume þin rice. Gewurðe þin willa on eorðan swa swa on heofonum. Urne gedæghwamlican hlaf syle us to dæg. And forgyf us ure gyltas swa swa we forgyfaþ urum gyltendum. And ne gelæd þu us on costnunge ac alys us of yfele. Soðlice.

Some of the differences between this and Modern English are merely differences in orthography. For instance, the sign *æ* is what Old English writers used for a vowel sound like that in modern *hat* or *and*. The *th* sounds or modern *thin* or *then* are represented in Old English by þ or ð. But of course there are many differences in sound too. *Ure* is the ancestor of modern *our*, but the first vowel was like that in *too* or *ooze*. *Hlaf* is modern *loaf;* we have dropped the *h* sound and changed the vowel, which in *hlaf* was pronounced something like the vowel in *father*. Old English had some sounds which we do not have. The sound represented by *y* does not occur in Modern English. If you pronounce the vowel in *bit* with your lips rounded, you may approach it. /37/

In grammar, Old English was much more highly inflected than Modern English is. That is, there were more case endings for nouns, more person and number endings for verbs, a more complicated pronoun system, various endings for adjectives, and so on. Old English nouns had four cases — nominative, genitive, dative, accusative. Adjectives had five — all these and an instrumental case besides. Present-day English has only two cases for nouns — common case and possessive case. Adjectives now have no case system at all. On the other hand, we now use a more rigid word order and more structure words (prepositions, auxiliaries, and the like) to express relationships than Old English did.

Some of this grammar we can see in the Lord's Prayer. *Heofonum*, for instance, is a dative plural; the nominative singular was *heofon*. *Urne* is an accusative singular; the nominative is *ure*. In *urum gyltendum* both words are dative plural. *Forgyfaþ* is the third person plural form of the verb. Word order is different: "urne gedæghwamlican hlaf syle us" in place of "Give us our daily bread." And so on.

In vocabulary Old English is quite different from Modern English. Most of the Old English words are what we may call native English: that is, words which have not been borrowed from other languages but which have been a part of English ever since English was a part of Indo-European. Old English did certainly contain borrowed words. We have seen that many borrowings were coming in from Norse. Rather large numbers had been borrowed from Latin, too. Some of these were taken while the Anglo-Saxons were still on the Continent (*cheese, butter, bishop, kettle*, etc.); a larger number came into English after the Conversion (*angel, candle, priest, martyr, radish, oyster, purple, school, spend*, etc.). But the great majority of Old English words were native English. /38/

Now, on the contrary, the majority of words in English are borrowed, taken mostly from Latin and French. Of the words in *The American College Dictionary* only about 14 percent are native. Most of these, to be sure, are common, high-frequency words – *the, of, I, and, because, man, mother, road,* etc.; of the thousand most common words in English, some 62 percent are native English. Even so, the modern vocabulary is very much Latinized and Frenchified. The Old English vocabulary was not.

Sometime between the years 1000 and 1200 various important changes took place in the structure of English, and Old English became Middle English. The political event which facilitated these changes was the Norman Conquest. The Normans, as the name shows, came originally from Scandinavia. In the early tenth century they established themselves in northern France, adopted the French language, and developed a vigorous kingdom and a very passable civilization. In the year 1066, led by Duke William, they crossed the Channel and made themselves masters of England. For the next several hundred years, England was ruled by kings whose first language was French.

One might wonder why, after the Norman Conquest, French did not become the national language, replacing English entirely. The reason is that the Conquest was not a national migration, as the earlier Anglo-Saxon invasion had been. Great numbers of Normans came to England, but they came as rulers and landlords. French became the language of the court, the language of the nobility, the language of polite society, the language of literature. But it did not replace English as the language of the people. There must always have /39/ been hundreds of towns and villages in which French was never heard except when visitors of high station passed through.

But English, though it survived as the national language, was profoundly changed after the Norman Conquest. Some of the changes – in sound structure and grammar – would no doubt have taken place whether there had been a Conquest or not. Even before 1066 the case system of English nouns and adjectives was becoming simplified; people came to rely more on word order and prepositions than on inflectional endings to communicate their meanings. The process was speeded up by sound changes which caused many of the endings to sound alike. But no doubt the Conquest facilitated the change. German, which didn't experience a Norman Conquest, is today rather highly inflected compared to its cousin English.

But it is in vocabulary that the effects of the Conquest are most obvious. French ceased, after a hundred years or so, to be the native language of very many people in England, but it continued – and continues still – to be a zealously cultivated second language, the mirror of elegance and civilization. When one spoke English, one introduced not only French ideas and French things but also their French names. This was not only easy but socially useful. To pepper one's conversation with French expressions was to show that one was well-bred, elegant, *au courant.* The last sentence shows that the process is not yet dead. By using *au courant* instead of, say, *abreast of things,* the writer indicates that he is no dull clod who knows only English but an elegant person aware of how things are done in *le haut monde.*

Thus French words came into English, all sorts of them. There were words to do with government: *parliament, majesty, treaty, alliance, tax, government;* church words: *parson, sermon, baptism, incense, crucifix, religion;* words for foods: /40/ *veal, beef, mutton, bacon, jelly, peach, lemon, cream, biscuit;* colors: *blue, scarlet, vermilion;* household words: *curtain, chair, lamp, towel, blanket, parlor;* play words: *dance, chess, music, leisure, conversation;* literary words: *story, romance, poet, literary;* learned words: *study, logic, grammar, noun, surgeon, anatomy, stomach;* just ordinary words of all sorts: *nice, second, very, age, bucket, gentle, final, fault, flower, cry, count, sure, move, surprise, plain.*

All these and thousands more poured into the English vocabulary between 1100 and 1500, until at the end of that time many people must have had more French words than English at their command. This is not to say that English became French. English remained English in sound structure and in grammar, though these also felt the ripples of French influence. The very heart of the vocabulary, too, remained English. Most of the high-frequency words — the pronouns, the prepositions, the conjunctions, the auxiliaries, as well as a great many ordinary nouns and verbs and adjectives — were not replaced by borrowings.

Middle English, then, was still a Germanic language, but it differed from Old English in many ways. The sound system and the grammar changed a good deal. Speakers made less use of case systems and other inflectional devices and relied more on word order and structure words to express their meanings. This is often said to be a simplification, but it isn't really. Languages don't become simpler; they merely exchange one kind of complexity for another. Modern English is not a simple language, as any foreign speaker who tries to learn it will hasten to tell you.

For us Middle English is simpler than Old English just because it is closer to Modern English. It takes three or four months at least to learn to read Old English prose and more than that for poetry. But a week of good study should put one /41/ in touch with the Middle English poet Chaucer. Indeed, you may be able to make some sense of Chaucer straight off, though you would need instruction in pronunciation to make it sound like poetry. . . .

Sometime between 1400 and 1600 English underwent a couple of sound changes which made the language of Shakespeare quite different from that of Chaucer. Incidentally, these changes contributed much to the chaos in which English spelling now finds itself.

One change was the elimination of a vowel sound in certain unstressed positions at the end of words. For instance, the words *name, stone, wine, dance,* were pronounced as two syllables by Chaucer but as just one by Shakespeare. The *e* in these words became, as we say, "silent." But it wasn't silent for Chaucer; it represented a vowel sound. So also the words *laughed, seemed, stored,* would have been pronounced by Chaucer as two-syllable words. The change was an important one because it affected thousands of words and gave a different aspect to the whole language.

The other change is what is called the Great Vowel Shift. This was a systematic shifting of half a dozen vowels and diphthongs in stressed syllables. For instance, the word *name* /42/ had in Middle English a vowel something like that in the modern word *father; wine* had the vowel of modern *mean; he* was pronounced something like modern *hey; mouse* sounded like *moose; moon* had the vowel of *moan.* Again the shift was thoroughgoing and affected all the words in which these vowel sounds occurred. Since we still keep the Middle English system of spelling these words, the differences between Modern English and Middle English are often more real than apparent.

The vowel shift has meant also that we have come to use an entirely different set of symbols for representing vowel sounds than is used by writers of such languages as French, Italian, or Spanish, in which no such vowel shift occurred. If you come across a strange word — say, *bine* — in an English book, you will pronounce it according to the English system, with the vowel of *wine* or *dine.* But if you read *bine* in a French, Italian, or Spanish book, you will pronounce it with the vowel of *mean* or *seen.*

These two changes, then, produced the basic differences between Middle English and Modern English. But there were several other developments that had an effect upon the language. One was the invention of printing, an invention introduced into England by William Caxton in the year 1475. Where before books had been rare and costly, they suddenly became cheap and common. More and more people learned to read and write. This was the first of many advances in communication which have worked to unify languages and to arrest the development of dialect differences, though of course printing affects writing principally rather than speech. Among other things it hastened the standardization of spelling.

The period of Early Modern English — that is, the sixteenth and seventeenth centuries — was also the period of the English /43/ Renaissance, when people developed, on the one hand, a keen interest in the past and, on the other, a more daring and imaginative view of the future. New ideas multiplied, and new ideas meant new language. Englishmen had grown accustomed to borrowing words from French as a result of the Norman Conquest; now they borrowed from Latin and Greek. As we have seen, English had been raiding Latin from Old English times and before, but now the floodgates really opened, and thousands of words from the classical languages poured in. *Pedestrian, bonus, anatomy, contradict, climax, dictionary, benefit, multiply, exist, paragraph, initiate, scene, inspire* are random examples. Probably the average educated American today has more words from French in his vocabulary than from native English sources, and more from Latin than from French.

The greatest writer of the Early Modern English period is of course Shakespeare, and the best-known book is the King James Version of the Bible, published in 1611. The Bible (if not Shakespeare) has made many features of Early Modern English perfectly familiar to many people down to present times, even though we do not use these features in present-day speech and writing. For instance, the old pronouns *thou* and *thee* have dropped out of use now, together with their verb forms, but they are still familiar to us in prayer and in Biblical quotation: "Whither thou goest,

I will go." Such forms as *hath* and *doth* have been replaced by *has* and *does;* "Goes he hence tonight?" would now be "Is he going away tonight?"; Shakespeare's "Fie on't, sirrah" would be "Nuts to that, Mac." Still, all these expressions linger with us because of the power of the words in which they occur.

It is not always realized, however, that considerable sound changes have taken place between Early Modern English and the English of the present day. Shakespearian actors putting /44/ on a play speak the words, properly enough, in their modern pronunciation. But it is very doubtful that this pronunciation would be understood at all by Shakespeare. In Shakespeare's time, the word *reason* was pronounced like modern *raisin; face* had the sound of modern *glass;* the *l* in *would, should, palm* was pronounced. In these points and a great many others the English language has moved a long way from what it was in 1600.

The history of English since 1700 is filled with many movements and countermovements, of which we can notice only a couple. One of these is the vigorous attempt made in the eighteenth century, and the rather half-hearted attempts made since, to regulate and control the English language. Many people of the eighteenth century, not understanding very well the forces which govern language, proposed to polish and prune and restrict English, which they felt was proliferating too wildly. There was much talk of an academy which would rule on what people could and could not say and write. The academy never came into being, but the eighteenth century did succeed in establishing certain attitudes which, though they haven't had much effect on the development of the language itself, have certainly changed the native speaker's feeling about the language.

In part a product of the wish to fix and establish the language was the development of the dictionary. The first English dictionary was published in 1603; it was a list of 2500 words briefly defined. Many others were published with gradual improvements until Samuel Johnson published his *English Dictionary* in 1755. This, steadily revised, dominated the field in England for nearly a hundred years. Meanwhile in America, Noah Webster published his dictionary in 1828, and /45/ before long dictionary publishing was a big business in this country. The last century has seen the publication of one great dictionary: the twelve-volume *Oxford English Dictionary,* compiled in the course of seventy-five years through the labors of many scholars. We have also, of course, numerous commercial dictionaries which are as good as the public wants them to be if not, indeed, rather better.

Another product of the eighteenth century was the invention of "English grammar." As English came to replace Latin as the language of scholarship it was felt that one should also be able to control and dissect it, parse and analyze it, as one could Latin. What happened in practice was that the grammatical description that applied to Latin was removed and superimposed on English. This was silly, because English is an entirely different kind of language, with its own forms and signals and ways of producing meaning. Nevertheless, English grammars on the Latin model were worked out and taught in the schools. In many schools they are still being taught. This activity is not often popular with school children, but it is sometimes an interesting and instructive exercise in logic. The principal harm in it is that it has tended to keep people from being interested in English and has obscured the real features of English structure.

But probably the most important force on the development of English in the modern period has been the tremendous expansion of English-speaking peoples. In 1500 English was a minor language, spoken by a few people on a small island. Now it is perhaps the greatest language of the world, spoken natively by over a quarter of a billion people and as a second language by many millions more. When we speak of English, we must specify whether we mean American English, British English, Australian English, Indian English, or what, since the differences are considerable. The American cannot /46/ go to England or the Englishman to America confident that he will always understand and be understood. The Alabaman in Iowa or the Iowan in Alabama shows himself a foreigner every time he speaks. It is only because communication has become fast and easy that English in this period of its expansion has not broken into a dozen mutually unintelligible languages. . . . /47/

3. SIMEON POTTER

Etymology and Meaning

The following discussion of how words change with time is from Simeon Potter, *Our Language* (London, 1950).

The most obvious semantic category is that involving specialization or narrowing. When a speech-form is applied to a group of objects or ideas which resemble one another in some respect, it may naturally become restricted to just one object or idea, and if this particular restriction gains currency in a speech community, a specialized meaning prevails. *Meat,* as in *sweetmeat* and as in the archaic phrase 'meat and drink', /107/ meant any kind of food. It now means 'edible flesh', a sense formerly expressed by *flesh* and *flesh meat. Deer,* like Dutch *dier* and German *Tier,* used to mean 'animal' in general, as in Shakespeare's 'mice and rats and such small deer'. Latin *animal* and French *beast* have taken its place as the general words and *deer* now means 'wild ruminant of a particular (antlered) species'. *Fowl,* like Dutch and German *Vogel,* denoted 'bird' in general as in Chaucer's 'Parlement of Foules' and Biblical 'fowls of the air' and as in modern names of larger kinds of birds used with a qualifying adjective, such as *sea fowl, water fowl,* and *wild fowl.* Otherwise, of course, *fowl* normally means a domestic cock or hen, especially when full grown. Hound formerly meant a dog of any breed and not, as now, a hunting-dog in particular. *Disease* was still conceived in Chaucer's day as being dis-ease 'absence of ease'. It might point to any kind of temporary discomfort and not, as now, to 'a morbid physical condition'. To *starve*, like Dutch *sterven* and German *sterben*, meant 'to die', not necessarily from lack of food. In modern Yorkshire dialect a body can still 'starve of cold'. A *wed* was a pledge of any kind. In conjunction with the suffix *-lock* forming nouns of action, it has come to be restricted to 'the marriage vow or obligation'. To the Elizabethans an *affection* was a feeling of any kind and both *lectures* and *lessons* were 'readings' of any kind. *Doctrine* was still teaching in general and *science* was still knowledge in general.

Sometimes a word has become restricted in use because a qualifier has been omitted. *Undertaker*, like French *entrepreneur* and German *Unternehmer*, used to mean 'contractor, one who *undertakes* to do a particular piece of work'. It is now used exclusively in the sense of *funeral undertaker*, although *mortician* has already superseded it in the cities and towns of America. In daily conversation *doctor* 'teacher' means 'medical doctor' and normally refers to a 'general practitioner'. Many words have both wider and narrower senses in the living language and many others have varying senses according to the /108/ persons addressed. *Pipe*, for example, evokes different images in the mind of the smoker, the plumber, the civil engineer, the geologist, the organist, and the boatswain. The *line* means a clothes-line to the laundry-woman, a fishing line to the fisherman, the equator to the seaman (as in Joseph Conrad's *Crossing the Line*), a communication wire to the telephonist, a succession of descent to the genealogist, and a particular kind of article to the man of business. To the geographer *cataract* means a cascade or waterfall, to the engineer a hydraulic controller, but a disease of the crystalline lens to the oculist.

The processes of specialization and extension of meaning may take place in a language side by side. For instance, as we have just seen, *hound* has been restricted in the course of a thousand years from a dog in general to a hunting-dog in particular; contrariwise, *dog* . . . has been extended from 'a dog of ancient breed' to include any sort of dog, ranging from a formidable Alsatian to a puny and insignificant lap-dog. *Bird* meant 'young birdling', just as *pigeon* meant 'young dove' and *pig* 'young swine'. *Place* has had a remarkable history in English, where it has largely superseded the older words *stead* and *stow*. It derives from the feminine form of the Greek adjective meaning 'broad', as in *plateîa hodós* 'broad way'. In one of its senses it still means 'a group of houses in a town or city, now or formerly possessing some of the characters (positive or negative) of a square', like its well-known cognate in French, as in *Place de la Concorde*, or like Italian *piazza*, Spanish *plaza*, and German *Platz*. Now, however, it is also used in a hundred ways: 'Keep him in his place', 'It is not my place to inquire into that', 'The meeting will not take place', 'There is a place for everything', 'I have lost the place (in reading)', 'That remark was quite out of place (inappropriate, improper)', 'In the first, second place (first, secondly)'. /109/

If we assume that the central meaning of *place* is still 'square' and that these other diverse uses *radiate* from that centre, we might equally well put it into our third semantic category: radiation, polysemia, or multiplication. Another excellent example is the word *paper*. It is the same as *papyrus*, the paper-reed of the Nile from the thin strips of which writing-sheets were first made as a substitute for parchment. The name was naturally transferred to paper made of cotton and thence to paper of linen and other fibres. To-day a paper may mean a document of any kind, for instance, a Government White Paper; an essay, dissertation or article on some particular topic, especially a communication read or sent to a learned society; a set of questions in an examination; a journal or a daily newspaper. *Power* 'ability to do, state of being able' may hold radiating meanings as diverse as 'capacity for mental or bodily action' (power of intellect, power of movement); 'mechanical or natural energy' (horse-power, candle-power, electric power-station); 'political or national strength' (the balance of power); 'possession of control or command over others, dominion, sway' (the power of the Cabinet); 'a political state' (the four great powers); and 'a mathematical conception' (5^4 or five to the fourth power). Because the *head* is that part of the human body containing the brain, it may be the top of anything, literally or metaphorically, whether it resembles the head in shape (the head of a nail, screw, pin, hammer, walking-stick, flower, or cabbage) or in position (the head of the page, the list, the bed, the table or the stairs); or it may signify the person who is the chief or leader (the head of the school, the business, the family, the house, the State, the Church). It may denote the head of a coin (that side of a coin bearing the sovereign's head); a headland or promontory (St Bees Head, Great Ormes Head, or Beachy Head, from tautologous Beau Chef Head); a single person or beast (lunch at five shillings a head, fifty head of cattle); or one of the main points or logical divisions of a subject or discourse (dealing with a /110/ theme under several heads). These and other senses do not derive from one another. They radiate from a common centre and are therefore mutually independent. Some of these senses will be translated by German *Kopf*, by French *tête*, by Spanish *cabeza* or by the ordinary word for *head* in other languages, but many senses will not permit of such direct translation. Each sense must be considered separately and, in the process of translating, our linguistic knowledge may be severely put to the test. It is surprising that in ordinary conversation in English there is so little ambiguity.

It is surprising, too, that every day we use words in both literal and metaphorical senses and that there is little danger of being misapprehended. We may speak as we will of 'bright sunshine' or 'a bright boy'; 'a sharp knife', 'a sharp frost' or 'a sharp rebuke'; 'a cold morning' or 'the cold war'; 'the Black Country' or 'the black market'. A person who is slow-witted may be described metaphorically as 'dull', 'obtuse', or 'dim', the latter term being associated with the German *dumm* meaning 'stupid', although cognate with our *dumb*. 'Dumb' in German is now *stumm*, which is related etymologically to our *stammer*. Many words are themselves old metaphors: *dependent* 'hanging from' (Latin dē-pendens); *egregious* 'selected from the herd' (Latin *ē* for *ex* + *grex, gregis* 'herd'); *precocious* 'too early ripe' (Latin *praecox* from *prae* 'before' + *coquere* 'to cook, ripen').

Our next category of semantic changes may be labelled concretization. The naming of abstract qualities, such as *whiteness, beauty*, and *justice*, comes late in the evolution of a language because it results from conscious or unconscious comparison in the mind of man. Does *beauty* really exist apart from beautiful things? On this question the medieval schoolmen argued for centuries. No sooner are abstract nouns formed than men tend to think of each appearance of a quality or action in the abstract as a separate entity and so, by concretization, they make abstractions tangible and visible once /111/ more. *Youth*, 'youngness' in the abstract, becomes a 'young man'. In the form *geogoþ* this word occurs eleven times in *Beowulf*, five times with the abstract meaning 'youth', but six times with the concrete and collective meaning 'young men'. In much the same way Latin *multitūdo* 'manyness, the quality of being many' came to signify 'a crowd' and *congregātio* 'flocking together' came to mean 'a body of people assembled'. Barristers appointed counsel to the Crown are named *King's Counsel*. A judge is addressed as *Your Honour* and an archbishop as *Your Grace*. *Health* is the quality of being *hale* or *whole*, soundness of body and mind. Modern man seeks diligently to maintain physical, mental, and social health. It is Greek *hugíeia* (from the adjectival form of which comes our *hygiene*), Latin *salūs*, French *la santé*, and German *die Gesundheit*. Clearly these are all highly abstract forms. Nevertheless, even *health* becomes concrete in the sense of a toast drunk — 'Here's a health unto His Majesty!' *Wealth* was primarily 'weal', 'welfare', or 'well-being', the state of being 'well'. In the old assonantal formula 'health and wealth' the two abstract substantives were practically synonymous. But side by side with this meaning of *wealth* the concretized sense of 'worldly goods, riches, affluence' also developed. The expression *wealth of nations*, denoting 'the collective riches of a people or country', was certainly current before it was adopted by Adam Smith in 1776 as the title of his epoch-making book. 'Money', wrote John Stuart Mill in 1848, 'being the instrument of an important public and private purpose, is rightly regarded as wealth'. 'Let us substitute welfare for wealth as our governing purpose', said Edward Hallett Carr in 1948, exhorting us, in fact, to restore to the word *wealth* its older meaning. *Kindness, mercy, opportunity*, and *propriety* are historically abstractions, but to-day we speak of *kindness* in the plural in the sense of 'deeds of kindness', *mercies* as 'instances or manifestations of mercy', *opportunities* as 'favourable chances or occasions', and *proprieties* as 'proper forms of /112/ conduct'. Similarly *provision* 'foreseeing, foresight' has come to be applied in the plural to 'stores of food'.

Sometimes words, like men, 'fall away from their better selves' and show deterioration or catachresis. *Silly* once meant 'happy, blissful, holy', as in the 'sely child' of Chaucer's *Prioress's Tale*. Later it signified 'helpless, defenceless', becoming a conventional epithet in the 'silly sheep' of Milton, Cowper, and Matthew Arnold. Then it descended yet lower and came to imply 'foolish, feeble-minded, imbecile'. *Crafty* 'strong' and *cunning* 'knowing' were once attributes of unmingled praise. A crafty workman was one skilled in a handicraft; a cunning workman was one who knew his trade. To *counterfeit* meant simply 'to copy, reproduce', conveying no suggestion of fraud. 'What finde I here?' asked Bassanio, as he opened the leaden casket, 'Faire Portias counterfeit.' (*The Merchant of Venice*, III, ii, 115.) It was, in fact, no counterfeit in the modern sense, but a true and lifelike delineation that came 'so near creation'. A *villain* once meant 'a slave serving in a country-house or *villa*', a man occupying a lowly station in life. Chaucer's *vileynye* already showed depreciation, for it connoted the opposite of *courteisye*, that comprehensive term for a noble and chivalrous way of life, implying high courtly elegance and politeness of manners. A *knave*, like German *ein Knabe*, was just 'a boy'; later, as in 'the kokes knave, thet wassheth the disshes' of the *Ancrene Riwle*, 'a boy or lad employed as a servant'; later still, 'a base and crafty rogue'. Like *rogue* and *rascal*, *knave* may still be used jocularly without seriously implying bad qualities. *Varlet*, a variant of *valet*, has shown an almost identical catachresis. *Nice* has become just a pleasant verbal counter: anything or everything may be nice. But *nescius*, its Latin antecedent, had the precise meaning 'ignorant, unaware', a meaning maintained in Chaucer side by side with that of 'foolish'. From 'foolish' it developed the sense 'foolishly particular about small things', and so 'fastidious, precise', as in 'nice in one's dress'. Later it was made to /113/ refer to actions or qualities, as in 'a nice discrimination' and 'a nice sense of honour'. Since then, as H. W. Fowler has sagaciously observed in *A Dictionary of Modern English Usage*, 'it has been too great a favourite with the ladies, who have charmed out of it all its individuality and converted it into a mere diffuser of vague and mild agreeableness'. It is a pleasant, lazy word which careful speakers are bound to avoid using in serious contexts. *Propaganda*, which now implies an organized and vicious distortion of facts for a particular purpose, has suffered sad depreciation in recent years. In 1622 Pope Gregory XV founded a special Committee or Congregation of Cardinals for the Propagation of the Faith, in Latin *Congregātio dē propāgandā fide*. That marked the beginning of the history of this word, which, you see, is the ablative singular feminine form of the gerundive of *propāgāre* 'to fasten or peg down slips of plants for growth, to multiply plants by layering'. Most appropriately the Latin metaphor is agricultural and botanical. *Propaganda* should mean, in its extended sense, the dissemination of news of any kind. Unfortunately, since the year 1880 the meaning of the word has been poisoned. Propaganda and truthworthy news are dissociated in our minds. We even hear of propaganda and counter-propaganda! /114/

4. CHARLTON LAIRD

The Way of a Man with a Word

> The following "biography" of a word is from Charlton Laird,
> *The Miracle of Language* (Cleveland, 1953).

Before we talk about principles, we should perhaps look at a few of the words which illustrate those principles. Any common word would suffice for our first example, one such as *tap*. Presumably the syllable came from an Indo-European base resembling **dap*, "something cut out," from a base-like **dai*, "to cut" or "to tear." [The asterisks signify that the Indo-European bases are hypothetical, reconstructed words.] By the time this word got into Anglo-Saxon as *tæppe*, it meant "something cut out and used to stop a hole." Anglo-Saxon also had a verb form corresponding to this, as did many other Germanic languages, which meant "to draw forth liquid by means of a tap." By Middle English times the situation had become complicated, for a new word *tappe* appeared, a noun meaning "a light sound," or "a light blow which would produce the sound"; there was also a verb meaning "to give a light blow." Thus, when King Arthur split a giant from head to crotch with one stroke, and buried the axe deep in the ground, the writer could remark, "It was not a light tap." No one knows where this word *tap* came from. In Middle English it was imported from Old French *tapper*, but where did the French get the word? They may have used it in imitation of the sound of a light blow, but there are, in various Germanic dialects, enough similar words meaning "to strike a blow" so that there is at least strong suspicion that the French word came from a Germanic dialect, perhaps by way of the Low Countries. Meanwhile, a *tap* in a /54/ bunghole had to be pounded in, and usually *tapped* sideways to get it out; no doubt the association helped.

Thus, by Middle English times the word *tap* could mean "to pound in" or "to draw out" and it could mean also the names of these actions and the names of a number of things connected with these actions. Now things start happening to this word. The sort of tap which is also a spigot was so convenient that it started replacing other taps, and when running fluids became essential to industry and to modern living, taps became faucets but were still called taps, and the stuff which comes out of taps, *tap water*. These taps are not tapped at all, in the sense of being pounded; they are screwed with a thread. Consequently we now have implements for inside threading, whether or not a tap in the sense of "a faucet" is to be attached by the threads, and these implements are taps: *hand taps, machine taps, taper taps, plug taps, bottoming taps, pipe taps, collapsing taps, tap chucks, tap extractors, tap reamers, tap grinders, tap gauges,* and so on, ad infinitum, even to *tapper taps*, in which the two types of *tap* fall together again. A *tapping hole* can be distinguished from a *clearing hole* — it is now a question of size — and a *taplet* is at first a small tap, and then becomes no tap at all, but an insulator. Meanwhile in England, the place where liquor is drawn becomes a *tap*, a *taphouse*, or a *taproom*, the woman who draws the liquor a *tapstress*, and the imbiber who swallows too much is in slang *tap-shackled*. To acquire liquid refreshment surreptitiously is to *tap the admiral*, the legend being that a dead admiral was brought home by sea preserved in alcohol, or rather he was preserved until the sailors drew off the liquor and consumed it.

But this is only the beginning. Not only are there many more sorts of tap which represent objects, sights, or sounds; the word *tap* is used figuratively. One can make an opening in order to *tap*. A railroad *taps* a productive area, and the railroad line which runs into the area is called a *tap line*. Resources can be *tapped*. Even mental, moral, and physical resources can be tapped. A water main can be *tapped* to divide its flow, and a telephone wire can be *tapped* to obtain information. Because the funeral sound for a soldier was a tap on a drum, a bugle call became *taps*, a /55/ piece of music became *taps*, and *it's taps for him* can be an indication of certain death. A patch fastened on the bottom of a shoe with taps became a *tap*, a leather-thick layer of liquor in the bottom of a glass a *heeltap*, and the dancer who taps with the metal taps on his shoes is a *tap dancer*. One was *tapped* for Bones, the senior society at Yale, physically tapped, and now one can be *tapped* for any kind of appointment, and the *tapping* can be done by long-distance telephone. Anything ready to be tapped is *on tap*, whether the commodity be beer or gossip. And so it goes.

One meaning of a word leads to another meaning; words which were separate fall together and become indistinguishable; new meanings lead to other new meanings. Some meanings disappear, and from some meanings, perhaps very minor meanings on the periphery of the whole body of meaning of a word, will suddenly blossom new meanings of various sorts and in considerable number. A change in society has created a demand for new words; we get the new words by juggling the old ones.

Psychologically, what has happened? How have we been able to make an old word serve a new purpose, take on a new meaning? Scrutiny of the uses of *tap* will suggest that two complementary changes operate with overwhelming frequency. For instance, *to tap* means to draw liquor out of a barrel by means of a bung-stop. By extension, by generalizing this idea, *to tap* means to draw upon any resources whatever by making an actual or an imaginary opening into these resources. That is, a concrete or specific object or action has been seen in its general aspect, and the word for the concrete thing now becomes a word for a generality.

This tendency can be observed constantly. The Nazi army developed a highly successful land offense, which they called *Blitzkrieg*, that is, "lightning-war." We adopted the word to describe the tactic, and promptly made a verb of it: *Rommel blitzkriegs Monty*. But the word was too long, so that soon we had *Monty blitzes Rommel.* The word was handy, too handy to be left only to military opponents, and soon one prize fighter could *blitz* another by hitting him on the jaw. The German word for *lightning* had become an American verb describing any fast, /56/ devastating attack. At this writing the word seems to be dying, but if it had enjoyed more support, critics would now presumably be *blitzing* novels and Senator A. would be *blitzing* Senator B.'s bill. This sort of change in meaning is called *generalization.*

There is an opposite tendency. Since a *tap* was an object to keep liquor in its container, but could also be the means of letting liquor out, the instrument which regulated the flow of liquor by turning a handle became a *tap.* As we have said earlier, this taproom convenience came into great demand with modern plumbing and with the use of flowing liquids in industry. Most taps were threaded into the inside of pipes, and accordingly all instruments for cutting an inside screw were *taps.* Here, by a series of changes, the word for a relatively general concept has become the name of a highly specialized, specific object. The word for the general thing has become the word also for a particular part of the general concept, or for an object used in connection with something already associated with the word. If the word alone cannot be made sufficiently specific it is combined with another, and a *tapper tap* becomes a particular type of tap. Like generalization, this tendency, *specialization,* is always with us. A *shrimp* gets its name from an Anglo-Saxon word meaning "shriveled" — specialization from the concept of being shriveled to an object which looks shriveled. But a shrimp is an insignificant creature and the word sounds insignificant. Thus *shrimp* applied to a human being becomes an insult, specialization of the idea of insignificance. My class in phonetics calls one of the phonetic symbols which troubles them [ɔ] "the little shrimp." Unaware that *shrimp* etymologically means "shriveled," they specialized on the fact that a shrimp is curved.

This long dissertation on the word *tap,* then, illustrates two . . . principles . . . : new words and new meanings for words are added to the language both by specialization and by generalization. /57/

5. EDWARD SAPIR

Grammatical Relationships

Edward Sapir (1884-1939) became known first for his work on languages of the North American Indian, later as one of the century's most significant analysts of the nature and working of language. The following is from *Language: An Introduction to the Study of Speech* (New York, 1921).

In dealing with words and their varying forms we have had to anticipate much that concerns the sentence as a whole. Every language has its special method or methods of binding words into a larger unity. The importance of these methods is apt to vary with the complexity of the individual word. The /109/ more synthetic the language, in other words, the more clearly the status of each word in the sentence is indicated by its own resources, the less need is there for looking beyond the word to the sentence as a whole. The Latin *agit* "(he) acts" needs no outside help to establish its place in a proposition. Whether I say *agit dominus* "the master acts" or *sic femina agit* "thus the woman acts," the net result as to the syntactic feel of the *agit* is practically the same. It can only be a verb, the predicate of a proposition, and it can only be conceived as a statement of activity carried out by a person (or thing) other than you or me. It is not so with such a word as the English *act*. *Act* is a syntactic waif until we have defined its status in a proposition — one thing in "they act abominably," quite another in "that was a kindly act." The Latin sentence speaks with the assurance of its individual members, the English word needs the prompting of its fellows. Roughly speaking, to be sure. And yet to say that a sufficiently elaborate word-structure compensates for external syntactic methods is perilously close to begging the question. The elements of the word are related to each other in a specific way and follow each other in a rigorously determined sequence. This is tantamount to saying that a word which consists of more than a radical element is a crystallization of a sentence or of some portion of a sentence, that a form like *agit* is roughly the psychological [27] equivalent of a form like *age is* "act he." Breaking down, then, the wall that separates word and sentence, we may ask: What, at last analysis, are the fundamental methods of relating word to word and element to element, in short, of passing from the isolated notions symbolized by each word and by each element to the unified proposition that corresponds to a thought?

The answer is simple and is implied in the preceding remarks. The most fundamental and the most /110/ powerful of all relating methods is the method of order. Let us think of some more or less concrete idea, say a color, and set down its symbol — *red;* of another concrete idea, say a person or object, setting down its symbol — *dog;* finally, of a third concrete idea, say an action, setting down its symbol — *run*. It is hardly possible to set down these three symbols — *red dog run* — without relating them in some way, for example *(the) red dog run(s)*. I am far from wishing to state that the proposition has always grown up in this analytic manner, merely that the very process of juxtaposing concept to concept, symbol to symbol, forces some kind of relational "feeling," if nothing else, upon us. To certain syntactic adhesions we are very sensitive, for example, to the attributive relation of quality *(red dog)* or the subjective relation *(dog run)* or the objective relation *(kill dog)*, to others we are more indifferent, for example, to the

[27] Ultimately, also historical—say, *age to* "act that (one)."

attributive relation of circumstances (*to-day red dog run* or *red dog to-day run* or *red dog run to-day*, all of which are equivalent propositions or propositions in embryo). Words and elements, then, once they are listed in a certain order, tend not only to establish some kind of relation among themselves but are attracted to each other in greater or in less degree. It is presumably this very greater or less that ultimately leads to those firmly solidified groups of elements (radical element or elements plus one or more grammatical elements) that we have studied as complex words. They are in all likelihood nothing but sequences that have shrunk together and away from other sequences or isolated elements in the flow of speech. While they are fully alive, in other words, while they are functional at every point, they can keep themselves at a psychological distance from their neighbors. As they gradually lose much of their life, they fall back into the embrace of the sentence as a whole and the sequence of independent words regains the importance it had in part /111/ transferred to the crystallized groups of elements. Speech is thus constantly tightening and loosening its sequences. In its highly integrated forms (Latin, Eskimo) the "energy" of sequence is largely locked up in complex word formations, it becomes transformed into a kind of potential energy that may not be released for millennia. In its more analytic forms (Chinese, English) this energy is mobile, ready to hand for such service as we demand of it.

There can be little doubt that stress has frequently played a controlling influence in the formation of element-groups or complex words out of certain sequences in the sentence. Such an English word as *withstand* is merely an old sequence *with stand*, i.e., "against [28] stand," in which the unstressed adverb was permanently drawn to the following verb and lost its independence as a significant element. In the same way French futures of the type *irai* "(I) shall go" are but the resultants of a coalescence of originally independent words: *ir* [29] *a'i* "to-go I-have," under the influence of a unifying accent. But stress has done more than articulate or unify sequences that in their own right imply a syntactic relation. Stress is the most natural means at our disposal to emphasize a linguistic contrast, to indicate the major element in a sequence. Hence we need not be surprised to find that accent too, no less than sequence, may serve as the unaided symbol of certain relations. Such a contrast as that of *go' between* ("one who goes between") and *to go between'* may be of quite secondary origin in English, but there is every reason to believe that analogous distinctions have prevailed at all times in linguistic history. A sequence like *see' man* might imply some type of relation in which *see* qualifies the following /112/ word, hence "a seeing man" or "a seen (or visible) man," or is its predication, hence "the man sees" or "the man is seen," while a sequence like *see man'* might indicate that the accented word in some way limits the application of the first, say as direct object, hence "to see a man" or "(he) sees the man." Such alterations

[28] For *with* in the sense of "against," compare German *wider* "against."
[29] Cf. Latin *ire* "to go"; also our English idiom "I have to go," i.e., "must go."

of relation, as symbolized by varying stresses, are important and frequent in a number of languages.[30]

It is somewhat venturesome and yet not an altogether unreasonable speculation that sees in word order and stress the primary methods for the expression of all syntactic relations and looks upon the present relational value of specific words and elements as but a secondary condition due to a transfer of values. Thus, we may surmise that the Latin -*m* of words like *feminam*, *dominum*, and *civem* did not originally [31] denote that "woman," "master," and "citizen" were objectively related to the verb of the proposition but indicated something far more concrete,[32] that the objective relation was merely implied by the position or accent of the word (radical element) immediately preceding the -*m*, and that gradually, as its more concrete significance faded away, it took over a syntactic function that did not originally belong to it. This sort of evolution by transfer is traceable in many instances. Thus, the *of* in an English phrase like "the law of the land" is now as colorless in content, as purely a relational indicator as the "genitive" suffix -*is* in the Latin *lex urbis* "the law of the city." We know, however, that it was originally an adverb of considerable concreteness of meaning,[33] "away, moving from," and that the syntactic relation was originally expressed by /113/ the case form [34] of the second noun. As the case form lost its vitality, the adverb took over its function. If we are actually justified in assuming that the expression of all syntactic relations is ultimately traceable to these two unavoidable, dynamic features of speech — sequence and stress [35] — an interesting thesis results: — All of the actual content of speech, its clusters of vocalic and consonantal sounds, is in origin limited to the concrete; relations were originally not expressed in outward form but were merely implied and articulated with the help of order and rhythm. In other words, relations were intuitively felt and could only "leak out" with the help of dynamic factors that themselves move on an intuitional plane. /114/

. . . The observant reader has probably been surprised /116/ that all this time we have had so little to say of the time-honored "parts of speech." The reason for this is not far to seek. Our conventional classification of words into parts of speech is only a vague, wavering approximation to a consistently worked out inventory of experience. We imagine, to begin with, that all "verbs" are inherently concerned with action as such, that a "noun" is the name of some definite object or personality that can be pictured by the mind, that all qualities are necessarily expressed by a definite group of words to which we may appropriately apply the term "adjective." As soon as we test our vocabulary, we discover that the parts of speech are far from cor-

[30] In Chinese no less than in English.

[31] By "originally" I mean, of course, some time antedating the earliest period of the Indo-European languages that we can get at by comparative evidence.

[32] Perhaps it was a noun-classifying element of some sort.

[33] Compare its close historical parallel *off*.

[34] "Ablative" at last analysis.

[35] Very likely pitch should be understood along with stress.

responding to so simple an analysis of reality. We say "it is red" and define "red" as a quality-word or adjective. We should consider it strange to think of an equivalent of "is red" in which the whole predication (adjective and verb of being) is conceived of as a verb in precisely the same way in which we think of "extends" or "lies" or "sleeps" as a verb. Yet as soon as we give the "durative" notion of being red an inceptive or transitional turn, we can avoid the parallel form "it becomes red, it turns red" and say " it reddens." No one denies that "reddens" is as good a verb as "sleeps" or even "walks." Yet "it is red" is related to "it reddens" very much as is "he stands" to "he stands up" or "he rises." It is merely a matter of English or of general Indo-European idiom that we cannot say "it reds" in the sense of "it is red." There are hundreds of languages that can. Indeed there are many that can express what we should call an adjective only by making a participle out of a verb. "Red" in such languages is merely a derivative of "being red," as our "sleeping" or "walking" are derivatives of primary verbs.

Just as we can verbify the idea of a quality in such cases as "reddens," so we can represent a quality or an action to ourselves as a thing. We speak of "the /117/ height of a building" or "the fall of an apple" quite as though these ideas were parallel to "the roof of a building" or "the skin of an apple," forgetting that the nouns (*height, fall*) have not ceased to indicate a quality and an act when we have made them speak with the accent of mere objects. And just as there are languages that make verbs of the great mass of adjectives, so there are others that make nouns of them. In Chinook, . . . "the big table" is "the-table its-bigness"; in Tibetan the same idea may be expressed by "the table of bigness," very much as we may say "a man of wealth" instead of "a rich man."

But are there not certain ideas that it is impossible to render except by way of such and such parts of speech? What can be done with the "to" of "he came to the house"? Well, we can say "he reached the house" and dodge the preposition altogether, giving the verb a nuance that absorbs the idea of local relation carried by the "to." But let us insist on giving independence to this idea of local relation. Must we not then hold to the preposition? No, we can make a noun of it. We can say something like "he reached the proximity of the house" or "he reached the house-locality." Instead of saying "he looked into the glass" we may say "he scrutinized the glass-interior." Such expressions are stilted in English because they do not easily fit into our formal grooves, but in language after language we find that local relations are expressed in just this way. The local relation is nominalized. And so we might go on examining the various parts of speech and showing how they not merely grade into each other but are to an astonishing degree actually convertible into each other. The upshot of such an examination would be to feel convinced that the "part of speech" reflects not so much our intuitive analysis of reality as our ability to compose that reality into a variety of formal patterns. A part of speech outside of the limitations of syntactic form is but a /118/ will o' the wisp. For this reason no logical scheme of the parts of speech — their number, nature, and necessary confines — is of the slightest interest to the linguist. Each language has its own scheme. Everything depends on the formal demarcations which it recognizes.

Yet we must not be too destructive. It is well to remember that speech consists of a series of propositions. There must be something to talk about and something must be said about this subject of discourse once it is selected. This distinction is of such fundamental importance that the vast majority of languages have emphasized it by creating some sort of formal barrier between the two terms of the proposition. The subject of discourse is a noun. As the most common subject of discourse is either a person or a thing, the noun clusters about concrete concepts of that order. As the thing predicated of a subject is generally an activity in the widest sense of the word, a passage from one moment of existence to another, the form which has been set aside for the business of predicating, in other words, the verb, clusters about concepts of activity. No language wholly fails to distinguish noun and verb, though in particular cases the nature of the distinction may be an elusive one. It is different with the other parts of speech. Not one of them is imperatively required for the life of language. */119/*

6.   HANS KURATH

Linguistic Geography: Atlantic Seaboard

Among the modern approaches to language is linguistic geography, intended to reveal the geographical spread of various locutions within a language. The investigator collects data in a controlled manner calculated to determine who says what; these data are plotted on maps, and the resulting boundaries of speech, represented in what are called *isoglosses*, suggest the spread of a locution and accordingly the dialects within a language. Linguistic geography is now being actively pursued in most parts of the United States, but thus far the most extensive results available are for the Atlantic seaboard. The following is taken from Hans Kurath, *A Word Geography of the Eastern United States* (Ann Arbor, 1949).

One fact of major importance seems to me to be fully established: *There is an extensive Midland speech area that lies between the traditionally recognized "Northern" and "Southern" areas.* This Midland area, which is linguistically distinct from the Northern and Southern areas and is in part set off by sharp boundaries, corresponds to the Pennsylvania settlement area. */v/* The common notion of a linguistic Mason and Dixon's Line separating "Northern" from "Southern" speech is simply due to an erroneous inference from an oversimplified version of the political history of the nineteenth century. The widely accepted assumption that there is a "General American" type of English proves to be equally unfounded in fact; no Southerner or New Englander would ever have made such a generalization. /*vi*/

. . . Every word that is not in nation-wide use has its own spread geographically as well as socially; yet the word boundaries tend to coalesce in some sectors and to be spaced more or less widely in others. Wherever they coalesce to form more or less close-knit strands or bundles, we have speech boundaries of varying importance. If we have at our disposal a sufficiently large number of regionally or locally restricted words, we are able to draw dialect boundaries.

In the Eastern states there are two boundaries of the first degree of importance, one running in a westerly direction through northern Pennsylvania, the other in a southwesterly direction along the Blue Ridge in Virginia.

Boundaries of the second degree run (1) in a northerly direction from the mouth of the Connecticut River to the Green Mountains of Vermont, (2) from the fork of the Susquehanna in Pennsylvania to Sandy Hook in New Jersey, (3) from Dover in Delaware in an arc through Baltimore to the Blue Ridge, (4) from the lower James in Virginia through the piedmont of North Carolina to Roanoke in the Blue Ridge, (5) between the Peedee and the Santee in South Carolina, (6) along the northern watershed of the Kanawha in West Virginia, and (7) from Roanoke in the Blue Ridge through the piedmont of North Carolina to the Blue Ridge in South Carolina. /*11*/

. . . The Northern speech area corresponds to the New England settlement area, together with the Dutch settlement area which lies embedded in it. The southern boundary of this area runs in a westerly direction through northern Pennsylvania. On the East Branch of the Susquehanna (near Scranton) the line turns off in a southeasterly direction and cuts through New Jersey to the Atlantic coast below Sandy Hook.

The subareas of the North are (1) Western New England and the New England settlement area west of the Hudson to the Great Lakes, (2) Eastern New England, including the upper Connecticut Valley, and (3) the Hudson Valley, including western Long Island and East Jersey.

Eastern New England and the Hudson Valley have many local expressions, which make them stand out as distinctive subareas in the broad expanse of the Northern Area. /*12*/

The northern boundary of the Midland area coincides with the southern boundary of the Northern area, which has been described above (*p. 12*). It is more sharply defined in Pennsylvania than in New Jersey, where a complicated settlement history and the old lines of communication between Philadelphia and New York City intersecting the settlement boundary have frayed the word lines. We shall also have occasion to note the spreading of some Northern expressions from the New York area to Philadelphia and environs.

The southern boundary of the Midland runs along the crest of the Blue Ridge in Virginia. North of the Potomac the line turns east and sweeps in an arc through Baltimore to the Atlantic below Dover in Delaware. In

Maryland west of Chesapeake Bay this line is clearly defined. On the Eastern Shore, where Delaware Bay expressions have often spread far southward under Philadelphia influence, the boundary is less sharp.

South of the James River the Midland boundary swerves out into the piedmont and embraces a large section of the North Carolina piedmont. This southern section of the Midland boundary is less sharply defined than the middle sector in Virginia because Southern expressions have mingled with the old Midland terms in the Blue Ridge south of the James and in the Appalachians to a much greater extent than farther north. Moreover, some Midland features have been carried down the valleys of the Cape Fear and the Yadkin-Peedee to the Atlantic coast.

The Midland area extends westward to the Ozarks and beyond. West of Pennsylvania its northern boundary runs through the central part of Ohio, northern Indiana, and central Illinois. The systematic survey of the speech of the Great Lakes Basin and the Ohio Valley, which is being carried out under the direction of A. H. Marckwardt of the University of Michigan, provides the localized material. . . .

The southern boundary of the Midland in Georgia and farther west is as yet unknown. It probably runs somewhat to the north of the cottonlands. . . .

The Delaware Bay area and the Pennsylvania German area — the oldest parts of the Midland area in point of settlement — are the most distinctive subareas of the Midland.

The Midland is not a uniform speech area, but it has a considerable body of words that sets it off from the North and the South. Its chief subareas are (1) Eastern Pennsylvania and West Jersey, in which the Pennsylvania German area is embedded, (2) Western Pennsylvania and Northern West Virginia, and (3) the Southern /27/ Appalachians and the Blue Ridge south of the James River. The crest of the Alleghenies separates Eastern Pennsylvania from Western Pennsylvania; the northern watershed of the Kanawha forms the boundary of the Southern Appalachians. It will be convenient to refer to Eastern Pennsylvania and West Jersey as the Philadelphia area, to Western Pennsylvania as the Pittsburgh area, and to group them together as the North Midland. The Southern Appalachians and the Blue Ridge south of the James are conveniently called the South Midland. The Pittsburgh area and the South Midland together constitute the West Midland, i.e., the Midland exclusive of the Philadelphia area. /28/

. . . The wheelless horse-drawn vehicle made of heavy planks, which is used for dragging stones from the fields, is known as a *stone sled* or *drag sled* in the Midland and as a *stone boat* in the North, except for the coastal area of New England, which has *drag* or *stone drag*.

Stone boat is a Connecticut Valley and Hudson Valley expression that was carried westward to the Great Lakes. In Pennsylvania and Ohio it has spread rather farther south than other New Englandisms, especially in the Pittsburgh area.

In the entire Connecticut Valley we find both the "western" *stone boat* and the "eastern" (*stone*) *drag;* also on Long Island and in East Jersey. . . .

The word *seesaw* is used everywhere, but in the New England settlement area other expressions are more widely current than *seesaw.* The same is true of parts of the South and the South Midland. It is only in Pennsylvania, and the greater parts of northern Maryland, Virginia, and South Carolina that *seesaw* is not paralleled by other terms.

Teeter, teeter board, teetering board are characteristic of New England and the entire New England settlement area to the Great Lakes. We find these expressions also in the New England settlements around Marietta and even on the West Virginia side of the Ohio.

On the lower Hudson, on Long Island, and in New Jersey *teeter* (*board*) is uncommon. Here we encounter *teeter-totter,* an expression that occurs also in New England settlements of New York State, Pennsylvania, and Ohio. In New England *teeter-totter* can now be heard only on the Housatonic and west of the Green Mountains, but its predominance in northern New Jersey and its widespread use in the New England settlement area lead to the inference that it was formerly more widely current in western New England.

It is fairly clear that *teeter* (*board*) is supplanting the earlier local expressions in New England: *tinter* in New Haven and on the lower Connecticut River; *dandle* in Rhode Island; *tilt, tilting board, tilter board* in Essex County, Massachusetts, and on the coast of Maine; *teedle board, tiddle board* on Cape Anne. However, on Cape Cod, Buzzards Bay, Martha's Vineyard, Nantucket, and on Aquidneck (Newport) in Narragansett Bay the Plymouth Colony expression *tilt, tilting board* is still firmly established; and Block Island has its *tippity-bounce* beside *tilt.*

The expressions for the seesaw in New England illustrate admirably the general trend in the development of the vocabulary of the Eastern States: the old (Colonial) local expressions /58/ are yielding ground to the regional term *teeter* (*board*), which in turn is being supplanted by the national (literary) expression *seesaw* in urbanized areas.

In the Southern area and in the Appalachians *seesaw* is in rather general use on all social levels. The most widespread regional term is *ridy-horse* (*riding horse*). It occurs (1) in the Appalachians from central West Virginia southward, and (2) in the coastal area of the Carolinas between the Neuse and the Peedee; and (3) relics of it occur on Albemarle Sound and on upper Chesapeake Bay.

Local expressions are: *cocky-horse, cock horse* in southern Delaware and in adjoining parts of the Eastern Shore of Maryland, and around St. Marys in southern Maryland; *hicky-horse, hick horse* between Albemarle Sound and the lower Neuse. /59/

. . . *Cottage cheese* is the trade name for curds in all the Eastern States; it is especially common in the urbanized areas. The earlier regional terms, however, are still in rather general use, even in the cities.

Maine and adjoining parts of New Hampshire have *curds, curd cheese.* In coastal New England, from the mouth of the Connecticut River to Cape

Cod and northward to the Kennebec River, *sour-milk cheese* predominates.

The remaining greater part of New England, except for southwestern Connecticut, has *Dutch cheese*, a term that also competes with *sour-milk cheese* on Narragansett Bay, in the back-country of Boston, and in the Merrimack Valley of New Hampshire. *Dutch cheese*, named with reference to the Dutch in the Hudson Valley, has also become established in the New England settlements of New York State, Pennsylvania, and Ohio, and has spread to some extent into West Virginia from Marietta.

The Hudson Valley expression is *pot cheese*, which is modeled on Dutch *pot kees*. . . . This term is now in general use in the Dutch settlement area and has spread eastward into Connecticut (the Housatonic Valley) and the New England settlements of Long Island, and westward to the Delaware and the head of the Mohawk.

Smear case (*shmear case*, *smear cheese*), borrowed from the Pennsylvania German (*schmierkäs*), is current throughout the North Midland and has spread to all of Delaware and Maryland and into the Shenandoah Valley. It has even gained a foothold on the Northern Neck of Virginia and on the Kanawha in West Virginia.

In the Southern area *curds* (*curd cheese*) and *clabber cheese* are widely used, the former on Chesapeake Bay, and the Carolina coast, the latter in the greater part of the Carolinas and in parts of West Virginia. A third term, *homemade cheese*, has considerable currency in western North Carolina and parts of the Appalachians. /71/

. . . Adverbial expressions for coasting "face-down" on a sled are numerous and display a striking geographic pattern reflecting settlement areas.

Belly-bump, belly-bumper(s), belly-bumping are characteristic (1) of coastal New England and (2) of Eastern Pennsylvania to the Alleghenies; *belly-bunt* predominates in the upper Connecticut Valley, in Worcester County, Massachusetts, and in parts of Maine; *belly-gut, belly-gutter* are found from the lower Connecticut to the Great Lakes and on the Allegheny River in Pennsylvania; *belly-wop, belly-wopper(s)* dominates (1) the lower Hudson, Long Island and East Jersey, and (2) Maryland; *belly-bust, belly-buster* occur in the South Midland and in parts of Virginia.

There are also some expressions that are local or individual or occur in scattered fashion: *belly-whack*, sporadically throughout the North; *belly-kəchunk*, around New London, Connecticut; *belly-flop, belly-flopper*, in Western New England and on Delaware Bay; *belly-whomper(s)*, on the Susquehanna; *belly-bunker*, in Western Pennsylvania; *belly-grinder*, in the Wheeling area; *belly-booster*, in southern Ohio. /80/

7. ALBERT H. MARCKWARDT

Linguistic Geography: North-Central States

> Field records for the *Linguistic Atlas of the North-Central States*
> have been virtually completed, and scholars have been able to
> reach some conclusions about Midland and Northern speech areas.
> The following selection is from Albert H. Marckwardt, "Prin-
> cipal and Subsidiary Dialect Areas in the North-Central States,"
> *Publication of the American Dialect Society*, No. 27 (April,
> 1957), 3-15.

What we see indicated here is symptomatic of the overlapping spread in
the North-Central territory of a number of individual items which maintain
a well-defined regional distribution to the east. For example, Kurath's *Word
Geography* shows a clear-cut line of demarcation between *sweet corn* and
roasting ear, following the general direction of the isoglosses separating
the North and the Midland.[5] In the North-Central territory, *sweet corn*,
though concentrated in the North, is found throughout the area. No state
is without an instance of it, and even as far south as Kentucky there were
seven occurrences. *Roasting ear* has a complementary distribution, heavy in
the south but thinning out as one goes northward. It was not recorded in
Ontario, only twice in Wisconsin and once in the Upper Peninsula of
Michigan, but it turned up no less than thirteen times in the Michigan
Lower Peninsula. Although space does not permit the presentation of additional examples, we now know that many items, between which the line of
cleavage was sharp in the East, have invaded each other's territories in the
North-Central states, resulting in broad belts of multiple usage. The nature
of these items, their general cultural patterning, the extent to which they
may have developed distinctions in meaning, are all matters for future
investigation.

We shall find it convenient to consider next certain of the features whose
boundaries in the Eastern United States generally follow the line separating
the eleventh and twelfth of Kurath's divisions. . . . One is the southern
limit of a Northern and North Midland term, *hay mow*. The remaining
three isoglosses represent the northern limits of South Midland features. In
general the lines follow the Ohio River. On occasion they veer upward,
but rarely do they penetrate north of the line of the Old National Road,
which connected Wheeling, Columbus, Indianapolis, Vandalia, and St. Louis.

Judging from the general configuration of these isoglosses, we are led to
the conclusion that the New England speech island /ʃ/ consisting of the
area around Marietta, namely the Ohio Company lands, offered an initial

---

[5] Kurath, *Word Geography*, Figure 41.

obstacle to the introduction of South Midland features. The dips in two of the isoglosses reflect this, and in them there are no significant bulges to the north until they cross Indiana and Illinois. The remaining two items apparently did gain acceptance in the Marietta area, but their spread north of that was prevented by the prior establishment of terms current in Pennsylvania. Nevertheless, they did spread north as far as the line of the Old National Road. At all events, these extensions of the boundary between what Kurath cails the Northern and Southern West Virginia areas do present a fairly clear-cut picture, one which is repeated in other items which have not been charted here.

Much less predictable is the behavior of the features which constitute the boundary between the tenth and eleventh of Kurath's subdivisions. . . . The isogloss of *nicker*, though entering Ohio just a little north of Wheeling, quickly rises toward the Western Reserve and follows generally the major boundary between the Northern and Midland speech areas. In addition, we find the term current in the Galena Lead Region, which though mixed in settlement history was originally developed by a Kentuckian. The northern limit of *gutters* follows the Old National Road in Ohio, but upon reaching Indiana again jumps northward almost to the principal Northern-Midland boundary. *Dogbit* as a participial form behaves in a decidedly different fashion. Though not charted by Kurath, this item does appear in Atwood's analysis of verb forms in the Eastern United States.[6] He shows it to be current throughout all of West Virginia and extending into Pennsylvania up to the Monongahela. This isogloss, after following the Old National Road two-thirds of the way across Ohio, suddenly dips toward the Ohio River, and in fact veers considerably below it over a large part of Kentucky.

This raises a question. How are we to account for the erratic behavior of these items? Any explanation undoubtedly can be little more than conjectural, but up to the present there is little ground even for conjecture. It is true, of course, that between the Old National Road and the principal dialect boundary separating /6/ the Northern and Midland areas there were no natural barriers, no important pathways of communication and travel, nor patterns of settlement which might have helped to create a second east-west line continuing the division between the tenth and eleventh of Kurath's areas. Moreover, a glance at the last map in the series will suggest that whatever items current in the area between the Monongahela and the Kanawha might have entered Ohio at this point, they would have been in competition with the northern features of the Western Reserve and the Ohio Company lands and also with the Southern or extreme South-Midland features of the Virginia Military District. Consequently, a deflection of these isoglosses either upward or downward is not too surprising.

More important still, perhaps, is the fact that features of the language spreading westward from the West Virginia panhandle and along the Monongahela were thrown into competition with others current throughout

[6] E. Bagby Atwood, *A Survey of Verb Forms in the Eastern United States* (Ann Arbor, 1953), Figure 3.

Pennsylvania, which were also penetrating the Ohio territory. . . . *Spouting*, as the term for gutters or eavestroughs, is now found in a band running all the way across central Ohio, crossing slightly into Indiana. *Run*, as the term for a small stream tributary, covers somewhat more territory, with one point heading into southeastern Michigan as well. *Serenade*, as an alternate for *belling*, *horning*, or *chivaree*, has an even larger radius; it does not go quite as far north as the others but includes the Kentucky bluegrass and part of the hill country. *Fishing worm* . . . is more extensive in its coverage than any of those charted.

This points to the fact that in the North-Central area we must reckon with three major population movements and corresponding transmissions of speech features. Heretofore much of our thinking has been primarily in terms of two: the migration from New York and New England into the northern part of the territory, and that from Virginia and the Carolinas into Kentucky and then northward across the Ohio River into southern Ohio and Illinois and most of Indiana. In fact, the census figures for 1870 do explain very satisfactorily the predominance of Northern items in Michigan and Wisconsin, of Midland terms in Indiana, and the division between Northern and Midland in Ohio and Illinois. Convincing and helpful as all of this is, as far as explaining the Hoosier apex is concerned, it does not take into account the migration from Penn- /7/ sylvania as a third factor, which suggests an historical reason for what may be called an Ohio wedge.

This brief account does not exhaust the possibilities of subsidiary dialect areas which a further examination of our records will enable us to chart. The Northern items entering the area were not all of one piece, and we may confidently expect to find belts or islands in which coastal New England terms are current. We have seen that with respect to at least one feature, the Galena Lead Region constitutes a distinct island. There are others as well, and indeed I am confident that we shall find the movement of settlers up and down the Mississippi River reflected in the distribution of a number of items.

Thus far our analyses do seem to verify the existence of a bundle of isoglosses cutting through our three central states in an apical line, thus constituting the principal dialect boundary between Northern and Midland speech. In general these isoglosses form a relatively broad band, and in many instances they must be interpreted as representing the limits of areas of concentration rather than of actual occurrence. For many terms there is considerable spreading throughout much of the area.

Another band, bounded on the north by the Old National Road and on the south by the Ohio River, constitutes a second transition belt, north of which Southern and South-Midland features fail to penetrate. A third group of South-Midland items, entering the area slightly to the north, have failed to establish a well-defined boundary of their own but have either spread as far as the Northern-Midland boundary or have been squeezed behind the subsidiary belt to the south. Finally, a wedge-like intrusion of Pennsylvania terms into and across Ohio has immensely complicated the dialect picture in the latter state.

At this point it is clear that we are dealing with a challenging and highly complex dialect situation: one which will require our drawing upon every available facet of cultural and settlement history to give it meaning and to make it understandable. /8/

8. HAROLD B. ALLEN

Minor Dialect Areas: Belly Buster, Dutch Cheese, Ranch Terms

> The following discussion shows something of the way in which usage boundaries (isoglosses) for selected words reveal minor dialect areas. It is from Harold B. Allen, "Minor Dialect Areas of the Upper Midwest," *Publication of the American Dialect Society*, No. 30 (November, 1958), 3-16.

Year by year new data from the regional linguistic atlases expand the outline of the great panorama of the westward extension of the principal eastern seaboard dialect patterns. Recent analyses of the field records of both the North Central [1] and the Upper Midwest [2] atlases clearly reveal that the major isogloss bundles are projections of the same basic Northern-Midland contrast first made specific by Hans Kurath in 1949 in his *Word Geography of the Eastern United States*. But the study of the Upper Midwest records reveals also the presence of significant independent minor dialect areas within this five-state region of Minnesota, Iowa, the two Dakotas, and Nebraska.

The major division in this region is indicated in Map 1 in terms of the items chosen by Marckwardt to illustrate his article on the North Central states.[3] Here the isoglosses marking the southern limit of the Northern *stone boat* and the northern limit of the Midland *belly buster* and *snake feeder* suggest that Northern speech may be receding in the Upper Mid-

[1] Albert H. Marckwardt, "Principal and Subsidiary Dialect Areas in the North-Central States," *Publication of the American Dialect Society*, No. 27 (Apr. 1957), pp. 3-16.

[2] Harold B. Allen, "Primary Dialect Areas of the Upper Midwest," an article included in the festschrift for Charles C. Fries, due to be published soon by the University of Michigan Press.

[3] It is hardly necessary to review here the methodology of dialect geography in the United States, as several recent articles in various journals have described it in some detail. The 208 informants interviewed in their Upper Midwest homes are of the accepted three types: I, oldest and least educated lifelong resident; II, middle-aged high school graduate; III, younger graduate of regional college or university, also a lifelong resident. Data from these persons have been supplemented in the Upper Midwest by replies to 137 checklist or questionnaire items returned by mail from 1069 informants representing all but two of the 400 counties.

west. Other evidence is confirmatory. Although some Northern terms have expanded into Nebraska, the general spread is only into the northeastern diagonal half of South Dakota. *Stone boat*, for example, has an incidence of 95% in Minnesota, 92% in North Dakota, 85% in South Dakota, and only 16% in Nebraska. Midland features, on the other hand, often extend north of the main dialect division and even in Minnesota may occur with statistically significant frequency. *Belly buster*, with a frequency of 58% in Iowa, has an incidence of 4% in Minnesota and 6% in North Dakota (12% and 21%, respectively, by the less reliable checklists), in contrast with zero frequency for *snake feeder* in these two Northern speech states.

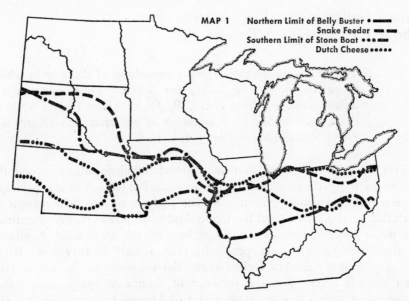

MAP 1   Northern Limit of Belly Buster •━━━
Snake Feeder ━━ ━━
Southern Limit of Stone Boat ••• ▰▰
Dutch Cheese •••••

But a number of lexical terms do not occur in geographical patterns corresponding to the isogloss divisions for known Northern and Midland features. Most of these aberrant terms, on the contrary, reveal an East-West contrast which correlates rather with the differences between the farm lands and occupations of the Midwest and the ecology of the dry Western prairies. /3/

. . . In Map 2 appear isoglosses illustrating this important subdialect split. *Flat*, or *hayflat*, when a specific use is to be indicated, is a term applied to a topographical feature common in this region, level bottomland near a lake or prairie stream, or a somewhat higher area such as a shelf of land between a stream and a plateau. Although *flat(s)* is not infrequent in New York and Pennsylvania, the term does not appear in Minnesota or Iowa, where a feature roughly similar would have one of the more common Eastern designations *meadow*, *bottoms* or *bottomland*, or perhaps *swale*.

Map 2 shows also the eastern limit of *range*, signifying open grazing land. Although much of the range country is now fenced, /5/ open expanses of thousands of acres still occur in such cattle-producing areas as Cherry

County, Nebraska; and elsewhere the word infrequently is still heard with application to very large pastures. But it does not occur in Minnesota or Iowa.

Ranch, denoting an establishment for cattle-raising and not for tilling the soil, is distributed pretty much as is *range,* although the somewhat prestigious nature of the word has spread it eastward through its adoption by farmers who have large wheat-farms or who both farm and also raise beef-cattle. A man with such a dual establishment in central Nebraska or South Dakota is more likely to identify himself as a rancher rather than as a farmer. Areal statistics for *ranch* are not available, since the item was added to the work-sheets after the completion of field work in Minnesota and Iowa.

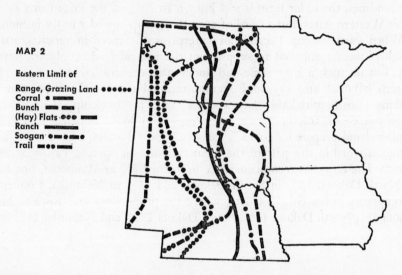

MAP 2

Eastern Limit of

Range, Grazing Land ●●●●●●
Corral ● ▬▬
Bunch ▬▬ ▬▬
(Hay) Flats ●●● ▬▬
Ranch ▬▬▬▬▬
Soogan ●▬●▬●
Trail ▬●●▬▬

With its referent a man-made feature found on a ranch, the term *corral* has almost the same distribution and frequency. It is absent in Iowa, occurs with only 1.7% of the Minnesota informants, but appears with a frequency of 73% in North Dakota, 53% in South Dakota, and 62% in Nebraska — and most of the instances are in the western two-thirds of each state. Semantically this term is peculiar in the ambiguity of the referent. Many informants use the term indifferently to apply to the enclosure itself and also to the wooden fence which forms the enclosure. The context ordinarily prevents misunderstanding. One rancher in Nebraska admitted to me in some surprise, "I guess I could say that Jim was sittin' on the corral watchin' the horses in the corral, but I sure never thought of it that way before."

Two other Western terms appear now only as relics; like their referents they have become archaic and may well disappear with this generation. One is *soogan,* of Irish origin, the name for the wool-filled comforter in a cow-puncher's bedroll. The word was reported only in the extreme western fringe of the area, and then only by informants with memories of round-up days of a generation and more ago. The other term is *jerky,* folk-etymolo-gized from Mexican Spanish *charqui,* and sometimes further transformed into *jerked-beef*, a designation for beef (or venison or, formerly, buffalo meat) sun-dried in strips. Mostly it is older Type I speakers who recall the expression, but even then only 25% in South Dakota and 20% in Nebraska.[4] In Iowa only one old-timer remembered the word; it did not turn up at all in North Dakota or Minnesota. /6/ The distribution suggests the spreading influence of the northward-traveling cattlemen from the Spanish-speaking Southwest, the source also of *lasso, lariat, rodeo, remuda,* and *canyon,* terms having their own but related distribution patterns in the plains country.

What soon may be another archaism is *trail* as the name for the meandering way over the prairie to a distant ranch. Although in most of the area the early trails have been replaced by surveyed roads that generally can follow section-lines, the older term is still known to 30% of the informants in the three Western states. But a third of even this group consider it old-fashioned.

When cattle-raising became an enterprise of fenced-in ranches, many ranchers were compelled to supplement the natural feed supply by raising hay, but on such a large scale and under such climatic conditions that the eastern *haycock* and *hayshock* seemed unsuitable terms. Lack of summer soaking rains required the "hay-waddies" only to "buck up" the hay with huge horse- or tractor-drawn haysweeps into loose bunches instead of smaller hand-prepared "cocks," "shocks," or "doodles." So *bunch* is a common word in this part of the country, with the specific variant *sweep-bunch.* The term has zero occurrence in Iowa, 3.7% in Minnesota, but 29% in North Dakota, 16% in South Dakota, and 15% in Nebraska. Confirmation appears in the checklist data, where the proportions are: Iowa 0, Minnesota 2%, North Dakota 11%, South Dakota 23%, and Nebraska 15%. /7/

9. THOMAS PYLES

Bible Belt Onomastics

> Onomastics, the study of names, is fascinating in itself; it can also make important contributions to a general understanding of how language works. The following selection is from Thomas Pyles, "Bible Belt Onomastics or Some Curiosities of Anti-Pedobaptist Nomenclature," *Names: Journal of the American Name Society,* 7 (June 1959), 84-100.

In a youth agreeably misspent *in partibus infidelium,* I was little conscious of the tendencies in name-giving with which I am here concerned. It is true that names which were thought strange or amusing did in those days occasionally come to one's attention, but they were almost invariably cited as

---

[4] One South Dakotan living not far from the Pine Ridge Indian reservation said that while he had used the term *jerky* the usual designation when he was a young man was the Sioux equivalent ['tado].

curiosa and equated with naïveté, inferior social standing, and ignorance. They were more or less sporadic even on the social level at which they were believed most likely to occur and were regarded as the creations of those who led drab and lowly lives – the onomastic *bijouterie* of the underprivileged.

It was not indeed until my translation, fairly late in life, first to the south-western and later to the southeastern sector of the Bible Belt – in Mencken's classic definition, as utilized by M. M. Mathews in the *Dictionary of Americanisms*, "those parts of the country in which the literal accuracy of the Bible is credited and clergymen who preach it have public influence" – that I first became aware of such names in high places. To what extent the onomastic mores with which I am here concerned have become nationwide I do not really know. Mr. Thomas L. Crowell in *American Speech* (XXIII [1948], 265-272) contributes some very fruity specimens from /85/ Washington, a city which has a more or less transient population, and has collected similar examples in New York City. Mencken also cites a good many from outside the Bible Belt. It is likely that the isoglosses demarcating the Fancy Names Belt have by now spread considerably beyond the limits of the Bible Belt. Two World Wars have brought hosts of anti-pedobaptists from the hills to the towns and cities, where their fecundity has shown no signs of abating. Their places of worship have moved from deserted stores to gaudy, neon-illuminated erections and, among the more sophisticated, to tabernacles of neo-Gothic and colonial meeting-house architecture. But the moral, social, and ecclesiastical customs of the rural Bethels linger on, as do also the naming habits of the remoter areas, despite increasing prosperity, superficial sophistication, and considerable distinction in business, politics, and the professions on the part of many. In the towns of the inland South and even to a large extent in the cities, the pastors of these formerly more or less obscure religious bodies [1] have retained much of the public influence which they and their predecessors had in the hill country, but unlike the pedo-baptist men of God whom they have displaced in prestige, they exert no influence over the name-giving habits of those committed to their charge. The naming of Christians is no part of their ghostly office. . . .

The effect of these circumstances peculiar to our American religious life in the matter of name-giving is obvious. Where name-giving is no part of the sacrament of baptism, and where consequently a clergyman with some sense of traditional onomastic decorum has no say, individual taste and fancy may run riot – and usually do. It is highly unlikely /86/ that any man of God, even though the canons of his church were not explicit in the matter, would consent in the course of his sacerdotal duties to confer upon hapless infants such names as Buzz Buzz, Coeta, Merdine, Aslean, La Void, Arsie,

[1] The Baptists were of course never obscure in American life. But there are now, according to my friend and former student, the Reverend James Sims, himself a Baptist pastor, at least 117 other anti-pedobaptist denominations among the 272 listed in the 1956 *World Almanac*. (Of still others he was not sure.) The groups most prominent in the inland South, in addition to the various Baptist bodies, are the Assemblies of God, the Churches of Christ, the Disciples of Christ, Jehovah's Witnesses, the Churches of God, the Pentecostal Assemblies, and the Church of the Nazarene.

Phalla, and Raz — all legal names borne by Bible Belters of repute. And it is certain that Ima Hogg, the *grande dame* of Houston society, whose father was once governor of Texas, was so named without the connivance of any anointed priest.

One result of the increasing numbers and prestige of anti-pedobaptists has thus been, ironically enough, the decline of the Christian name in what is certainly the most self-consciously and vocally Christian of all lands, where God's name is minted into the very currency and He runs on all sides of every political campaign. It has also, incidentally, given rise to a new type of urban Christianity, quite unlike anything ever known in Europe and probably never before known even in this nation under God.

The proud bearers of the names which I shall shortly begin to cite are all, unless otherwise specified, Christian Caucasians of good standing in their communities — people of sufficient importance that their engagements, their marriages, their parturitions, and, alas, their deaths are recounted fairly fully on "society" pages and in full-length obituaries in the newspapers,[2] which are a veritable onomastic treasure-trove. Other important sources have been class lists, yearbooks, official lists of voters and of property owners, telephone directories, and commencement programs. These last have provided entertainment and instruction during many commencement addresses by atomic physicists, business executives, industrialists, generals, and presidents of neighboring colleges and universities panting after yet another honorary doctorate to add to their string. Many of my handsomest specimens were collected under such otherwise depressing circumstances. It should be obvious that the names culled from these sources are not those of the underprivileged, the economically depressed, or whatever the current term for "poor and lowly" happens to be. Nor are such names to be regarded as nicknames, since they appear in formal and digni- /87/ fied surroundings — those in the commencement programs being obviously the same as those which appear in Old English calligraphy on diplomas.

The formal and official use of diminutives by adults is quite common in the Belt. The most popular of these diminutives is Billy (with "clear" *l*), usually masculine, though considered perfectly appropriate for women also, with Bobby, Johnny, and Jimmy — also bisexual — running slightly behind. In a single year (1950), no fewer than eighteen Billys, including two Billy Joes, two Billy Genes, and one feminine Billye, received degrees from the University of Oklahoma. In addition, there were four Willies.[3] At the University of Florida in the same year, three Billys graduated from a single college, Business Administration.

So prestigious is Billy, in fact, that one of Florida's representatives in Congress, Hon. Donald Ray Matthews, has adopted the name, using the official style D. R. (Billy) Matthews. It is unlikely that many of his con-

[2] Among my richest sources are the Oklahoma City *Daily Oklahoman*, the Norman (Okla.) *Transcript*, the Jacksonville *Florida Times-Union*, and the Gainseville (Fla.) *Sun*.
[3] The preferred spelling of the *W*-form seems to be *Willie* rather than *Willy*.

stituents are even aware that *Billy* is a *nom de guerre*. For similar reasons, doubtless, Rev. Dr. Billy Graham long ago abandoned the full form of his name, which happens really to be William. ("We don't put on airs in God's family.") Diminutive forms occur frequently in combination with clipped forms, as in the previously mentioned Billy Joe and Billy Gene, and with non-hypocoristic forms, as in Billy Donald, Larry Leroy, and Jerry Roscoe.

I have collected scores of printed instances of diminutives and apparent diminutives used as legal names by adults, some of them adults of advanced years, some recently gone to their Great Reward. Most of these are commonplace enough (like Dannie, Davie, and Maxie), most are bisexual, and some are diminutives by virtue of their endings, without being necessarily derivative. Only Zippie (Mrs. Billy), Sippie, Vandie, Watie, Beadie, Lamie, Collie, Cossie, Ossie, Carlie (Mrs. Bobby), Omie (f.), Fonzy, Lonzie, Lokie, Mammie, Toppy, Schiley, Mealy, Bussie, Jadie Obie (m.), Nicy, Dicey, Ledgie, Raffie, Dilly, Coarsey, Sugie, Urksey, Skeety, and Ripsie seem to me particularly noteworthy, though I confess to a personal fondness for the comparatively conventional Early Bill and Jody Elijah. /88/

. . . Often a hypocoristic name becomes so closely identified with a person that it is customarily inserted in parentheses after his legal /90/ given names or initials. This retention of what in some instances must be by-names acquired in school is by no means confined to the Bible Belt though it is probably of more frequent occurrence in anti-pedobaptist civilization than in the Sodoms and Gomorrahs of the Atlantic Coast. I must confess that I was brought up suddenly by the following item from the Gainesville *Sun* (Oct. 1, 1952, p. 5): "Friends of Mr. A. W. (Poopy) Roundtree, Sr., will be interested to know that he is recuperating following an operation in Lake City." Similar, if less colorful, specimens, all taken from printed sources, are Tootie, Tucky, Bus, Tiny (male principal of an elementary school), and Lefty. Hon. Juanita (Skeet), a former mayor of High Springs, Florida, is now languishing in durance vile at the State Penitentiary for moonshining activities. Hon. E. L. (Tic) Forester is a representative of Georgia in the U. S. Congress. Rev. Charles E. (Stoney) Jackson came into national prominence some time back as a participant in one of the TV quiz shows. Hon. J. Emory (Red) Cross represents his home county in the Florida State Legislature; his hair is not red. . . .

I am convinced that such forms as Buddy, Bubba, Bud, Buck, Sonny, Bunnie, and Buster, which occur with an almost nauseating frequency, are legal names, not merely alternate names like those cited just previously, since they appear alone in formal connotations without quotation marks. They are frequently preceded by honorifics, as in an account of a reception following a large church wedding at which Mrs. Buddy was "floor hostess" — whatever that is — and Mrs. Buster greeted guests. (*Times-Union*, Feb. 20, 1949, /91/ p. 11.) The ceremony might have been performed either by Rev. Buck or by Rev. Buddy, both of whom are in my files, but I regret to say that it was not. A third-generation Buddy is indicated in "A.O.M. 2-c. Buddy E. C. Kelly III, son of Mrs. Clara Kelly and the late Mr. Buddy E. C.

Kelly, Jr." [6] A new trend may be indicated by the fact that a Mr. and Mrs. Buddy named their son Ronald Eugene (*Times-Union*, Aug. 18, 1958, p. 22) and a Mr. and Mrs. Sonny named theirs Randy Allen (*loc. cit.*).

Because they share a certain indefinable folksy quality which is highly regarded in the inland South, I have grouped the following names, some of them derivative forms, together; all are borne by substantial citizens: Lum, Dub, Teet, Quince, Zack, Zeph, Zeb, Clem, Wash, and Sim. Had I never been privileged to live in the Bible Belt, I should have thought to this day that their only existence was in the literature of backhouse humor. *Ish*, though it had no previous associations for me, seems to me nevertheless to have the same homely, down-to-earth flavor. It is borne by Hon. Ish W. Brant, Superintendent of Public Instruction of Duval County, Florida (the county seat of which is Jacksonville), who has the additional distinction of being governor of the Florida District of Kiwanis International. When Hon. Ish was merely a candidate for the political office which he now holds with grace and distinction, his campaign slogan was "Ish Is Everybody's Wish." His opponents were Mr. Coke L. Barr and Mrs. Iva Sprinkle. /92/

. . . The armed services have been a prolific source of names. My collections include General Phillips and Lieutenant Tisdale who were inducted into the army as privates at Knoxville, Tennessee (*Times-Union*, March 11, 1952, p. 5); Major General Williams, who at the age of 17 enlisted in Birmingham, Alabama, as a member of the Marine Corps, explaining to reporters that his parents decided to name him something "everybody else wasn't" (*Times-Union*, Jan. 11, 1958, p. 17); and General Morgan, who died in Waycross, Georgia, in 1952, survived by a son named Colonel. But it is unnecessary to multiply examples of generals who have never heard the roar of cannon fire; I have many more. I consider General Salor [*sic*] (*Sun*, Sept. 24, 1954, p. 8) and General Ulysses Grant (his full name) who graduated from the University of Florida in 1956 with a B.S. in Education, to be my prize specimens. I pray that General Grant does not encounter discrimination if he is now practicing his chosen profession in the Confederacy. Colonel and Major are also popular, but I have only a single Cap, a single Ensign, a single (aforementioned) Lieutenant, and, it is perhaps needless to say, no Sergeants, Corporals, or Privates. Bishop and Judge occur a number of times, but these are probably family names, particularly the first when borne by anti-episcopalians. Missie Frankie was a first-year student in the University of Florida in 1957-58, and may well now be a sophomore for all I know.

When one has the same surname as a great man or woman, the temptation to confer his or her given name (or names) upon one's /93/ offspring — and in the case of the aforementioned General Ulysses Grant, a title as well — is for many Bible Belters practically irresistible. (In the examples which follow I shall of course be required to give surnames.) Enrollment records at the University of Florida since 1900 disclose the fact that its student body has included, as is to be expected, a good many Robert E. Lees, along with

---

[6] This gem appeared in the Gainesville *Sun*. The cutting is in my possession, but I carelessly neglected to take down the date.

a number of Andrew Jacksons and Benjamin Franklins. My researches in the newspapers and telephone directories have brought to light Lon Chaney, Gloria Swanson, Jefferson Davis, Woodrow Wilson, George K. Washington and his daughter Martha, William H. Taft, Dick Whittington, and Josh Billings. When Abe Lincoln of Oklahoma City made a contribution to that city's United Fund, the fact was considered newsworthy by the Associated Press (*Sun*, Dec. 4, 1958, p. 7), but no Oklahoman would consider it anything out of the ordinary, for in that state alone Daniel Boone, Oliver Cromwell, Joe E. Brown, Mae West, Joan Crawford, Brigham Young, Al Jennings, Will Rogers, Huey Long, Jack Dempsey, William Cullen Bryant, and Robert Burns have all aspired to, and some have held, political office. As Secretary of the American Dialect Society, I was always delighted to receive a cheque for subscription of the University of Texas signed by, of all people, Jesse James, Texas State Treasurer. Bryan Jennings, of Norman, Oklahoma, Lee Grant, formerly of the University of Florida, and De Leon Ponce, late of Jacksonville, Florida, present interesting anomalies. /94/

. . . A number of bisexual names have already been cited. Lee, Pat, Jo(e), Robin, and Lynn are doubtless given to boys and girls indiscriminately all over the country nowadays, and can hardly be considered Bible Belt names. The following names, which are usually feminine or which one would expect to be feminine, are borne by males in the inland South: Paulyne, Pearlie, Delories, Fay, Adell, Ardelle, Ellie, Bonnie, June, Junell, Merrilett Jessie, Loice, Jewell, Bernice (also Burnice), Ivy, Buna Joe, Pink, Jonice, Dixie, Beryl, Nance, Bronzell, Alvine, Nolia, Cledith, Dee, Elizie, Gayle, Rae, Ovida, Jackie Jo, Sam Ella, Laurie, Carman, Verdell, Juadean, Lorraine, Sharon Lee, Amander, Berta, and Euzema, Jr. Conversely, the following apparently masculine names are borne by females: Terry (also -ie), Gil, Stacy, Tracy, Bobbie, Laddie, Mick, Mickie, Ira, Bennie, Benjie, Mackie, Willie, Jimmie, Tommy, Kimberly Ann, Kelley, Nigel, Vincent, Juan, Billie Joe, Danny, Deane, /95/ Don, Page, Toni, Maxie, Montez, Nathan, Sandy, Glen, Sammie, and Henri.[8] The popularity of LaVoid and LaVerne, both bisexual, I am totally at a loss to explain. It may be that some of these onomastic reversals of sex may be due to the desire to name a male child after his mother, or a female child after her father. A number of names borne by females are somehow formed from the given name of a male relative, usually the father, e.g., Julie Anne (dau. of Julian), Philelle, Lloydene, Gina (dau. of Gene), Basilene (dau. of Alfred Basil), Charlsie, Dennisteen, Donita (dau. of J. Don), Elmerine, Johnita (dau. of Johnny), Orvillyne, Harolyn (dau. of Harold), and Methadene (dau. of Metha). /96/

. . . I hasten to cite a few miscellaneous whimsicalities, all full names, which have appealed to me for one reason or another: Oleander Lafayette Fitzgerald III, Ed Ek, Shellie Swilley, Early Hawaiian McKinnon, Sandy Gandy, Earl Curl, Jr., Percy Nursey, Rev. Fay de Sha (m.), Lovie Slappey, Esperanza LeSocke, Pamela Gay Day, Staff-Sgt. Mehogany Brewer, Girlie

---

[8] This last is also cited by Crowell, *loc. cit.*, p. 271, along with other bisexual names which I have not encountered.

Burns, Fawn Grey Trawick Dunkle, Alure Sweat (f., sister of Alfa, Alta, Sabry, and the late Cleveland Sweat [*Times-Union*, Feb. 12, 1958, p. 22]), Bloomer Bedenbaugh, Martha Magdalene Toot, Okla Bobo, and Melody Clinkenbeard. The last-cited given name may be bisexual, for a fellow townsman of Miss Clinkenbeard's is Hon. Melody Reynolds, an officer of the Veterans of Foreign Wars in Norman, Oklahoma. The same bisexuality seems to be characteristic of Memory: Hon. Memory Martin is lieutenant governor of division 6, Florida Kiwanis district, as well as a former school teacher and principal; my files also disclose Memorie Frances Griner, whom I take to be female from the spelling of the second name. Hon. Cowboy Pink Williams, former Lieutenant Governor of Oklahoma, was defeated to succeed himself in 1958 despite a style which should have endeared him to all Southwesterners. It is possible that Cowboy Pink is merely a *nom de guerre,* but the hon. gentleman is so listed in the 1958 *World Almanac* and in the *Britannica* Yearbook.

In the whimsies which follow I omit surnames: Dawn Robin, Kitty Bit, Lance Amorus, Lovely, Charme, Greek (f.), Pearl Garnet, Dimple, Dixie, Pixianne, Cherry, Orchid Favia (f.), Rose Bud, Satire, Fairy (a missionary of the Church of the Nazarene to Africa, *Times-Union*, Jan. 26, 1952, p. 6), Acid, Buzz Buzz, Tyty, Hubert Herbert, Kae Rae, Mary Sunshine, Boysy, Madonna Ruth, Delyte, Doe, Dovey, Echo, Edelweiss, and Brunette (who turned out to be a blond). The children of Mr. Stanford Bardwell, a realtor and a graduate of Louisiana State University, and his wife Loyola, are Stanford, Jr., Harvard, Princeton, Cornell, Auburn, and the twins Duke and T'lane. When the Bardwells go on a holiday they travel in a specially equipped school bus called the "Collegiate Caravan." (*Times-Union*, Aug. 29, 1954, p. 13.) /97/

The following combinations of given name and surname represent the conscious, if misguided, humor of parents with no priestly hand to guide or restrain them, though some are doubtless to be attributed simply to parental naïveté: Pleasant Weathers, Honey Combs, French Crown, Golden Gamble, Royal Child, Goode Carr, Early Priest, Robin Starling, Paris Singer, Paris Miracle, Etta Turnipseed, Summer Robbins, Shari Glass, Fannie Bottom, Love Snow (f.), Rocky Mountain, Alto Hooten, Early Wages, Drew Swords, English Piper, Candy Barr, and Minor Peeples. Everyone has by now doubtless heard of Dill L. Pickle, of Rolling Fork, Mississippi, who grew up to be a pickle salesman for Paramount Foods, a Louisville concern. Less widely publicized are Never Fail of Oklahoma City, who did fail to graduate from Harding Junior High School in that city (*Sun*, May 26, 1950, p. 7) and Dr. Safety First of Tulsa, Oklahoma. I have elsewhere recorded Bunker Hill, Charming Fox, Ima Fox, Diamond Queen, France Paris, Jack Frost, Winter Frost, Merry English, Erie Lake, Pinky Bottom, Virgin Muse, and Fairy Guy, among a good many other such jocular and would-be jocular names (*American Speech*, XXIII [1947], 263). It seems to me unlikely than any of these names — and they are legal names, not nicknames — were conferred in the course of administering the sacrament of baptism. /98/

Subjects for Discussion

1. How do languages of the same family reveal their kinship?

2. In what sense is Grimm's Law a law?

3. How can one account for the similarity of such words as English *mother*, Celtic *mathaer*, Latin *mater*, and Persian *mader?*

4. What are some of the characteristics common to languages of the Teutonic group?

5. List, with illustrations, the types of semantic change distinguished by Potter. Which of Potter's terms is the equivalent of Laird's *generalization?*

6. By studying examples of words you know, distinguish between specialization and extension of meaning.

7. What does Sapir apparently mean by the word *grammar* and how does his use of the word differ from any way in which you have usually used the word?

8. How does the linguistic geographer plot an isogloss?

Suggestions for Investigation, Reports, or Brief Papers

1. Use the story of *tap* as a model for a similar "biography" of a word; common words, like *dig, place, mill,* or *hand,* are likely to prove the most interesting. Use several dictionaries, especially the detailed ones such as the *Century, A Dictionary of Americanisms,* and particularly the *Oxford English Dictionary,* also called the *New English Dictionary.*

2. From your own observation collect words that have acquired use and meaning metaphorically; slang is often a fruitful field for such words.

3. Write down a few dozen words from a field of study or work in which you are interested; for example, in printing you might have *type, press, paper, ink, serif, matrix, column, stick, chase, justify, stereotype,* and the like. Find out which of these words have come down within the language from Old English and which have been borrowed, and if possible, when (the *Oxford English Dictionary* — the *OED* — gives dates). Then ask yourself the most interesting questions you can about these words. How do they illustrate the history of their subject? What do they suggest about the times when English was borrowing words from French, Latin, or another language? What kinds of semantic change do they illustrate?

4. Try your hand at linguistic geography. This is too complicated and specialized to be much pursued by amateurs, but you can make a start with your friends. For instance, *seesaw* occurs throughout the United States and *teeter-totter* is common. On the other hand, *teetering board, dandle, tilt, tippity-bounce, hicky-horse* and some others have only very limited currency. Try to find out whether your community is unusual in some of its speech habits. Can you find words, slang or standard, that seem to have developed only in one college or in a limited group of colleges; what, for example, is your term for failing a course? Words listed below, for example, have interesting regional distribution. You might endeavor to discover which are current in your community, and whether they show any social variation. Which words are known to which sorts of people? Which words are known but not normally used? You may also encounter forms not listed here. Count only synonyms as you find them used; for example, *loft* is used as a term for a storage room where it is not used as a term for a haymow, and *meadows* is restricted to bottom lands only in certain areas.

1. parlor, living room, sitting room (settin' room)
2. kindling wood, fat pine, pitch pine, rich pine, lightwood
3. andirons, fire dogs, dog irons, dogs, irons
4. roller shades, curtains, blinds
5. porch, piazza, stoop, veranda, gallery
6. eaves troughs (eaves), gutters, spouts, spouting, water troughs
7. (hay) mow, loft, overhead, over-den
8. rail fence, worm fence, zigzag fence, snake fence, Virginia rail fence
9. frying pan, skillet, spider, fry pan
10. paper bag (sack), poke, toot, tote bag
11. singletree, whippletree, whiffletree, swiveltree, swingletree
12. bottom lands, bottoms, flats, low-lands, meadows, savannahs
13. lake, pond, playa, pool, eye, meer
14. creek, brook, river, run, branch, kill
15. bull, sire, brute, beast, critter, animal, seed ox, masculine
16. co-boss, co-bossie, sook, sookie, co-wench, co-inch, wookie
17. doughnut, fried cake, cruller, cookie, fat-cake, nut cake, ring
18. dragon fly, snake feeder, (devil's) darning needle, snake doctor, mosquito hawk, snake guarder
19. sick at (to, on, in) the stomach
20. play truant, play hooky, skip school, lay out, hook Jack

5. On the basis of Pyles's article, make a study of naming practices. For example, compare the first names of adults on a page of the telephone directory, with the first names of the students in your class, or in a section of the student directory. Reading of early American writing will reveal that Ebenezer, Obadiah, and Shadrach were not uncommon. By using a copy of *Who's Who in America* can you find out when they declined? Continuing to use *Who's Who* and other sources of the kind mentioned by Pyles — newspapers, graduation lists, directories, etc. — answer other questions about naming. Have Bible names decreased or increased, and in what parts of the country? Which Biblical or holy names are used as given names and which are not? (*Jesus* is a common name for boys in Mexico, but not in the United States; *Mary* is common for girls, *Angel* is rare.) What has become of *Prudence, Hope,* and *Charity* as names? Why was *Woodrow* a popular name for boys about the time of the first World War? Did the 1950's show any increase in the popularity of *Ike* as a name? When did *Sharon* and *Nancy* become popular and *Lulu* decline? What influence has foreign nationality, say Italian or Danish, had upon given names? How many occupations do you find represented as the sources of names? Can you make up further questions about names?

III. THE LANGUAGE AS IT WAS

The preceding section provided background information about language; this and the following sections provide materials for the study of language. The selections are arranged for historical study; we shall look first at an early form of English, compare it with intermediate forms, and eventually consider contemporary English as we speak it and write it. Although the historical study of English may not provide the most important approach to an understanding of how language works, it may provide the most revealing way to begin. We can often understand what is happening if we see how similar events have happened.

For example, in Section II it was frequently asserted that language is changing, and this assertion was based partly on the fact that language always has changed. Presumably the reader accepted this statement, even though he may have accepted it on faith, but the statement can scarcely mean much to him until he has seen evidence of the change. Language changes so slowly that no man in his lifetime can observe much alteration; he can see the change dramatically only if he compares the language at different stages over the centuries. Furthermore, he is not likely to know what the word "change" means specifically in this context. How does language change? What changes? How fast does it change? Does one part or aspect of language change while another remains? These questions require at least something by way of answer.

Accordingly in this section we shall start with a simple example of an early form of our language and work toward the present. To begin, we have a version of the Gospels written in the English of the late tenth century. It is not the earliest example of English; Old English, also called Anglo-Saxon, exists in verse that probably was composed as early as the seventh century. But this early verse is complicated and difficult, too difficult to begin with, and we can find ample evidence of changes in the language if we start with the English of about a thousand years ago.

From the Old English version of the Gospels we have selected the Sermon on the Mount. It is printed in diplomatic text, which reproduces the original manuscript as exactly as is reasonably possible in modern print, including the old spellings, obsolete letters, and lost forms of words. We have provided a verbatim translation to help the student find which word is which and what it is doing in the sentence. Examination of the passage and comparison with later versions of the same material reveal that English has changed in spelling, punctuation, word form, word meaning, and grammar in the past thousand years. It has also changed in sound, although demonstrating these changes is harder. We may have to be content with only token evidence of changes in sound, but the careful student may be able to observe, tracing the versions down through the centuries, that these changes reveal at least some continuing tendencies.

Demonstrating that the language as a whole has changed, however, is not enough; we might start by recalling the statement in the preceding section that language grows and changes at least in part by dialects. Observing dialects in our own time is quite easy; everyone knows that people who have grown up in Boston speak differently from those who have lived their lives in Dallas, that natives of the New York East Side do not speak like natives of Portland, Oregon. But appreciating and remembering that such dialectal differences have been characteristic of all languages at all times — or so we suppose — is not so easy. Accordingly, we shall study differences in dialect in Middle English times, differences that reflect levels of society and geographical areas. Geoffrey Chaucer, a sophisticated courtly gentleman, spoke and wrote differently from his contemporary, Sir John Mandeville; although we know too little about Mandeville, compared with Chaucer he must have been a mundane person. Sir Thomas Malory, a rural gentleman by breeding if not by manners, probably would have had difficulty understanding his literary contemporary Robert Henryson, who lived a few hundred miles to the north.

The samples of English in this section span six hundred years in which the language was changing relatively rapidly, probably more rapidly than it had ever changed or is likely to change again. Why it changed so rapidly we cannot be sure. We assume it changed because it was in conflict with other languages; languages tend to change more rapidly when they are fighting for their lives. During the first half of this period English won two big battles. First the Danes and Norwegians came, bringing their languages with them and settling down all over northern England. Then the Normans came and made their Norman French the official language. When English had triumphed over these two rivals it embarked on a period of unprecedented borrowing from Continental French and from Latin and Greek. Thus, whatever the reason, the half millennium 1100-1600 provides remarkable evidence of linguistic change.

Within limits this sample half millennium of change in English may be accepted as exemplary — provided one makes sufficient allowance for the reservations involved in that phrase, "within limits." All languages are different, all exist under different conditions and are used by differing peoples; accordingly, we must surely assume that no two languages ever change in precisely the same ways. In fact, we should probably assume that they will change in notably different ways in different times and places. Thus, many of the changes revealed in English may be characteristic only of English, but others will inevitably be characteristic of many or even all languages. If we study English with an eye for essentials we shall also, to a degree, be studying language.

10.

Old English to the Present:
Versions of the Sermon on the Mount

One of the best records of the development of the English language is the English Bible, in its many versions dating from before 1000 A.D. Following are nine versions of the Sermon on the Mount as recorded in Matthew 5:1-16.

The first three are samples of Old and Middle English. The first column contains an Old English or Anglo-Saxon version, essentially that in Corpus Christi College, Cambridge, MS. Ii.2.11, of the period just before 1000. The second column is a verbatim modernization of the Old English, intended not as a translation, but only as an aid in understanding the original. The word order has been preserved, and where possible the original word has been suggested, even though the translation thereby becomes awkward; thus *menigu* is rendered *manyness* to suggest that it is the noun related to *many*, although *multitude* would provide a smoother translation. The third version is associated with John Wycliffe; it is Middle English, and can be accepted as a fair sample of English a little before 1400. Both of these old versions are presumably based upon the Latin version of St. Jerome, known as the Vulgate. The Old English and Wycliffite versions, along with William Tyndale's of 1526, are taken from *Gothic and Anglo-Saxon Gospels*, edited by Joseph Bosworth (3rd ed., London, 1888).

Punctuation and capitalization in the Old and Middle English versions have been modernized; the spelling of the originals has been preserved. Old English letters were made somewhat differently from modern English letters, but since they are obviously the same letters they are printed here in modern type. A few which have not survived will probably be strange to you. Two symbols, þ and ð, are equivalents of *th* in *this* or *think*, and by late Old English times were used interchangeably. The symbol ȝ was used for various sounds, sometimes for a sound like *y* in *yellow*, for sounds now indicated by *h* or *g*, and for a sound that we have lost, although it survives in German. It can be approximated by trying to pronounce *khkhkh*. The ligature *æ* is the same as that which appears in many Latin words and modern spellings like *æsthetic*, but it was probably pronounced about like the *a* in *hat* in most American speech. Other letters that seem to have been used interchangeably are *v* and *u*, *y* and *i*.

The next three translations exemplify the many versions which grew from the religious controversies of the sixteenth century. The first of these, Tyndale's translation, served as a basis for the King James version in the next century. The next version is a selection from the Geneva Bible of 1560, also known as the Breeches Bible from its rendering of Genesis 3:7 as "They sewed fig leaves together, and made themselves breeches." Even though its use was prohibited in Anglican churches, the Geneva Bible was one of the most popular Protestant versions of the century, with nearly a hundred and fifty editions between 1560 and 1644. Like Tyndale's it did not rely exclusively on the Latin of Jerome but went back to the original Greek and Hebrew texts. In 1582 an English-language Roman Catholic New Testament, based on the Vulgate, was printed at Rheims to compete with the many Protestant Bibles that had appeared. This New Testament together with the Old Testament which was translated and published in Douai in 1609-10 comprise the modern Roman Catholic Bible in English, called the "Douay." A selection from the Rheims translation appears as the sixth version. All the versions preserve original spelling and punctuation except for modernization of some conventions of sixteenth-century printing.

The seventh version is a selection based on the King James translation, which appeared in 1611 after several years of work by some fifty-four clergymen and scholars, and which has been called "the noblest monument of English prose." The eighth and ninth are modern versions of the Bible based primarily on the King James version: James Moffatt, *The Bible, a New Translation* (New York, 1922), and *The Holy Bible, Revised Standard Version*, sponsored by the National Council of the Churches of Christ (New York, 1952).

OLD ENGLISH, *995*

1. Soþlice ða se Hælend geseh ða menigu, he astah on ðone munt; and ða he sæt, ða genealæhton his leorning-cnihtas to him.

2. And he ontynde his muþ, and lærde hi, and cwæth,

3. Eadige synd ða gastlican þearfan, forðam hyra ys heofena rice.

5.* Eadige synd ða liþan, forðam ðe hi eorþan agun.

[*So numbered in the original.]

TRANSLATION OF OLD ENGLISH

1. Truly, when the Holy One saw the manyness [of people], he climbed on the mount [i.e., hill], and there he sat, then near-came his learning-knights to him.

2. And he opened his mouth and taught them and said,

3. Blessed are the spirits poor, for theirs is of heavens [the] kingdom.

5.* Blessed are the lithe [i.e., mild], for that they earth [will] own.

[*So numbered in the original.]

4. Eadige synd ða ðe nu wepaþ, forðam ðe hi beoþ gefrefrede.

6. Eadige synd ða ðe for riht-wisnesse hingriaþ and þyrstaþ, for-þam ðe hi beoþ gefyllede.

7. Eadige synd ða mild-heortan, forðam ðe hi mild-heortnysse begytaþ.

8. Eadige synd ða clæn-heortan, forðam ðe hi God geseoþ.

9. Eadige synd ða gesybsuman, forðam ðe hi beoþ Godes bearn genemnede.

10. Eadige synd ða ðe ehtnysse þoliaþ for rihtwisnysse, forðam ðe hyra ys heofonan rice.

11. Eadige synd ge, þonne he wyriaþ eow, and ehtaþ eow, and secgeaþ ælc yfel ongen eow leogende, for me.

12. Geblissaþ and gefægniaþ, for-ðam ðe eower med ys mycel on heofonum; swa he ehtun ða witegan ðe beforan eow wæron.

13. Ge synd eorþan sealt; gyf ðæt sealt awyrþ, on ðam ðe hit gesylt biþ? Hit ne mæg syððan to nahte, buton ðæt hit sy ut-aworpen, and sy fram mannum fortreden.

14. Ge synd middan-eardes leoht; ne mæg seo ceaster beon behyd ðe byþ uppan munt aset.

15. Ne hi ne ælaþ hyra leoht-fæt, and hit under cyfe settaþ, ac ofer candel-stæf, ðæt hit onlihte eallum ðam ðe on ðam huse synd.

16. Swa onlihte eower leoht beforan mannum, ðæt he geseon eowre godan weorc, and wuldrian eowerne fæder ðe on heofonum ys.

4. Blessed are they who now weep, for that they are [i.e., will be] joyed.

6. Blessed are they that for righteousness hunger and thirst, for that they are [i.e., will be] filled.

7. Blessed are the mild-hearted, for that they mild-heartedness [will] get.

8. Blessed are the clean-hearted, for that they God [will] see.

9. Blessed are the sib-group [i.e., peaceful], for that they are [i.e., will be] God's children called.

10. Blessed are those that punishment suffer for righteousness, for that theirs is of the heavens kingdom.

11. Blessed are [i.e., will be] you, when they curse you, and hurt you, and say all evil against you lying, for me.

12. Be blissful and be fain [related to *fair* and *peace*] for that your need is [i.e., will be] great in heaven; so they did [to] the knowing ones that before you were.

13. You are of the earth salt; if the salt away-does, with what that it salted is [i.e., will be]? It not may since to nothing; but that it be out-thrown, and be by man down-trodden.

14. You are middle-earth's light; nor may the castle [*chester* as in *Winchester*, meaning *camp, town*] be hidden that is up on mount [or *mound*, meaning *hill*] set.

15. Nor they not make-burn their light-fat [i.e., lamp], and it under sieve [basket] set, but on candle-staff, that it light all those that in the house are.

16. So out-light your light before men, that they see your good work and glorify your father who in heaven is.

WYCLIFFE GOSPELS, *1389*

1. Jhesu forsothe, seynge cumpanyes, wente vp in to an hill; and when he hadde sete, his disciplis camen niȝe to hym.

2. And he, openinge his mouthe, tauȝte to hem, sayinge,

3. Blessed be the pore in spirit, for the kingdam in heuenes is heren.

5.* Blessid be the mylde men, for thei shuln welde the eerthe.

4. Blessid be thei that mournen, for thei shuln be comfortid.

6. Blessid be thei that hungren and thristen riȝtwisnesse, for thei shuln ben fulfillid.

7. Blessid be mercyful men, for thei shuln get mercye.

8. Blessid be thei that ben of clene herte, for thei shuln see God.

9. Blessid be pesible men, for thei shuln be clepid the sonys of God.

10. Blessid be thei that suffren persecucioun for riȝtwisnesse, for the kyngdam of heuenes is herun.

11. ȝee shulen be blessid, when men shulen curse ȝou, and shulen pursue ȝou, and shulen say all yuel aȝeins ȝou leeȝing, for me.

12. Ioye ȝee with yn forth, and glade ȝee with out forth, for ȝoure meede is plenteuouse in heuenes; forsothe so thei han pursued and prophetis that weren before ȝou.

13. ȝee ben salt of the erthe; that ȝif the salt shal vanyshe awey, wherynne shal it be saltid? To no thing it is worth ouer, no bot that it be sent out, and defoulid of men.

14. ȝe ben liȝt of the world; a citee putt on an hill may nat be hid.

15. Nether men tendyn a lanterne, and putten it vndir a busshel, but on a candilstike, that it ȝeue liȝt to all that ben in the hous.

16. So shyyne ȝoure liȝt before men, that thei see ȝoure good werkis, and glorifie ȝoure fadir that is in heuens.

TYNDALE GOSPELS, *1526*

1. When he sawe the people, he went vp into a mountayne; and when he was set, his disciples cam vnto hym.

2. And he openned his mought, and taught them, saynge,

3. Blessed are the poore in sprete, for theirs is the kyngdome off heven.

4. Blessed are they that morne, for they shalbe comforted.

5. Blessed are the meke, for they shall inheret the erth.

6. Blessed are they which honger and thurst for rightewesnes, for they shalbe filled.

7. Blessed are the mercifull, for they shall obteyne mercy.

8. Blessed are the pure in herte, for they shall se God.

9. Blessed are the maynteyners of peace, for they shalbe called the chyldren of God.

[*So numbered in the original.]

10. Blessed are they which suffre persecucion for rightewesnes sake, for theirs ys the kyngdome off heven.

11. Blessed are ye, when men shall revyle you, and persecute you, and shall falsly say all manner of yvell saynges agaynst you, ffor my sake.

12. Reioyce, and be glad, for greate is youre rewarde in heven; for so persecuted they the prophets which were before youre dayes.

13. Ye are the salt of the erthe; but and if the salt be once vnsavery, what can be salted ther with? It is thence-forthe goode for nothynge, but to be cast oute at the dores, and that men treade it vnder fete.

14. Ye are the light of the worlde; a cite that is set on an hill cannot be hid;

15. Nether do men lyght a candell, and put it vnder a busshell, but on a candelstick, and it lighteth all them which are in the housse.

16. Se that youre light so shyne before men, that they maye se youre good workes, and glorify youre father which is in heven.

GENEVA BIBLE, *1560*

1. And when he sawe the multitude, he went vp into a mountaine: and when he was set his disciples came to him.

2. And he opened his mouthe and taught them, saying,

3. Blessed are the poore in spirit, for theirs is the kingdome of heauen.

4. Blessed are they that mourne, for they shalbe comforted.

5. Blessed are the meke: for they shal inherite the earth.

6. Blessed are they which honger & thirst for righteousnes: for they shal be filled.

7. Blessed are the merciful: for thei shal obteine mercie.

8. Blessed are the pure in heart: for they shal se God.

9. Blessed are the peace makers: for they shalbe called the children of God.

10. Blessed are they which suffer persecution for righteousnes sake: for theirs is the kingdome of heauen.

11. Blessed are ye when men reuile you, and persecute you, and say all maner of euil against you for my sake, falsely.

12. Reioyce and be glad, for great is your rewarde in heauen: for so persecuted they the Prophets which were before you.

13. Ye are the salte of the earth: but if the salte haue lost his sauour, wherewith shal it be salted? It is thenceforthe good for nothing, but to be cast out & to be troden vnderfote of men.

14. Ye are the light of the worlde. A citie that is set on an hill, can not be hid.

15. Nether do men light a candel, and put it vnder a bushel, but on a candelsticke, & it giueth light vnto all that are in the house.

16. Let your light so shine before men, that they may se your good workes, & glorifie your Father which is in heauen.

RHEIMS (DOUAI) BIBLE, *1582*

1   †And seeing the multitudes, he vvent vp into a mountaine: and
2   vvhen he vvas set, his Disciples came vnto him, †and opening his
      mouth he taught them, saying
3   †Blessed are the poore in Spirit: for theirs is the Kingdom of
4   heauen. †Blessed are the meeke: for they shall possesse the land.
5, 6 †Blessed are they that mourne: for they shall be comforted. †Blessed
      are they that hunger & thirst after iustice: for they shall haue
7   their fil. †Blessed are the merciful: for they shal obtayne mercie.
8, 9 †Blessed are the cleane of hart: for they shal see God. †Blessed are
      the peace-makers: for they shal be called the children of God.
10   †Blessed are they that suffer persecution for iustice: for theirs is
11   the Kingdom of heauen. †Blessed are ye vvhen they shal reuile
      you, and persecute you, & speake al that naught is agaynst you,
12   vntruely, for my sake: †be glad & reioyce, for your revvard is
      very great in heauen. For so they persecuted the Prophets, that
      vvere before you.
13, 14   †You are the salt of the earth. †But if the salt leese his vertue,
      vvherevvith shal it be salted? It is good for nothing any more but
15   to be cast forth, and to be troden of men. †You are the light of
16   the vvorld. A citie cannot be hid, situated on a mountaine. †Neither
      do men light a candel and put it vnder a bushel, but vpon a candle-
17   sticke, that it may shine to al that are in the house. †So let your
      light shine before men: that they may see your good vvorkes, and
      glorifie your father vvhich is in heauen.

KING JAMES, *1611*

And seeing the multitudes, he went up into a mountaine: and when he
was set, his disciples came unto him.

2. And he opened his mouth, and taught them, saying,

3. Blessed are the poore in spirit: for theirs is the kingdome of heauen.

4. Blessed are they that mourne: for they shall be comforted.

5. Blessed are the meeke: for they shall inherit the earth.

6. Blessed are they which doe hunger and thirst after righteousnesse: for
they shall be filled.

7. Blessed are the mercifull: for they shall obtaine mercie.

8. Blessed are the pure in heart: for they shall see God.

9. Blessed are the peacemakers: for they shall bee called the children of
God.

10. Blessed are they which are persecuted for righteousnesse sake: for
theirs is the kingdome of heauen.

11. Blessed are ye, when men shall reuile you, and persecute you, and
shall say all manner of euil against you falsly for my sake.

12. Reioyce, and be exceeding glad: for great is your reward in heauen: For so persecuted they the Prophets which were before you.

13. Yee are the salt of the earth: But if the salt haue lost his sauour, where-with shall it bee salted? It is thenceforth good for nothing, but to be cast out, and to be troden under foote of men.

14. Yee are the light of the world. A citie that is set on an hill, cannot be hid.

15. Neither doe men light a candle, and put it under a bushell: but on a candlesticke, and it giueth light unto all that are in the house.

16. Let your light so shine before men, that they may see your good workes, and glorifie your father which is in heauen.

MOFFATT TRANSLATION, *1922*

So when he saw the crowds, he went up the hill and sat down; his
2 disciples came up to him and he opened his lips and began to teach them. He said:

3 "Blessed are those who feel poor in spirit!
the Realm of heaven is theirs.

4 Blessed are the mourners!
they will be consoled.

5 Blessed are *the humble!*
they *will inherit the earth.*

6 Blessed are those who hunger and thirst for goodness!
they will be satisfied.

7 Blessed are the merciful!
they will find mercy.

8 Blessed are the pure in heart!
they will see God.

9 Blessed are the peacemakers!
they will be ranked sons of God.

10 Blessed are those who have been persecuted for the sake of goodness!
the Realm of heaven is theirs.

11 Blessed are you when men denounce you and persecute you and utter all manner of evil against you for my sake;

12 rejoice and exult in it, for your reward is rich in heaven; that is how they persecuted the prophets before you.

13 You are the salt of the earth. But if the salt becomes insipid, what can make it salt again? After that it is fit for nothing, fit only to be thrown outside and trodden by the feet of men.

14 You are the light of the world. A town on the top of a hill cannot
15 be hidden. Nor do men light a lamp to put it under a bowl; they put it on a stand and it shines for all in the house. So your light
16 is to shine before men, that they may see the good you do and glorify your Father in heaven."

REVISED STANDARD, *1952*

Seeing the crowds, he went up on the mountain, and when he sat down his disciples came to him.

2 And he opened his mouth and taught them, saying:

3 "Blessed are the poor in spirit, for theirs is the kingdom of heaven.

4 "Blessed are those who mourn, for they shall be comforted.

5 "Blessed are the meek, for they shall inherit the earth.

6 "Blessed are those who hunger and thirst for righteousness, for they shall be satisfied.

7 "Blessed are the merciful, for they shall obtain mercy.

8 "Blessed are the pure in heart, for they shall see God.

9 "Blessed are the peacemakers, for they shall be called sons of God.

10 "Blessed are those who are persecuted for righteousness' sake, for theirs is the kingdom of heaven.

11 "Blessed are you when men revile you and persecute you and utter all kinds of evil against you falsely on my account. 12 Rejoice and be glad, for your reward is great in heaven, for so men persecuted the prophets who were before you.

13 "You are the salt of the earth; but if the salt has lost its taste, how shall its saltness be restored? It is no longer good for anything except to be thrown out and trodden under foot by men.

14 "You are the light of the world. A city set on a hill cannot be hid.

15 "Nor do men light a lamp and put it under a bushel, but on a stand, and it gives light to all in the house. 16 Let your light so shine before men, that they may see your good works and give glory to your Father who is in heaven."

11. SIR JOHN MANDEVILLE

Middle-Class Middle English

The following purports to be the account of a journey to the Holy Land by one Sir John Mandeville, Gentleman. It probably is not, but whoever wrote or translated this version must have been a contemporary of Wycliffe and Chaucer, writing in Middle English. It is obviously not the work of a skilled mind, and it can be accepted as an approximation of speech of upper middle-class people about 1400. The first version is diplomatic; it preserves the original, including the punctuation and capitalization. Letters printed in italics are not in the original, but are represented by a sign of abbreviation. For instance, the word for *marvel* appears *m'uaylle*, since frequently in Middle English the sound we represent with *v* is represented by *u*, and the *er* is represented by a curved sign not unlike an inverted apostrophe. This extract is taken from *Mandeville's Travels* as edited by P. Hamelius for the Early English Text Society, Original Series, No. 153 (London, 1909). For symbols like þ see the introduction to the Old English passage above. The modernization in the second version preserves the word order of the original.

In Ethiope all the Ryueres & all the watres ben trouble & þei ben somdell salte for the gret hete þat is þere. And the folk of þat contree ben lyghtly dronken & han but litill appetyt to mete And þei han comounly the flux of the wombe & þei lyuen not longe. In Ethiope ben many dyuerse folk And Ethiope is clept Cusis. In þat contree ben folk þat han but o foot & þei gon so blyue þat it is meruaylle And the foot is so large þat it schadeweth all the body aзen the sonne Whanne þei wole lye & reste hem. In Ethiope whan the children ben зonge & lytill þei ben all зalowe And whan þat þei wexen of age þat зalowness turneth to ben all blak. In Ethiope is the cytee of Saba & the lond of the whiche on of the .iij. kynges þat presented oure lord in Bethleem was kyng offe. Fro Ethiope men gon into ynde be manye dyuerse contreyes And men clepen the high ynde Emlak. And ynde is devyded in .iij. princypall parties þat is [ynde] the more þat is a full hoot contree & ynde the less þat is a full atempree contrey þat streccheth to the londe of Mede. And the .iij. part toward the Septentrion is full cold so þat for pure cold & contynuell frost the water becometh Cristall. And vpon the roches of cristall growen the gode dyamandes þat ben of trouble colour; зalow Cristall draweth colour lyke oylle And þei ben so harde þat noman may pollysch hem & men clepen hem dyamandes in þat contree & Hamese in anoþer contree. Othere dyamandes men /105/ fynden in Arabye þat ben not so gode & þei ben more broun & more tendre. And oþer dyamandes also men fynden in the Ile of Cipre þat ben зit more tendre & hem men may wel pollischen; And in the lond of Macedoyne men fynden dyamaundes also, But the beste & the moste precyiouse ben in ynde. And men fynden many tyme harde dyamaundes in a masse þat cometh ut of gold whan men puren it & fynen it out of the myne whan men breken þat mass in smale peces. And sum tyme it happeneth þat men fynden summe as grete as a pese & summe lasse & þei ben als harde as þo of ynde. And all be it þat men fynden gode dyamandes in ynde, зit natheles men fynden hem more comounly vpon the roches in the see & vpon hilles where the myne of gold is; And þei growen many to gedre on lytill another gret And þer ben summe of the gretness of a bene & summe als grete as an hasell note & þei ben square & poynted of here owne kynde boþe abouen & benethen withouten worchinge of mannes hond & þei growen togedre male & female And þei ben norysscht with the dew of heuene And þei engendren comounly & bryngen forth smale children þat multiplyen & growen all the зeer. I have often tymes assayed þat зif a man kepe hem with a lityll of the roche, & wete hem with may dew ofte sithes þei schull growe eueryche зeer, & the smale wole wexen grete. For right as the fyn perl congeleth and wexeth gret of the dew of heuen right so doth the verray dyamand, And right as the perl of his owne kynde taketh roundness right so the dyamand be ve*r*tu of god taketh squareness. And me*n* schall bere the dyamaund on his left syde for it is of grettere ve*r*tue þa*n*ne þan on the right syde; For the strengthe of here growynge is toward the north þ*a*t is the left syde of the world, & the left p*a*rtie of ma*n* is whan he turneth his face toward the est.

In Ethiope [northeast Africa] all the rivers and all the waters are troubled, and they are somewhat salt for the great heat that is there. And the people of that country are lightly drunk [easily become drunk] and have but little appetite for food and they have commonly the flux of the belly and they live not long. In Ethiopia are many diverse people, and Ethiopia is called Cusis. In that country are people that have but one foot, and they go so rapidly that it is a marvel, and the foot is so large that it shadows all the body from the sun when they wish to lie and rest them. In Ethiopia when the children are young and little they are all yellow, and when that they grow of age that yellowness turns to be all black. In Ethiopia is the city of Saba [a supposed city, probably not in Ethiopia, but across the Red Sea in southwest Arabia], and the land of which one of the three kings that presented our Lord in Bethlehem was king of. From Ethiopia people go into India by many diverse countries, and men call the high India *Emlack*. And India is divided in three principal parts, that is [India] the Greater, that is a very hot country, and India the Less that is a very temperate country that stretches to the land of Media [a country between the Caspian Sea to the north and the ancient city of Ecbatan to the south]. And the third part toward the Septentrion [the north, since the Great Bear was called the Seven Plow Oxen] is very cold so that for pure cold and continual frost the water becomes crystal. And upon the rocks of crystal grow the good diamonds that are of cloudy color; yellow crystal draws color like oil, and they are so hard that no man may pollish them, and people call them diamonds in that contree and *hamese* in another country. Other diamonds people /105/ find in Arabia that are not so good and they are browner and more tender. And other diamonds, also, people find in the Isle of Cyprus that are yet more tender, and them people can easily pollish. And in the land of Macedonia people find diamonds, also, but the best and the most precious are in India. And people find many times hard diamonds in a mass that come out of gold when they purify it and refine it out of the mine when they break that mass into small pieces. And sometimes it happens that people find some as large as peas and some less, and they are as hard as those of India. And although people find good diamonds in India, yet nevertheless people find them more commonly upon the rocks in the sea and upon hills where the mine of gold is; and they grow many together, one little, another large. And there are some of the size of a bean, and some as great as a hazelnut, and they are square pointed of their own nature, both above and beneath, without working of man's hand, and they grow together, male and female, and they are nourished with the dew of heaven, and they engender together and bring forth small children that multiply and grow all the year. I have often proposed that if a man keep them with a little of the rock, and wet them with May dew often times they would grow every year, and the small would grow great. For just as the fine pearl congeals and grows great from the dew of heaven, just so does the true diamond, and just as the pearl of its own nature takes roundness, just so the diamond by virtue of God takes squareness. And people should wear the diamond on the left side, for it is of greater virtue then than on the right side, for the strength of their growing is toward the north, that is the left side of the world, and the left part of man is when he turns his face toward the east.

12. GEOFFREY CHAUCER

The Language of One Who Would Gladly Learn and Gladly Teach

Geoffrey Chaucer (d. 1400) was a contemporary of the trans- lators of *Mandeville's Travels* and the Wycliffite gospels, but he was a learned man writing for a sophisticated audience at the king's court. His language not only differs somewhat in dialect from that of the two other writers of Middle English, but it dif- fers also in social level. The first passage describes the Clerk in the *Canterbury Tales*, a young man who might be compared to an advanced graduate student in our society; it is reprinted from *The Text of the Canterbury Tales*, edited by John M. Manly and Edith Rickert (Chicago, 1940).

Canterbury Tales

A CLERK ther was of Oxenford also 285
That vn to logyk hadde longe ygo
  As leene was his hors as is a rake
And he was nat right fat I vndertake
But looked holwe and ther to sobrely
Ful thredbare was his ouereste courtepy 290
For he hadde geten hym yet no benefice
Ne was so worldly for to haue office
For hym was leuere haue at his beddes heed
Twenty bookes clad in blak or reed
Of Aristotle and his philosophie 295
Than robes riche or fithele or gay sautrie
  But al be that he was a philosophre
Yet hadde he but litel gold in cofre
But al that he myghte of his frendes hente
On bookes and on lernynge he it spente 300
And bisily gan for the soules preye
Of hem that yaf hym wher with to scoleye

> Of studie took he moost cure and moost heede
> Noght oo word spak he moore than was neede
> And that was seid in forme and reuerence   *305*
> And short and quyk and ful of heigh sentence
> Sownynge in moral vertu was his speche
> And gladly wolde he lerne and gladly teche.

There was also a student from Oxford, who had devoted himself [hadde] long since to logic. His horse was as lean as is a rake, and I will bet you [vndertake] that he was not very fat, but he looked hollow and also somewhat solemn [sobrely]. His jacket [ouereste courtepy] was quite threadbare, for he had as yet got himself no benefice [an ecclesiastical appointment], and he was not worldly enough to accept a job [office; that is, employment outside the church]. For to him it was preferable [leuere] to have at his bed's head twenty books, bound in black or red, of Aristotle and his philosophy, than rich clothes, or a fiddle, or gay music [sautrie]. But although he was a philosopher, yet he had but little gold in his coffer. [Chaucer is joking about the tradition that the "philosopher's stone," sought by alchemists, could change base metals into gold.] But all that he could borrow [myghte . . . hente], he spent it on books and learning, and busily went about [gan] praying for the souls of those that gave him the wherewithall to go to school [to scoleye]. Of learning he took the most concern [cure] and most care [heede]. He spoke not one word more than necessary [neede], and that was said in form [probably rhetorical form] and with due respect [reuerence] and brief and lively and full of lofty meaning; his speech tended to [was sownynge (sounding) in] moral virtue, and gladly would he learn and gladly teach.

> The following passage is the introduction to a textbook which Chaucer apparently wrote for his son; for older students such books would have been written in Latin. It is reprinted from *The Works of Geoffrey Chaucer*, edited by F. N. Robinson, second edition (Boston, 1957). The punctuation is modern.

A Treatise on the Astrolabe

Lyte Lowys my sone, I aperceyve wel by certeyne evydences thyn abilite to lerne sciences touching nombres and proporciouns; and as wel considre I thy besy praier in special to lerne the tretys of the Astrelabie. Than for as mochel as a philosofre saith, "he wrappith him in his frend, that condescendith to the rightfulle praiers of his frend," therfore have I yeven the a suffisant Astrolabie as for oure orizonte, compowned after the latitude of Oxenforde; upon which, by mediacioun of this litel tretys, I purpose to teche the a certein nombre of conclusions aperteynyng to the same instrument. I seie a certein of conclusions, for thre causes. The first cause is this: truste wel that alle the conclusions that han be founde, or ellys possibly might be founde in so noble an instrument as is an Astrelabie ben unknowe parfitly to eny mortal man in this regioun, as I suppose. Another cause is this, that sothly in any tretis of the Astrelabie that I have seyn there be somme conclusions that wol not in alle thinges parformen her bihestes; and somme of hem ben to harde to thy tendir age of ten yeer to conceyve.

This tretis, divided in 5 parties, wol I shewe the under full light reules and naked wordes in Englissh, for Latyn ne canst thou yit but small, my litel sone. But natheles suffise to the these trewe conclusions in Englissh as wel as sufficith to these noble clerkes Grekes these same conclusions in Grek; and to Arabiens in Arabik, and to Jewes in Ebrew, and to the /545/ Latyn folk in Latyn; whiche Latyn folk had hem first out of othere dyverse langages, and writen hem in her owne tunge, that is to seyn, in Latyn. And God woot that in alle these langages and in many moo han these conclusions ben suffisantly lerned and taught, and yit by diverse reules; right as diverse pathes leden diverse folk the righte way to Rome. Now wol I preie mekely every discret persone that redith or herith this litel tretys to have my rude endityng for excusid, and my superfluite of wordes, for two causes. The first cause is for that curious endityng and hard sentence is ful hevy at onys for such a child to lerne. And the secunde cause is this, that sothly me semith better to writen unto a child twyes a god sentence, than he forgete it onys.

And Lowys, yf so be that I shewe the in my light Englissh as trewe conclusions touching this mater, and not oonly as trewe but as many and as subtile conclusiouns, as ben shewid in Latyn in eny commune tretys of the Astrelabie, konne me the more thank. And preie God save the king, that is lord of this langage, and alle that him feith berith and obeieth, everich in his degre, the more and the lasse. But considre wel that I ne usurpe not to have founden this werk of my labour or of myn engyn. I n'am but a lewd compilator of the labour of olde astrologiens, and have it translatid in myn Englissh oonly for thy doctrine. And with this swerd shal I sleen envie. /546/

Little Lewis, my son, I perceive well by certain evidences your ability to learn sciences involving numbers and proportions, and also I consider your busy prayer to study an exposition of the astrolabe. In as much as a philosopher says, "He wraps himself in his friend who condescends to the reasonable prayers of his friend," I have given you a sufficient astrolabe for our horizon, calculated according to the latitude of Oxford; by means of this little treatise I intend to teach you certain conclusions pertaining to this same instrument. I say certain conclusions for three causes. The first cause is this: you may well believe that all the conclusions that have been found, or else possibly might be found in so noble an instrument as is an astrolabe, are not perfectly known to any mortal in this region, as I suppose. Another cause is this, that truly in any treatise of the astrolabe that I have seen there are some conclusions that will not live up to their promises in all things; and some of them are too hard for your tender age of ten years to conceive.

This treatise, divided into five parts, I shall show you with very easy rules and simple words in English, for of Latin you as yet know but little, my young son. Nontheless, these true conclusions suffice in English as well as they sufficed the noble learned Greeks in Greek, and the Arabians in Arabic, and the Jews in Hebrew, and the Latin people in Latin, which Latin people had them first out of other various languages, and wrote them in their own tongue, that is to say, in Latin. And God knows that in all these languages and in many more these conclusions have been sufficiently taught and by diverse rules, just as various paths lead various people the right way to Rome. Now I shall pray every understanding person who reads or hears this little treatise that for two reasons he will excuse my crude composition and my superfluity of words. The first cause is that elaborate constructions and difficult meaning are very hard for such a little child to comprehend at once. And the second is this, that truly it seems to me better to write a good idea to a child twice than that he forget it once.

And Lewis, if I am able to show you in my easy English as true conclusions in this subject, and not only as true but as many and sharply reasoned conclusions, as have been shown in Latin in any common treatise of the astrolabe, you may thank me the more. And pray God save the King, who is lord of this language, and all that bear faith to him and obey him, each in his social station, greater or less. But remember that I do not pretend to have discovered this learning by my own labor or by my ingenuity. I am but an ignorant compiler of the work of old astrologers, and have translated it into English only for your education. And with this sword shall I slay envy.

13. SIR THOMAS MALORY

Early Printed English

Although Sir Thomas Malory (ca. 1410-1471) fought in France, sat in Parliament, and attended the king's court, he can perhaps best be described as a gentleman gangster of the fifteenth century. He was accused, plausibly, of collecting gangs of toughs who stole cattle and sheep, and who broke into the Abbey of the Blessed Mary of Coombe carrying off money and vestments, and terrorizing the nuns. He was often thrown into jail and often broke out. While incarcerated he occupied his time by making a compilation of stories about King Arthur and his knights, *Le Morte Darthur*, which has become the source for most later English versions of the Arthurian story. Malory's manuscript came into the hands of William Caxton, his younger contemporary and presumably England's first printer, who published it in 1485. Thus the following passage can be accepted as a sample of late fifteenth-century English and of early English printing procedures. Obviously, Caxton is continuing some practices of medieval scribes; he uses *u* for either *u* or *v*, and he uses a line over a vowel for a subsequent *m* or *n*, as in *laūdes* for *laundes*, our word *lands*. In this reprinting, these spellings have been expanded, with the omitted letter italicized; that is, the word printed lau*n*des below was laūdes in the original. If you have trouble recognizing a word, say it aloud and you will probably guess it. The version reproduces Caxton's spelling, capitalization, and punctuation, except that it does not employ the printer's long *s*, which looked much like an *f*. No modernization has been provided, but the first sentence with modern spelling and punctuation would read as follows:

> "Sire," said the Damsel Lynet unto Sir Beaumaynes, "look you be glad and light, for yonder is your deadly enemy, and at yonder window is my lady's sister, Dame Lyones."

The text is taken from *Le Morte Darthur by Syr Thomas Malory*, edited by H. Oskar Sommer (London, 1889), Vol. I, which preserves the original pagination.

SYre sayd the damoysel Lynet vnto syr Beaumayns loke ye be gladde and lyght / for yonder is your dedely enemy / and at yonder wyndowe is my lady syster dame Lyones / where sayd Beaumayns / yonder said the damoysel & pointed with her fynger / that is trouthe sayd Beaumayns / She besemeth a ferre the fayrest lady that euer I loked vpon and truly he said I aske no better quarel than now for to do bataylle / for truly she shalle be my lady / and for her I wylle fyghte / And euer he loked vp to the wyndowe with gladde countenaunce / And the lady Lyones made curtosy to hym doune to the erthe with holdynge vp bothe their handes / Wyth that the reed knyghte of the reed laundes [Red Knight of the Red Lands] callid to syr Beaumayns / leue syr knyghte thy lokynge / and behold me I cou*n*ceille the / for I warne the wel she is my lady / and for her I haue done many stronge batails / Yf thou haue so done said Beaumayns / me semeth it was but waste labour / for she loueth none of thy felauship / and thou to loue that loueth not the / is but grete foly / For and I vnderstode that she were not glad of my comynge / I wold be auysed or I dyd bataille for her / But I vnderstande by the syegyng of this castel she may forbere thy felauship / And therfor wete thou wel thou rede knyghte of the reed laundes / I loue her / and wille rescowe her or els to dye / Saist thou that said the reed knyghte / me semeth / thou oughte of reson to beware by yonder knyghtes that thow sawest hange vpon yonder trees / Fy for shame said Beaumayns that euer thou sholdest saye or do so euyl / for in that thou shamest thy self and knyghthode / and thou mayst be sure ther wylle no lady loue the that knoweth thy wycked custommes And now thou wenest that the syghte of these hanged knyghtes shold fere me / Nay truly not so / that shameful syght causeth me to haue courage and hardynes ageynste the more than I wold haue had ageynst the / and thou were a wel ruled kynght / make the redy said the reed knyghte of the reed laundes / and talke no lenger with me / Thenne syre Beamayns badde the damoysel goo from hym / and thenne they putte their speres in their reystes and came to gyders with alle their myȝt /237/ that they had bothe / and eyther smote other in myddes of their sheldes that the paytrellys [poitrels, breast plates for the horses] / sursenglys and crowpers braste [burst] / and felle to the erthe bothe / and the reynys of their brydels in their handes / and soo they laye a grete whyle sore stonyed [unconscious; cf. astonished] that al that were in the castel and in the sege wende [weened, that is, believed] their neckes had ben broken / and thenne many a straunger and other sayd the straunge hnyȝt was a bygge man / and a noble Iuster / for or [ere] now we sawe neuer noo knyghte matche the reed knyghte of the reed laundes / thus they sayd bothe within the castel and withoute / thenne lyghtly they auoyded theyr horses and put their sheldes afore them / and drewe their swerdes and ranne to gyders lyke two fyers lyons / and eyther gafe other suche buffets vpon their helmes that they relyd bacward bothe two strydys / and thenne they recouerd both and hewe grete pyeces of theire harneis and theire sheldes / that a grete parte felle in to the feldes.

ANd thenne thus they foughte tyl it was past none / and neuer wold stynte tyl att the laste they lacked wynde bothe / and thenne they stode wagyng and scateryng pontyng / blowynge and bledynge that al that be-helde them for the moost party wepte for pyte / Soo whan they had restyd them a whyle / they yede [went] to bataille ageyne / tracyng racyng foynyng as two bores / And at some tyme they toke their renne as hit had ben two rammys & hurtled to gyders that somtyme they felle grouelyng to the erthe / And at somtyme they were so amased that eyther took others swerd in stede of his owne / Thus they endured tyl euensong tyme / that there was none that beheld them myghte knowe whether was lyke to wynne the bataill / and their armour was so ser [sore] hewen that men myȝt see their naked sydes / and in other places / they were naked / but euer the naked places they dyd defende / and the rede knyghte was a wyly knyght of werre / and his wyly fyghtyng taughte syr Beaumayns to be wyse / but he aboughte hit [it] fulle sore or he dyd aspye his fyghtynge / And thus by assente of them bothe they graunted eyther other to rest / and so they sette /238/ hem doune vpon two molle hylles there besydes the fyghtynge place / and eyther of hem vnlaced his helme / and toke the cold wynde / for either of their pages was fast by them to come whan they called to vnlace their harneis and to sette hem on ageyn at their commaundement/ And thenne whan syr Beaumayns helme was of / he loked vp to the wyn-dowe / and there he sawe the faire lady Dame Lyones / and she made hym suche countenaunce that his herte waxed lyghte and Ioly / and ther with he bad the reed knyghte of the reed laundes make hym redy and lete vs doo the bataille to the vtteraunce / I will wel said the knyghte / and thenne they laced vp their helmes / and their pages auoyded / & they stepte to gyders & foughte fresshely / but the reed knyghte of the reed laundes awayted

hym/ & at an ouerthwart smote hym within the hand / that his swerd felle
oute of his hand / and yet he gaf hym another buffet vpon the helme that he
felle grouelynge to the erthe / & the reed kynghte felle ouer hym / for to
holde hym doune / Thenne cryed the maiden Lynet on hyghe / O syr
Beaumayns where is thy courage become / Allas my lady syster beholdeth
the and she sobbeth and wepeth / that maketh myn herte heuy / when syr
Beaumayns herd her saye soo / he abrayed vp with a grette myght and gate
hym vpon his feet / and lyghtely he lepte to his swerd and gryped hit in his
hand and doubled hys paas vnto the reed knyghte and there they foughte a
newe bataille to gyder / But sir Beaumayns thenne doubled his strokes /
and smote soo thyck that he smote the swerd oute of his hand / and thenne
he smote hym vpon the helme that he felle to the erthe / and sir Beaumayns
felle vpon him / and vnlaced his helme to haue slayne hym / and thenne he
yelded hym and asked mercy / and said with a lowde vois O noble knyghte
I yelde me to thy mercy / Thenne syr Beaumayns bethoughte hym vpon
the knyghtes that he had made to be hanged shamefully / and thenne he
said I may not with my worship saue thy lyf / for the shameful dethes that
thou has caused many ful good knyghtes to dye / Syre saide the reed
knyghte of the reed laundes hold your hand and ye shalle knowe the causes
why I put hem to so shameful a dethe / saye on said sir Beaumayns / Syre
I loued ones a lady a fair damoisel / and she /239/ had her broder slayne /
and she said hit was syr launcelot du lake / or els syr gawayn [Gawayne] /
and she praide me as that I loued her hertely that I wold make her a promyse
by the feith of my knyghthode for to laboure dayly in armes vnto I mette
wyth one of them / and alle that I myghte ouercome I shold putte them
vnto a vylanous dethe / and this is the cause that I haue putte all these
knyghtes to dethe / and soo I ensured her to do all the vylony vnto kynge
Arthurs knyghtes / and that I shold take vengeaunce vpon alle these
knyghtes and syr now I wille the telle that euery daye my strengthe en-
creaceth tylle none [noon] / and al this tyme I haue seuen mens strengthe

THenne came ther many Erles and Barons and noble knyghtes and praid
that knyghte to saue his lyf and take hym to your prysoner / And all they
felle vpon their knees and prayd hym of mercy / and that he wolde saue his
lyf / and syr they all sayd it were fairer of hym to take homage and feaute
[fealty] / and lete hym holde his landes of you than for to slee hym / by
his deth ye shall haue none auauntage and his mysdedes that ben done maye
not ben vndone / And therefor he shal make amendys to al partyes & we al
wil become your men and doo you homage and feaute / Fayre lordes said
Beaumayns / wete [know] you wel I am ful lothe to slee this knyʒt neuer-
theles he hath done passyng ylle and shamefully / But in soo moche al that
he dyd was at a ladyes request I blame hym the lesse / and so for your
sake I wil releace hym that he shal haue hys lyf vpon this couenaunt / that
he goo within the castel / and yelde hym there to the lady / And yf she wil
forgyue and quyte hym / I wil wel / with this he make her amendys of al
the trespas he hath done ageynst her and her landes / /240/

Following are three differing printings of a brief passage from the colophon of *Le Morte Darthur:* (1) as it was reprinted from Caxton by Wynkyn de Worde, 1529; (2) by William Copland, presumably from Worde in 1557; and (3) by Thomas Stansby in 1634. The passage is reprinted from Sommer, vol. II, folded sheet to face p. 17.

[1529]   Thus endeth this noble and ioyous boke entytled la mort darthur / notwithstandynge it treateth of the byrthe / lyfe and actes of the sayd kyng Arthur / and of his noble knyghtes of the rounde table / theyr meruaylous enquestes & aduentures / the achyeuynge of the holy Sancgreall. An in yᵉ ende the dolorous deth and departynge out of this world of them all / whiche boke was reduced in to Englysshe by the moost well dysposed knyght afore named.

[1557]   Thus endeth this noble and ioyous booke entytuled la mort darthur, notwithstandynge it treateth of the byrthe lyfe and actes of the sayd king Arthur, and of his noble knyghtes of the round table, their meruaylous enquestes and aduentures, the achieuynge of the holy Sancgreall. And in the ende the dolorous death and departynge out of this worlde of them all, whiche booke was reduced in to Englysshe by the mooste well dysposed knyght afore named.

[1634]   Thus endeth this noble and ioyous booke entituled La Mort Darthur, not-withstanding it treateth of the birth, life, and acts, of the said King Arthur and of his noble Knights of the round table, and their meruailous enquests and aduentures, the achieueing of the Holy Sancgreall.

And in the end the dolorous death and departing out of this world of them all.

14.   ROBERT HENRYSON

Dialectal English

The following stanzas from one of Robert Henryson's fables may seem more like early than late Middle English, but Henryson was a younger contemporary of Malory; he died in 1506. Dialect accounts for the difference between Henryson's language and that of the other fifteenth-century writers represented in this section, who lived in or near London. Henryson was a northerner, and his speech characteristic of Lowland Scotch. The word *quhy* presumably represents a northern sound; it would have been *why* farther south. *Quhylis* is *whiles* and often means sometimes. *Scho* is *she*, pronounced like our *show*. Northern scribes often indicate a long vowel by putting an *i* after it, as in the words *deir, cheir,* the equivalents of *dear* and *cheer*, pronounced about like our words *dare* and *chair*. The selection is from *The Poems of Robert Henryson*, edited by G. Gregory Smith (Edinburgh and London, 1906), 2 volumes. This version is printed only on odd-numbered pages; the punctuation is modern.

The story is the old fable of the Town Mouse and the Country Mouse. The selection begins with the Town Mouse speaking; the Country Mouse has been frightened by a "spenser," a sort of butler, and has fallen in a faint.

'Quhy ly ȝe thus? ryse vp my sister deir,
Cum to ȝour meit, this perrell is ouerpast.'
The vther answerit hir *with* heuie cheir,
'I may not eit, sa sair I am agast;
I had leuer thir fourtie dayis fast,
With watter caill and to gnaw benis and peis,
Than all ȝour feist in this dreid and diseis.'

With fair tretie ȝit scho gart hir vpryse,
And to the burde thay went and togidder sat;
And scantlie had thay drunkin anis or twyse,
Quhen in come Gid hunter, our Iolie Cat,
And bad God speid: the Burges vp with that,
And till the hole scho went as fyre on flint:
Bawdronis the vther be the bak hes hint. /25/

Fra fute to fute he kest hir to and fra,
Quhylis vp, quhylis doun, als cant as ony kid;
Quhylis wald he lat hir rin vnder the stra,
Quhylis wald he wink, and play *with* hir buk heid.
Thus to the selie Mous greit pane he did,
Quhill at the last, throw fortune and gude hap,
Betuix ane burde and the wall scho crap. /27/

"Why lie you thus? Rise up my dear sister, come to your meat; this peril is past." The other answered her with heavy cheer; "I can not eat, so sorely I am frightened; I had rather fast these forty days, with cold water and gnaw beans and peas, than all your feast with this dread and trouble."

With fair entreaty she got her up, and they went and sat together to the board, but they had only drunk once or twice when in came Gid the Hunter, our jolly cat, and bade them Godspeed; the Town Mouse jumped up with that, and to her hole she went like fire on flint; Bawdronis (the cat) grabbed the other by the back.

From foot to foot he cast her to and frow, sometimes up, sometimes down, as gay as any kid; sometimes he would let her run under the straw, sometimes he would pretend to sleep, and play cutting off hedge thorns with her. Thus he did the poor mouse great pain, until at last, through fortune or good luck, she crept in between a board and the wall,

15. WILLIAM SHAKESPEARE

Early Modern English

Seven years after Shakespeare's death, two of his friends brought out his collected plays under the title *Mr. William Shakespeares Comedies, Histories, & Tragedies* (London, 1623), an edition known as the First Folio. It was an elaborate printing job, and done with more than usual care. Whether the spelling represents Shakespeare's, that of various copyists, or that of the printer is not easy to determine, but the capitalization, punctuation, use of italics, and the like probably reflect printing practices in the early seventeenth century. Numbers between bars in the text indicate volume and page in the Folio.

The first selection is from *Love's Labour's Lost,* in modern editions Act V, scene i, lines 18-29. It is a speech of the schoolmaster Holofernes, whose insistence on making pronunciation conform to spelling humorously reveals the ridiculousness of his pedantry.

PEDA[NT]. He draweth out the thred of his verbositie, finer then the staple of his argument. I abhor such phanaticall phanatasims, such insociable and poynt deuise companions, such rackers of ortagriphie, as to speake dout fine, when he should say doubt; det, when he shold pronounce debt; d e b t, not det: he clepeth a Calf, Caufe: halfe, haufe: neighbor *vocatur* nebour; neigh abreuiated ne: this is abhominable, which he would call abhominable: it insinuateth me of infamie: *ne inteligis domine,* to make franticke, lunaticke? /I, 136/

The following selection is from *King Lear,* I, i, lines 35-190, in modern numbering.

Sennet. Enter King Lear, Cornwall, Albany, Gonerill, Regan, Cordelia, and attendants.

Lear. Attend the Lords of France & Burgundy, Gloster.
Glou. I shall, my Lord. *Exit.*
Lear. Meane time we shal expresse our darker purpose.
Giue me the Map there. Know, that we haue diuided
In three our Kingdome: and 'tis our fast intent,
To shake all Cares and Businesse from our Age,
Conferring them on yonger strengths, while we
Vnburthen'd crawle toward death. Our son of *Cornwal,*
And you our no lesse louing Sonne of *Albany,*
We haue this houre a constant will to publish

Our daughters seuerall Dowers, that future strife
May be preuented now. The Princes, *France & Burgundy*
Great Riuals in our yongest daughters loue,
Long in our Court, haue made their amorous soiourne,
And heere are to be answer'd. Tell me my daughters
(Since now we will diuest vs both of Rule,
Interest of Territory, Cares of State)
Which of you shall we say doth loue vs most,
That we, our largest bountie may extend
Where Nature doth with merit challenge. *Gonerill*,
Our eldest borne, speake first.

personal

    Gon. Sir, I loue you more then word can weild ye matter,
Deerer then eye-sight, space and libertie,
Beyond what can be valewed, rich or rare,
No lesse then life, with grace, health, beauty, honor:
As much as Childe ere lou'd, or Father found.
A loue that makes breath poore, and speech vnable,
Beyond all manner of so much I loue you.
    Cor. What shall *Cordelia* speake? Loue, and be silent.
    Lear. Of all these bounds euen from this Line, to this,
With shadowie Forrests, and with Champains rich'd
With plenteous Riuers, and wide-skirted Meades

proclimation

We make thee Lady. To thine and *Albanies* issues
Be this perpetuall. What sayes our second Daughter?
Our deerest *Regan*, wife of *Cornwall*?
    Reg. I am made of that selfe-mettle as my Sister,
And prize me at her worth. In my true heart,
I finde she names my very deede of loue:
Onely she comes too short, that I professe
My selfe an enemy to all other ioyes,
Which the most precious square of sense professes,
And finde I am alone felicitate

personal

In your deere Highnesse loue.
    Cor. Then poore *Cordelia*,
And yet not so, since I am sure my loue's
More ponderous then my tongue.

proclimation

    Lear. To thee, and thine hereditarie euer,
Remaine this ample third of our faire Kingdome,
No lesse in space, validitie, and pleasure
Then that conferr'd on *Gonerill*. Now our Ioy,
Although our last and least; to whose yong loue,
The Vines of France, and Milke of Burgundie,
Striue to be interest. What can you say, to draw
A third, more opilent then your Sisters? speake.
    Cor. Nothing my Lord.
    Lear. Nothing? /II, 283/

Cor. Nothing.

Lear. Nothing will come of nothing, speake againe.

Cor. Vnhappie that I am, I cannot heaue

personal My heart into my mouth: I loue your Maiesty

According to my bond, no more nor lesse.

personal *Lear.* How, how *Cordelia?* Mend your speech a little,

Least you may marre your Fortunes.

Cor. Good my Lord,

personal You haue begot me, bred me, lou'd me.

I returne those duties backe as are right fit,

Obey you, Loue you, and most Honour you.

Why haue my Sisters Husbands, if they say

They loue you all? Happily when I shall wed,

That Lord, whose hand must take my plight, shall carry

Halfe my loue with him, halfe my Care, and Dutie,

Sure I shall neuer marry like my Sisters.

official question *Lear.* But goes thy heart with this?

Cor. I my good Lord.

Lear. So young, and so vntender?

Cor. So young my Lord, and true.

official in sense *Lear.* Let it be so, thy truth then be thy dowre:

For by the sacred radience of the Sunne,

The miseries of *Heccat* and the night:

By all the operation of the Orbes,

From whom we do exist and cease to be,

Heere I disclaime all my Paternall care,

Propinquity and property of blood,

And as a stranger to my heart and me,

Hold thee from this for euer. The barbarous *Scythian,*

Or he that makes his generation messes

To gorge his appetite, shall to my bosome

Be as well neighbour'd, pittied, and releeu'd,

As thou my sometime Daughter.

Kent. Good my Liege.

Lear. Peace *Kent,*

Come not betweene the Dragon and his wrath,

I lou'd her most, and thought to set my rest

On her kind nursery. Hence and avoid my sight:

So be my graue my peace, as here I giue

Her Fathers heart from her; call *France,* who stirres?

Call *Burgundy, Cornwall,* and *Albanie,*

With my two Daughters Dowres, digest the third,

Let pride, which she cals plainnesse, marry her:

official I doe inuest you ioyntly with my power,

Preheminence, and all the large effects

That troope with Maiesty. Our selfe by Monthly course,

With reseruation of an hundred Knights,
By you to be sustain'd, shall our abode
Make with you by due turne, onely we shall retaine
The name, and all th' addition to a King: the Sway,
Reuennew, Execution of the rest,
Beloued Sonnes be yours, which to confirme,
This Coronet part betweene you.
    Kent. Royall *Lear,*
Whom I haue euer honor'd as my King,
Lou'd as my Father, as my Master follow'd,
As my great Patron thought on in my praiers.
    Lear. The bow is bent & drawne, make from the shaft.
    Kent. Let it fall rather, though the forke inuade
The region of my heart, be *Kent* vnmannerly,
When *Lear* is mad, what wouldest thou do old man?
Think'st thou that dutie shall haue dread to speake;
When power to flattery bowes?
To plainnesse honour's bound,
When Maiesty falls to folly, reserue thy state,
And in thy best consideration checke
This hideous rashnesse, answere my life, my iudgement:
Thy yongest Daughter do's not loue thee least,
Nor are those empty hearted, whose low sounds
Reuerbe no hollownesse.
    Lear. Kent, on thy life no more.
    Kent. My life I neuer held but as pawne
To wage against thine enemies, nere feare to loose it,
Thy safety being motiue.
    Lear. Out of my sight.
    Kent. See better *Lear,* and let me still remaine
The true blanke of thine eie.
    Lear. Now by *Apollo,*
    Kent. Now by *Apollo,* King
Thou swear'st thy Gods in vaine.
    Lear. O Vassall! Miscreant.
    Alb. Cor. Deare Sir forbeare.
    Kent. Kill thy Physition, and thy fee bestow
Vpon the foule disease, reuoke thy guift,
Or whil'st I can vent clamour from my throate,
Ile tell thee thou dost euill.
    Lear. Heare me recreant, on thine allegeance heare me;
That thou hast sought to make vs breake our vowes,
Which we durst neuer yet; and with drain'd pride,
To come betwixt our sentences, and our power,
Which, nor our nature, nor our place can beare;
Our potencie made good, take thy reward.

Fiue dayes we do allot thee for prouision,
To shield thee from disasters of the world,
And on the sixt to turne thy hated backe
Vpon our kingdome; if on the tenth day following,
Thy banisht trunke be found in our Dominions,
The moment is thy death, away. By *Iupiter*,
This shall not be reuok'd,
    Kent. Fare thee well King, sith thus thou wilt appeare,
Freedome liues hence, and banishment is here;
The Gods to their deere shelter take thee Maid,
That iustly think'st, and hast most rightly said:
And your large speeches, may your deeds approue,
That good effects may spring from words of loue:
Thus *Kent*, O Princes, bids you all adew,
Hee'l shape his old course, in a Country new. *Exit.   /II, 284/*

Subjects for Discussion

1. What kinds of words had inflectional endings in Old English that no longer have them? In Middle English? For example, what has happened to verb endings? In Old English you can safely assume that all vowels were pronounced, but your conclusions about Middle English will be questionable because a final *e* was sometimes pronounced, but not always.

2. Is there any difference in the word order of Old English, Middle English, Early Modern English, and Modern English?

3. Study the development of punctuation during these years. Certain passages are printed diplomatically; note which punctuation marks were used in them when they were used, and what they seem to have been used for.

4. Obviously, some words used in Old English are still in use, although they may have changed in several ways. Have some apparently disappeared? Can you find out whether they disappeared in Middle English, Early Modern English, or Modern English?

5. Clearly, the history of spelling from 1000-1600 was not simple; that is, it did not follow any one consistent pattern of change. Can you work out any of the apparent sorts of changes in spelling? For example, was there more change in vowels or in consonants?

6. Some of the grammatical words or relationship words were used differently than they are now—*which*, for example. Can you find others?

7. Count the native and borrowed words in a brief passage of Old English, one of Middle English, one of Early Modern English, and one of Modern English. Calculate roughly the percentage of native words as against words borrowed from the Greek-Latin-French tradition. What seem to have been the times of great borrowing? You are likely to find that even in modern English about half the words are native, although eighty or ninety per cent of the words which appear as entries in your dictionary may be borrowed. How would you account for this apparent discrepancy?

8. Compare closely the versions of the Sermon on the Mount. What ideas appear in modern translations which were not in the Old English? When do they seem to have appeared?

9. Study the growth or decay of verb forms. For example, what was the third person singular and plural in Old English? In Chaucer? In Shakespeare?

10. You may have been told not to end a sentence with a preposition. Do you find any medieval writer ending a sentence with a word like *of*, however he may have spelled the word? Mandeville would be one good place to look.

11. Presumably the passages of Middle English represent various levels of usage. In the *Canterbury Tales*, Chaucer was addressing a sophisticated audience; *Mandeville's Travels* was probably intended for middle-class people, somewhat cultured; the Gospels were intended for everybody; including the most ignorant, and especially for those who would not know Latin or French. Can you see any reflections of these social levels in the levels of language usage? The *Astrolabe* was intended for a child, but a bright child who was presumably learning rapidly; how does it compare with Chaucer's writing for adults? With *Mandeville?*

12. See if you can figure out how the pedant (Holofernes) in *Love's Labour's Lost* thought certain words should be pronounced. What evidence is there that he thought pronunciation should follow spelling?

13. When he is banishing Kent, Lear says "nor nature, nor our place" where we would say "neither our nature nor our place." Do you find other words and phrases used as they would not be used today?

14. Notice ways in which the selection from Henryson differs from that of his contemporary, Malory. In which words does the scribe apparently use *i* to indicate a preceding long vowel? The spelling *anis* (once) indicates that it was a two-syllable word. Are there other words which now have one syllable which Henryson apparently spoke with two? Notice that in the last line the word for modern *crept* is *crap*, probably pronounced about like modern *crop*. It had a similar pronunciation in Old English. Would this suggest that Scottish was more or less conservative than dialects farther south? The word *disease* (dis-ease) formerly meant a state lacking ease; does it have that meaning here?

Suggestions for Investigation, Reports, or Brief Papers

1. From the passage in Old English, try to make up a paradigm (that is, an outline of all the forms) of the verb *to be*, and of the personal pronoun.

2. Study Middle English spelling to see if you can discover any medieval principles of spelling. State the principles, and illustrate them with examples.

3. Repunctuate a portion of Malory; then try to describe how Malory uses his maid-of-all-work punctuation, a slanting line. Does he use it for end punctuation, internal punctuation, or both? Does he use no punctuation where a modern editor would require it?

4. Try to describe what one scribe or printer seems to think capitals are good for.

5. Compare the vocabulary of Chaucer with that of his contemporaries. Which used more words from Latin? From French?

6. In Chaucer's time two sets of third person plural pronouns were in use; forms which were spelled something like *hie, her,* and *hem,* which had survived from Old English, and the ancestors of our pronouns *they, their, them,* which had presumably come from Old Norse. Do Chaucer and his contemporaries quoted here use either set consistently, or do they use them interchangeably, or

use some from one list and some from the other consistently? Describe your findings.

7. Obviously Caxton has some spelling principles. Can you work them out?
Is he entirely consistent? Is it possible that he sometimes added letters or left
them out in order to make his line of type set full to the margin?

✓8. On the basis of the various printings of *Le Morte Darthur*, what would you
infer about the times at which modern spelling, punctuation, and capitalization
were being standardized? Organize your evidence and describe it.

9. There is a theory that the First Folio was punctuated in order to indicate
the actor's pauses. Study the punctuation and try to establish or invalidate this
theory.

✓10. Notice the use of the second personal pronouns, forms of *thee* and *you*, in
Shakespeare. Several characters use both forms. Can you discover any reason
for this apparent inconsistency? Did the two sets of forms apparently have
different uses? You might consider, for instance, that Cordelia may sometimes feel
she is speaking to her father, and sometimes to the King of England, that Lear
is always a king, but sometimes he speaks officially and sometimes he speaks
like an angry man. Try to develop a theory and to support it with evidence.

IV. EARLY OBSERVATIONS ON LANGUAGE

The preceding section provides materials for the study of early English, the way it worked, the way it has changed. This section has a dual purpose. In one sense it is like the preceding section: it includes no Anglo-Saxon, but it includes samples of English from the thirteenth to the late sixteenth century. It can be used, as the writing in that section was used, to study early characteristics of the English language which have subsequently vanished or altered.

In another sense, however, the writings in this section are unlike those in Section III. They are characteristic examples of writing, but of a rather different sort, writing that is essentially expository — as is most of the writing of modern men. Much of the preceding section is narrative or dramatic; the writing in this section is all expository in purpose — even though Caxton may tell a story to illustrate his point. Furthermore, all the examples in this section are *about* language. They are examples of language, but they are also discussions of language; or if too brief and sketchy properly to be called discussions, they are at least comments upon language.

The first selection consists of a few lines from a long and dull poem by a monk named Orm, who apparently set out to save souls and reform spelling, hoping to stone two formidable birds with one piece of composition. One trusts he saved souls; we have no evidence that he had any impact at all upon English orthography. His brief admonishment is interesting, however, because it provides us evidence that by the thirteenth century one Englishman, at least, cared enough about right and wrong spelling to write verses about it. Not many people in Orm's time, if we are to trust the extant evidence, had that much interest.

Orm and his admonitions about spelling at least remind us that although thinking about language may be very useful in a sophisticated society, it is an esoteric occupation. Barbarians of today do not do it much, and presumably yesterday's never did. If our ancestors did, they left few records. Although not all the early references to language have been included here, we have tried to include all the interesting early writings on English in English. They are few, and writings on English continued to be few until about the time of Shakespeare. Then, with a growing native zeal for learning, with the importation of French and Italian writings on language, not to mention a growing acquaintance with Latin and Greek grammarians, and a growing native pride in anything English, works about language and the use of it have become so plentiful that we have been able to include only a small part of the existing later material.

Although the contents of this section are to a degree curiosa, they are evidence; the writings of Orm and Mulcaster are samples of language just as the writings of Chaucer and Shakespeare are samples of language — a different sort of language, but still an important sort. As significant discussion of language, most of the writing in this section is now curious and not much more; yet the observations of Orm and Caxton and Mulcaster, for example, are interesting in that they reflect the linguistic knowledge and the linguistic ignorance of the day, even though they do not help us much to understand language. Caxton's anecdote convinces us that there were two current words for a *hen's egg* in his time, but it does not reveal the nature and working of language as do the writings of a modern scholar like Edward Sapir or Leonard Bloomfield. Still, it is important to know what Englishmen had to say about English when they first became aware that language was one of the proper studies of mankind.

16. ORM

Spelling in the Ormulum

About 1200 one Orm, who was perhaps the dullest monk who ever supposed he was writing English seriously, compiled a digest of Biblical and ecclesiastical lore, which he called the *Ormulum*. We possess what may have been the original manuscript, written in his own hand. He apparently invented his own means of spelling, which he considered the only right one. The passage has been often reprinted; this is taken from *Mittelenglische Sprach-und Literaturproben*, edited by Alois Brandl and Otto Zippel, second edition (Berlin, 1927). The spelling of the original is preserved, but the punctuation is modern; the modernized version preserves the original order of the words.

Forr itt maȝȝ hellpenn alle þa	þatt bliþelike itt herenn	46
Annd lufenn itt annd follȝhen itt	Wiþþ þohht, wiþþ word, wiþþ dede,	
Annd whase wilenn shall þiss boc	Efft oþerrsiþe writtenn,	
Himm bidde icc þatt het write rihht	Swasumm þiss boc himm taecheþþ,	
All þwerrtut affterr þatt itt iss	Uppo þiss firrste bisne,	50
Wiþþ all swillc rime alls her iss sett	Wiþþ allse fele wordess;	
Annd tatt he loke wel þatt he	An bocstaff write twiȝȝess	
Eȝȝewhaer þaer itt uppo þiss boc	Iss writenn o þatt wise.	
Loke he well þatt het write swa;	Forr he ne maȝȝe nohht elless	
Onn ennglissh writenn rihht te word,	þatt wite he wel to soþe.	55

For it [the *Ormulum*] may help all those	that gladly it hear
And love it and follow it	with thought, with word, with deed,
And whoso wish shall this book	Again anothertime write,
Him bid I that it write right	As this book him teaches,
All throughout after that it is	Upon this first example

With all such rhyme as here is set   With as many words;
And that he look well that he   One letter write twice
Everywhere there it upon this book   Is written in that wise.
Look he well that he write so;   For he may not else
In English write right the word,   That knows he well for truth.

17. WILLIAM CAXTON

A Changing Language

William Caxton (see pp. 68-69) was a translator as well as a printer and publisher. The following selection recounts observations on the language of his day, which he arrived at in his translation of the *Aeneid*, published in 1490. The text is diplomatic, reproducing Caxton's printing; it has been reprinted in Nellie Slayton Aurner, *Caxton, Mirrour of Fifteenth Century Letters* (Boston and New York, 1926), from which this version is taken.

I delybered and concluded to translate it [the *Aeneid*] in to englysshe And forthwyth toke a penne & ynke and wrote a leef or tweyne / which I ouersawe agayne to correcte it / And whan I sawe the fayr & straunge termes therin / I doubted that it sholde not please some gentylmen whiche late blamed me sayeng yᵗ [that] in my translacyons I had ouer curyous termes whiche coude not be vnderstande of comyn peple / and desired me to vse olde and homely termes in my translacyons. and fayn wolde I satysfye euery man / and so to doo toke an olde boke and redde therin / and certaynly the englysshe was so rude and brood that I coude not wele vnderstande it. And also my lord abbot of westmynster [Westminster] ded do shewe to me later certayn euydences wryton in olde englysshe for to reduce it in to our englysshe now vsid / And certaynly it was wreton in such wyse that it was more like to dutche than englysshe   I coude not reduce ny brynge it to be vnderstonden / Ande certaynly our langage now vsed varyeth ferre from that. whiche was vsed and spoken whan I was borne / For we englysshe men ben / born vnder the domynacyon of the mone. whiche is neuer stedfaste / but euer wauerynge / wexynge one season / and waneth & dyscreaseth another season / And that comyn englysshe that is spoken in one shyre varyeth from another. In so much that in my dayes happened that certayn marchauntes were in a shippe in tamyse [Thames] for to haue sayled ouer the see into zelande [Holland] / and for lacke of wynde thei taryed atte forlond [at the foreland]. and wente to lande for to refreshe them And one of theym named sheffelde a mercer [Sheffield, a clothier] came into a hows and axed for mete. and specyally he axyd after eggys And the good wyfe answerde. that she coude speke no frenshe. And the merchaunt was angry. for he also coude speke no frenshe. but wolde

haue hadde egges / and she vnderstode hym not / And thenne at last a nother
sayd that he wold haue eyren / [*cf.* modern German *Eier*, eggs] then the good
wyf sayd that she vnderstod hym wel / Loo what sholde a man in thyse
dayes now wryte. egges or /*286*/ eyren / certaynly it is harde to playse
euery man / by cause of dyuersite & chau*n*ge of langage. For in these dayes
euery man that is in ony reputacyon in his cou*n*try. wyll vtter his comyny-
cacyon and maters in suche maners & termes / that fewe men shall vnderstonde theym / And som honest and grete clerkes haue ben wyth me and
desired me to wryte the moste curyous termes that I coude fynde / And thus
betwene playn rude / & curyous I stande abasshed. but in my Iudgement /
the comyn terms that be dayli vsed ben lyghter to be vndersonde than the
olde and au*n*cyent englysshe / And for as moche as this present booke is
not for a rude vplondysshe man to laboure therin / ne rede it / but onely
for a clerke & a noble gentylman that feleth and vnderstondeth in faytes
of armes in loue & noble chyualrye / Therfor in a meane bytwene bothe
I haue reduced & translated this sayd booke in to our englysshe not ouer
rude ne curyous but in such termes as shall be vnderstanden by goddys
grace accordynge to my copye. and yf ony man wyll intermete in redyng
of hit and fyndeth suche termes that he can not vnderstande late hym goo
rede and lerne vyrgyll / or the pystles of ouyde (*Epistles* of Ovid) and ther
he shall see and vnderstonde lyghtly all / /*287*/

18. ALBERT C. BAUGH

Sixteenth-Century Observations on Language

> The following selection is from *A History of the English Lan-*
> *guage*, second edition (New York, 1957) by Albert C. Baugh,
> Felix E. Schelling Memorial Professor at the University of Penn-
> sylvania. It is the standard one-volume work on the subject.

That the problem of bringing about greater agreement in the writing of
English is one the importance of which was recognized in the sixteenth
century is apparent from the attempts made to draw up rules and to devise
new systems. The earliest of these, *An A. B. C. for Children* (before 1558),
is almost negligible. It consists of only a few pages, and part of the space is
devoted to "precepts of good lyvynge", but the author manages to formulate
certain general rules such as the use of the final *e* to indicate vowel length
(*made, ride, hope*). Certain more ambitious treatises attacked the problem
in what their authors conceived to be its most fundamental aspect. This
was the very imperfect way in which the spelling of words represented their
sound. These writers were prepared to discard the current spelling entirely
and re-spell the language phonetically with the use of additional symbols
where needed. Thus in 1568 Thomas Smith published a *Dialogue concern-*

ing the Correct and Emended Writing of the English Language. He increases the alphabet to thirty-four letters and marks the long vowels. Smith's reform did not win much favor. His work, moreover, was in Latin, and this would further limit its chance of popular influence. The next year another /252/ attempt at phonetic writing was made in a work by John Hart called *An Orthographie,* elaborated in the following year in *A Method or Comfortable Beginning for All Unlearned, Whereby They May Bee Taught to Read English* (1570).[1] Hart makes use of special characters for *ch, sh, th,* etc., but his system seems to have won no more favor than Smith's. A more considerable attempt at phonetic reform was made in 1580 by William Bullokar in his *Booke at Large, for the Amendment of Orthographie for English Speech.* He confesses that he has profited by the mistakes of Smith and Hart, whose works were "not received in use (the chiefe cause whereof, I thinke, was their differing so farre from the old)". So he says, "My chiefe regard (from the beginning) was to follow the figures of the old letters and the use of them . . . as much as possible." He accordingly invents few special characters, but makes liberal use of accents, apostrophes, and numerous hooks above and below the letters, both vowels and consonants. If his innovations in this way had been more moderate, English spelling might have come to the use of accents such as were being adopted for French at this time, but one glance at a specimen page printed according to his system shows why it could not possibly win acceptance. We cannot pursue the history of such attempts further. They continued well into the seventeenth century. Many of them represented mere exercises in ingenuity, as when Charles Butler, in *The English Grammar, or The Institution of Letters, Syllables, and Woords in the English Tung* (1634), substitutes an inverted apostrophe for final *e*'s and *ɪ* for *th* (*boɪ, wiɪout, ɪird*). Efforts at such a radical reform as these enthusiasts proposed were largely wasted.

This was clearly perceived by Richard Mulcaster, the teacher of Spenser, whose *Elementarie* (1582), "which entreateth chefelie of the right writing of our English tung", is the most extensive and the most important treatise on English spelling in the sixteenth century. Mulcaster's great virtue is his moderation. He saw the futility of trying to make English spelling phonetic in any /253/ scientific sense. He was therefore willing to compromise between the ideal and the practical. He did not believe that the faults of English spelling were so desperate that they could only be removed by desperate remedies. The way to correct an existing difficulty was not to substitute a new and greater one. This seemed to him to be the effect of all those proposals that took into consideration only the sound of words. Even at its best, he did not think that spelling could ever perfectly represent sound. The differences between one sound and another were often too subtle. "Letters," he says, "can expresse sounds withall their joynts & properties no fuller than the pencill can the form & lineaments of the face." It was inevitable, he thought, that the same letter must sometimes be used for

---

[1] On Hart see Bror Danielsson, *John Hart's Works on English Orthography and Pronunciation,* Part I (Stockholm, 1955), a model of scholarly editing.

different sounds, but this was no worse than to use the same word, as we often do, in very different senses. Another difficulty that he saw was that pronunciation constantly changes. These were his theoretical reasons for refusing to go along with the phonetic reformers. His practical reason was that their systems were too cumbersome ever to be accepted. "But sure I take the thing to be to combersom and inconvenient, . . . where no likeliehood of anie profit at all doth appear in sight." Every attempt to force people against established custom "hath alwaie mist, with losse of labor where it offered service."

The basis of his reform, therefore, was custom or usage. This he defines not as the practice of the ignorant, but that "wherein the skilfull and best learned do agre." "The use & custom of our cuntrie hath allredie chosen a kinde of penning wherein she hath set down hir relligion, hir lawes, hir privat and publik dealings." This cannot now be completely changed, although it can be pruned "so that the substance maie remain, and the change take place in such points onelie as maie please without noveltie and profit without forcing." "I will therefor do my best," he says, "to confirm our custom in his own right, which will be easilie obtained where men be acquainted with the matter allredie and wold be verie glad to se wherein the right of their writing standeth." In making usage his point of departure he does not ignore sound; he merely insists that it shall not be given an undue share /254/ of attention. We must use common sense and try to remove defects in the existing system, not substitute a new one. He thinks ease and convenience in writing should be considered, for popular approval is the final authority. Only a general goodness, not perfection in each detail, can be expected. No set of rules can cover all points; some things must be left to observation and daily practice.

The details of his system we cannot enter into here. We must be content with a statement of his general aims. He would first of all get rid of superfluous letters. There is no use in writing *putt, grubb, ledd* for *put, grub, led,* "and a thowsand such ignorant superfluities". On the other hand, we must not omit necessary letters such as the *t* in *fetch* or *scratch*. He allows double consonants only where they belong to separate syllables (*wit-ting*), and almost never at the end of a word except in the case of *ll* (*tall, generall*). Words ending in *-ss* he writes *-sse* (*glasse, confesse*). Otherwise final *-e* is used regularly to indicate a preceding long vowel, distinguishing *made* from *mad, stripe* from *strip,* and at the end of words ending in the sound of *v* or *z* (*deceive, love, wise*). An *e* is added to words that end in a lightly pronounced *i; daie, maie, trewlie, safetie;* but when the *i* is sounded "loud and sharp" it is spelled *y: deny, cry, defy.* Analogy, or as he calls it "proportion", plays a justly important part in his system. Since we write *hear,* we should therefore write *fear* and *dear.* This principle, he admits, is subject to exceptions which must be made in deference to "prerogative", that is, the right of language to continue a common custom, as in employing an analogous spelling for *where, here, there.* In such a case he becomes frankly the apologist, justifying the common practice. He is really more interested in having every one adopt the same spelling for a given word than he is in phonetic consistency. It is not so much a question of whether one should write *where* as that he should adopt a single spelling and use it regularly instead of writing *where, wher, whear, wheare, were, whair,* etc. To this end he prints in the latter part of his book a *General Table* giving the recommended spelling for some 7000 of the commonest words. Mulcaster's spelling is not always /255/ that which ultimately came to be adopted. In spite of his effort for the most part to follow current usage, he seems sometimes to have gone counter to the tendency of his own and later times. He advocates spelling *guise, guide, guest,* and the like without the *u* and writes *băble, dăble,* indicating the length of the vowel by a short mark over it. But his book had the great merit — or demerit — of standardizing a large number of current spellings, justifying them, and advocating the consistent use of them. /256/

19. WILLIAM CAMDEN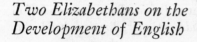

Two Elizabethans on the Development of English

> William Camden (1551-1623), antiquarian, chronicler, trenchant observer of his day, is little read today because he wrote mainly in Latin. The following is from extracts and digests from his monumental *Brittaniae,* printed as *Remaines, Concerning Britaine: But especially England, and the Inhabitants thereof,* third edition (London, 1623), and translated by an anonymous contemporary who signs himself M. N. The translator deprecates his version as "onely the rude rubble and out-cast rubbish . . . of a greater and more serious worke."

First, the British tongue or Welsh (as we now call it) was in use onely in this Iland, hauing great affinity with the old *Galliqua* of *Gaule,* now *France,* from whence the first inhabitants in all probability came hither. Afterward the *Latine* was taken vp when it was brought into the forme of a Prouince, by little and little. /16/

Notwithstanding in this Isle the *British* ouergrew the *Latine,* and continueth yet in *Wales,* and some Villages of *Cornewall* intermingled with *Prouinciall Latine,* being very significatiue, copious, and pleasantly running vpon agnominations, although harsh in asperations. After the Irish tongue was brought into the Northwest parts of the Isle, out of *Ireland* by the ancient Scottishmen, and there yet remaineth. Lastly, the *English Saxons* out of *Germany,* who valiantly and wisely performed here all the three things, which imply a full conquest, *viz.* the alteration of lawes, language, and attire.

This English tongue is extracted, as the Nation, from the Germans the most glorious of all now extant in Europe for their morall, & martial vertues, & preseruing the liberty entire, as also for propagating their Language by happy victories in *France* by the *Francs*, & *Burgundians*, in this Ile by the *English-Saxons*, in *Italy* by the *Heruli*, West-*Gothes*, *Vandales*, & *Lombards*, in *Spaine* by the *Sueuians* and *Vandales*. /17/

But the *English-Saxon* Conquerors, altered the tongue which they found here wholly: so that no *British* words, or prouinciall *Latine* appeared therein at the first: & in short time they spread it ouer this whole *Island*, from the *Orcades* to the Isle of *Wight*, except a few barren corners in the *Westerne* parts, whereunto the reliques of the *Britans* and *Scots* retired preseruing in them both their life and Language. For certainly it is, that the greatest and best parts, the East and South of *Scotland*, which call themselues the *Law-land men*, speake the English tongue varied only in Dialect, as descended from the *English-Saxons* and the old [original has olp] *Scottish*, which is the very *Irish*, is vsed onely by them of the West, called the *Hechtland-men*, who call the other as the Welsh call vs *Sassons*, *Saxons*, both in respect of Language and originall, as I shewed before.

I dare not yet here affirme for the antiquity of our Language, that our great-great-great-Grandsires tongue came out of *Persia*, albeit the wonderfull Linguist *Iosoph Scaliger* hath obserued, *Fader, Moder, Bruder, band, &c.* in the Persian tongue in the very sence as we now vse them.

It will not be vnproper I hope to this purpose, if I note out of the Epistles of that learned Ambassour *Busbequius*, how the inhabitants of *Taurica Chersonessus*, in the vttermost part of *Europe* Eastward, haue these words, *Wind, Siluer, Korne, Salt, Fish,* /18/ *Son, Apple, Waggen, Singen, Ilanda, Beard*, with many other in the very same sence and signification, as they now are in vse with vs, whereat I maruelled not a little when I first read it. But nothing can be gathered thereby, but that the *Saxons* our progenitours, which planted themselues here in the West, did also to their glory place Colonies likewise there in the East.

As in the Latine tongue, the learned make in respect of time, foure *Idioms*, the *Ancient*, the *Latine*, the *Romane*, the *Mixt:* so we in ours may make the *Ancient English-Saxon*, and the *Mixt.* But that you may see how powerable *Time* is in altering tongues as all things else, I will set downe the Lords Prayer as it was translated in sundry ages, that you may see by what degrees our tongue is risen, and thereby coniecture how in time it may altar and fall againe.

If we could set it downe in the ancient *Saxen*, I meane in the tongue which the Enlish vsed at their first arriuall here, about 440. yeeres after Christs birth, it would seeme most strange and harsh Dutch or Gebrish, as women call it; or when they first embraced Christianity, about the yeere of Christ 600. But the ancientst that I can find, was about 900. yeere since, about the yeere of Christ 700. found in ancient *Saxon* glossed *Euangelists*, in the hands of my good friend Master *Robert Bowyer*, written by *Eadfride* the eight Bishop of *Lindisfarne*, (which after was translated to *Durham*) and diuided according to the ancient *Canon of Eusebius,* not into Chapters: for *Stephen Langton,* Archbishop of *Canterbury,* first diuided the holy Scripture into Chapters, as *Robert Stephan* did lately into Verse, and thus it is.

> *Our   Father   which   art   in   heauen*
> Vren Fader thic   arth in heofnas,
>
> *be   hallowed   thine name.   come*
> Sic [1] gehalgud thin noma. to cymeth
>
> *thy   Kingdome. Be   thy   will   so   as   in*
> thin ric.   Sic [1] thin willa sue is [2] in /19/
>
> *Heauen and in earth.   Oure lofe*
> heofnas, and in eortho. Vren hlaf
>
> *Super-substantiall giue vs to day, and*
> ofer   wirtlic [3] sel vs to dæg, and
>
> *forgiue vs debts ours so we for-*
> forgef   vs scylda urna, sue we for-
>
> *giue   debts   ours, and do not leade*
> gefan scyldgum vrum, and do inlead [4]
>
> *vs   into temptation. But deliuer euery one*
> vsith [5] in   custnung. Ah gefrig vrich [5]
>
> *from euill.*
> from ifle. Amen.

Some two hundred yeeres after, I find this somewhat varied in two translations.

	Thu vre fader the eait on heofenum
	Si thin nama gehalgod. Cum thin ric.
*Gewurth thin willa.	*Si thin willa on eorthan, swa on heofe-
	dayly
	num. Syle vs to dæg vrn dægthanlican [6] hlaf.
	trespasses
	And forgif vs vre glytas swa, swa we for-
	against vs haue trespassed
*Vrum Gyltendum.	gifath* tham the with vs agyltath. And ne
	led the vs on costnung, Ac alys vs from
	Be it so.
*Sothlice.	yfle. *Si it swa./20/

[1 Probably a transcriptural error for *sie.*]

[2 The misprint here must be in the Anglo-Saxon, which should read something like *sue,* since *sue sue* means *even as.*]

[3 Presumably a misprint for *oferwistlic.* Since *wist* can mean *reality,* this translation is possible, but *wist* can also mean a *feast, plenty,* giving the more probable translation *plentiful, abundant.*]

[4 *Inlead* means *lead into,* not *not lead; do* may be an error for *no* or *ne.*]

[5 *Vsith* and *vrich* should probably read *vsich,* meaning *us.*]

[6 Presumably an error for *dægwhamiican,* which means *daily.*]

About an hundred and threescore yeares after, in the time of King *Henry* the second, I finde this rime sent from *Rome* by Pope *Adrian* the English-man, to be taught to the people.

> *Vre fadyr in heauen rich,*
> *Thy name be halyedeuer lich,*
> *Thou bring vs thy michell blisse,*
> *Als hit in heauen y-doe,*
> *Evar in yearth beene it also:*
> *That holy bread that lasteth ay,*
> *Thou send it ous this ilke day.*
> *Forgiue ous all that we haue don,*
> *As wee forgivet vch other mon:*
> *Ne let ous fall into no founding,*
> *Ac shield ous fro the fowle thing. Amen.*

. . . In the time of King *Richard* the second about a hundred and odde yeares after, it was so mollified, that it came to be thus, as it is in the Trans-lation of *Wickeliffe*, with some Latine words now inserted, whereas there was not one before.

> *Our fadyr, that art in heauen, halloed be thy name,*
> *thy kingdom comto, be thy will done, so in heauen, /21/*
> *and in erth: gif to vs this day our bread ouer other*
> *substance: and forgif to vs our* dettis, *as we forge-*
> *uen to our* detters, *and leed vs not into* temptation,
> *but* deliuer *vs fro euill. Amen.*

Hitherto will our sparkefull Youth laugh at their great grandfather *English*, who had more care to do wel, than to speak minion-like, and left more glory to vs by their exployting of great actes, than we shall do by our forging a new words, and vncuth phrases.

Great verily was the glory of our tongue before the *Norman* Conquest, in this, that the old *English* could expresse most aptly, all the conceipts of the minde in their owne tongue, without borrowing from any. As for example:

The holy seruice of God, which the *Latines* called *Religion*, because it knitted the mindes of men together, and most people of *Europe* haue bor-rowed the same from them they called most significantly *Ean-fastnes*, as the one and onely assurance and fast anker-hold of our soules health.

The gladsome tidings of our saluation, which the *Greekes* called *Euan-gelion*, and other Nations in the same word, they called *Godspell*, that is *Gods speech*.

For our *Sauiour*, which we borrowed from the *French*, and they from the *Latine Saluator*, they called in their owne word, *Hae-lend* from *Hael*, that is, *Salus*, safety, which we retaine still in *Al-hael*, and *Was-hael*, that is *Aue, Salue, Sis, saluus*.

They could call the disciples of Christ, *Leorning Cnihtas* that is, *Learn-ing Seruitours*. For *Cniht* which is now a name of worship, signified with them an *Attendant*, or seruitour.

They could name the *Pharises* according to the *Hebrew Sunder-halgens*, as holy religious men, which had sundred and seuered themselues from other.

The Scribes they could call in their proper signification, as *Booke-men*, *Bocer*. So they called parchment, which we haue catcht from the Latine *Pergamenum, Boc-fell* in respect of the vse.

So they could call the Sacrament *Haligdome*, as holy iudgement. For so it is according as we receiue it.

They could call *Fertility* and fruitfulnesse of land signi /22/ ficatiuely *Eordes-wela*, as wealth of the earth.

They could call a *Comet*, a *Faxed starre;* which is all one with *Stella Crinita*, or *Cometa*. So they did call the iudgment seate *Domesettle*.

That which we call the *Parliament*, of the *French Parler* to speake, they called a *Witten mot*, as the Meeting and assembly of wisemen.

The certaine and inward knowledge of that which is in our minde, be it good or bad, which in the Latine word we call *Conscience*, they called *Inwit*, as that which they inwardly wit and wote, that is, know certainely.

That in a riuer which the Latines call *Alueus*, and *Canalis*, and from thence most nations of *Europe* name *Chanell, Kanell, Canale, &c.* they properly called the *Streame-race*.

Neither in the degrees of kindred they were destitute of significatiue words; for he whom we of a (*French* and *English* compound word; call *Grandfather*, they called *Eald-fader*, whom we call *Great Grandfather*, they called *Thirdafader*). So, which we call *Great Great Grandfather*, they called *Fortha-fader*, and his father, *Fiftha-fader*. . . . /23/

The alteration and admiration in our tongue as in all others, hath beene brought in by entrance of Strangers, as *Danes, Normans*, and others which haue swarmed hither; by trafficke, for new words as well as for new wares, haue alwayes come in by the tyranne *Time*, which altereth all vnder Heauen, by *Vse*, which swayeth most, and hath an absolute command in words, and by *Pregnant wits:* specially since that learning after long banishment, was recalled in the time of King *Henry* the eight, it hath beene beautified and enriched out of other good tongues, partly by enfranchifying and endenizing strange words, partly by refining and mollifying old words, partly by implanting new words with artificiall composition, happily containing themselues within the bounds prescribed by *Horace*. So that our tongue is (and I doubt not but hath beene) as copious, pithy, and significatiue, as any other tongue in *Europe:* and I hope we are not yet and shall not hereafter come to that which *Seneca* saw in his time, *When mens minds beginne once to inure themselues to dislike, whatsoeuer is vsuall, is disdained. They affect nouelty in speech, they recall forworne and vncuth words, they forge new phrases, and that which is newest, is best liked; there is presumptuous and farre fetching of words. And some there are that thinke it a grace if their speech do houer, and thereby hold the hearer in suspence:* you know what followeth.

Omitting this, pardon me and thinke me not ouerballanced with affection, if I thinke that our English tongue is (I will not say as sacred as the *Herbew*, or as learned as the *Greeke*,) but as fluent as the *Latine*, and as courteous as the *Spanish*, as courtlike as the *French*, and as amorous as the *Italian*, as some Italianated amorous haue confessed. Neither hath any thing detracted more from the dignity of our tongue, than our owne affecting of forraine tongues, by admiring praysing, and studying them aboue measure: whereas the wise *Romans* thought no small part of their honour to consist in the honour of their language, As for a long time the English placed in the Boroughs townes of *Ireland* and *Wales*, would admit neither Irish or Welsh, among them. And not long since for the honour of our natiue tongue, *Henry Fitz-Allan*, Earle of *Arun-* /24/ *dell*, in trauaile into *Italy*, and the Lord *William Howard* of *Effingham*, in his gouernment of *Calice*, albeit they were not ignorant of other forraine tongues, would answere no strangers by word of writing, but onely in English. As in this consideration also (before them) Cardinall *Wolsey* in his ambassage into *France*, commanded all his seruants to vse no French, but meere English to the French, in all communication whatsoeuer.

As for the *Monosyllables* so rife in our tongue, which were not so originally, although they are vnfitting for verses and measures, yet are they most fit for expressing briefly the first conceipts of the minde, or *Intentionalia*, as they call them in Schooles: so that we can set downe more matter in fewer lines, then any other language. Neitheir do we or the Welsh so curtall the *Latine*, that we make all therein *Monosyllables*, as *Ioseph Scaliger* chargeth vs; who in the meane time forgetteth, that his French men haue put in their *Proviso* in the edict of *Pacification* in the *Grammaticall* warre, that they might not pronounce *Latine* distinctly, and the Irish not to obserue quantity of syllables. I cannot yet but confesse that we haue corruptly contracted most names both of men and places, if they were of more then two syllables, and thereby hath ensued no little obscurity.

Whereas our tongue is mixed, it is no disgrace, when as all the tongues of *Europe* do participate interchangeably the one of the other, and in the learned tongues, there hath beene like borrowing one from another. As the present *French* is composed of *Latine*, *Germane*, and the old *Gallique*, the *Italian* of *Latine* and *Germane-Gotish*, and the *Spanish* of *Latine*, *Gotish-Germane*, and *Arabique*, or *Morisquo*. Yet it is false which *Gesner* affirmeth, that our tongue is the most mixt and corrupt of all other. For if it may please any to compare but the Lords Prayer in other languages, hee shall finde as few *Latine* and borrowed forraine words in ours, as in any other whatsoeuer. Notwithstanding the diuersity [the *t* is printed upside down] of Nations which haue swarmed hither, and the practise of the Normans, who as a monument of their Conquest, would haue yoaked the English vnder their tongue, as they did vnder their /25/ command, by compelling them to teach their children in schooles nothing but French, by setting downe their lawes in the Norman-French, and enforcing them (most rigorously) to pleade and to bee impleaded in that tongue onely for the space of three hundred yeares, vntill King *Edward* the third enlarged them first from that bondage. Since which time, our language hath risen by little, and the prouerbe proued vntrue, which so long had beene vsed, *lacke would be a gentleman, if he could speake French.*

Herein is a notable argument of our Ancestors stedfastnesse in esteeming and retaining their owne tongue. For as before the Conquest, they misliked nothing more in King *Edward* the Confessor, than that he was Frenchified, and accounted the desire of forraigne language then, to be a foretoken of the bringing in of forraine powers, which indeede happened. In like manner after the Conquest, notwithstanding those enforcements of the Normans in supplanting it, and the nature of men, which is most pliable with a curious iolity, to fashion and frame themselues according to the manners, attire and language of the Conquerours: Yet in all that long space of 300. yeares, they intermingled very few French-Norman words, except some termes of law, hunting, hawking, and dycing, when as wee within these 60. yeares, haue incorporate so many Latine and French, as the third part of our tongue consisteth now in them. But like themselues continue still those old Englishmen which were planted in *Ireland,* in *Fingall* and the Countrey of *Weysford,* in the time of King *Henry* the second, who yet still continue their ancient attire and tongue, in so much that an English Gentleman not long since, sent thither in Commission among them, sayd that hee would quickely vnderstand the Irish, when they spake the ancient English. So that our ancestors seemed (in part) as iealous of their natiue language, as those *Brittaines* which passed hence into *Armorica* in *France,* and marrying strange women there, did cut out their tongues, lest their children should corrupt their language with their mothers tongues, or as the *Germans* (which haue most of all Nations) opposed themselues against all innouations in habite and language. /26/

Whereas the *Hebrew Rabbines* say, and that truely, that Nature hath giuen man fiue instruments for the pronouncing of all letters, the lips, the teeth, the tongue, the palate, and throate; I will not deny but some among vs do pronounce more fully, some flatly, some broadly, and no few mincingly, offending in defect, excesse, or change of letters, which is rather to bee imputed to the persons and their education, than to the language. When as generally wee pronounce (by the confession of strangers), as sweetely, smoothly, and moderately, as any of the Northerne Nations of the world, who are noted to foupe [fop?] their words out of the throate with fat and full spirits.

This variety of pronunciation hath brought in some diuersity of Orthography, and hereupon Sir *Iohn Price,* to the derogation of our tongue, and glory of his *Welsh,* reporteth that a sentence spoken by him in *English,* and penned out of his mouth by foure good Secretaries, seuerally for triall of our Orthography, was so set downe by them, that they all differed one from the other in many letters: whereas so many *Welsh,* writing the same likewise in tongue, varied not in any one letter at all. Well, I will not derogate from the good Knights credite; yet it hath beene seene where tenne English, writing the same sentence, haue all so concurred, that among them all there hath beene no other difference, than the adding, or omitting once or twise of our silent *E*, in the end of some words. As for the *Welsh*, I could neuer happen on two of that nation together, that would acknowledge that they could write their owne language. /27/

> The following appears in Camden's volume, under the title "The Excellency of the English *tongue*," pp. 32-39, attributed to one "R. C. of Anthony," who may have been the antiquary Sir Robert Cotton, of whom Camden wrote, "at his torch he willingly suffered me to light my taper."

For our owne parts we imploy the borrowed ware so far to our aduantage, that we raise a profit of new words from the same stocke, which yet in their owne Country are not marchantable. For example, we deduce diuers words from the Latine, which in the Latine it selfe cannot be yeelded, as the verbs, *To Aire, to beard, to crosse, to flame*, and their deriuations, ayring, ayred, bearder, bearding, &c. as also closer, closely, closenesse, glosingly, hourely, maiesticall, maiestically. In like sort we graffe vpon French words those buds, to which that soile affoordeth no growth, as *chiefly, faulty, slauish, precisenesse*. Diuers words also we deriue out of the Latine at second hand by the French, and make good English, though both Latine and French haue their hands closed in that behalfe, as in these verbes, *Pray, Point, Paze, Prest, Rent, &c.* and also in the Aduerbes *carpingly, currantly, actiuely, colourably, &c.* . . .

Moreouer, the copiousnesse of our Language appeareth in the diuersity of our Dialects, for we haue Court and we haue Country English, we haue Northerne, and Southerne grosse and ordinary, which differ each from other, not only in the terminations, but also in many words, termes, and phrases, and expresse the same things in diuers sorts, yet all right English alike, neither can any tongue (as I am perswaded) deliuer a matter with /37/ more varietie then ours, both plainely and by Prouerbes and Metaphors: for example, when wee would bee rid of one, wee vse to say, *bee going, trudge, packe, bee faring, hence, away, shift*, and by circumlocution; *Rather your roome then your company, lets see your backe, come againe when I bid you, when you are called, sent for, intreated, willed, desired, inuited, spare vs your place, another in your stead, a Ship of Salt for you, saue your credite, you are next the doore, the doore is open for you, there is no body holdeth you, no body teares your sleeue, &c.* likewise this word *Fortis* wee may sinonymize after all these fashions, stout, hardy, valiant, doughty, couragious, aduentrous, &c.

And in a word, to close vp these proofes of our copiousnesse, looke into our Imitations, of all sorts of Verses affoorded by any other Language, and you shall finde that Sir *Philip Sidney*, Master *Puttenham*, Master *Stanihurst*, and diuers more haue made vse how farre we are within compasse of a fore-imagined possibility in that behalfe.

I come now to the last and sweetest point of the sweetenesse of our tongue, which shall appeare the more plainely, if like two Turkeyses or the London

Drapers, we match it with our neighbors. The Italian is pleasant but without sinewes, as a still fleeting water. The French, delicate, but euen nice as a woman, scarce daring to open her lippes for feare of marring her countenance. The Spanish Maiesticall, but fulsome, running too much on the O. and terrible like the Diuell in a Play. The Dutch manlike but withall very harsh, as one ready at euery word to picke a quarrell. Now we in borrowing from them, giue the strength of consonants to the Italian, the full sound of words to the French, the variety of terminations to the Spanish, and the mollifying of more vowels to the Dutch, and so (like Bees) gather the hony of their good properties, and leaue the dregs to themselues. And thus when substantialnesse combineth with delightfulnesse, fulnesse with finenesse, seemlinesse with portlinesse, and currantnesse with stayednesse, how can the Language which consisteth of all these, sound other then most full of sweetnesse? /38/

20. RICHARD MULCASTER

A Schoolmaster on Spelling and Punctuation

Richard Mulcaster (1530?-1611), the teacher of Edmund Spenser, was the first headmaster of the Merchant Taylors' School and high-master of St. Paul's School. Among his important writings on the education of children is the *Elementarie*, available in a modern edition, *Mulcaster's Elementarie*, edited by E. T. Campagnac (London, 1925), from which the following passages are taken.

OF DISTINCTION

THis title of *distinction* reacheth verie far, bycause it conteineth all those characts, and their vses, which I called before signifying, but not sounding, which help verie much, naie all in all to the right and tunable vttering of our words and sentences, by help of those characts, which we set down, and se in writing. The number of them be thirtene, and their names be *Comma, Colon, Period, Parenthesis, Interogation, long time, shorte time, sharp accent, flat accent, streight accent, the seuerer, the uniter, the breaker.* Whose forces, & vses I will run thorow in order as theie ar named. *Comma,* is a small crooked point, which in writing followeth som small branch of the sentence, & in reading warneth vs to rest there, and to help our breth a litle, as *Who so shall spare the rod, shall spill the childe. Colon* is noted by two round points one aboue another, which in writing followeth some full branch, or half the sentence, as *Tho the daie be long: yet at the last commeth euensong. Period* is a small round point, which in writing followeth a perfit sentence, and in reading warneth vs to rest there, and to help our breth at

ful, as *The fear of God is the beginning of Wisdom. Parenthesis* is expressed by two half circles, which in writing enclose some perfit branch, as not mere impertinent, so /166/ not fullie concident to the sentence, which it breaketh, and in reading warneth vs, that the words inclosed by them, ar to be pronounced with a lower & quikker voice, then the words either before or after them, as *Bycause we ar not able to withstand the assalt of tentation (such is the frailtie of our natur) therefor we praie God, that our infirmitie be not put to the hasard of that triall. Interogation* is expressed by two points one aboue another, wherof the vpper is sometimes croked which both in writing & reading teacheth vs, that a question is asked there, where it is set, as *Who taught the popiniaye to speak? the bellie:* These fiue characts, that I haue allredie named, ar helps to our breathing, & the distinct vtterance of our speche, not ruling within the word, as al those do which follow, but by the word, & therefor com her in note, bycause theie ar creaturs to the pen, & distinctions to pronoune by, & therefor, as theie ar to be set down with iudgement in writing, so theie ar to be vsed with diligence in the right framing of the tender childes mouth. The two next concern the time, that is, the long or short pronouncing of syllabs, and ar not allwaie to be marked ouer that syllab, whereon theie shew their force, but with discretion & vpon great cause for som manifest *distinction,* which rule we haue of the *Latins,* who vse their accents in that sort, and truble not their writing therewith, so much as the *Grekes* do, much less so much as the Hebrewes. *The long time,* is expressed by a streight outright line, which being set ouer anie vowell or diphthong, telleth vs, that the same vowell or diphthong, must be pronounced long, as *repīning, perūsing, repēnting. The short time,* is expressed by an half circle opening vpward, which standing avoue [*v* for *b* may be a printer's error] anie vowell or consonant, signifieth that the same is to be pronounced short and quik, as *perfïting, natŭrell, periŭrie, tormĕnter, carpĕnter.* In the other fiue I haue no further note then that theie were to be well markt, euen for that theie were writen to such an end, bycause the matter of their periods and branching, whereof manie learned men haue writen /167/ hole treatises, belongeth not to this place, but onelie their form to the eie, and their vse to the ear, which tendeth to the qualifying of our voice. /168/

OF PREROGATIUE

. . . This secret misterie, or rather quikning spirit in euerie spoken tung, and therefor in ours, call I *prerogatiue,* bycause when *sound* hath don his best, when *reason* hath said his best, when *custom* hath effected, what is best in both, this *prerogatiue* will except against anie of them all, and all their rules, be theie neuer so generall, be theie neuer so certain. Whereby it maketh a waie to a new change that will follow in some degree of the tung, if the writers period be chosen at the best. I cannot compare this customarie *prerogatiue* in speche to anie thing better, than vnto those, /177/ which deuise new garments, and by law ar left to the libertie of deuise. Hence cummeth it in apparell, that we be not like our selues anie long time, tho the best & most semelie (like an artificial rule) do best please the wisest peple. But by the waie is it not a maruell, that the period of a tu*n*g, being so quik an instrume*n*t, shall continew lo*n*ger, when the fashio*n* of apparell, being a thing so thought on, & sadlie misformd? Vpon the like libertie in speche, to be hir own caruer, com our exceptions against our generall rules. He*n*ce coms the writing of *com*, the simple with, o, the compound with, u, *cumfort cumpasse*. Hence, *whom*, & *most* sound lik, *rome* & *roste*, tho not qualifyed with, e. Hence cometh it that, *enough, bough, tough* & such other primitiues be so stra*n*glie writen, and more strangelie sounded. Whereby *prerogatiue* semeth to be a quiksiluer in *custom*, euer stirring, and neuer staied tho the generall *custom*, as a thing of good staie do still offer it self to be ordered by *rule*, as a nere frind to *reason*. This stirring quintessence the leader to change in a thing that is naturallie changeable, and yet not blamed for the change, some not verie well aduised peple, esteme as an error, and a priuat misuse contrarie to *custom*, bycause it semes to be a verie imperious controller, but theie ar deceiued. For in dede this *prerogatiue*, tho it chek general conclusions, thorough priuat oppositions, yet that opposition came not of priuat men, but it is a priuat thing it self, and the verie life blood, which preserueth tungs in their naturall best from the first time that theie grew to accou*n*t, till theie com to decaie, & a new period growen, different from the old, tho excellent in the altered kinde, and yet it self to depart, and make roum for another, when the circulat turn shall haue ripened alteration. */178/*

> NOTE: Mulcaster discusses all the letters of the alphabet; selected in the following are his comments on *E* and *V*. He does not treat the symbol *U*.

E Besides the common difference of time, and tune, is a letter of maruellous vse in the writing of our tung, and therefor it semeth to be recommended vnto vs speciallie aboue anie other letter, as a chefe gouernour in the right of our writing. Which e, tho it be somtime idlelie writen, either of ignorance, if the writer be vnlearned, and know not how to write, or of negligence, if he be learned, and mark not his hand, yet most times it is writen to great purpos, even where it semeth idle, before the force of it be considered, and hath a verie great saying in ech of the seuen precepts, and shalbe declared in euerie of them particularie.

And first for *rule*, the first of the seuen precepts, this is to be noted of E, that it either soundeth or is silent, and that either in the former or in the last syllabs. But first of the last, where it either endeth the syllab it self, or with som other consonant, or consonants after. Whensoeuer E, is the last letter, and soundeth, it soundeth sharp, as *mé, sé, wé, agré*. sauing in *the*, the article, ye the pronown, and in Latin words, or of a Latin form, when theie be vsed English like, as, *certiorare quandare*, where e, soundeth full and brode after the originall Latin.

Whensoeuer e, is the last, and soundeth not, it either qualifieth som letter going before, or it is mere silent, and yet in neither kinde encreaseth it the number of syllabs. I call that E, qualifying, whose absence or presence, sometime altereth the vowell, sometime the consonant going next before it. It altereth the sound of all the vowells /123/ euen quite thorough one or mo consonants as, máde stéme, éche, kínde, strípe, óre, cúre, tóste sound sharp with the qualifying E in their end: whereas, màd, stèm, èch, frind, strip, or, cur, tost, contract of tossed sound flat without the same E, And therefor the same loud and sharp sound in the word, calleth still for qualifying e, in the end, as the flat and short nedeth it not. It qualifyeth no ending vowell, bycause it followeth none in the end, sauing i. as in daie, maie, saie, trewlie, safetie. where it maketh i, either not to be heard, or verie gentlie to be heard, which otherwise wold sound loud and sharp, and must be expressed by y. as, deny, aby, ally. Which kinde of writing shalbe noted hereafter. It altereth also the force of c, g, s, tho it sound not after them, as in hence, for that, which might sound henk, if anie word ended in e. in swinge differing from swing, in vse differing from vs. /124/ . . . Some vse the same silent e, after r, in the end, as *lettre, cedre, childre*, and such, where methink it were better to be the flat e, before r, as *letter, ceder, childer*, and so *childern* rather than *children*, onelesse ye will form of *childe, childer, childeren*, and so by contraction *children*, cutting awaie the former e: or *childern*, cutting awaie the latter.

E. when it endeth the last sillab, with one or mo consonants cumming after it, either soundeth flat and full, and maketh a syllab, as in *rest, wretch, discent*, or it is passant & soundeth quik like the fine gentle i, mostwhat not encreasing the number of sullabs as *writen, goten, saieth*. This e, *passant* and the gentle i, be of such affinitie, as theie do oftimes enterchange places, as *indite, induce, intent*, or *endite, enduce, entent*. Generallie words that end in the qualifying or silent e, when theie put s, vnto them in their deriuatiues, theie make the e passant, as *time, times, wife, wiues, pipe, pipes*, without encrease of the syllabs, and ar therefor to be speld together.

E, ending anie former sullab soundeth of it self brode, and longish, as, reprehend, delegate, onelesse it be a deriuatiue or compound of some sharp ending e, which answereth the primatiue or simple in the first sound, as *agréing*, of *agrée, foreséeth*, of *foresé*. If it end the syllab with anie consonant after, it is flat, as *entending, repentant. /125/*

It is neuer silent in anie former syllab, but in composition, where the hole simple word is to be writen, as in *wherefor, herevpon, hencefurth*, in the two former, the prerogatiue of custom vsing e, in the end, *where, here*, contrarie to the proportion, in *hear, wear, ear:* in the last the qualifying e, accompanying hir simple *hence*. In the titles of *distinction* and *derivation* there shalbe more said of the silent and qualifying e, both where theie be to be vsed, and where not in the respect of the timing and tuning of words. /126/

. . . V besides the notes of his form, besides his time and tune, is to be noted also not to end anie English word, which if it did it should sound sharp, as *nú, trú, vertú*. But to auoid the nakednesse of the small u, in the end we vse to write those terminations with ew the diphthong, as *new, trew, vertew.* It is vsed consonantlike also as well as i, when it leadeth a sounding vowell in the same syllab, as *vantage, reuiue, deliuer,* or the silent e, in the end, as beleue, reproue. This duble force of both i, and v, is set from the latin, and therefor it is neither the vncertaintie of our writing, nor the vnstedfastnesse of our tung, for to vse anie letter to a duble vse. */129/*

21.   RICHARD HODGES

True Writing of the Letter E

> The following selection is from Richard Hodges, *A Special Help to Orthographie* (London, 1643); it is available in a facsimile reprint (Ann Arbor, 1932).

Take heed that you never put a double consonant with an *e,* in the end of any word: for there is no necessitie thereof. And the rather wee may be the bolder so to do, because the Learned, both in Printing and Writing, do dayly practise it. Therefore, you must not write such words as these, thus, *ladde, bedde, lidde, rodde, budde,* but thus, *lad, bed, lid, rod, bud:* and in like manner, you are to write al other words which end /17/ with any other consonant: as *al, hal, bal, wal, gal, cal, stal:* only for your satisfaction heerin, you are to know, that whensoever *a* cometh before *l,* in the end of any word, it must bee pronounc't like *au:* and then, what need wil there be of a double *l,* in the word *cal,* when it signifieth as a verb, to *cal,* more than there is in *caul,* the substantive, when it signifieth a *caul* or tire to wear upon the head? Besides, forasmuch as wee use to write the word *al,* with a single *l,* in *al-*most, and *al-*together, by the same reason, wee may aswel write *al* with a single *l,* when it is a simple word, as when it is compounded. Only in such words, as end with *f,* or *s,* they are commonly writen, with *a double f and an e,* and with *a double s and an e,* as in *chaffe* and *brasse:* yet I see no reason why custom should be offended, if the two words aforegoing were writen thus, *chaf* and *bras,* & so, al other words of this kinde: but I submit my self to the judgment of the Learned: and therefore, howsoever I have practised the same, in the Worke aforegoing, yet I have withal, set down each word, as it is the other way writen, that so both ways may bee known. . . . */18/*

It is also needles, (needlesse) to put a double consonant in the midle of such words as these, namely, in *saddle, meddle, fiddle, cobble, bubble:* but rather write them thus, *sadle, medle, fidle, coble, buble:* for what use is there of a double *b,* in *bubble,* more than there is in *double* and *trouble?*

I give you farther to understand, that if the vowels were so distinguisht one from another, as that their sounds might bee certainly known, when they are long, and when they are short, there is no necessitie that any word whatsoever, should have a double consonant, either in the middle, or any part of it, unles it bee to shewe the Etymologie thereof: and this may plainly appeare, even by our own practice, in the writing of many English words: as for example, what use is there of a double *t* in *dittie*, more than there is in *Citie;* or of a double *d* in *ruddy*, more than in *studie;* or of a double *d* in *sodden*, more than there is in *troden?* But forasmuch as our vowels are not so distinguisht, as to know when they are long and when they are short, wee are inforc't to use a double consonant, where a single might serve: as for example, these two words, *fill'd* and *fil'd*, as they are exprest in *fill'd* up to the brim, and *fil'd* with a file, they might either of them, bee writen with a single l, if their vowels were so distinguisht, that the long vowel in the one word, might bee known from the short vowel in the other: as also, these two words, /20/ *pinn'd* and *pin'd*, might either of them bee writen with a single *n*, if there were the like distinction. Multitudes of examples might bee given in this kinde, but these may suffice.

But although the sounds of our vowels, are not so distinguisht one from another, as they should bee, yet I see no reason, why *a double* l, should bee writen, in any derivative word, where the vowel in the simple word, is known by custom, to bee long of it self, as for example, in these three simple words, namely, *cal, wal, fal*, where the vowel *a* is wel known to have the sound of *au:* and therefore, why may not these three derivatives, *ca-ling*, *wa-ling*, and *fa-ling*, be so writen, forasmuch as their syllables are to be pronounc't, like *cau-ling, wau-ling*, and *fau-ling?* Again, forasmuch as the sound of *o*, is wel known to bee long *before* l, in the end of many simple words, as in *roll, poll, toll*, which may as wel bee writen thus, *rol, pol, tol*, why may not their derivatives bee writen thus, *ro-ling, to-ling, po-ling?* But heerin, (as in other things before) I submit my self to the judgement of the Learned.

You are to know also, that whensoever *e* cometh in the end of any English word whatsoever, except the article *the*, it hath no use for sound of it self; and therefore might bee altogether left out, if wee had long vowels to expres our words withal: but forasmuch as this is wanting, wee are inforc't to make use of *e* in the end of a word, to shewe thereby, the vowel going before to bee long: as in these words, *vale, male, mane, mare;* to distinguish them from *val, mal, man, mar:* as also in these words, *wine* and *wile*, to distinguish them from *win* and *wil*, whose vowels are short. But it were to bee wisht, that the vowels might bee so distinguisht, as that their sounds might bee certainly known, to bee long of themselves, without any other help. And surely, in some cases, there is an absolute necessitie for the doing of it; if wee desire that there should bee any certaintie in the pronouncing of our words. an example thereof, you may see in these two words, *win-der*, and *wil-der*, where the first syllable in either of them must bee pronounc't long, as in *wine*, and *wile*. The neglect of distinguishing the long vowels from the short, is the cause, why many words are pronounc't two several ways: for some men cal the *winde*, the *wind;* and so accordingly, they mispronounce the derivatives of the same word. Again, in the word *wil-der*, the first syllable thereof, must be pronounc't like the word *wile*, but in the word *wil-der-nes*, it must bee pronounc't like *wil*. What great uncertaintie is this for the learner! And how great a benefit might the whole Nation receive thereby, if these things were amended! I wish therefore, that al such as love Learning, would take this into their serious consideration. /21/

Thus much have I though good to speak, by way of digression. And now I return again to my former discourse, concerning the use of *e* in the end of a word, which (as I said before) is onely useful, to shewe the vowel to be long which went before: and therefore, in al such words, where the vowel or the diphthong, that went before, is wel known to bee long of it self, what need wil there be of an *e*, in the end thereof? As for example, in these words, *lead, land, seed, fool, pail, void, cloud*, and the like, the vowels and diphthongs, are so wel known to bee long, of themselves, as that there needs no *e* in the end, to make them known. Nevertheles, you are to observe, that there are many words, wherein such vowels are, which are commonly known to bee long in the most words, and yet in some, they are to bee pronounc't short, as in these words, *head, read, stead, hea-dy, rea-dy, stea-dy*, and such like: it is therefore (for the present) very meet, to put an *e* in the end of some such words, as in *reade*, the present tense, to distinguish it from the short sound of *read*, the preterimperfect tense. Also, there is no need of an *e* in the end of such words, as *harm, learn, corn, burn, part, hurt, hand, bound, hang, thing, sing, song, hung*, and such like: You are therefore to bee careful, that you never put an *e*, in the end of any such words as these aforegoing, but specially, in the latter words, whereof the word *sing*, is one, for, if you should put an *e*, to the end of it, it would alter the sense thereof, and make it in stead of sing, to become singe. Also, it is to bee observed, that where it is not needful to use *e*, in the end of the singular number, it shall not bee needful, to use *e* in the plural, and therefore the plurals are to be written thus, *seeds, fools, pails, clouds, harms, parts, hands, bands, bounds, things, songs, rings, strings, swings*: but not thus, *seedes, fooles, pailes, cloudes, harmes, partes, handes, bandes, boundes, thinges, &c.* In such words as these aforegoing, custom hath already given way, for the leaving out of *e* in the end, and therefore wee may boldly practise it. But there are diverse words, which as yet would seem strange, and therefore, for customs sake wee use it, although there bee no more necessity, for the using of it in these words, than was in the former: as in *fee-ble, stee-ple, nee-dle, tem-ple, peo-ple*, and such like. And heer it may bee observed, from such syllables as these aforegoing, that some kinde of syllables, may be exprest without a vowel: for what use hath *e* for sound in the last syllable of the word *fee-ble?* And therefore, if custom would give way thereto, such words, might rather bee writen thus, *fee-bl, stee-pl, nee-dl, tem-pl, peo-pl*. And heer by the way, we may take it into consideration, whether *o* in *peo-ple*, were not better to bee left out, and the word to bee writen thus, *pee-ple*. /22/

There bee also, many other words, wherein *e* might very wel bee spared, as in *give, live, five,* and the like: for, the vowel which went before in either of them is short, and therefore needs no *e* in the end, to shewe it to be long; such words therefore might be writen thus, *giv, liv, fiv.* As also, such words as these, *mouse, house,* and the like, forasmuch as the diphthong going before, in either of them, is wel known to bee long of it self, what need is there of an *e* in the end, to make it known? The words therefore, they might bee writen thus, *mous, hous,* and so, al other words of this kinde. But I leave these things to the consideration of the Learned.

You ought also to observe, that it is not needful to write *e* after *y,* in the end of any word: because *y,* will serve sufficiently of it self, to expres the sound of *ie* in the end of a word, as *y* in *cry,* is wel known to expres the like sound as *ie* doth in *crie:* and therefore we ought not to write *crye, trye, &c.*

It is also very needful, for the help of True writing, that you diligently observe, when you are to write *y,* for *i* the vowel: understand therefore in the first place, that it ought most naturally, and truly to bee writen, in al such words as are borrowed of the Greek, as *Synagogue, Physician, hypocrite, mystery,* and such like. But forasmuch as custom hath received it, and withal the Learned do so frequently practise it, I see no reason, why wee may not use it for a vowel, as formerly we have done: for, in many words (according to our custom in writing) it is, as if it were naturalliz'd, as in *my, by, thy, why:* for these words are always so writen: but in many other words, they are differently writen: as for example, some write thus, *die, tie, lie, stie, crie, spie:* and some write thus, *dy, ty, ly, sty, cry, spy:* for mine owne part, I think, that both these ways of writing, may stil be reteined: yet so, as that the first sort may bee constantly used for nouns, and the last for verbs, for in so doing, by adding *s,* to the first sort, they wil become nouns of the plural number: as *die dies, tie ties, lie lies, stie sties, crie cries, spie spies:* and by adding *ing,* to the last sort, which are verbs, they wil become participles: as *dy dy-ing, ty ty-ing, ly ly-ing, sty sty-ing, cry cry-ing, spy spy-ing.* As for *y,* which is used for a vowel, in the diphthong *ay,* forasmuch as it is so constantly used, in the end of a word, as in *may, lay, say, day, way, pay:* it may therefore, be constantly used, both in nouns and verbs: and not onely, in the singular number of a noun, but also in the plural, as *day days, way ways, stay stays;* and it is not onely to bee used before *ing,* as in *stay-ing,* but also before *eth* as in *stayeth,* and before *ed* as in *stayed:* and so in al other words, which have the like endings. /23/

It is our custom in writing, to use *y* for *i,* in multitudes of words: yea I think, that there is scarcely any word (not beeing a substantive) that, ends in *i,* but may (according to our custom) bee writen with *y:* as *tary, cary, very, weary, heady, ready, fully, happy, trusty, lusty:* and what not?

It is very meet therefore, that any word, which is a substantive, should never end in *y,* but always in *ie,* as *Citie, dittie, treatie, bellie:* and so al others, save onely in some words, where *l* and *n* went before: as in *alley, valley, journey, Atturney,* and the like. Any of these words aforegoing, by putting *s* to the end, wil make nouns of the plural number, as *Citie Cities, dittie ditties, treatie treaties, bellie bellies, alley alleys, valley valleys, journey journeys, Atturney Atturneys:* and so in al others whatsoever, of either kinde. /24/

22. JOHN AWDELEY, THOMAS HARMAN

Language of the Underworld

As printing developed in the sixteenth and seventeenth centuries, pamphlets appeared which we should classify as sensational journalism. Among them were exposés of the cheats and thieves of the day, who had their own cant in order to discuss shady matters without revealing secrets. One pamphlet by John Awdeley has the elaborate title: *The Fraternitye of Vacabondes both rusling and beggerly, Men and women, Boyes and Gyrles, with their proper names and qualities. Whereunto are adioyned the company of Cousoners and Shifters.* The original appeared in 1565; the following selections are from the diplomatic reprint of the Early English Text Society, extra series, 9, edited by Edward Viles and F. J. Furnivall (London, 1869).

AN ABRAHAM MAN. An Abraham man is he that walketh bare armed, and bare legged, and fayneth hym selfe mad, and caryeth a packe of wool, or a stycke with baken on it, or such lyke toy, and nameth himselfe poore Tom.

A RUSSELER. A Russeler goeth wyth a weapon to seeke seruice, saying he hath bene a Seruitor in the wars, and beggeth for his reliefe. But his chiefest trade is to robbe poore wayfaring men and market women.

A PRYGMAN. A Prygman goeth with a stycke in hys hand like an idle person. His propertye is to steale cloathes of the hedge, which they call storing of the Rogeman: or els filtch Poultry, carying them to the Alehouse, whych they call the Bowsyng In, & ther syt playing at cardes and dice, tyl that is spent which they haue so fylched. /3/

A WHIPIACKE. A whypiacke is one, that by couler of a counterfaite Lisence, (which they call a Gybe, and the seales they cal Iarckes) doth vse to beg lyke a Maryner, But hys chiefest trade is to rob Bowthes in a Faire, or to pilfer ware from staules, which they cal heauing of the Bowth.

A FRATER. A Frater goeth wyth a like Lisence to beg for some Spittlehouse or Hospital. Their pray is commonly vpon poore women as they go and come to the Markets.

A QUIRE BIRD. A Quire bird is one that came lately out of prison, & goeth to seeke seruice. He is commonly a stealer of Horses, which they terme a Priggar of Paulfreys.

AN VPRIGHT MAN. An Vpright man is one that goeth wyth the trunchion of a staffe, which staffe they cal a Filtchman. This man is of so much

authority, that meeting with any of his profession, he may cal them to ac-
compt, & commaund a share or snap vnto him selfe, of al that they haue
gained by their trade in one moneth. And if he doo them wrong, they haue
no remedy agaynst hym, no though he beate them, as he vseth commonly to
do. He may also commaund any of their women, which they cal Doxies, to
serue his turne. He hath ye chiefe place at any market walke, & other as-
sembles, & is not of any to be controled.

A CURTALL.   A Curtall is much like to the Vpright man, but hys authority
is not fully so great. He vseth commonly to go with a short cloke, like to
grey Friers, & his woman with him in like liuery, which he calleth his
Altham if she be hys wyfe, & if she be his harlot, she is called hys Doxy.

A PALLIARD.   A Palliard is he that goeth in a patched cloke, and hys Doxy
goeth in like apparell. /4/

AN IRISHE TOYLE.   An Irishe toyle is he that carieth his ware in hys wallet,
as laces, pins, poyntes, and such like. He vseth to shew no wares vntill he
haue his almes. And if the good man and wyfe be not in the way, he
procureth of the ch[i]lldren or seruants a fleece of wool, or the worth of
xij.d of some other thing, for a peniworth of his wares.

A IACK MAN.   A Iackeman is he that can write and reade, and somtime
speake latin. He vseth to make counterfaite licences which they call Gybes,
and sets to Seales, in their language called Iarkes.

A SWYGMAN.   A Swygman goeth with a Pedlers pack.

A WASHMAN.   A Washman is called a Palliard, but not of the right making. He vseth to lye in the hye way with lame or sore legs or armes to beg.
These men ye right Pilliards wil often times spoile, but they dare not com-
playn. They be bitten with Spickworts, & somtime with rats bane.

A TINKARD.   A Tinkard leaueth his bag a sweating at the Alehouse, which
they terme their Bowsing In, and in the meane season goeth abrode a begging.

A WYLDE ROGE.   A wilde Roge is he that hath no abiding place but by his
coulour of going abrode to beg, is commonly to seeke some kinsman of
his, and all that be of hys corporation be properly called Roges.

A KITCHEN CO.   A Kitchin Co is called an ydle runagate Boy.

A KITCHEN MORTES.   A Kitchin Mortes is a Gyrle, she is brought at her full
age to the Vpryght man to be broken, and so she is called a Doxy, vntil she
come to ye honor of an Altham. /5/

DOXIES.   Note especially all which go abroade working laces and shirt
stringes, they name them Doxies.

A PATRIARKE CO.   A Patriarke Co doth make mariages, & that is vntill
death depart the maried folke, which is after this sort: When they come to
a dead Horse or any dead Catell, then they shake hands and so depart euery
one of them a seurall way /6/

> This following, presumably imaginary but roughly authentic,
> purports to be the conversation between two scamps. It is taken
> from Thomas Harman, *A Caueat or Warening, for Commen*

Cvrsetors Vvlgarely Called Vagabones (London, 1567), which was reprinted in Viles and Furnivall.

The vpright Cofe canteth to the Roge.
The vpright man speaketh to the Roge.

VPRIGHTMAN. Bene Lightmans to thy quarromes, in what lipken has thou lypped in this darkemans, whether in a lybbege or in the strummell? /84/
God morrowe to thy body, in what house hast thou lyne in all night, whether in a bed, or in the strawe?

ROGE. I couched a hogshead in a Skypper this darkemans.
I layd me downe to sléep in a barne this night.

VPRIGHT MAN. I towre the strummel trine vpon thy nabchet *and* Togman.
I sée the strawe hang vpon thy cap and coate.

ROGE. I saye by the Salomon I will lage it of with a gage of benebouse; then cut to my nose watch.
I sweare by the masse, I wull washe it of with a quart of good drynke; then saye to me what thou wylt.

MAN. Why, hast thou any lowre in thy bonge to bouse?
Why, hast thou any money in thy purse to drinke?

ROGE. But a flagge, a wyn, and a make.
But a grot, a penny, and a halfe penny.

MAN. Why, where is the kene that hath the bene bouse?
Where is the house that hath good drinke?

ROGE. A bene mort hereby at the signe of the prauncer.
A good wyfe here by at the signe of the hors.

MAN. I cutt it is quyer bouse, I bousd a flagge the laste dark mans.
I saye it is small and naughtye drynke. I dranke a groate there the last night.

ROGE. But bouse there a bord, *and* thou shalt haue beneship.
But drinke there a shyllinge, and thou shalt haue very good.

Tower ye yander is the kene, dup the gygger, and maund that is bene shyp.
Se you, yonder is the house, open the doore, and aske for the best. /85/

MAN. This bouse is as benshyp as rome bouse.
This drinke is as good as wyne.

Now I tower that bene bouse makes nase nabes.
Now I se that good drinke makes a dronken heade.

Maunde of this morte what bene pecke is in her ken.
Aske of this wyfe what good meate shee hath in her house.

ROGE. She hath a Cacling chete, a grunting chete, ruff Pecke, cassan, and popplarr of yarum.
She hath a hen, a pyg, baken, chese and mylke porrage.

MAN. That is beneshyp to our watche.
That is very good for vs.

Now we haue well bousd, let vs strike some chete.

Nowe we haue well dronke, let us steale some thinge.

Yonder dwelleth a quyere cuffen, it were beneship to myll him.

Yonder dwelleth a hoggeshe and choyrlyshe man, it were very well donne to robbe him.

ROGE. Nowe bynge we a waste to the hygh pad, the ruffmanes is by.

Naye, let vs go hence to the hygh waye, the wodes is at hand.

MAN. So may we happen on the Harmanes, and cly the Iarke, or to the quyerken and skower quyaer cramprings, and so to tryning on the chates.

So we maye chaunce to set in the stockes, eyther be whypped, eyther had to prison house, and there be shackled with bolttes and fetters, and then to hange on the gallowes.

Gerry gan, the ruffian clye thee.

A torde in thy mouth, the deuyll take thee.

MAN. What, stowe your bene, cofe, and cut benat whydds, and byng we to rome vyle, to nyp a bong; so shall we haue lowre for the bousing ken, and when we byng back to the deuseauyel, we wyll fylche some duddes of the Ruffemans, or myll the ken for a lagge of dudes.

What, holde your peace, good fellowe, and speake better wordes, and go we to London, to cut a purse; then shal we haue money for the ale house, and /87/ when wee come backe agayne into the country, wee wyll steale some lynnen clothes of one [off'n?] hedges, or robbe some house for a bucke of clothes. /88/

23. NATHANIEL BAILEY

The Advantages and Alteration of Old English

> Nathan Bailey (d. 1742), sometimes called Nathaniel Bailey, was the first great English lexicographer. One of his significant contributions was attention to the history of the language and to etymology, illustrated in the following selection from the preface to his dictionary. It is taken, with Bailey's transcriptions of Old English modernized, from the fourth edition of his *An Universal Etymological Dictionary* (London, 1728), enlarged and revised from the first edition, 1721.

Before I proceed to account for the Alteration of the *English Saxon*, by the two other Causes, I shall mention something relating to the *Saxon* Tongue, of a great Part of which the *Normans* despoil'd us, giving a worse for a better. "Great verily (says *Camden*) was the Glory of our Tongue before the *Norman* Conquest, in this, that the Old *English* could express most aptly all the Conceptions of the Mind in their own Tongue, without borrowing from any," and of this gives the following Examples.

The service of God, called *Religion,* they called Sal-fastness, as the only Assurance and fast Anchor-hold of our Souls Health.

The *Gladsome Tidings of Salvation* . . . they call'd Gods-spel, *i.e.* God's Speech.

Our *Saviour,* in French *Savieur,* of *Salvator,* Lat. they called Al-hael, *i.e.* All Health.

Pharisees, Sunder-halʒens, *i.e.* Religious Men, which had sundred and separated themselves from the Men of the World.

The *Scribes,* Boc-men, *i.e.* Book-men.

The *Sacrament,* Haliʒdom, *i.e.* Holy Judgment.

Fertility Eorðes-Wele, *i.e.* the Wealth of the Earth.

The *Judgment,* Dome-settle, *i.e.* the Settling of Doom.*

A *Parliament,* Witten-mot, *i.e.* an Assembly of Wise Men.

Conscience, Inwit, *i.e.* that which they did inwardly wot or know certainly.

Also the Names they gave to their Months were significant, as,

JANUARY [Wulfe-Monað, *Sax. i.e.* Wolf-month] because in that Month the Wolves were most mischievous to them, for that thro' the Extremity of Cold and Snow, they could not find Beasts sufficient to satisfy their ravenous Appetites.

FEBRUARY [Sprout-Kele, *Sax. i.e.* Cole-Wort or Spring-Wort] because then Worts begin to sprout.

MARCH [Lenct-Monað, *Sax. i.e.* the Lengthening Month] because then the Days begin in Length to exceed the Nights.

APRIL [Easter-Monað, *Sax.*] because their Easter generally fell in April.

MAY [Tri-milci, *Sax. i.e.* 3 Milkings] because then they milk'd their Cattle three Times a Day.

JUNE [Mede-Monað, *Sax. i.e.* Meadow Month] because then their Cattle were turned out to feed in the Meadows.

JULY [Hey-Monað, *Sax. i.e.* Hay Month] because then they generally cut their hay.

AUGUST [Arn-Monað, *Sax. i.e.* Barn-Month] because they then fill'd their Barns. [*Arn* is presumably an error for *Barn.*—Eds.]

SEPTEMBER [Gerst-Monað, *Sax. i.e.* Grist-Month] because then they carried their Corn to Mill.

OCTOBER [Wyn-Monað, *Sax. i.e.* Wine Month] because then Grapes were usually press'd to make Wines.

NOVEMBER [Wynde-Monað, *Sax. i.e.* Windy-Month] because of the high Winds happening commonly in that Month.

DECEMBER [Wynter-Monað, *Sax. i.e.* Winter Month, because of the Cold then growing intense; and afterwards Halig-Monað, *Sax. i.e.* Holy Month] on Account of the Nativity of Christ. /a/

[*More accurately, *dom* means judgment, *setl* means seat.]

I shall only add one piece of Saxon Antiquity more, and so proceed, which is the Lord's Prayer in the Saxon Language, written about the Year of Christ 900, by Alfred Bishop of Durham.

Vren fader ðic   arð in Heafnas sie gehalgud
Our Father which art in Heavens be hallowed

ðin noma tocymeð ðin ric   sie ðin   willa sue
thine Name come   thy Kingdom be they* will so

is in Heafnas and in Eorðo. Vren half ofer wirtlic
as in Heavens and in Earth. Our Loaf supersubstantial

sel vs to dæʒ and forʒef vs scylda urna sue we
give us to Day and forgive us Debts our so we

forʒefan scyldʒum vrom and no inlead vsið in   custnunʒ,
forgive Debts   ours, and do notlead us into Temptation,

Ah ʒefriʒ vrich   from ifle Amen.
but deliver every one from Evil Amen.

By these Instances it does appear that the *English Saxon* Language, of which the *Normans* despoiled us in great Part, had its Beauties, was Significant and Emphatical, and preferable to what they imposed upon us.

This may suffice for the Mutation of our Language upon the first Cause of it, which was Conquest: I now proceed to the other Two.

Secondly, As to *Commerce,* the *Britains* having been of a long Time a Trading Nation, as it generally happens, we have had many Words introduc'd by that Means; and besides, *Britain* having been a considerable Time under Subjection to the See of *Rome,* in Ecclesiastical Affairs, the *Italians* coming over hither to manage the Pope's Concerns, and others for Church Dignities, and many *Britains* going hence to *Rome* on Account of Ecclesiastical Suits, Priesthoods, Abbacies, and Bishopricks, must unavoidably introduce some *Italian* Words among us.

Thirdly, As to the particular Properties of a Language, our Tongue has undergone no small Mutation, or rather has received no small Improvement upon that Account; for as to the *Greek* and *Latin,* the Learned have, together with the Arts and Sciences, (now rendered very familiar among us) introduced abundance, nay almost all the Terms of Art, in the *Mathematicks, Philosophy, Physick,* and *Anatomy,* with many others from them; and many more have we entertained from the *Latin, French,* &c. for the sake of Nearness and Elegancy.

So that at this Day our Language, which 1800 Years ago was the ancient *British* or *Welsh,* is now a Mixture of *Saxon, Teu-/aˣ/tonic, Dutch, Danish, Norman,* and Modern *French,* imbellish'd with the *Greek* and *Latin.*

Yet is not this, I think, any Disparagement to the *English* Tongue as now

[*Presumably a misprint for *thy;* Bailey certainly knew better. For other revisions, see notes on the version in Camden, p. 89 above.]

spoke (for this Change is nothing but what all Languages have been liable to, and have undergone, and do interchangeably participate each with other, having likewise enfranchised many Words from the *Latin* and *Greek*, tho' perhaps not so many as we) but it rather makes to the Advantage of its Character; for transplanting Foreign Words into our Native Soil, and new forming them, we have so enrich'd it, that now it is become the most Copious and Significant Language in *Europe*, if not in the World. /a 2/

24. JAMES GREENWOOD

Changes in the English Language

James Greenwood (d. 1737), surmaster of St. Paul's School, published one of the earliest grammars written in English, *An Essay Towards a Practical English Grammar, Describing the Genius and Nature of the English Tongue* (London, 1711); the selections below are from the third edition, London, 1729. Greenwood explains that his preface is mainly a translation from John Wallis, *Grammatica Lingua Anglicanae* (Oxford, 1652), but that he has added some materials: "The *Additions* have this Mark before them (")." Thus Greenwood is saying, in effect, that the portions printed below without quotation marks are translated from Wallis' Latin, but that the portions printed with quotation marks are his own. His use of a pair of quotation marks for each line is not unusual.

When *William* Duke of *Normandy*, called the Conqueror, brought over his *Normans* hither, having got Possession of *England*, he attempted an Alteration of the Language, endeavouring to introduce the *French* Tongue; that being the Language which he himself used in *Normandy;* for tho' the *Normans*, or *Northmans*, while they were a People of *Norway*, as formerly they were, spoke the same Tongue with the *Saxons* who had been their Neighbours, namely, that which /8/ was then spoken by the *Saxons* in *England;* but after the *Normans* came into *Neustria* (which was long after called *Normandy*) they chang'd their Native Language for the *French*, which was made up of the *Romans*, or *France Gallick;* and this was the Language which the Conqueror had a Mind should be settled in *England* with himself, wherefore he took no small Care to have all *Diploma's* Publick Edicts, and other judicial Matters, written and performed in the *Neustrian*, or *French* Tongue. But his Attempts prov'd unsuccessful, because the Number of the *Normans* that came hither, was very small, in Comparison of the *English* with whom they were embodied or mix'd; wherefore the *Normans* left or forgot their own Language, sooner than they could make any Change in the *English*. But tho' for this Reason the old *English* Tongue kept its grounds, yet this Disadvantage arose from these Endeavours of the Conqueror, that many *French* words, tho' for the most part of *Latin* Original, crept into the *English,* and many *English* Words by Degrees grew out of Use. For as to the Derivation of some Words, we may thus judge; that the Words which the *French* have, that are of *German* Original, brought thither by the *Franks,* altho' they may now chance to be common to us, with the *French,* yet we are to reckon them originally our own, rather than borrow'd from them: So likewise as to the old *Gaulish* Words which they retain, now common to them with the *Welch,* and which we likewise have kept from the old *British* Language, we are to think, that we received them from the *Welch,* rather than from the *French.*

And I am of Opinion, that a tolerable Reason may be given why the Names of these living Creatures, are originally *German,* whose Flesh, when prepar'd for Food, we call by *French* Names; as for Instance, *an Ox, a Cow, a Calf, a Sheep, a Hog, a Boar, a Deer,* &c. are *German* Names; but *Beef, Veal, Mutton, Pork, Brawn, Venison,* &c. are *French:* The Reason then, I take to be, is that the *Norman* Soldiers did not so much concern themselves with Pastures, Parks, Pens, and other Places, where these Creatures were looked after and kept, which therefore preserv'd their ancient Names; as with Markets, Kitchins, Feasts and Entertainments, where the Food was either prepar'd or sold, whence it receiv'd new Names. . . . /9/

"Having thus done with what we had to say about the *Mother-Tongues,*
"we shall now proceed to give some Examples of the Changes which our
"own Language has suffered. Now, besides the common Fate and Corrup-
"tion to which Languages, as well as all other human Things are subject,
"there are many particular Things which may occasion the Changes of a
"Language: The Mixture with other Nations in Commerce; Marriages in
"Royal Families, which do usually bring some common Words into a Court-
"Fashion; that Affectation incident to some Eminent Men in all Ages, of coin-
"ing new Words, and altering the common Forms of Speech for greater
"Elegancy; the Necessity of making other Words, according as new Things
"and Inventions are discovered: Besides the Laws of foreign Conquests
"usually extended to Letters and Speech, as well as Territories; the Con-
"queror commonly endeavouring to propagate his own Language, as far
"as his Dominions; which is the Reason why the *Greek* and *Latin* are so
"universally known. For as no Person in the Provinces could enjoy the
"Benefit of the *Roman* Freedom with any Honour, and remain ignorant of
"the *Roman* Tongue: So in Embassies, Suits, Appeals, or whatever Provincial
"Business happened, nothing was allowed to be handled or spoken in the
"*Senate* at *Rome,* but in the *Latin* Tongue. The Laws also whereby the
"Provinces were governed, were all written in that Language, as being in
"all of them, except the Municipal Cities, the ordinary *Roman* Law. More-
"over the *Pretors* of the Provinces, were not allowed to deliver their Judg-
"ments but in that Language: And we read, in *Dion Cassius,* of a principal
"Man in *Greece,* that by *Claudius* was /16/ put from the Order of Judges,

"for being ignorant of the *Latin* Tongue: And to the same Effect in *Va-
"lerius Maximus, 1. 2. c. 2.* that the *Roman* Magistrates would not give audi-
"ence to the *Grecians* (therefore much less to the barbarous Nations) but in
"the *Latin* Tongue. Besides this there were publick Schools erected in
"sundry Cities of the Provinces, which we find mentioned in *Tacitus,*
"*Hierom,* and others, in which Schools the *Roman* Tongue was the ordinary
"and allowed Speech: These things were no small furtherance to that Lan-
"guage. But instead of following these brave Examples, we, for the Advance-
"ment of our Language, send our Boys and Girls to learn *French,* a Custom,
"especially as it relates to the Female Sex, very ridiculous and nonsensi-
"cal; . . . /17/

25. JAMES BARCLAY

In Praise of English

> Many writers of the eighteenth century apologized for English
> grammar, pointing out that it has fewer inflectional endings than
> have Latin and Greek; but James Barclay boldly asserted that
> English was better off without numerous inflectional endings, and
> many modern students would agree with him. The following is
> from his *A Complete and Universal English Dictionary* (London,
> 1792), revised from the first edition of 1774.

Having thus said all we think absolutely necessary, and consistent with
our intended Brevity, we shall proceed to the last Topic proposed; namely,
the Excellency of the *English Language.*

Now its Beauties are most conspicuous in the Four particular Articles here
undermentioned that is to say, it is free and easy; and in short more sweet
and harmonious, and by consequence preferable to any living Language
whatsoever.

Its Freedom and Facility, in the first Place, is demonstrable, since it is in
a great Measure exempt from that Multiplicity of Cases and Flexions, which
clog or incumber almost all others, and render them for that Reason extremely intricate, difficult, and abstruse. Our *Adjectives* being all invariable,
make their Concordance with their *Substantives* remarkably plain and easy:
Our *English Pronouns,* likewise, are not half so confused and perplexed as
either those of the *Latin* or the *French.* And scarce any thing can more
easily be conquered than the Conjugation of our *English* Verbs: Besides,
our Language is burdened with no such Thing as *Verbs reciprocal,* which
render the *French Tongue* in particular very dark and obscure; and very
often discourage Foreigners from the Study of it.

To illustrate its Copiousness, very little need be said, since it is too manifest and self-evident to be denied; for besides the ancient *Dutch,* which

the *English* retain in the *Saxon* Monosyllables, the Literati of *England*, like so many industrious Bees, have collected the Quintessence of divers foreign Languages, and rejected their Refuse or Dross; by which artful Management, and their Assiduity, they have improved their Mother-Tongue to that prodigious Degree, that all such Foreigners as have an adequate Idea of the Genius of it, are perfectly charmed to observe, that neither their own, nor any other Language whatsoever, can stand in Competition with it; and at the same Time, to find a great Variety of their own Terms so happily transplanted and blended with it, that they seem to thrive better in *England* than in their own native soil.

And whereas the *French* is too much limited and constrained, and through its Over-niceness is grown in some Measure barren, spiritless, and insipid; the *English*, on the other hand, is become prodigiously copious and luxuriant, through its innate power of making such *Compounds* and *Derivatives* as are very comprehensive, emphatical, and proper to contract any Expression into a narrow Compass; it must be allowed, that neither the *Greek* itself, nor the *Latin* can compound, or join many Words together, in a more agreeable Manner, which is one of the most shining Beauties that any Language can possibly boast of. In a Word, there is no Sentiment or Thought that can be expressed in a greater Flow of Words, or with more Propriety and a better Grace, than in the *English Tongue*.

As to its Energy or Significance, there is scarce any Variety, that any other Nation can boast of, but what the *English* have almost with equal Happiness made its own. With what Propriety has the celebrated Lord *Bacon* taught us to speak all the Terms of Art in our Mother-tongue, which was looked upon as impracticable, till we saw it actually carried into Execution! What inimitable Pieces of Oratory or Elocution, of our own Growth, have we seen published within these few Years; And what Collection of Poems bears a more sublime Sense, /*xiii*/ is more manly and majestic, more strong and nervous, than what has been exhibited to the Public by those universally admired Poets, Mr. *Milton*, Mr. *Addison*, and Mr. *Pope?*

As to its Harmony and Sweetness, it must be confessed, that the *Italian* abounds with Vowels, as the *Dutch* does with Consonants, which renders the first too effeminate, and the last too rugged and uncouth; whereas the *English* has, through a happy Intermixture, the Advantage of them both. We cannot but allow that the *Italian* Language is peculiarly delicate, soft and pleasing to the Ear; but then it glides along like a purling Stream. The *French*, doubtless, is very nice and courtly, but then it has too much in it, that savours of Effeminacy and Affectation. The *Spanish*, it is true, is very solemn and majestic; but then it is too apt to be stormy and tempestuous, and carries a Kind of Terror along with it. The *German* is very manly indeed, but then it is harsh and unpolite; whereas the *English* by judiciously borrowing a little here and a little there, from each of them, gives strength of Consonants to the *Italian*, the full and perfect Sound of Syllables to the *French*, the Variety of Terminations with much gentler Accents to the

Spanish, and dissolves the *Dutch* Consonants with greater Facility and Ease.

Now what can possibly be wanting to the Perfection of that Language, where Substance and Solidity combine with Pleasure; where Copiousness unites with Delicacy, Beauty with Majesty, and Expedition with Gravity and Sedateness? — And such doubtless is the Composition of the *English.*

That all these Advantages are inherent in our Mother-tongue, all Foreigners in general are become at length highly convinced; and notwithstanding indeed, in former Days, they spoke of it with an Air of Indifference at least, and looked upon it with an Eye of Contempt; yet as those groundless Prejudices are now removed, they stand in Admiration at the Sound of it.

The principal Objection that some Hyper-critics have urged against it, are these two; namely, Its being a Language compounded of divers others; and its being subject and liable to frequent Variations. The former, however, is so very natural to all Languages in general, that we have never heard hitherto of any one entirely free from it, the *Hebrew* only excepted, as some say; but whether that be real Factor not, we ingenuously acknowledge our Inability to determine. The *Latin* Language has a great Mixture of that which was spoken by the *Greeks* and *Goths;* the *French* is a Composition of *Latin, Dutch,* and the ancient *Gallic;* the *Spanish,* of *Latin* principally, with some Spice or Smattering of the *Gothic* and *Morisco;* and the *German* itself, tho' by some peremptorily insisted upon to be an Original, has some Savour of the *Roman* Empire, and its neighboring Nations.

As to its being subject to various Changes and Mutations, the Objection is altogether as groundless as the former: For it is universally allowed, that all Languages, as well as Kingdoms, have their Infancy and Age, their Perfection and Decay. /*xiv*/

26. NOAH WEBSTER

Origin of Language

The reputation of Noah Webster (1750-1843) rests mainly upon his great quarto dictionary, the basis of the American lexicographical tradition, and one of the most important books ever issued in this country. Less can be said for some of his linguistic assertions; his observations on the origin and growth of language, for example, may be revealing of the bizarre phantasies of the eighteenth-century speculative thinkers, but they are not very useful if one wishes to know how and when language grew. One can only pity poor Eve, having to learn by human means the language that her husband had acquired through a miracle. The following selection is from the preface to the first edition of *An American Dictionary of the English Language* . . . (New York, 1828), 2 vols.

We read, in the Scriptures, that God, when he had created man, "Blessed them and said to them, be fruitful and multiply and replenish the earth and subdue it; and have dominion over the fish of the sea, &c." God afterwards planted a garden, and placed in it the man he had made, with a command to keep it, and to dress it; and he gave him a rule of moral conduct, in permitting him to eat the fruit of every tree in the garden, except one, the eating of which was prohibited. We further read, that God brought to Adam the fowls and beasts he had made, and that Adam gave them names; and that when his female companion was made, he gave her a name. After the eating of the forbidden fruit, it is stated that God addressed Adam and Eve, reproving them for their disobedience, and pronouncing the penalties, which they had incurred. In the account of these transactions, it is further related that Adam and Eve both replied to their Maker, and excused their disobedience.

If we admit what is the literal and obvious interpretation of this narrative, that vocal sounds or words were used in these communications between God and the progenitors of the human race, it results that Adam was not only endowed with intellect for understanding his Maker, or the signification of words, but was furnished both with the faculty of speech, and with speech itself, or the knowledge and use of words, as signs of ideas, and this before the formation of the woman. Hence we may infer that language was bestowed on Adam, in the same manner as all his other faculties and knowledge, by supernatural power; or in other words, was of divine origin; for supposing Adam to have had all the intellectual powers of any adult individual of the species, who has since lived, we cannot admit as probable, or even possible, that he should have invented and constructed even a barren language, as soon as he was created, without supernatural aid. It may even be doubted, whether without such aid, men would ever have learnt the use of the organs of speech, so far as to form a language. At any rate, the invention of words, and the construction of a language must have been a slow process, and must have required a much longer time, than that which passed between the creation of Adam and of Eve. It is therefore probable that *language* as well as the faculty of speech, was the *immediate gift of God.* We are not however to suppose the language of our first parents in paradise to have been copious, like most modern languages; or the identical language they used, to be now in existence. Many of the primitive radical words may and probably do exist in various languages; but observation teaches that languages must improve and undergo great changes as knowledge increases, and be subject to continual alterations, from other causes incident to men in society.

A brief account of the origin and progress of the principal languages, ancient and modern, that have been spoken by nations between the Ganges and the Atlantic ocean.

We learn from the Scriptures that Noah, who, with his family, was preserved from destruction by the deluge, for the purpose of re-peopling the earth, had three sons, Shem, Ham and Japheth. This fact, a little obscured by tradition, was retained by our rude German ancestors, to the age of Tacitus.

Japheth was the eldest son; but Shem, the ancestor of the Israelites, and of the writers of the Scriptures, is named first in order.

The descendants of Shem and Ham peopled all the great plain, situated north and west of the Persian Gulf, between that Gulf and the Indian ocean on the east and the Arabic Gulf and the Mediterranean Sea on the west, with the northern coast of Africa; comprehending Assyria, Babylonia or Chaldea, Syria, Palestine, Arabia, Egypt, and Lybia. The principal languages or dialects used by these descendants, are known to us under the names of Chaldee, or Chaldaic, which is called also Aramean, Syriac, Hebrew, Arabic, Ethiopic, Samaritan and Coptic. Of these, the Chaldee, and Hebrew are no longer living languages, but they have come down to us in books; the Samaritan is probably extinct or lost in the modern languages of the country, but the language survives in a copy of the Pentateuch; the Coptic is nearly or quite extinct, and little of it remains; the Syriac, Arabic and Ethiopic are yet living languages, but they have suffered and are continually suffering alterations, from which no living language is exempt.

These languages, except the Coptic, being used by the descendants of Shem, I call *Shemitic*, or *Assyrian*, in distinction from the *Japhetic*. As the descendants of Japheth peopled Asia Minor, the northern parts of Asia, about the Euxine and Caspian, and all Europe, their languages, have, in the long period that has elapsed since their dispersion, become very numerous.

All languages having sprung from one source, the original words from which they have been formed, must have been of equal antiquity. That the Celtic and Teutonic languages in Europe are, in this sense, as old as the Chaldee and Hebrew, is a fact not only warranted by history and the common origin of Japheth and Shem, but susceptible of proof from the identity of many words yet existing, in both stocks. But there is a marked difference between the Shemitic and Japhetic languages; for even when the radical words are unquestionably the same, the modifications, or inflections and combinations which form the compounds are, for the most part, different.

As it has been made a question which of the Shemitic languages is the most ancient, and much has been written to prove it to be the Hebrew, I will state briefly my opinion on what appears to me to be one of the plainest questions in the history of nations. We have for our certain guides, in determining this question — Ist. The historical narrative of facts in the book of Genesis, and 2d. The known and uniform progress of languages, within the period of authentic profane history.

1. The Scripture informs us that, before the dispersion, the whole earth was of one language and of one or the same speech; and that the descendants of Noah journeyed from the east, and settled on the plain of Shinar, or in Chaldea. The language used at that time, by the inhabitants of that /[*A4*] [1]/

[1 In unpaged books reference is made to signature marks.]

plain, must then have been the oldest of the primitive language of man. This must have been the original Chaldee.

2. The Scripture informs us, that in consequence of the impious attempts of the people to build a city and a tower, whose top might reach to heaven, with a view to make themselves a name and prevent their dispersion, God interposed and confounded their language, so that they could not understand each other; in consequence of which they were dispersed "from thence over the face of all the earth."

3. If the confusion of languages at Babel originated the differences which gave rise to the various languages of the families which separated at the dispersion, then those several languages are all of equal antiquity. Of these the Hebrew, as a distinct language, was not one; for the Hebrew nation was of posterior origin.

4. All the words of the several great races of men, both in Asia and Europe, which are vernacular in their several languages, and unequivocally the same, are of equal antiquity, as they must have been derived from the common Chaldee stock which existed before the dispersion. The words common to the Syrians and Hebrews, could not have been borrowed from the Hebrew, for the Hebrews originated from Heber and Abram, several centuries after Syria and Egypt were populous countries. This fact is attested by the Scripture history, which declares that when Abram migrated from Chaldea, and came into Canaan or Palestine, "The Canaanite was then in the land"; and when he returned from Egypt, "the Perizzite dwelt in the land." These declarations, and the history of Abimelech, and of the war of four kings or chieftains with five; as also of the cities of Sodom and Gomorrah, prove Syria to have been, at that time, well-peopled. The language of the inhabitants then must have been coeval with the nation, and long anterior to the Hebrew as a distinct dialect. It may be added that in the early periods of the world, when no books existed, nations, living remote or distinct, never borrowed words from each other. One nation, living in the midst of another, as the Hebrews did among the Egyptians, may adopt a single word, or a few words; but a family of words thus adopted is an occurrence rarely or never known. The borrowing of words, in modern times, is almost wholly from the use of books.

5. It is probable that some differences of language were produced by the confusion; but neither that event or any supernatural event is necessary to account for the differences of dialect or of languages, now existing. The different modern languages of the Gothic or Teutonic stock, all originated in the natural course of events; and the differences are as great between them as they are between the languages of the Shemitic stock.

6. Soon after two races of men of a common stock have separated and placed themselves in distant countries, the language of each begins to diverge from that of the other, by various means. — 1. One tribe or nation will suffer one word to become obsolete and be forgotten; another, will suffer the loss of another; sometimes a whole family of words will be lost; at other times, a part only; at other times, a single word only of a numerous

family will be retained by one nation, while another nation will retain the whole. 2. The same word will be differently applied by two distant races of men, and the difference will be so great as to obscure the original affinity. 3. Words will be compounded by two nations in a different manner, the same radical words making a different prefix or suffix, in different languages. Thus *wisdom* in English is in German *weisheit*, (wisehead, wisehood) from *wise*, *weis*. In English *mislead* is in Danish *förleder*, from *lead*, *leder*. 4. The pronunciation and orthography of words will often be so much changed, that the same word in two languages, cannot without difficulty, be recognized as identical. No person, without a considerable attention to the changes which letters have suffered, would at once suspect or believe the English *let* and the French *laisser* to be the same word.

7. As Abram migrated from Chaldea, he must have spoken the Chaldee language, and probably, at that time, the Syriac, Arabic and Egyptian, had not become so different, as to render it impracticable for him to converse with the inhabitants of Palestine and Egypt. /[*A4ᵛ*]/

Subjects for Discussion

1. Try to determine on what principles Orm was doubling letters. One student of language has suggested that he was using a doubled letter after any vowel that would have been long in Latin. If you have studied Latin, you might check this theory.

2. By consulting a good dictionary try to account for the two pronunciations of *eggs* in Caxton's time.

3. What can you infer about dialects in Caxton's time? You might try to find out what he meant by "uplandish" men. Is the word in any way related to our word *outlandish?*

4. Some people would like to fix language to try to keep it from changing. In the light of Caxton's experience, and changes since Caxton's time, are they likely to be able to do so?

5. How does Caxton account for linguistic change among Englishmen? If he is right, what do you need to assume about the natures of early Frenchmen, Spaniards, and Italians?

6. What is the importance for usage of Mulcaster's notion of what he calls *prerogative?*

7. Study levels of usage in the late sixteenth century. The Upright Man and the Rogue speak two sorts of slang or cant; Mulcaster and Hodges write good familiar nonfictional prose; most of the characters in Shakespeare speak familiar English with poetic overtones, but when Lear makes official pronouncements, promises, or condemnations, he speaks almost formal English. Holofernes speaks a strange mixture, much of it pedantic. What difference do you notice among the speakers, in diction, usage, grammatical forms, order of words, and the like?

8. What does Mulcaster seem to feel is the function of italics? Does he differ in this from the translator of Camden? From Hodges?

9. Camden speaks of the "endenizing of strange words." Which of the writers employ such unusual words, borrowed from foreign languages, that have not survived in modern dictionaries? Give examples.

10. What was the basis of punctuation according to Mulcaster? Modern students of language relate punctuation to stress and pitch in speaking; does Mulcaster take any account of oral expression as a basis of punctuation?

11. What do you infer from Mulcaster's treatment of *v* and from his omission of *u* among the symbols he treats? Does he seem to be treating *v* mainly as a vowel or a consonant?

12. Awdeley provides a glossary of terms for thieves in his day. What information does he fail to give you that the maker of a modern dictionary would include?

13. On whose authority does Awdeley rely for his definitions? Is he like or unlike a modern lexicographer in his selection of sources of reliable information?

14. Camden endeavors to account for similarities between English and certain Oriental languages. In the light of modern knowledge, can you provide any plausible guesses that he missed?

15. By the eighteenth century a few scholars, but not many, could read Old English, or, as they called it, Saxon. Which of the writers in this section seem to give clear evidence that they had a working knowledge of Old English?

16. Which writers have taken material or ideas directly from their predecessors, especially from Camden? Which acknowledge their debts; which don't?

17. Walter Scott is often given credit for discovering and recording, in *Ivanhoe*, the etymological distinction between words like *pig* and *calf*, *pork* and *veal*. Does this seem plausible in light of the readings in this section?

18. Various eighteenth-century writers endeavored to defend English against the common notion that it was inferior to the classical languages Latin and Greek, and even to contemporary Continental languages. Which of their arguments would probably be accepted by a modern student of language?

19. Webster seems to feel that he can trace language from Adam to his own time. Modern students, with much more material at their disposal than Webster had, doubt that anybody can do this. Unless all modern thinkers are wrong, Webster must be misusing his evidence. Examine his argument to see if you can detect the flaws in it.

20. Webster derived English spelling from what he called Saxon, that is, Old English. Does he seem aware of what happened to spelling during Middle English times?

21. Camden, noticing similarities between English and other languages, assumed that these similarities came about through borrowing and suggested as the only possible explanation that the "Saxons" had established colonies in the Orient. Would other explanations account for his evidence?

Suggestions for Investigation, Reports, or Brief Papers

1. Can you phrase what seem to be Caxton's ideas about proper usage?

2. In a day when even great scholars did not know Old English, Camden collected and compared it. He worked, of course, with great handicaps; of what modern idea or ideas of language does he seem to be ignorant? Can you demonstrate your thesis?

3. Compare Mulcaster and Hodges; which seems the more learned, which the more authoritarian?

4. Summarize as exactly as you can in about two hundred words what Mulcaster thought the letter *e* should be used for.

5. How does Mulcaster's system of punctuation differ from modern punctuation? Consider his treatment of each punctuation symbol.

6. What similarities do you find between the cant of Awdeley's underworld and modern cant or slang?

7. Does Hodges follow Mulcaster's rules of punctuation? Does Mulcaster follow Hodges' rules of spelling? Do they follow their own rules?

8. Consider the problem of usage in the various writers in this section. Orm is quite sure he is right about usage in spelling; does he ever indicate how he knows he is right? Caxton is aware of the problem of usage; how do you know this? Could you formulate a statement of Mulcaster's belief in usage? Hodges appeals to both "custom" and "the learned." How does he seem to arrive at proper usage? Obviously these writers do not entirely agree about usage; can you state precisely in what they agree and in what they seem to differ?

9. Mulcaster and Hodges consider spelling symbols and sounds and the relations of the two in considerable detail. Can you find any modern writer on spelling who considers these questions in as much detail? Can you think of reasons for differences between modern and sixteenth-century discussions of spelling?

10. Compare medieval spelling with later spelling; do the differences seem to reflect any awareness of the principles that Mulcaster and Hodges are laying down?

11. The First Folio of Shakespeare was printed after both Mulcaster and Hodges. Does the printer seem to have been following either Mulcaster or Hodges scrupulously? If not, does he seem to be working generally along the lines that these men recommend in spelling and punctuation?

12. Consider the writers on language in this section and try to decide which is the most reliable. Defend your choice with evidence.

13. Webster says that people who could not read and write probably did not borrow many words and that "the borrowing of words, in modern times, is almost wholly from the use of books." He does not define "modern times," but you might assume he means after about 1600. On the basis of what you know by now, is Webster probably right — are words today being borrowed exclusively from books and other printed material? If you wrote the history of a word in Section II, you might consider the evidence you found about borrowing. Can you infer from the form of a borrowed word whether it was borrowed as a sound or a sequence of letters?

V. DEVELOPMENT OF THE DICTIONARY

Modern man has devised various tools and techniques with which to study language; the first of these to be brought to something like perfection, at least in English, was the dictionary. Most non-European languages known today have no dictionaries, and apparently never have had them, except as scholars in the European tradition imitated the conventional dictionaries characteristic of all important European languages. Apparently the dictionary is a western European invention; it was not an English invention, but students of English have played a respectable part in its development. The dictionaries surveyed in this section reveal clearly the way dictionaries and the concept of lexicography have grown.

Apparently dictionaries grew from glosses — notes in a manuscript intended to explain it. In Anglo-Saxon times, manuscripts written in Latin might be glossed with Old English words, very much as students in college today will write the English words over troublesome locutions in their French or German or Russian language texts. Later, when Old English became little known, the process was sometimes reversed, with Latin written over the Old English; Latin or Greek might be glossed with French, or Anglo-Norman glossed with French or Latin. Eventually, lists of equivalents were prepared, Latin with the Anglo-Norman equivalents, Anglo-Norman with the English equivalents. By the seventeenth century, what we should call dictionaries of English were appearing, although they were not dictionaries in a modern sense, since they listed only words that the editor thought of as "hard," words which the user would not know without help.

At this point we might pause for a moment to look at these dictionaries, from the earliest glosses to books edited about 1700. They were all intended to be helpful, a fact which may at first seem insignificant, but is not. None of the earlier dictionaries were calculated to determine what was right and what was wrong, what was elegant and what was crude, what could be justified because it was like Greek and Roman and what was barbarian because it was used only in Yorkshire or Sussex. The books said, in effect, this word is used in Latin, and roughly speaking it is the equivalent in use of this word in Anglo-Norman, or Middle English, or whatever the language concerned. Or the dictionary said, in effect, this word is not very common; you may want to use it, or you may encounter it in speech or in written form; if so, this is probably about the way you should use it if you are to be understood, and this is about the way you can expect to find it used.

Interestingly enough, this is essentially the attitude of a modern lexicographer. He does not try to tell a user of his dictionary how to speak, although some publishers of dictionaries still pretend that their books are "authorities." He tries to describe the language of his time. He tries to include important words current in his day and to describe them in all ways and as accurately as he can, granted his limitations in knowledge and space. He feels that his job is to be as revealing about words as he can be. He does not dictate usage; he provides information to help users of the language make their own decisions about usage.

As a group, the men and women who make modern dictionaries are confident of what they are doing and why they are doing it, although not all the users of dictionaries understand how and why such books are made. This is the modern practice, and the early practice, but it has not always been the practice. During the eighteenth century quite a number of students of language were less interested in understanding their subject than in prescribing what it should be. This often rather blind dictatorialness was more characteristic of the grammarians than of the dictionary makers, but lexicographers toyed with the idea, also. Even so keen a man as Dr. Samuel Johnson started his great dictionary with the laudable hope that he could "purify" and "fix" the language from then until eternity. He outgrew that notion, as he confesses in his introduction. He was, after all, a learned and intelligent man, who had the perspicacity to realize his mistake and the honesty to admit it.

Not all of Johnson's fellow lexicographers were so intelligent nor so honest. Not the least of the charms of the present section is to be sought in a comparative study of the dictionary makers. For example, it is interesting to note how one characteristic after another of the modern dictionary appears in the work of successive lexicographers. One might also observe how long dictionary makers entertained the savioristic notion that a lexicographer can remake the language and reform muddleheaded mankind. Or, one might trace the development of the modern understanding of the use of a dictionary — to describe the language as fully and as accurately as present knowledge and available wood pulp permit.

In fact, the student can profitably observe the growth of the concept of the modern dictionary in some detail. First, what is a modern dictionary? What does it contain? Obviously, a modern dictionary differs from an early dictionary in that it tries to include all the important words in the language, not just the hard words. How else does it differ? For one thing, it makes a point, sometimes a great to-do, of indicating the pronunciation of words. Early dictionaries ignored pronunciation; how and when did this change come about? Most etymologies in early dictionaries are absent or meager or even ridiculous. When and how did lexicographers become aware that etymologies are important, and when did they learn to write them? What essential information had to be discovered before revealing etymologies became possible? How was spelling revealed in dictionaries? Modern America has made a fetish of spelling; students are seldom failed for writing meaningless sentences but they are frequently failed for faulty spelling. Where did our spelling conventions come from, and how did they get fixed? Most early dictionaries give but few uses of most words; early dictionaries of hard words, for instance, entered the word *horse* but gave no indication that it was a domesticated quadruped. When did dictionaries start being exhaustive in their descriptions of word usages, and which ones started the trend? Dictionaries now try to describe the currency of words with such tags as *obs.*, *colloq.*, and *slang;* how did these practices grow?

In this section we are endeavoring to understand the dictionary as a language tool; to understand it in its totality, we must understand its parts.

27. DAVID B. GURALNIK

Early English Dictionaries

> The following brief sketch of the history of the English dictionary is from David B. Guralnik, *The Making of a New Dictionary* (Cleveland, 1953), the published version of a paper read before the Rowfant Club in 1951.

The beginnings of dictionary history were not national, but were concerned with the international language of Medieval European civilization — Latin. They consisted of lists of relatively difficult Latin terms, usually those of a Scriptural nature, accompanied by glosses, i.e. explanations, in easier or more familiar Latin. Early in the Anglo-Saxon period, however, we find glosses containing native English (Anglo-Saxon) equivalents for the hard Latin terms. Such glosses, whether Latin-Latin or Latin-English, continued to be compiled during the entire Anglo-Saxon period.

Around the year 1400, numbers of these isolated glosses began to be collected into what were called "glossaria," an early kind of Latin-English dictionary. A later edition of one of the earliest of these, issued by Wynkyn de Worde in 1499 with the title /4/ *Promptorum Parvulorum sive clericorum*, was the first dictionary ever to be printed on English soil. Significantly enough, it places the English term first and its Latin equivalent second.

The rapid development of international trade in the 16th century created a great demand for foreign-language dictionaries, and so there appeared in rapid succession throughout the century a number of French-English, Welsh-English, English-Spanish, and English-Italian word books. In 1565, the first great classical dictionary appeared, Cooper's *Thesaurus*. Incidentally, the publication of this work was delayed five years because Cooper's wife, fearing that too much lexicography would kill her husband, had burned the first manuscript of this opus. I think her fears were exaggerated, and so does my wife, but only a little. It should be noted that none of these 16th-century word books actually used the title "dictionary." They were called by various fanciful names of which *hortus* (a garden) and *thesaurus* (a hoard) were the most popular.

The first English word book to use the name "dictionary" was Cokeram's *The English Dictionary* (published in 1623) and this was one of the numerous dictionaries of "hard words" which circulated at that time. The Renaissance had bred a race of pedants who preferred the Latin or Greek term to the English one. Their Latino-Greek-English "inkhorn terms" eventually affected English to such a degree that no non-Latinate Englishman could hope to read many works in his own language unless he was provided with explanations of *abequitate, bulbulcitate, sullevation,* and their exotic kinfolk.

It wasn't, thus, until the 18th century, with its simple elegance in literary usage and its self-assured /5/ dogmatism re its own standards of refinement, that the first modern dictionaries appeared. In 1721, Nathaniel Bailey published his *Universal Etymological Dictionary of the English Language,* and this revolutionary book was the first to pay attention to current usage, the first to feature etymology, the first to syllabify, the first to give illustrative quotations, the first to include illustrations, and the first to indicate pronunciation. An interleaved copy of the 1731 folio edition was the basis of Samuel Johnson's *Dictionary* of 1755. Through Johnson, it influenced all subsequent lexicographical practice. The position of dictionary pioneer, therefore, commonly granted to Johnson or to Noah Webster, belongs in all right to Nathaniel Bailey.

Johnson's *Dictionary* of 1755 greatly extended the techniques developed by Bailey. However, after emphatically affirming that his dictionary is a remarkable achievement, I should like, with your permission, a few minutes to examine the effects of this book, both the salutary and the deleterious, on all succeeding dictionaries. The general veneration of "rules" in the middle of the 18th century — implicit in the doctrine of Pope's *Essay on Criticism* that literature is to be both produced and judged according to a formula — lends weight to the treatment of languages as something that must be adjudged, once and for all, as either correct or incorrect. Dr. Johnson, in this respect at least, epitomizing the 18th century, purported to give the correct meaning, spelling, and accent of all words then in accepted usage, and these words Johnson conceived to be all that would ever be necessary. This unfortunate approach to language, which has since been rejected by all linguists of note, is still adhered /6/ to by many — perhaps most — dictionary-makers and by almost all dictionary-users. It was perhaps this aspect of the modern dictionary that led Ambrose Bierce to define a dictionary as "a malevolent literary device for cramping the growth of a language and making it hard and inelastic."

English spelling prior to the middle of the 18th century was "unsettled and fortuitous." Dictionaries as "supreme authorities" did not exist as courts of higher appeal to adjust the varying rules. Johnson set out to "ascertain" English orthography, to iron out existing inconsistencies mainly by conforming with long-established custom and by applying, where necessary, the principles of analogy. *Ascertain* Johnson himself defines as "to make certain; to fix; to establish." Make certain, establish, and fix Johnson certainly did, for as a result of his general prestige, the absurdities and illogicalities of

Modern English spelling remain with us today as a monument to Johnson's primitive etymological science and to his complete disregard for a phonetic evaluation of the language. Unwittingly, the weight of Johnson's authority has resulted in a conservatism and standardization that today appear an impassable barrier. Attempts at reform spelling from Benjamin Franklin's first efforts through the Funk & Wagnalls *Standard Dictionary's* respelling of basic words have all proved abortive. The general pessimism with which any large-scale modification of English orthography is viewed for the near future is reflected in the Basic English of Ogden and Richards,* which in spelling remains Basic Johnson.

Of Johnson's etymologies, the less said, the better. Largely because he lacked, of necessity, the linguistic apparatus of modern etymologists, but partly because /7/ of his natural exuberance and prolific imagination, he came up with some ingenious etymologies that approximate Mark Twain's derivation of *Middletown* from *Moses* by dropping the *-oses* and adding *-iddletown*.

It is in the sphere of definition writing that Johnson did his most remarkable and ageless work. He has been equaled but never surpassed in the particularly nerve-straining exercise of tearing a word down into all the senses in which it is used. He was almost never guilty of falling into the common error of redefining in alternative terms or of mistaking a mere nuance for a sense. True, a number of his definitions reveal a highly subjective slant (but here the bias was generally overt, and so harmless), true his overly precise pedantry, his superelaboration of thesis frequently results in something like "a convulsion of the lungs, vellicated by some sharp serosity," — obviously something to be shunned like the plague, but actually only the good doctor's definition for a "cough." Still, in this most difficult task of extracting the kernel from the shell and exposing it for all to see and recognize, Johnson had no master, and all succeeding lexicographers owe him a debt of gratitude for the standards and techniques that he elaborated.

The first American dictionaries were unpretentious little schoolbooks based chiefly on Johnson's *Dictionary* of 1755, via various English abridgments. The most famous work of this class, Noah Webster's *Compendious Dictionary of the English Language* (1806) was an enlargement of a British work, Entick's *Spelling Dictionary* (London, 1764). This book contributed little either to Webster's own reputation or to the development of the American dictionary. /8/

The first important date in American lexicography is 1828, in which year was published Noah Webster's *An American Dictionary of the English Language*. Despite its many deficiencies, this work, in its insistence upon American spellings and in definitions keyed to the American scene, provided the country with its first native dictionary comparable in scope with that of Johnson. Probably its greatest contribution to succeeding American dictionaries was the style of definition writing, writing of a clarity and pithiness

[*A proposed international language, requiring a vocabulary of 800 English words, introduced in C. K. Ogden, *The System of Basic English* (New York, 1934).]

never approached before its day. This book, and others of Noah Webster's, eventually gave birth to a line of offspring which in turn reproduced others so that ultimately there appeared on the American scene a whole series of Webster dictionaries of varying size and quality.

In 1830, Joseph Worcester brought out his dictionary, actually a thoroughly revised abridgment of the Webster work of 1828, and this book, because of its compactness and low price, became extremely popular. There have been other excellent dictionaries published in America, notably the *Century Dictionary* of 1889 and the *New Standard Dictionary* of 1893. I need not, of course, mention that I have been touching upon only a few of the dictionaries published for general use. The great *Oxford English Dictionary* and its analogues, the *Dictionary of American English* and the *Dictionary of Americanisms*, are very special cases that need no discussion here. /9/

28. ELISHA COLES

"Difficult" Words; Dictionary Entries

> The first English dictionary, Robert Cawdrey's *A Table Alphabeticall* (1604) was followed by a number of seventeenth-century dictionaries which list "hard words" or "difficult terms." The following selection is from a later edition of one of these which first appeared in 1676: E[lisha] Coles, *An English Dictionary, explaining Difficult Terms . . . containing Many thousand hard Words* (London, 1685). Coles, who died in 1680, was one of a number of seventeenth-century schoolmasters who published dictionaries. The entries from *horror* to *hortation* and *wicket* to *weight* are consecutive; obviously Coles omitted many words which he did not consider "difficult." Coles appends to his preface a table of abbreviations, including the following which appear in the selection: "*A*. Arabick; *C*. Canting; *F*. French; *I*. Italian; *L*. Latin; *No*. North Country; *O*. Old Word; *Ss*. Sussex."

To the Reader

The several Climates of the World, have influenced the inhabitants with Natures very different from one another. And their several Speeches bear some proportion of Analogy with their Natures. The *Spanish* and the *Spaniard* both are grave, the *Italian* and th' *Italians* amorous, the *Dutch* as boisterous as the *Germans*, and the *French* as light as they themselves are. But the moderate Clime of England has indifferently temper'd us as to both; and what excess there is in either, must be attributed to the accession of something Foraign. Our changes are all professedly owing to the Conquests, especially of *Sax* and *Normandy*.

The first was far the greater, and by virtue of that the body of our Language is still Teutonick: But the last is that which more nearly concerneth us; because, though its first irruption was not a violent inundation, yet it forced us to such a communication with *France*, that our Genius is wrought into some resemblance of theirs: and (to imitate them) we bring home Fashions, Terms and Phrases from every Nation and Language under Heaven. Thus we should fill one another with Confusion and Barbarity, were it not for some such faithful Interpreter as is here presented to the Prince of Isles.

Not that I am ignorant of what's already done. I know the whole Succession from Dr. *Bulloker*, to Dr. *Skinner*, from the smallest Volume to the largest Folio. I know their difference and their defects. Some are too little, some are too big; some are too plain (stufft with obscenity not to be named) and some so obscure, that (instead of expounding others) they have need themselves of an Expositor. The method of some is Foolish, and supposes things to be known before they are explained. For when the terms of Art are reduced to their several Heads, you must know (in general) what your word is, before you can possi- /A2/ bly tell where to seek it; or else (as they say) you must look a Needle in a bottle of Hay. . . .

It is excusable in a *World* of *Words* to say that Contemtible and Contemptuous, Ingenious and Ingenuous are all one: that *Decomposite* signifies compounded of two other words: Ember-week is the week next before Lent: Froise, a Pancake or Tansie: Gallon, a measure of two Quarts: Gomer, nine Gallons (instead of one). *Limbus Patrum*, where the Saints reside till the Resurrection: *Nazareth*, the place where Christ was born; *Redstert*, a Robin-red-breast, *&c.*

And a thousand more such, which simple Children would be apt to contradict, but Men of Judgement (for whom they were not writ) know where the mistake might lie. Yet sure't would have made his Worship smile, to have read, how that *Argus* King of *P.* for his singular wisdom and circumspection was feigned by the Poets to have had no eyes. . . . /A2ᵛ/

Poetical expressions may be allowed to Poetical Relations and Dictions; yet here and there I give a hint, to let you know, that I like them not for real verities.

The History of the Bible I suppose to be so well known, as that I onely give the plain *English* of the *Hebrew, Chaldee, Syriack,* and *Greek* Names.

Here is a large addition of many words and phrases that belong to our English Dialects in the several Counties, and where the particular Shire is not exprest, the distinction (according to the use) is more general into North and South Country words.

Here are also added all the Market-towns (and other considerable places) in *England,* with all the places of note in other Countries, especially the Neighbour Nations. Where it is to be observed, that (as Dr. *Heylin* says of *Hungary*) it were infinite labour to express every little place which the seat of a War gives occasion for History to mention.

'Tis no disparagement to understand the Canting Terms. It /*A3*/ may chance to save your throat from being cut, or (at least) your pocket from being pickt.

I have not onely retain'd, but very much augmented the number of Old Words. For though Mr. *Blount* (as he says expressly) shunn'd them, because they grew obsolete; yet doubtless their use is very great: not onely for the unfolding those Authors that did use them, but also for giving a great deal of light to other words that are still in use. Those that I call Old Words are generally such as occurr in *Chaucer*, *Gower*, *Pierce*, *Ploughman* [sic; the reference is to *Piers Plowman*] and *Julian Barns*.

And whosoever has a mind, instead of them (or other vulgar Terms) to use expressions that are more polite; he sees what words are markt for *Latin*, *Greek* or *French*, and may himself make such Collections as will be far more advantageous, than if they had been gathered to his hand.

Finally, that I might be the more comprehensive (for here is very much in very little room) I have signified the derivation of the words from their several Originals, and the names of the Counties in which they are used, by one or two of their initial letters. /*A3ᵛ*/

Horror, l. a quaking for fear or cold, astonishment.

Horrow, o. nasty, base.

Hors de son fée, f. (out of his fee) an exception to avoid an Action (brought by the pretended Lord) for rent or other service.

Horse, a rope fasten'd to the fore-mast shrouds, to keep the sprit-sail sheats clear of the anchor-flooks.

Horse-habet, a horse-danse.

Horsham, a town in *Sussex*.

Horse-heal, Elicampane.

Horse-tail, an herb good for inward wounds or ulcers.

Hortative, -tatory, belonging to.

Hortation, l. an exhorting. . . .

Wicket, c. a casement.

Wickham, a town in *Bucks*.

Wicklivists, -vians, followers of.

Wicklif, Curate of *Lutterworth* in *Leicestershire*, (1380.)

Wickware, a town in *Glocestershire*.

Widows-bench, Ss. a share of their Husbands Estate which they enjoy beside their joynture.

Wiegh, Waagh, No. a leaver or wedge.

Wieres, o. Witches, Destinies.

Wigan, a town in *Lancashire*.

Wight, an Isle on the South of *England.*

Wight, o. swift.

29. NATHANIEL BAILEY

Dictionary Entries

Nathaniel Bailey's dictionary was the first to pay adequate attention to current usage, to etymology, to syllabification, and to pronunciation. Samuel Johnson wisely used it as the basis for his *Dictionary* of 1755, correcting some of Bailey's errors — notably in the etymologies — as subsequent scholars have been required to correct Johnson's errors. The following entries are from the fourth edition, *An Universal Etymological Dictionary* (London, 1728), enlarged and revised from the first edition of 1721. In general, abbreviations used in Bailey's entries are self-explanatory or similar to modern practices: for example, L. for Latin, F. for French, *Teut.* for Teutonic, *Sax.* for Saxon (that is, Old English), *Dan.* for Danish.

HORROR [*horreur*, F. of *horror*, L.]   such a Shuddering and Quivering as precedes an Ague Fit, and is often joined with *Rigores*, and *Lumbagines*.

HORS *de son Fée*, an Exception to quash an action brought for Rent. . . .

HOR'SA, a famous Saxon Commander, brother to *Hengist*, so called from the Figure of an Horse, which he and his Brother had upon their Coats of Arms.

HORSE [Horsa, *Sax.*]   a Beast well known, the generical Name of it's kind, taking in both Male and Female.

HORSE [in a *Ship*] is a Rope made fast to one of the Fore-mast Shrouds, having a dead Man's Eye at it's End, through which the Pendant of the Sprit-sail Sheet is reeved.

It is a good horse that never stumbles.

This Proverb intimates to us, that there is no Creature that ever went upon four *Legs*, but has made some false Step or other; and that every Mother's Son of us, who goes upon two, hath his *Slips*, and his *Imperfections;* that there is no Person in the World without his *weak Side;* and therefore pleads a Pardon for Mistakes, either in *Conversation*, or *Action*, and puts a Check upon intemperate *Mockery*, or uncharitable *Censure*. And so the *French* say, *Il n'y a bon cheval, qui ne bronche;* and *Quandoque bonus dormitat Homerus*, says *Horace*.

HORS'HAM [*q.d.* Horsa and Ham, or *Horsa's* Town] in *Sussex*, so called from *Horsa*, a famous *Saxon* General, Brother of *Hengist*.

HORSE-*Knobs*, Heads of Knapweed.

HORSE-*Leechery*, the Art of curing Horses of Diseases.

HORSEMANSHIP, the Art of riding or managing Horses.

HORSE-*Measure*, a Measuring Rod, divided into Hands and Inches, for measuring the Height of Horses.

HORSE-*Shoe* [in *Fortification*] is a Work either of a round or oval Figure, raised in the Ditch or a marshy Place, and bordered with a Parapet, either to secure a Gate, or to lodge Soldiers in, to Prevent a Surprize.

HORSE-*Twitchers*, a Tool used by Farriers to hold unruly Horses by the nostrils.

HORSTED [of Horsa Steð, *Sax. q.d. Horsa's* Place; so called from being the Place where *Horsa's* Corpse was buried] a Village in *Kent.*

HORTATION, an Exhorting. *L.* . . .

HUGE [probably from hefiᵹ, *Sax.*] heavy; but *Minshew* derives of *augere, L.* to increase] great, large, high, vast.

To HUG [hoᵹan, *Sax.* of hagen, to tender, to cherish, *Teut.*] to be tender of, to embrace.

A *Cornish* HUG [among *Wrestlers*] is when one has his Adversary on his Breast, and there holds him.

HUG'GER-*Mugger*, [perhaps of hoᵹan, *Sax.* hugghen, *Du.* and mozker, *Dan.* Darkness] privately, clandestinely.

HUGH [hew, *Eng.* hawen, *Teut.* to cleave, or hooch, *Belg.* high] a Name.

HUGUENO'TE, a kind of Kettle for a Stove, or an earthen Stove, for a Pot to boil on. *F.* Hence,

A la HUGUENO'TE [in *Cookery*] a particular Way of dressing Eggs with Gravy.

HU'GUENOTISM, the Profession, or Principles of an *Huguenot.*

HU'GUENOTS [either from *huc nos venimus*, the beginning of the first Protestation of the Apologetical Oration made before Cardinal *Lotharingius*, in the Time of *Francis* II. of *France;* or from *Hugon* a Gate in the City of *Tours*, where they assembled when they first stirred; or *q.d. les Guenots de Husse, i.e.* John Huss's *Imps*] a Nickname given by the *Papists* in *France*, to the Protestants there.

HU'LET [of *hulette, F.* a Shepherd's Crook] a Sirname.

HULFERE, Holly. *Chauc.*

HULK [Hulcke, *Belg.*] a great broad Ship, chiefly in Use for setting in Masts into Ships, and the like.

To HULK [*Hunting Term*] to take out the Garbage of a Hare or Coney.

HULL [Hulle, *Teut.*] the Chaff of Corn, the Cod of Pulse.

HULL [*Sea Term*] the main Body or Bulk of a Ship without her rigging.

To HULL [*Sea Term*] to float, to ride to and fro upon the Water.

To *lie a* HULL [*Sea Term*] is said of a Ship, when she takes all her Sails in, so that nothing but her Masts, Yards, and Rigging are abroad, either in a dead Calm, or a Storm, when she cannot carry them.

To *strike a* HULL [*Sea Term*] is to lie close or obscurely in the Sea in a Storm, or tarry for some Consort, bearing no Sail, with the Helm *lashed a Lee.*

HULL [of Hu*l*en, *L. S.* Heu*l*en, *Teut.* to howl, from the Noise the River makes, when it meets with the Sea] in *Yorkshire.* This Town was famous for it's good Government; and thence arose this Saying, called the Beggars and Vagrants Litany, *From* Hell, Hull, *and* Halifax, *Good Lord deliver us; Hull,* for the severe Chastisement they met with there; *Halifax* for a Law instantly beheading with an Engine those who were taken in the Fact of stealing Cloth, without any further legal Proceedings, being probably more terrible to them than *Hell* itself. . . .

HUMO'RES [with *Physicians*] the several Humors of the Animal Bodies; all that are contained in Canals or Vessels, and which are distinguished from one another by some manifest Qualities, as healthful, vitiated, sanguine, cholerick, and the like.

HU'MOUR [*humeur*, F. *humor*, L.] Moisture, Juice; also Temper of Mind, Fancy, Whim.

HU'MOURIST [*humerista*, Ital.] one full of Humours, Whimsies, or Conceits; a fantastical or whimsical Person.

HU'MOUROUS, belonging to Humours, fantastical, whimsical, wedded to his own Humours or Conceits.

HU'MOURSOME, peevish, hard to please.

To HUNCH [of Husch, *Teut.* a Blow] to give a Thrust with the Elbow. . . .

HUSBAND [probably of Hus, *Sax.* an House, and Band, *Eng. q.d.* the Tie of the House, or Hus, *Sax.* and *Bon*da, a Master of a Family] a Wife's Consort.

HUS'BANDMAN, one employed in Husbandry.

HUS'BANDRY, the Art of tilling and improving Land, also Management of Expences.

HUS'CARLE, a Household Servant. *Sax.*

HUSE, a Fish, of which is made the white Glue called Isinglass.

HU'SEANS [*hoseau*, F.] a sort of Boots or Spatterdashes. . . .

HUSEFASTINE [of hus and fast, *Sax.*] one who holds House and Lands. . . .

HUS'HABLE, House-Rents. *O.R.*

A HUSK [husche, *Dan.*] the Coat of Corn, Grain, Seed, &c.

HUS'SARS, *Hungarian* Horsemen, so called from the Huzza or Shout they give at the first Charge. . . .

HUS'SELING-*People*, Communicants at the Sacrament.

HUS'SEY [*housse*, F. a sordid Garment] a Sirname.

HUS'SY [corrupt. of *Housewife*] a Name given to a Woman by way of Contempt.

HUS'TINGS [of hus, an House, and þing, a Cause or Trial, *Sax.*] a principal, and very ancient Court of Pleas, held before the Lord-Mayor and Court of Aldermen of *London*.

HUS'WIFE [of hus, and wif, *Sax. q.d.* the Wife of the House] a Manager of Household Affairs. . . .

A WIDOW [widwa, *Sax. wittow*, Teut. *Gwedow*, C. Br. *Wiedwe*, L. S. *Vidua*, L.] a Woman whose Husband is dead.

WIDOW *of the King,* she who after the Death of her Husband, who was the King's Tenant, in *Capite,* was forced to recover her Dower by the Writ *de dote assignandi,* and could not marry again without the King's Consent.

WIDOW-*Bench* [in *Sussex*] is that Share which a Widow is allowed of her Husband's Estate besides her Jointure.

WIDOW-*Wail,* a Shrub.

WID'OWER [weduwer, of weduwe, a Widow, and wer, a Man, B. weit-wer, Teut.] a Man who survives his deceased Wife.

WID'OWHOOD [wuduw and hade, *Sax.*] the State and Condition of a Widow or Widower.

To WIELD] [wealdan, and wedan, *Sax.* Walten, Teut.] to handle, to
To WEILD ſ manage, to sway.

WIERDES [of wird, *Sax.*] Fates, Destinies. *Chauc.*

A WIFE [wif of wifian, *Sax.* to marry a Wife, Wift, L. S. Weth, Teut. and *wif,* Dan.] a married Woman, whose Will, in the Judgment of the Law, is subject to that of her Husband, whence it is said, *She has no Will,* but *Fulget radiis mariti, i.e.* Shines with her Husband's Lustre.

30. BENJAMIN MARTIN

Spelling, Pronunciation, and Fuller Definitions; Dictionary Entries

> Benjamin Martin's dictionary, which appeared first in 1749, was notable particularly for its improved definitions, but it also had an ambitious plan for improving generally the quality of dictionaries. The following excerpts are from his *Lingua Brittanica Reformata* [*The British Language Reformed*] (London, 1765).

Orthoepy teaches the true Method of spelling and pronouncing Words; and is therefore a principal Requisite in a Dictionary. And since Speech is much more common and public, than our Writing, it greatly behoves us to be as just and correct as possible, in that Particular. For what can reflect more on a Man's Reputation for Learning, than to find him unable to pronounce or spell many Words in common Use? Yet how often do we hear the grating Sounds of *A'n-ti-podes,* for *An-ti''po-des; Ho''-ri-zon,* for *Ho-ri'-zon; Cy-cloi'd,* for *Cy'-clo-id; Di'-a-stole,* for *Di-a''-sto-le;* and many others in like Manner. But whom shall we blame for such false Pronunciation? Not those, surely, who make the Mistake, but more justly those who occasion them; that is, those who, as Dictionary Writers, are no others than blind Leaders of the Blind. For by what Dictionary extant can a Man regulate his Pronunciation, or correct his Errors in this Respect? Certainly, by no one at all. No Man that has not the Happiness of a learned Education or Conversation, can possibly guard against this Imperfection of Speech. To remedy which, I have

been more than ordinarily anxious, and hope I have in a great measure succeeded by the following Expedient. For, (I.) where I have observed the Number of Syllables in a Word to be any ways doubtful or uncertain to the
Unlearned, I have shewn the Number by a Figure at the End of the Word.
Thus in the Word *Antipodes*[4], the Figure (4) shews there are *four* Syllables; in the Word *Cycloid*[3], the Figure (3) shews there are *three* Syllables;
and so in others throughout the Book. Again, (2dly,) In order that no Mistake, or even Doubt, about the true Emphasis may arise, I have taken Care to
set that Affair right by single and double Accents placed over the proper
Syllables in every Word, where they could be supposed in the least necessary;
some very few Words ex- /*vii*/ cepted, in which I could arrive at no Certainty myself. The single Accent shews the Syllable on which the Emphasis
or Stress of the Voice lies, and the double one shews the same Thing if alone.
But the Use of the double Accent is everywhere to denote that the Letter
which begins the Syllable to which it is prefix'd has a double Sound, one of
which belongs to the preceding Syllable. Thus the Word *A"nimal* is sounded
with a double *n*, as *An-nimal*. So *Mi"croscope* is sounded *Mic-croscope; Cen-
tri"fugal* is sounded *Centrif-fugal;* and the like of others. I imagine this Matter is hereby rendered so very easy, that if a Person gives but the least Attention to it, it must be rarely possible for him to be at any Loss about an accurate Pronunciation. There are a few Words of French Extraction, which
are not to be pronounced as they are written; thus the *c* before *h* is always
sounded like an *s*, as in *Machine, Chagrine, Chaise*, &c. which are sounded
Masheen, Shagreen, Shaise, &c. There are also many other particular Words,
wherein some Letters are not sounded at all; and others in which Letters
have sometimes an *hard*, sometimes a *soft Sound;* but to direct in such Cases
is the Province of a Grammarian; and of which we shall treat more fully in
another Place. /*viii*/

HO"RROUR (of *horror*, lat. of *horreo* to tremble) 1 a trembling for fear,
such an excess of fear as makes a person tremble. 2 fright, dread. 3 awe,
veneration.

HORROUR (in Physic) such a shuddering or quivering as precedes an
ague fit.

HORSE, 1 a beast well known. 2 horsemen, or cavalry. 3 a stand to
put barrels of beer or wine upon. 4 an utensil used by women to air linen
on. 5 a place for school-boys to be whipped upon. 6 an instrument used by
labourers to saw wood upon.

HORSE-*leech*, 1 a sort of insect that lives in the water, which, if it sticks
to the flesh, will not let go till he is full of blood. 2 a farrier, or horse-doctor.

HORSE-*shoe* (in Fortification) is a work of a round, and sometimes oval
figure, raised in the ditch of a marshy place, or in low ground, and bordered
with a parapet. It is made to secure a gate, or to serve as a lodgment for soldiers to prevent surprizes, or to relieve over-tedious defence.

HO'RSEMANSHIP, 1 the art of breaking, disciplining, and managing
horses. 2 the art of riding, or of directing a horse to advantage.

HORSHAM, (W. lon. 22 min. lat. 51°. 10'.) an ancient borough town in Bramberrape in Sussex, reckoned one of the largest towns in the county. It is incorporated with the title of two bailiffs and burgage-holders within and without the borough, who elect the two members to parliament. Here is a very fine church, and a well endowed free-school. It has a market on saturday, and fairs on May the 3d, monday before Whit-sunday, June the 24th, July the 7th, for nine days, and November the 19th. Distant from London 28 computed, and 35 measured miles; and 19 from Lewes.

HO'RTICULTURE, (of *hortus* a garden, and *colo* to till) the art of gardening. . . .

HOU'SEWIFE, a woman prudent in the management of domestic affairs.

HOU'SING, 1 the action of putting any one into a house. 2 a horse-cloth worn beneath the saddle.

HOW, See Hoe.

HOW? in what manner? . . .

HU'RDLE, a frame of hazle rods, wattled together to make sheep-folds, &c.

HU'RDLES, or CLAYS (in Fortification) are made of thick and small twigs of willow, or osiers, being five or six foot high, and from three to four foot broad. They are interwoven very close together, and usually laden with earth, that they may serve to render batteries firm, or to consolidate passages over muddy ditches, or to cover traverses and lodgments for the defence of the workmen against the artificial fires or stones that may be cast upon them.

To HURL, to fling, or cast.

HU'RLIBAT, or WHO'RLEBAT, a kind of weapon with plummtes [sic] of lead, used in games for exercise, by the ancient Romans.

HU'RLY-*burly*, tumult, uproar, or confusion.

HU'RRICANE (of *hurracan*, sp.) a most violent storm arising from a contrariety and opposition of several winds.

HU'RRY, 1 confusion, or disorder. 2 great haste, or precipitation.

HURST, a little wood, or thicket of trees.

HURT, 1 prejudice, loss, damage. 2 wound, or damage. 3 mischief, or crime.

HU'SBAND, a married man.

To HUSBAND, 1 to manage in the spending. 2 to till, or cultivate.

HU'SBANDRY, 1 managing in one's expences. 2 agriculture, or the art of tilling and improving land.

HUSH, an interjection of silence.

To HUSH, 1 to keep silence. 2 to quiet, or make silent. 3 to quash, or overthrow. 4 to calm, or make easy.

HUSK, 1 the outside coats of most sorts of grain. 2 (in Botany) the part which a flower grows out of.

HUSSA'RS, Hungarian horsemen, so called from their giving a huzza at the first onset.

HUSSY, 1 a contemptuous name for a woman. 2 a woman's case for needles, thread, &c.

HUSTINGS, (of hus, sax. a house, and þinᵹ a tryal) a court of common-pleas, held before the lord mayor and aldermen of London, in Guild-hall, and is the highest court held in all the city, and is very ancient; it being in the laws of Edward the Confessor.

HU'SWIFE. See Housewife.

31. JOHN WESLEY

"Hard" Words Again; Dictionary Entries

> Dictionaries of hard words continued to appear; the following is from the anonymous "*The Complete English Dictionary, Explaining most of the HARD WORDS, which are found in the BEST ENGLISH WRITERS,* by a lover of *Good English* and *Common Sense.* N.B. The Author assures you, he thinks this is the best *English* DICTIONARY in the World" (Bristol, 1764). The author was presumably John Wesley, leader of the Methodist movement, who may have had the needs of his poor priests in mind when he compiled it.

As incredible as it may appear, I must avow, that this dictionary is not published to get money, but to assist persons of common sense and no learning, to understand the best *English* authors: and that, with as little expence of either time or money, as the nature of the thing would allow.

To this end it contains, not a heap of *Greek* and *Latin* words, just tagged with *English* terminations: (for no good *English* writer, none but vain or senseless pedants, give these any place in their writings:) not a scroll of barbarous *law expressions*, which are neither *Greek, Latin,* nor good *English:* not a croud of *technical* terms, the meaning whereof is to be sought in books expresly wrote on the subjects to which they belong: not such *English* words as *and, of, but;* which stand so gravely in Mr. *Baily's, Pardon's,* and *Martin's* dictionaries: but "most of those hard words which are found in the best *English* writers." I say, *most;* for I purposely omit not only all which are not *hard,* and which are not found in the best writers: not only all law-words and most technical terms, but likewise all, the meaning of which may be easily gathered from those of the same derivation. And this I have done, in order to make this dictionary both as short and as cheap as possible. /A2/

The COMMENCE'MENT, the time when they take their degrees at CAMBRIDGE. . . .

A CU'LVERIN, a sort of cannon.

CU'POLA, the round, arch'd top of a building.

The CU'RFEW, the eight o'clock bell.

CU'RRENT, that goes or passes; common.

A CU'RRENT, a stream.
A CU'RRIER, a leather-dresser.
A CU'RSITOR, a chancery-clerk.
CU'RSORY, slight, hasty. . . .
The CY'CLOPS, a sort of giant.
A CY'GNET, a young swan.

32. SAMUEL JOHNSON

Perplexity Disentangled, Confusion Regulated; Dictionary Entries

In his dictionary, Johnson, the most famous of English lexicographers, defines *lexicographer* as "a writer of dictionaries, a harmless drudge that busies himself in tracing the original and detailing the significance of words." Johnson was obviously more than a harmless drudge, and his dictionary was by far the most significant that had appeared, in spite of some whimsical definitions and some erroneous etymologies. The dictionary was first published in 1755; the following selections are from the preface and vocabulary of the third edition of the *Dictionary of the English Language* (London, 1765).

It is the fate of those who toil at the lower employments of life, to be rather driven by the fear of evil, than attracted by the prospect of good; to be exposed to censure, without hope of praise; to be disgraced by miscarriage, or punished for neglect, where success would have been without applause, and diligence without reward.

Among these unhappy mortals is the writer of dictionaries; whom mankind have considered, not as the pupil, but the slave of science, the pioneer of literature, doomed only to remove rubbish and clear obstructions from the paths through which Learning and Genius press forward to conquest and glory, without bestowing a smile on the humble drudge that facilitates their progress. Every other author may aspire to praise; the lexicographer can only hope to escape reproach, and even this negative recompense has been yet granted to very few.

I have, notwithstanding this discouragement, attempted a Dictionary of the *English* language, which, while it was employed in the cultivation of every species of literature, has itself been hitherto neglected; suffered to spread, under the direction of chance, into wild exuberance; resigned to the tyranny of time and fashion; and exposed to the corruptions of ignorance, and caprices of innovation.

When I took the first survey of my undertaking, I found our speech copious without order, and energetick without rules: wherever I turned my view, there was perplexity to be disentangled, and confusion to be regulated; choice was to be made out of boundless variety, without any established principle of selection; adulterations were to be detected, without a settled test of purity; and modes of expression to be rejected or received, without the suffrages of any writers of classical reputation or acknowledged authority.

Having therefore no assistance but from general grammar, I applied myself to the perusal of our writers; and noting whatever might be of use to ascertain or illustrate any word or phrase, accumulated in time the materials of a dictionary, which, by degrees, I reduced to method, establishing to myself, in the progress of the word, such rules as experience and analogy suggested to me; experience, which practice and observation were continually increasing; and analogy, which, though in some words obscure, was evident in others. . . .

From . . . uncertain pronunciation arise in a great part the various dialects of the same country, which will always be observed to grow fewer, and less different, as books are multiplied; and from this arbitrary representation of sounds by letters, proceeds that diversity of spelling observable in the *Saxon* remains, and I suppose in the first books of every nation, which perplexes or destroys analogy, and produces anomalous formations, that, being once incorporated, can never be afterwards dismissed or reformed.

Of this kind are the derivatives *length* from *long, strength* from *strong, darling* from *dear, breadth* from *broad,* from *dry, drought,* and from *high, height,* which *Milton,* in zeal for analogy, writes *highth; Quid te exempta juvat spinis de pluribus una?* to change all would be too much, and to change one is nothing. /a1/

This uncertainty is most frequent in the vowels, which are so capriciously pronounced, and so differently modified, by accident or affectation, not only in every province, but in every mouth, that to them, as is well known to etymologists, little regard is to be shown in the deduction of one language from another.

Such defects are not errours in orthography, but spots of barbarity impressed so deep in the *English* language, that criticism can never wash them away: these, therefore, must be permitted to remain untouched; but many words have likewise been altered by accident, or depraved by ignorance, as the pronunciation of the vulgar has been weakly followed; and some still continue to be variously written, as authors differ in their care or skill: of these it was proper to inquire the true orthography, which I have always considered as depending on their derivation, and have therefore referred them to their original languages; thus I write *enchant, enchantment, enchanter,* after the *French,* and *incantation* after the *Latin;* thus *entire* is chosen rather than *intire,* because it passed to us not from the *Latin integer,* but from the *French entier.* . . .

In this part of the work, where caprice has long wantoned without control, and vanity sought praise by petty reformation, I have endeavoured to proceed with a scholar's reverence for antiquity, and a grammarian's regard to the genius of our tongue. I have attempted few alterations, and among those few, perhaps the greater part is from the modern to the ancient practice; and I hope I may be allowed to recommend to those, whose thoughts have been perhaps employed too anxiously on verbal singularities, not to disturb, upon narrow views, or for minute propriety, the orthography of their fathers. It has been asserted, that for the law to be *known,* is of more importance than to be *right.* Change, says *Hooker,* is not made without inconvenience, even from worse to better. There is in constancy and stability a general and lasting advantage, which will always overbalance the slow improvements of gradual correction. Much less ought our written language to comply with the corruptions of oral utterance, or copy that which every variation of time or place makes different from itself, and imitate those changes, which will again be changed, while imitation is employed in observing them.

This recommendation of steadiness and uniformity does not proceed from an opinion, that particular combinations of letters have much influence on human happiness; or that truth may not be successfully taught by modes of spelling fanciful and erroneous: I am not yet so lost in lexicography, as to forget that *words are the daughters of earth, and that things are the sons of heaven.* Language is only the instrument of science, and words are but the signs of ideas: I wish, however, that the instrument might be less apt to decay, and that signs might be permanent, like the things which they denote.

In settling the orthography, I have not wholly neglected the pronunciation, which I have directed, by printing an accent upon the acute or elevated syllable. It will sometimes be found, that the accent is placed by the author quoted, on a different syllable from that marked in the alphabetical series; it is then to be understood, that custom has varied, or that the author has, in my opinion, pronounced wrong. Short directions are sometimes given where the sound of letters is irregular; and if they are sometimes omitted, defect in such minute observations will be more easily excused, than superfluity.

In the investigation both of the orthography and signification of words, their ETYMOLOGY was necessarily to be considered, and they were therefore to be divided into primitives and derivatives. A primitive word, is that which can be traced no further to any *English* root; thus *circumspect, circum-/al^v/ vent, circumstance, delude, concave,* and *complicate,* though compounds in the Latin, are to us primitives. Derivatives, are all those that can be referred to any word in *English* of greater simplicity.

The derivatives I have referred to their primitives, with an accuracy sometimes needless; for who does not see that *remoteness* comes from *remote, lovely* from *love, concavity* from *concave,* and *demonstrative* from *demonstrate?* but this grammatical exuberance the scheme of my work did not allow me to repress. It is of great importance, in examining the general fabric of a language, to trace one word from another, by noting the usual modes of derivation and inflection; and uniformity must be preserved in systematical words, though sometimes at the expense of particular propriety.

Among other derivatives I have been careful to insert and elucidate the anomalous plurals of nouns and preterites of verbs, which in the *Teutonick* dialects are very frequent, and, though familiar to those who have always used them, interrupt and embarrass the learners of our language.

The two languages from which our primitives have been derived are the *Roman* and *Teutonick:* under the *Roman* I comprehend the *French* and provincial tongues; and under the *Teutonick* range the *Saxon, German,* and all their kindred dialects. Most of our polysyllables are *Roman,* and our words of one syllable are very often *Teutonick.*

In assigning the *Roman* original, it has perhaps sometimes happened that I have mentioned only the *Latin,* when the word was borrowed from the *French;* and considering myself as employed only in the illustration of my own language, I have not been very careful to observe whether the *Latin* word be pure or barbarous, or the *French* elegant or obsolete. . . .

Our knowledge of the northern literature is so scanty, that of words undoubtedly *Teutonick,* the original is not always to be found in any ancient language; and I have therefore inserted *Dutch* or *German* substitutes, which I consider not as radical, but parallel, not as the parents, but sisters of the *English.* . . . */b1/*

My purpose was to admit no testimony of living authors, that I might not be misled by partiality, and that none of my contemporaries might have reason to complain; nor have I departed from this resolution, but when some performance of uncommon excellence excited my veneration, when my memory supplied me, from late books, with an example that was wanting, or when my heart, in the tenderness of friendship, solicited admission for a favourite name. */b2v/*

So far have I been from any care to grace my pages with modern decorations, that I have studiously endeavoured to collect examples and authorities from the writers before the restoration, whose works I regard as *the wells of English undefiled,* as the pure sources of genuine diction. Our language, for almost a century, has, by the concurrence of many causes, been gradually departing from its original *Teutonick* character, and deviating towards a *Gallick* structure and phraseology, from which it ought to be our endeavour to recall it, by making our ancient volumes the ground-work of style, admitting among the additions of later times, only such as may supply real deficiencies, such as are readily adopted by the genius of our tongue, and incorporate easily with our native idioms.

But as every language has a time of rudeness antecedent to perfection, as well as of false refinement and declension, I have been cautious lest my zeal for antiquity might drive me into times too remote, and crowd my book with words now no longer understood. I have fixed *Sidney's* word for the boundary, beyond which I make few excursions. From the authors which rose in the time of *Elizabeth,* a speech might be formed adequate to all the purposes of use and elegance. If the language of theology were extracted from *Hooker* and the translation of the Bible; the terms of natural knowledge from *Bacon;* the phrases of policy, war, and navigation from *Raleigh;* the dialect of poetry and fiction from *Spenser* and *Sidney;* and the diction of common life from *Shakespeare,* few ideas would be lost to mankind, for want of *English* words, in which they might be expressed.

It is not sufficient that a word is found, unless it be so combined as that its meaning is apparently determined by the tract and tenour of the sentence; such passages I have therefore chosen, and when it happened that any author gave a definition of a term, or such an explanation as is equivalent to a definition, I have placed his authority as a supplement to my own, without regard to the chronological order, that is otherwise observed. . . . /c1/

That many terms of art and manufacture are omitted, must be frankly acknowledged; but for this defect I may boldly allege that it was unavoidable: I could not visit caverns to learn the miner's language, nor take a voyage to perfect my skill in the dialect of navigation, nor visit the warehouses of merchants, and shops of artificers, to gain the names of wares, tools and operations, of which no mention is found in books; what favourable accident, or easy inquiry brought within my reach, has not been neglected; but it had been a hopeless labour to glean up words, by courting living information, and contesting with the sullenness of one, and the roughness of another. . . .

Nor are all words which are not found in the vocabulary to be lamented as omissions. Of the laborious and mercantile part of the people, the diction is in a great measure casual and mutable; many of their terms are formed from some temporary or local convenience, and though current at certain times and places, are in others utterly unknown. This fugitive cant, which is always in a state of increase or decay, cannot be regarded as any part of the durable materials of a language, and therefore must be suffered to perish with other things unworthy of preservation. . . . /c1ᵛ/

Of the event of this work, for which, having laboured it with so much application, I cannot but have some degree of parental fondness, it is natural to form conjectures. Those who have been persuaded to think well of my design, will require that it should fix our language, and put a stop to those alterations which time and chance have hitherto been suffered to make in it without opposition. With this consequence I will confess that I flattered myself for a while; but now begin to fear that I have indulged expectation which neither reason nor experience can justify. When we see men grow old and die at a certain time one after another, from century to century, we laugh at the elixir that promises to prolong life to a thousand years; and with equal justice may the lexicographer be derided, who being able to produce no example of a nation that has preserved their words and phrases from mutability, shall imagine that his dictionary can embalm his language, and secure it from corruption and decay, that it is in his power to change sublunary nature, and clear the world at once from folly, vanity and affectation.

With this hope, however, academies have been instituted, to guard the avenues of their language, to retain fugitives, and repulse intruders; but their vigilance and activity have hitherto been vain; sounds are too volatile and subtle for legal restraints; to enchain syllables, and to lash the wind, are equally the undertakings of pride, unwilling to measure its desires by its strength. The *French* language has visibly changed under the inspection of the academy; the style of *Amelot's* translation of father *Paul* is observed by *Le Courayer* to be *un peu passé;* and no *Italian* will maintain, that the diction of any modern writer is not perceptibly different from that of *Boccace, Machiavel,* or *Caro.*

Total and sudden transformation of a language seldom happen; conquests and migrations are now very rare: but there are other causes of change, which, though slow in their operation, and invisible in their progress, are perhaps as much superiour to human resistance, as the revolutions of the sky, or intumescence of the tide. Commerce, however necessary, however lucrative, as it depraves the manners, corrupts the language; they that have frequent intercourse with strangers, to whom they endeavour to accommodate themselves, must in time learn a mingled dialect, like the jargon which serves the traffickers on the *Mediterranean* and *Indian* coasts. This will not always be confined to the exchange, the warehouse, or the port, but will be communicated by degrees to other ranks of the people, and be at last incorporated with the current speech.

There are likewise internal causes equally forcible. The language most likely to continue long without alteration, would be that of a nation raised a little, and but a little, above barbarity, secluded from strangers, and totally employed in procuring the conveniencies of life; either without books, or, like some of the *Mahometan* countries, with very few: men thus busied and unlearned, having only such words as common use requires, would perhaps long continue to express the same notions by the same signs. But no such constancy can be expected in a people polished by arts, and classed by subordination, where one part of the community is sustained and accommodated by the labour of the other. Those who have much leisure to think, will always be enlarging the stock of ideas; and every increase of knowledge, whether real or fancied, will produce new words, or combinations of words. When the mind is unchained from necessity, it will range after convenience; when it is left at large in the fields of speculation, it will shift opinions; as any custom is disused, the words that expressed it must perish with it; as any opinion grows popular, it will innovate speech in the same proportion as it alters practice.

As by the cultivation of various sciences a language is amplified, it will be more furnished with words deflected from their original sense; the geometrician will talk of a courtier's zenith, or the eccentrick virtue of a wild hero, and the physician of sanguine expectations and phlegmatick delays. Copiousness of speech will give opportunities to capricious choice, by which some words will be preferred, and others degraded; vicissitudes of fashion will enforce the use of new, or extend the signification of known terms. The tropes of poetry will make hourly encroachments, and the metaphorical will become the current sense; pronunciation will be varied by levity or ignorance, and the pen must at length comply with the tongue; illiterate writers will, at one time or other, by public infatuation, rise into renown, who, not knowing the original import of words, will use them with colloquial licentiousness, confound distinction, and forget propriety. As politeness increases, some expressions will be considered as too gross and vulgar for the delicate, others as too formal and ceremonious for the gay and airy; new phrases are therefore adopted, which must, for the same reasons, be in time dismissed. *Swift,* in his petty treatise on the *English* language, allows that new words must sometimes be introduced, but proposes that none should be suffered to become obsolete. But what makes a word obsolete, more than general agreement to forbear it? and how shall it be continued, when it conveys an offensive idea, or recalled again into the mouths of mankind, when it has once by disuse become unfamiliar, and by unfamiliarity unpleasing? /c2/

There is another cause of alteration more prevalent than any other, which yet in the present state of the world cannot be obviated. A mixture of two languages will produce a third distinct from both, and they will always be mixed, where the chief part of education, and the most conspicuous accomplishment, is skill in ancient or in foreign tongues. He that has long cultivated another language, will find its words and combinations crowd upon his memory; and haste and negligence, refinement and affectation, will obtrude borrowed terms and exotick expressions.

The great pest of speech is frequency of translation. No book was ever turned from one language into another, without imparting something of its native idiom; this is the most mischievous and comprehensive innovation; single words may enter by thousands, and the fabrick of the tongue continue the same; but new phraseology changes much at once; it alters not the single stones of the building, but the order of the columns. If an academy should be established for the cultivation of our style, which I, who can never wish to see dependance multiplied, hope the spirit of *English* liberty will hinder or destroy, let them, instead of compiling grammars and dictionaries, endeavour, with all their influence, to stop the license of translators, whose idleness and ignorance, if it be suffered to proceed, will reduce us to babble a dialect of *France.*

If the changes that we fear be thus irresistible, what remains but to acquiesce with silence, as in the other insurmountable distresses of humanity? It remains that we retard what we cannot repel, that we palliate what we cannot cure. Life may be lengthened by care, though death cannot be ultimately defeated: tongues, like governments, have a natural tendency to degeneration; we have long preserved our constitution, let us make some struggles for our language. . . . /c2ᵛ/

CURMU'DGEON. *n. s.* [It is a vitious manner of pronouncing *coeur mechant,* Fr. an unknown correspondent.] An avaritious churlish fellow; a miser; a niggard; a churl; a griper. . . .

HORSE. *n. s.* [hors, Saxon.]

1. A neighing quadruped, used in war, and draught and carriage.

> Duncan's *horses,* the minions of the race,
> Turn'd wild in nature, broke their stalls. *Shakespeare.*

> A *horse!* a *horse!* my kingdom for a *horse! Shakespeare.*

> I would sell my *horse,* and buy ten more
> Better than he. *Shakespeare.*

> Thy face, bright centaur, Autumn's heats retain,
> The softer season suiting to the man;
> Whilst Winter's shivering goat afflicts the *horse*
> With frost, and makes him an uneasy course. *Creech.*

> We call a little horse such a one as comes not up to the size of that idea which we have in our minds to belong ordinarily to *horses. Locke.*

> I took *horse* to the lake of Constance, which is formed by the entry of the Rhine. *Addison.*

2. It is used in the plural sense, but with a singular termination, for horses, horsemen, or cavalry.

> I did hear
> The galloping of *horse:* who was't came by? *Shakespeare.*

> The armies were appointed, consisting of twenty-five thousand *horse* and foot, for the repulsing of the enemy at their landing. *Bacon.*

> If they had known that all the king's *horse* were quartered behind them, their foot might very well have marched away with their *horse. Clarendon.*

> Th' Arcadian *horse*
> With ill success engage the Latin force. *Dryden.*

3. Something on which any thing is supported: as, a *horse* to dry linen on.
4. A wooden machine which soldiers ride by way of punishment. It is sometimes called a timber-mare.
5. Joined to another substantive, it signifies something large or coarse; as, a *horseface,* a face of which the features are large and indelicate.

To HORSE. *v. a.* [from the noun.]

1. To mount upon a horse.

> He came out with all his clowns, *horsed* upon such cartjades, and so furnished, as in good faith I thought with myself, if that were thrift, I wisht none of my friends or subjects ever to thrive. *Sidney.*

> After a great fight there came to the camp of Gonsalvo, the great captain, a gentleman proudly *horsed* and armed: Diego de Mendoza asked the great captain, Who's this? Who answered, It is St. Ermin, who never appears but after the storm. *Bacon.*

2. To carry one on the back.
3. To ride any thing.

> Stalls, bulks, windows
> Are smother'd, leads fill'd, and ridges *hors'd*
> With variable complexions; all agreeing
> In earnestness to see him. *Shakespeare.*

4. To cover a mare.

If you let him out to *horse* more mares than your own, you must feed him well. *Mortimer.*

HO′RSEBACK. *n. s.* [*horse* and *back.*] The feat of the rider; the state of being on a horse.

> I've seen the French,
> And they can well on *horseback.* *Shakespeare.*
> I saw them salute on *horseback,*
> Beheld them when they lighted. *Shakespeare.*

He fought but one remarkable battle wherein there were any elephants, and that was with Porus, king of India; in which notwithstanding he was on *horseback.* *Brown's Vulg. Err.*

> When mannish Mevia, that two-handed whore,
> Astride on *horseback* hunts the Tuscan boar. *Dryden.*

If your ramble was on *horseback,* I am glad of it, on account of your health.

HORSEBEA′N. *n. s.* [*horse* and *bean.*] A small bean usually given to horses. Only the small *horsebean* is propagated by the plough. *Mort.*

HO′RSEBLOCK. *n. s.* [*horse* and *block.*] A block on which they climb to a horse.

HORSEBOA′T. *n. s.* [*horse* and *boat.*] A boat used in ferrying horses.

HORSEBO′Y. *n. s.* [*horse* and *boy.*] A boy employed in dressing horses; a stableboy.
Some *horseboys,* being awake, discovered them by the fire in their matches. *Knolles.*

HO′RSEBREAKER. *n. s.* [*horse* and *break.*] One whose employment it is to tame horses to the saddle.
Under Sagittarius are born chariot-racers, *horsebreakers,* and tamers of wild beasts. *Creech.*

HORSECHE′SNUT. *n. s.* [*horse* and *chesnut.*] A plant.
It hath digitated or fingered leaves: the flowers, which consist of five leaves, are of an anomalous figure, opening with two lips; there are male and female upon the same spike: the female flowers are succeeded by nuts, which grow in green prickly husks. Their whole year's shoot is commonly performed in three weeks time, after which it does no more than increase in bulk, and become more firm; and all the latter part of

the Summer is occupied in forming and strengthening the buds for the next year's shoots. *Miller.*

I may bring in the *horsechesnut*, which grows into a goodly standard. *Mortimer.*

HO'RSECOURSER. *n. s.* [*horse* and *courser.* *Junius* derives it from *horse* and *cose*, an old Scotch word, which signifies to change; and it should therefore, he thinks, be writ *horsecoser.* The word now used in Scotland is *horsecouper*, to denote a jockey, seller, or rather changer of horses. It may well be derived from *course*, as he that sells horses may be supposed to *course* or exercise them.]

1. One that runs horses, or keeps horses for the race.
2. A dealer in horses.

A servant to a *horsecourser* was thrown off his horse. *Wiseman.*

A Florentine bought a horse for so many crowns, upon condition to pay half down: the *horsecourser* comes to him next morning for the remainder. *L'Estrange.*

HO'RSECRAB. *n. s.* A kind of fish. *Ainsworth.*

HORSECU'CUMBER. *n. s.* [*horse* and *cucumber.*] A plant.

The *horsecucumber* is the large green cucumber, and the best for the table, green out of the garden. *Mortimer.*

HO'RSEDUNG. *n. s.* [*horse* and *dung.*] The excrements of horses.

Put it into an ox's horn, and covered close, let it rot in hot *horsedung.* *Peachum.*

HORSEE'MMET. *n. s.* [*horse* and *emmet.*] Ant of a large kind.

HO'RSEFLESH. *n. s.* [*horse* and *flesh.*] The flesh of horses.

The Chinese eat *horseflesh* at this day, and some gluttons have coltsflesh baked. *Bacon.*

An old hungry lion would fain have been dealing with a good piece of *horseflesh* that he had in his eye; but the nag he thought would be too fleet for him. *L'Estrange.*

HO'RSEFLY. *n. s.* [*horse* and *fly.*] A fly that stings horses, and sucks their blood.

HO'RSEFOOT. *n. s.* An herb. The same with coltsfoot. *Ains.*

HO'RSEHAIR. *n. s.* [*horse* and *hair.*] The hair of horses.

His glitt'ring helm, which terribly was grac'd
With waving *horsehair.* *Dryden.*

HO'RSEHEEL. *n. s.* An herb. *Ainsworth.*

HO'RSELAUGH. *n. s.* [*horse* and *laugh.*] A loud violent rude laugh.

A *horselaugh*, if you please, at honesty;
A joke on Jekyl. *Pope.*

HO'RSELEECH. *n. s.* [*horse* and *leech.*]

1. A great leech that bites horses.

> The *horseleech* hath two daughters, crying give, give. *Prov.*
>
> > Let us to France; like *horseleeches*, my boys,
> > The very blood to suck. *Shakespeare.*

2. A farrier. *Ainsworth.*

HO'RSELITTER. *n. s.* [*horse* and *litter.*] A carriage hung upon poles between two horses, in which the person carried lyes along.

> He that before thought he might command the waves of the sea, was now cast on the ground, and carried in a *horselitter.* 2. *Maccabees.*

HO'RSEMAN. *n. s.* [*horse* and *man.*]

1. One skilled in riding.

> A skilful *horseman*, and a huntsman bred. *Dryden.*

2. One that serves in wars on horseback.

> Encounters between *horseman* on the one side, and foot on the other, are seldom with extremity of danger; because as *horsemen* can hardly break a battle on foot, so men on foot cannot possibly chase *horsemen.* *Hayward.*

> In the early times of the Roman commonwealth, a *horseman* received yearly *tria milla aeris*, and a foot-soldier one mille; that is, more than sixpence a day to a *horseman*, and two-pence a day to a foot-soldier. *Arbuthnot.*

3. A rider; a man on horseback.

> > With descending show'rs of brimstone fir'd,
> > The wild Barbarian in the storm expir'd;
> > Wrapt in devouring flames the *horseman* rag'd,
> > And spurr'd the steed in equal flames engag'd. *Addison.*

> > > A *horseman*'s coat shall hide
> > > Thy taper shape, and comeliness of side. *Prior.*

HO'RSEMANSHIP. *n. s.* [from *horseman.*] The art of riding; the art of managing a horse.

> > He vaulted with such ease into his seat,
> > As if an angel dropt down from the clouds,
> > To turn and wind a fiery Pegasus,
> > And witch the world with noble *horsemanship.* *Shakespeare.*

> They please themselves in terms of hunting or *horsemanship.* *Wotton.*

> His majesty, to shew his *horsemanship*, slaughtered two or three of his subjects. *Addison.*

> > Peers grew proud, in *horsemanship* t' excel;
> > Newmarket's glory rose, as Britain's fell. *Pope.*

HO'RSEMARTEN. *n. s.* A kind of large bee. *Ainsworth.*

HO'RSEMATCH. *n. s.* A bird. *Ainsworth.*

HO'RSEMEAT. *n. s.* [*horse* and *meat.*] Provender.

Though green peas and beans be eaten sooner, yet the dry one [sic] that are used for *horsemeat* are ripe last. *Bacon.*

HO'RSEMINT. *n. s.* A large coarse mint.

HO'RSEMUSCLE. *n. s.* A large muscle.

The great *horsemuscle,* with the fine shell, that breedeth in ponds, not only gapes and shuts as the oysters do, but removes from one place to another. *Bacon.*

HO'RSEPLAY. *n. s.* [*horse* and *play.*] Coarse, rough, rugged play.

He is too much given to *horseplay* in his raillery, and comes to battle like a dictator from the plough. *Dryden.*

HO'RSEPOND. *n. s.* [*horse* and *pond.*] A pond for horses.

HO'RSERACE. *n. s.* [*horse* and *race.*] A match of horses in running.

In *horseraces* men are curious to foresee that there be not the least weight upon the one horse more than upon the other. *Bacon.*

Trajan in the fifth year of his tribuneship, entertained the people with a *horserace. Addison.*

HO'RSERADISH. *n. s.* [*horse* and *radish.*] A root acrid and biting: a species of scurvygrass.

Horseradish is increased by sprouts spreading from the old roots left in the ground, that are cut or broken off. *Mortimer.*

Stomachicks are the cress acrids, as *horseradish* and scurvygrass, infused in wine. *Floyer.*

HO'RSESHOE. *n. s.* [*horse* and *shoe.*]
1. A plate of iron nailed to the feet of horses.
    I was thrown into the Thames, and cool'd glowing hot in that surge, like a *horseshoe. Shakespeare.*
2. An herb. *Ainsworth.*

HORSESTEA'LER. *n. s.* [*horse* and *steal.*] A thief who takes away horses.

He is not a pickpurse, nor a *horsestealer;* but for his verity in love, I do think him as concave as a covered goblet, or a worm-eaten nut. *Shakespeare.*

HO'RSETAIL. *n. s.* A plant.

HO'RSETONGUE. *n. s.* An herb. *Ainsworth.*

HO'RSEWAY. *n. s.* [*horse* and *way.*] A broad way by which horses may travel.
    Know'st thou the way to Dover?
    —Both stile and gate, *horseway* and footpath. *Shakespeare.* . . .

HO'USEWIFE. *n. s.* [*house* and *wife.* This is now frequently written *huswife,* or *hussy.*]
1. The mistress of a family.
    You will think it unfit for a good *housewife* to stir in or to busy herself about her housewifery. *Spenser.*

I have room enough, but the kind and hearty *housewife* is dead. *Pope to Swift.*

2. A female oeconomist.

Fitting is a mantle for a bad man, and surely for a bad *housewife* it is no less convenient; for some of them, that be wandering women, it is half a wardrobe. *Spenser.*

Let us sit and mock the good *housewife*, fortune, from her wheel, that her gifts may henceforth be disposed equally. *Shakes.*

> Farmers in degree,
> He a good husband, a good *housewife* she. *Dryden.*

> Early *housewives* leave the bed,
> When living embers on the hearth are spread. *Dryden.*

The fairest among the daughters of Britain shew themselves good stateswomen as well as good housewives. *Addison.*

3. One skilled in female business.

He was bred up under the tuition of a tender mother, 'till she made him as good an *housewife* as herself: he could preserve apricocks, and make jellies. *Addison.* . . .

HU'SBAND. *n. s.* [*hossband,* master, Danish; from *house* and *bonda,* Runick, a master.]

1. The correlative to wife; a man married to a woman.

> Thy *husband* is thy lord, thy life, thy keeper,
> Thy head, thy sovereign. *Shakespeare.*

Why woman, your *husband* is in his old lunes again; he so takes on yonder with my *husband*, and so rails against all married mankind. *Shakespeare.*

> This careful *husband* had been long away,
> Whom his chaste wife and little children mourn. *Dryden.*

The contract and ceremony of marriage is the occasion of the denomination or relation of *husband*. *Locke.*

2. The male of animals.

> Ev'n though a snowy ram thou shalt behold,
> Prefer him not in haste, for *husband* to thy fold. *Dryden.*

3. An oeconomist; a man that knows and practises the method of frugality and profit. Its signification is always modified by some epithet implying bad or good.

Edward I. shewed himself a right good *husband;* owner of a lordship ill husbanded. *Davies.*

I was considering the shortness of life, and what ill *husbands* we are of so tender a fortune. *Collier.*

4. A tiller of the ground; a farmer.

Husband's work is laborious and hard. *Spenser.*

I heard a great *husband* say, that it was a common error to think that chalk helpeth arable ground. *Bacon.*

In those fields
The painful *husband* plowing up his ground,
Shall find, all fret with rust, both pikes and shields. *Hakew.*
If continu'd rain
The lab'ring *husband* in his house restrain,
Let him forecast his work. *Dryden.*

To HU'SBAND. *v. a.* [from the noun.]
1. To supply with an husband.

Think you I am no stronger than my sex,
Being so father'd and so *husbanded? Shakespeare.*

If you shall prove
This ring was ever her's, you shall as easy
Prove that I *husbanded* her bed in Florence,
Where yet she never was. *Shakespeare.*

In my right,
By me invested, he compeers the best.
— That were the most, if he should *husband* you. *Shakesp.*

2. To manage with frugality.

It will be pastime passing excellent,
If it be *husbanded* with modesty. *Shakespeare.*

The French, wisely *husbanding* the possession of a victory, kept themselves within their trenches. *Bacon.*

If thou be master-gunner, spend not all
That thou can'st speak at once; but *husband* it,
And give men turns of speech. *Herbert.*

3. To till; to cultivate the ground with proper management.

A farmer cannot *husband* his ground, if he sits at a great rent.
Bacon. . . .

HU'SWIFE. *n. s.* [corrupted from *housewife.*]
1. A bad manager; a sorry woman. It is common to use *housewife* in a good,
and *huswife* or *hussy* in a bad sense.

Bianca,
A *huswife,* that, by selling her desires,
Buys herself bread and cloth. *Shakespeare.*

2. An œconomist; a thrifty woman.

Why should you want?
The bounteous *housewife,* nature, on each bush,
Lays her fulness before you. *Shakespeare.*

To HU'SWIFE. *v. a.* [from the noun.] To manage with œconomy and
frugality.

But *huswifing* the little heav'n had lent,
She duly paid a groat for quarter-rent;
And pinch'd her belly, with her daughters two,
To bring the year about with much ado. *Dryden.*

WI'DOW. *n. s.* [*widwa*, Sax. *weduwe*, Dutch *weddw*, Welsh *vidua*, Latin.] A woman whose husband is dead.

> To take the *widow*,
> Exasperates, makes mad her sister Gonerill. *Shakespeare.*
>   Catharine no more
> Shall be call'd queen; but princess dowager,
> And *widow* to prince Arthur. *Shakespeare.*
>   Our fatherless distress was left unmoan'd,
> Your *widow*-dolours likewise be unwept. *Shakespeare.*
>   And will she yet debase her eyes on me,
> That cropt the golden prime of this sweet prince,
> And made her *widow* to a woeful bed. *Shakespeare.*
>   The barren they more miserable make,
> And from the *widow* all her comfort take. *Sandys.*
>   He warns the *widow*, and her houshold gods
> To seek a refuge in remote abodes. *Dryden.*

Who has the paternal power whilst the *widow*-queen is with child. *Locke.* . . .

WIFE. *n. s.* Plural *wives.* [*wif*, Saxon; *wiff*, Dutch.]

1. A woman that has a husband.

>   Your claim, fair sister,
> I bar it in the interest of my *wife*. *Shakespeare.*
>   There's no bottom, none
> In my voluptuousness; your *wives*, your daughters,
> Your matrons and your maids could not fill up
> The cistern of my lust. *Shakespeare.*

Why saidst thou, she is my sister? so I might have taken her to me to *wife*.

>   The *wife*, where danger or dishonour lurks,
> Safest and seemliest by her husband stays. *Milton.*

The *wife* her husband murders, he the wife. *Dryden.*

Fond of his friend, and civil to his *wife*. *Pope.*

2. It is used for a woman of low employment.

Strawberry *wives* lay two or three great strawberries at the mouth of the pot, and all the rest are little ones. *Bacon.*

33. FREDERICK BARLOW

Dictionary Entries

The appearance of Johnson's monumental work put no stop to dictionaries presented to the public as "complete." The following entries are from Frederick Barlow, *The Complete English Dictionary* (London, 1772).

CU'RFEW, S. [*couvre feu,* Fr. cover the fire] an evening bell, on the sound of which every man was obliged to extinguish his fire and candle, in the time of William the Conqueror. Figuratively, any bell which tolls constantly in the night time. A cover for a fire.

CURIO'SITY, S. a propensity to enquire after new objects, and to delight in viewing them. Figuratively, an act of curiosity, a nice experiment. A rarity.

CU'RIOUS, Adj. [*curiosus,* Lat.] disposed to enquire into novelties. Attentive to, or diligent. "*Curious of* antiquities." *Dryd.* Accurate, without impropriety. "Men were not *curious* what syllables or particles of speech they used." *Shakesp.* Exact; nice; artful; elegant; neat; composed with great care. Rigid, severe, strict, "*Curious* I cannot be with you." *Shak.*

CU'RIOUSLY, Adj. in an inquisitive, accurate, or elegant manner. Captiously.

CUR'L, S. a ringlet of hair formed into a kind of ring. Figuratively, a wave, or waving line.

To CU'RL, V.A. [*cyrlan,* Sax.] to place the hair in circles. To writhe, or twist round. To dress with curls. Neuterly, to form itself into ringlets, or circular lines. To twist.

CURMU'DGEON, S. [a corrupt pronunciation and spelling of *coeur mechant,* Fr. a bad heart] one who is void of generosity; a niggardly or avaritious person. A miser.

CURMU'DGEONLY, Adv. avariciously, covetously. After the manner of a curmudgeon. . . .

HO'RROR, S. [*horreur,* Fr. *horreo,* Lat.] a passion excited by a shocking object. Figuratively, a gloom or dreariness, which affects with horror. "Breathes a browner *horror* on the woods." *Pope.* In Medicine, a shuddering, quivering, or trembling preceding a fit of a fever, or ague.

HO'RSE, S. [*hors,* Sax.] a domestic beast. Used in the plural, without the plural terminations for the cavalry, or of the soldiers in an army that fight on horseback. "Five thousand *horse.*" In manufacturing, any thing used as a support, hence a horse to dry linen on. Joined with great or wooden, a machine made of wood, very sharp, on which soldiers sit astride by way of punishment. Joined to another substantive, something large or coarse. "A *horse* face," *i.e.* a face whose features are large or coarse.

To HO'RSE, V.A. [*hors,* Sax.] to mount upon a horse. To sit astride a thing. "Leads fill'd, and ridges *horsed.*" *Shak.* To cover. "To *horse* with mares." *Mortim.*

HU'RTLEBERRY, S. [*hiort bar,* Dan.] the bilberry.

HU'RTLESS, Adj. without doing injury or harm. Innocent, harmless. Receiving no injury or harm.

HU'SBAND, S. [*hossband,* Dan. master, from *hus,* Sax. a house, and *bonda,* Ron. a master.] a man married to a woman. Figuratively, one who understands and practices frugality. The male of animals. "*Husband* to thy fold."

Dryd. A farmer or tiller of ground. "The painful *husband* plowing up his ground." *Dryd.* A person who furnishes a ship with commodities, and answers the demands on it on shore, called a *ship's husband.*

To HU'SBAND, V.A. to supply with an husband. To manage frugally. To cultivate ground. "A farmer cannot *husband* his ground." *Bac.* . . .

HU'SKY, Adj. consisting of, husks.

HU'SSY, S. [a corruption of *housewife,* used in an ill sense] a bad manager; a bad or wanton woman.

HU'STINGS, S. [*hustinge,* Sax. a council, *husting,* Brit. a whisper] a court of Common Pleas held before the lord mayor and aldermen at Guildhall, London. It is the highest court belonging to the city; and existed so early as the reign of Edward the Confessor.

To HU'STLE, V.A. to shake or rattle together.

HU'SWIFE, S. [*huswif,* Sax.] a woman that is either a bad manager, or of any infamous character. An oeconomist. "The bounteous *huswife,* nature." *Shak.* Johnson says it is common to use *housewife* in a good sense, but *huswife* or *hussy* in a bad one.

To HU'SWIFE, V.A. to manage with frugality.

HU'SWIFRY, S. frugal management of household affairs. Management of such branches of farming as fall within the province of women; such as making cheese, &c.

34. WILLIAM KENRICK

Dictionary Attention to the Spoken Language; Dictionary Entries

> William Kenrick was remarkable for the attention he gave to the oral as against the written language; much of his discussion of language reads as though it had been written in the twentieth century. (When he says that languages were written before they were spoken he must have been guilty only of a slip of the pen; his whole discussion and the sentence in question presume the opposite.) The selections below come from *A New English Dictionary of the English Language* . . . (London, 1773).

The material elements of vocal language are sounds, which speak to the ears; those of literal language, written types or figures, which speak to the eyes: so that polished nations have in fact two distinct kinds of language, which may be called oral and ocular; the properties of which, though arbitrarily connected by use, have no natural or physical dependence on each other.

As languages were written before they were spoken, the elements of oral language, or speech, properly so called, present themselves first to our consideration. /2/

. . . it is evident that, there are rules for the utterance of speech in general, independent of particular languages. It is certain also that, although these rules have not been much attended to in theory, they have been adopted in practice; the language of every polished nation having been gradually refined, as well by the disuse of ill-sounding words and adoption of others more agreeable to the ear, as by the melioration of the sounds themselves; which in the infant state of most languages have been dissonant and barbarous. Not that languages have been improved by every such refinement. On the contrary, for want of a due attention to the theory of such improvements, many languages have lost in strength what they have gained in sweetness. For a language may as well be too smooth and sibilant as too rough and aspirate. Audibility is essential to speech, nor can any language be too sonorous while its articulation is distinct and clear. A man would not speak so loud, or in so high a key, in a drawing room as in a wood or in a plain; but the most sonorous language is the most easily spoken and best heard even in a whisper. At the same time, it is to be observed that the audibility of speech depends equally on the quality as the quantity of sound. It is in vain that we hear sounds if they are not distinct and intelligible; and they may be rendered equally indistinct by too great as by too small an exertion of voice. Distinct articulation therefore is the first and most essential part of speech. . . . /3/

Of Articulation, or the Formation of Syllables

By a syllable I mean an articulate sound; that is the voice, or a vocal sound, modified by some consonant or appulse of the organs of speech. A mere vowel, having no other distinction than the quality it acquires by simple emission through the mouth, wants that form, which is necessary to constitute it a compleat articulate sound, or syllable. We do indeed admit single vowels sometimes to pass for syllables, but they are the most equivocal and indeterminate of all others; ever causing an *hiatus* in pronunciation, for want of a formal consonant.

The great art of articulate pronunciation depending on the clear intonation of the vowel and suppressing the sound of the consonant, nothing can be more necessary to propriety of articulation, than to distinguish between those different modes of enunciation, and to attain the art of separating them with facility in practice. The former is essentially necessary to the latter. It is also the more necessary, as being what linguists seldom teach, and perhaps seldom know; nothing being so common as to blend the vowel and consonant so intimately together, in speaking, as to be hardly separated by the nicest ear. Nay the politest and best speakers of the French tongue maintain that, their nasal sounds, expressed by *ain, ein, an, in*, are really vowels, and have no formal termination at all. It is certain the English have not those sounds in their language, and represent them very imperfectly by *ang, ong,* and *ing.* But, though the final *g* certainly does not enter into that sound; there is something so exactly resembling a final *n,* at the close of it, that it cannot be generally distinguished from it. Indeed their typifying it by an *n* seems to be a proof of this; though, if it be useless it ought to be sunk as much as possible, and the sound thereby corrected; as the twang of the consonant makes it very harsh and disagreeable to the ear.

To this errour, of blending the surd and vocal modes of articulation together, may be added the too frequent use of compound articulations both vocal and surd. The first, distinguished in writing by the term diphthong, consists in the joining of two vocal sounds of different qualities in one note or syllable; but from this, little inconvenience arises; if the two are pronounced in the key and time of one. Triphthongs in speech we have few or none, nor will modern volubility admit of it.

The second, consists of the joining two or three surd forms together, which cannot be clearly distinguished, without the emission of an indistinct sound between each, as in the words *strength, breadth, whelm, lopt, lisp,* &c.

The author of the Elements of Criticism observes, that every articulate sound, into which a consonant enters, must necessarily be double; because consonants, being pronounced with a less cavity of the mouth than vowels, they are of a different tone. But this is not altogether the case; the tone or key of the voice is not formed by the aperture of the mouth, /5/ though it may be a little varied by it; but by the aperture in the wind-pipe. The audible consonants are formed, indeed, by the aperture and appulse of the organs of speech, but they have no musical tone. If they had they would be vowels; as is plain from the contraction and prolongation of such modes as take either form.

It is conjectured by some linguists, and that not without foundation, that most, if not all, these compound articulations are formed by the suppression of some vowel; which formerly intervened between each; as in common conversation and frequently in writing we say *lov'd* for *loved, stopt* for *stopped,* and so forth. But from whatever source they are derived, they tend evidently to load the remaining vowels with indistinct surds; and, as we have too many of them in our language already, I am not for encreasing their number, by taking too great a latitude even in the allowed contraction of the preterite of our verbs. On the other hand, I could wish that all such words were suffered to grow into disuse; of which the articulation is thus complicated and dissonant.

We cannot indeed new model our language, but we need not aggravate its imperfections. Nothing has contributed more to the adulteration of living languages, than the too extensive acceptation of Horace's rule in favour of custom.

Custom is undoubtedly the rule of present practice; but there would be no end in following the variations, daily introduced by caprice. Alterations may sometimes be useful, may be necessary; but they should be made in a manner conformable to the genius and construction of the language. Nothing can tend to greater confusion in speech, for instance, than the practice of adopting words of foreign growth, without the least variation either in sound or othography. And yet even this is better than what we sometimes do, in adopting the sound without the orthography, and the orthography without the sound. The French have in this particular carried their attention to the peculiar structure of their language to a ridiculous scrupulosity; having not only gallicised terms of art and appellatives; but even given Christian names to Pagans and frenchified the whole race of patriarchs, heroes and philosophers of antiquity. *Modus est in rebus.* Extremes in this, as in all other cases, are hurtful. We ought by no means to shut the door against the improvement of our language; but it were well that some criterion were established to distinguish between improvement and innovation.

The natives of a country are not so apt, indeed, to adopt the sounds of other languages, as to adapt their own to a foreign orthography. The adoption of different sounds is not easy, and is an affectation or an errour peculiar to those who have travelled, and have made the different modes of articulation familiar to their organs. A good speaker however will never mix the distinguishing tones of different languages together, any more than he would mix the words of one language with another. If he speak English, it will be in the tones of an Englishman; and if French, in those of a Frenchman. If he cannot do this, he cannot speak both languages with propriety; how great a master soever he may be of their construction or phraseology. /6/

CURMU'DGEON — CUR-MUDGE-ON. *n. s.* [probably a vitious manner of pronouncing *coeur mechant*, Fr.] A avaritous churlish fellow; a miser; a niggard; a churl; a griper.

Cu'rmudgeonly. *adj.* [from *curmudgeon.*] Avaricious; covetous; churlish; niggardly.

Cu'rrant — Cur-rant. *n. s.* A tree bearing sweet red berries in bunches. — A small dried grape, properly written *corinth.*

Ho'rrour — Hor-rour. *n. s.* [*horror*, Latin; *horreur*, French.] Terrour mixed with detestation; a passion compounded of fear and hate, both strong. — Gloom; dreariness — [In medicine.] Such a shuddering or quivering as precedes an ague-fit; a sense of shuddering or shrinking.

HORSE — HORSE. *n. s.* [hors, Saxon.] A neighing quadruped, used in war, and draught and carriage. — It is used in the plural sense, but with a singular termination, for horses, horsemen, or cavalry. — Something on which any thing is supported: as a *horse* to dry linen on. — A wooden machine which soldiers ride by way of punishment. It is sometimes called a timbermare. — Joined to another substantive, it signifies something large or coarse: as, a *horseface*, a face of which the features are large and indelicate.

To Horse. *v. a.* [from the noun.] To mount upon a horse. — To carry one on the back. — To ride any thing.

Ho'rseback. *n. s.* [*horse* and *back.*] The feat of the rider; the state of being on a horse.

Ho'rsebe'an. *n. s.* [*horse* and *bean.*] A small bean usually given to horses.

Ho'rseblo'ck. *n. s.* [*horse* and *block.*] A block on which they climb to a horse.

Ho'rseboa't. *n. s.* [*horse* and *boat.*] A boat used in ferrying horses.

Ho'rsebo'y. *n. s.* [*horse* and *boy.*] A boy employed in dressing horses; a stable-boy.

Ho'rsebre'aker. *n. s.* [*horse* and *break.*] One whose employment it is to tame horses to the saddle.

Ho'rseche'snut. *n. s.* [*horse* and *chesnut.*] The fruit of a tree so called.

Ho'rsecourser. *n. s.* One that runs horses, or keeps horses for the race. — A dealer in horses.

Ho'rsecu'cumber. *n. s.* [*horse* and *cucumber.*] The large green cucumber.

Ho'rsedung. *n. s.* [*horse* and *dung.*] The excrements of horses.

Ho'rse-e'mmet. *n. s.* [*horse* and *emmet.*] Ant of a large kind.

Ho'rseflesh. *n. s.* [*horse* and *flesh.*] The flesh of horses.

Ho'rsefly. *n. s.* [*horse* and *fly.*] A fly that stings horses, and sucks their blood.

Ho'rseha'ir. *n. s.* [*horse* and *hair.*] The hair of horses.

Ho'rsela'ugh. *n. s.* [*horse* and *laugh.*] A loud violent rude laugh.

Ho'rsele'ech. *n. s.* [*horse* and *leech.*] A great leech that bites horses. — A farrier.

Ho'rseli'tter. *n. s.* [*horse* and *litter.*] A carriage hung upon poles between two horses, in which the person carried lies along.

Ho'rseman. *n. s.* [*horse* and *man.*] One skilled in riding. — One that serves in wars on horseback. — A rider; a man on horseback.

Ho'rsemanship. *n. s.* [from *horseman.*] The art of riding; the art of managing a horse.

Ho'rseme'at. *n. s.* [*horse* and *meat.*] Provender.

Ho'rsemint. *n. s.* A large coarse mint.

Ho'rsemuscle. *n. s.* A large muscle.

Ho'rseplay. *n. s.* [*horse* and *play.*] Coarse, rough, rugged play.

Ho'rsepond. *n. s.* [*horse* and *pond.*] A pond for horses.

Ho'rsera'ce. *n. s.* [*horse* and *race.*] A match of horses in running.

Ho'rsera'dish. *n. s.* [*horse* and *radish.*] A root acrid and biting; a species of scurvy-grass.

Ho'rsesho'e. *n. s.* [*horse* and *shoe.*] A plate of iron nailed to the feet of horses. — An herb.

Ho'rsestea'ler. *n. s.* [*horse* and *steal.*] A thief who takes away horses.

Ho'rseway. *n. s.* [*horse* and *way.*] A broad way by which horses may travel.

HOSE — HOSE. *n. s.* plur. *hosen.* [hosa, Saxon; *hosan,* Welsh; *ossan,* Erse; *ossanen,* plur. *chausse,* Fr.] Breeches. — Stockings; covering for the legs.

Ho'sier — Ho-sier. *n. s.* [from *hose.*] One who sells stockings.

HU'SBAND — HUS-BAND. *n. s.* [*hossband,* master, Danish, from *house* and *bonda,* Runick, a master.] The correlative to wife; a man married to a woman. — The male of animals. — An oeconomist; a man that knows and practises the methods of frugality and profit. Its signification is always modified by some epithet implying bad or good. — A tiller of the ground; a farmer.

WI'CKED — WICK-ED. *adj.* (Of this common word the etymology is very obscure: wiccu, is *an enchanter;* wæccan, is *to oppress;* wiӡian, *to curse;* wiccd, is *crooked:* all these however *Skinner* rejects for *vitiatus,* Latin. Perhaps it is a compound of þic, *vile, bad*, and *head, malum, caput*.)   Given to vice; not good; flagitious; morally bad. — It is a word of ludicrous or slight blame. — Cursed; baneful; pernicious; bad in effect.

35. JOHN ASH

Dictionary Entries

John Ash, a Baptist minister, published an introduction to Lowth's grammar in 1763. Twelve years later he published his dictionary, from which the following entries are selected, *The New and Complete Dictionary of the English Language* (London, 1775).

CUR'FEW (*s. from the* Fr. couvrir, *to cover, and* feu, *fire*) A cover for a fire, a fireplate; the bell that was rung at eight in the evening, by order of William the conqueror, as a signal for all his English subjects to take up their fires, put out their lights and go to bed; the bell that rings about bed time. . . .

CURMUDG'EON (*s. from the* French coeur, *unknown, and* mechant, *a correspondent*) A miser, a churl, a griper. . . .

HOR'ROR (*s. a modern but correct spelling, from the* Lat.) Horrour, dread.

HOR'ROUR (*s. the common spelling, from the* French horreur) Horror, dread, terror; gloom, dreariness; a cold shaking fit.

HOR'SA (*s.*) A man's name, the brother of Hengist the Dane.

HORSE (*s. from the* Sax. hors) One of the most generous and useful of all quadrupeds; the cavalry of any army; a machine which soldiers ride by way of punishment; a machine on which any thing is supported by laying it across.

Horse (*v. t. from the sub.*) To mount upon a horse, to put one horseback, to carry on the back, to ride, to cover a mare.

Horse (*adj. an obsolete spelling*) Hoarse. *Chaucer.*

Horse (*s. a sea term*) A rope reaching from the middle to the end of a yard, a rope of a large size extended in a perpendicular direction near the side of a mast for the sail to ride on.

Horse'back (*s. from* horse, *and* back) The state of being on a horse, the seat of the rider.

Horse'ballet (*s. from* horse, *and* ballet) A horse dance. *C.* . . .

Horse'measure (*s. from* horse, *and* measure) A rod divided into hands and inches in order to measure horses.

Horse'meat (*s. from* horse, *and* meat) Provender, meat for horses.

Horse'mint (*s. in botany*) A lage [sic] kind of mint.

Horse'muscle (*s. from* horse, *and* muscle) A large muscle.

Horse'play (*s. from* horse, *and* play) Coarse rough play.

Horse'pond (*s. from* horse, *and* pond) A pond in which horses are washed and watered.

Horse'race (*s. from* horse, *and* race) A match of horses for running.

Horse'radish (*s. from* horse, *and* radish) A species of scurvygrass, an acrid kind of root.

Horse'shoe (*s. from* horse, *and* shoe) A plate of iron nailed to the foot of a horse.

Horse'shoehead (*s. from* horseshoe, *and* head) A disease in infants, in which the sutures of the skull are too open. *Scott.*

Horse'stealer (*s. from* horse, *and* steal) One that steals horses.

Horse'tail (*s. in botany*) The name of a plant.

Horse'tongue (*s. in botany*) The name of an herb.

Horse'twitchers (*s. from* horse, *and* twitchers) An instrument to hold an unruly horse by the nostrils.

Horse'way (*s. from* horse, *and* way) A road for horses.

HORSH'AM (*s.*) A borough town in Sussex; it has a market on Saturday, sends two members to parliament, and is 37 miles from London.

Horsh'am (*adj. from the sub.*) Belonging to Horsham, made at Horsham.

Hors'ing (*p. a. from* horse) Mounting on horseback, putting on a horse, covering a mare.

HOR'TA (*s. in heathen mythology*) A goddess among the Romans who was supposed to have excited persons to great and noble enterprises. . . .

Hose (*v. t. a local word*) To carry, to hug in the arms. *Cole.*

HOSE'A (*s. from the* Heb. *signifying* safety) A man's name, one of the prophetical books of scripture.

Hose'husk (*s. in botany*) A husk, a husk within another.

Ho'sen (*s. plu. of* hose, *but now grown nearly obsolete*) Hose, stockings.

HOSHE'A (*s. a different spelling*) Hosea, a man's name.

Ho'sier (*s. from* hose) One who deals in hose.

HOS'PITABLE (*adj. from the* Lat. hospes *a guest*) Kind to strangers, given to hospitality.

Hos'pitableness (*s. from* hospitable) Hospitality, kindness to strangers.

Hos'pitably (*adv. from* hospitable) With kindness to strangers, in a hospitable manner.

HOS'PITAL (*s. from the* Lat. hospes *a stranger*) A place for the reception of the poor and the sick, a place for shelter or entertainment. . . .

HUSKAN'NAWING (*s. with the Indians of Virginia*) An institution or discipline which their young men must pass through before they are permitted to hold any important office in their state. *Scott.*

Husk'ed (*adj. from* husk) Covered with a husk.

Husk'ing (*p. a. from* husk) Stripping off the husks.

Husk'y (*adj. from* husk) Full of husks.

HU'SO (*s. in ichthyology*) The isinglassfish.

HUSSA'R (*s. from* huzza) One of the Hungarian horsemen so called from the shout they generally make at the first onset.

Hussa'r (*s. from the foregoing*) A kind of coat or cloke such as is worn by the irregular horse of the Hungarian army.

Hus'sel (*s. obsolete*) The Sacrament. *Bailey.*

Hus'selling (*adj. from* hussel, *obsolete*) Going to the sacrament, receiving the sacrament. *Scott.*

Hus'sites (*s. in church history*) The followers of John Huss one of the first reformers.

Hus'sy (*s. corrupted from* housewife) A sorry woman, a worthless wench; a young woman in droll style; a kind of work bag, a contrivance to keep needles and thread.

Hust (*v. imp. mode, obsolete*) Be still, be silent. *Chaucer.*

HUST'INGS (*s. from the* Sax. husting) A council, the supreme court of the city of London; the place where the court is held.

36. THOMAS SHERIDAN

"Correct" Pronunciation; Dictionary Entries

Dictionaries of "hard words" did not bother much about pronunciation; presumably the authors assumed that pronunciation was not hard; even many of the "complete" dictionaries do not suggest that pronunciation had anything to do with completeness. The following selection and entries are from Thomas Sheridan, *A General Dictionary of the English Language, One MAIN Object of which, is, to establish a plain and permanent STANDARD OF PRONUNCIATION* (Dublin, 1784), revised from the first edition of 1780.

It must be obvious, that in order to spread abroad the English language as a living tongue, and to facilitate the attainment of its speech, it is necessary in the first place that a standard of pronunciation should be established, and a method of acquiring a just one should be laid open. That the present state of the written language is not at all calculated to answer that end, is evident from this; that not only the natives of Ireland, Scotland, and Wales, who speak English, and are taught to read it, pronounce it differently, but each county in England has its peculiar dialect, which infects not only their speech, but their reading also. All attempts to reform this by any alteration in our written language would be utterly impracticable: And the only plan which could possibly be followed with any prospect of success, is what the Author has pursued in his Rhetorical Grammar and Dictionary.

In his Grammar, he has laid open a method of teaching every thing which regards sound, from the first simple elements, to their most extended combinations in words and sentences. He has pointed out the principles upon which our pronunciation is founded, and the general rules by which it is regulated.

In his Dictionary he has reduced the pronunciation of each word to a certainty by fixed and visible marks; the only way by which uniformity of sound could be propagated to any distance. This we find effectually done in the art of music by notes; for in whatever part of the globe music is so taught, the adepts in it read it exactly the same way. A similar uniformity of pronunciation, by means of this Grammar and Dictionary, may be spread through all parts of the globe, wherever English shall be taught by their aid.

But it may be asked, what right the Author has to assume to himself the office of a legislator on this occasion, and what his pretensions are to establish an absolute standard in an article, which is far from being in a settled state among any class of people? It is well known, that there is a great diversity of pronunciation of the same words, not only in individuals, but in whole bodies of men. That there are some adopted by the universities; some prevail at the bar, and some in the senate-house. That the propriety of these several pronunciations is controverted by the several persons who have adopted them; and what right has this self-appointed judge to determine which is the best?

The Author allows the propriety of the objection, and therefore thinks it necessary to lay open the grounds upon which he puts in his claim to this arduous office. /*viii*/

There was a time, and that at no very distant period, which may be called the Augustan age of England, I mean during the reign of Queen Anne, when English was the language spoken at court; and when the same attention was paid to propriety of pronunciation, as that of French at the Court of Versailles. This produced a uniformity in that article in all the polite circles; and a gentleman or lady would have been as much ashamed of a wrong pronunciation then, as persons of a liberal education would now be of misspelling words. But on the accession of a foreign family to the throne, amid the many blessings conferred by that happy event, the English language suffered much by being banished the court, to make room for the French. From that time the regard formerly paid to pronunciation has been gradually declining; so that now the greatest improprieties in that point are to be found among people of fashion; many pronunciations, which thirty or forty years ago were confined to the vulgar, are gradually gaining ground; and if something be not done to stop this growing evil, and fix a general standard at present, the English is likely to become a mere jargon, which every one may pronounce as he pleases. It is to be wished, that such a standard had been established at the period before mentioned, as it is probable, that English was then spoken in its highest state of perfection. Nor is it yet too late to recover it in that very state. It was my fortune to receive the early part of my education under a master, who made that a material object of instruction to the youth committed to his-care. He was the intimate friend, and chosen companion of Swift; who had passed great part of his life in a familiar intercourse with the most distinguished men of the age, whether for rank or genius. Eminent as he was for the purity and accuracy of his style, he was not more attentive to that point in writing, than he was to exactness of pronunciation in speaking. Nor could he bear to hear any mistakes committed by his friends in that respect, without correcting them. I had the happiness to be much with him in the early part of my life, and for several months read to him three or four hours a day, receiving still the benefit of his instruction. I have since had frequent opportunities of being convinced that a uniformity of pronunciation had prevailed at the court of Queen Anne, by comparing Swift's with that of many distinguished personages who were there initiated into life; among the number of which were the Duke of Dorset and the Earl of Chesterfield. And that very pronunciation is still the customary one among the descendants of all the politer part of the world bred in that reign. Upon investigating the principles on which the pronunciation of that time was formed, I found, that though there were no rules laid down for its regulation, yet there was a secret influence of analogy constantly operating, which attracted the different words, according to their several classes, to itself as their center. And where there were any deviations from that analogy, the anomalies were founded upon the best principle by which speech can be regulated, that of preferring the pronunciation which was the most easy to the organs of speech, and consequently most agreeable to the ear. So far the Author has laid open his pretensions, upon a supposition that pronunciation depended only upon custom and fashion. But when he adds, that he is the first who ever laid open the principles upon which our pronunciation is founded, and the rules by which it is regulated, he hopes the claim he has laid in to the office he has undertaken, will not be considered as either vain or presumptuous.

When we reflect, that no evil so great can befall any language, as a perpetual fluctuation both in point of spelling and pronouncing, it is surely a point to be wished, that a permanent and obvious standard to both should at some certain period be established: and if possible, that period should be fixed upon, when probably they were in the greatest degree of perfection. Dr. Johnson's spelling has been implicitly followed in the present Dictionary. It scarce deviates from that used by the writers in Queen Anne's reign; as he had judiciously rejected several innovations attempted since that time by vain and pragmatical writers, who, from an affectation of singularity, have attempted to introduce changes, /ix/ upon principles which will by no means stand the test of examination: and it might indisputably be proved, that no alterations in that respect, productive of any real benefit, can be made, without new moulding our alphabet, and making a considerable addition to its characters; a point utterly impracticable. /*x*/

HORROUR, hor'-rur. s. Terrour mixed with detestation; gloom, dreariness; in medicine, such a shuddering or quivering as precedes an ague-fit; a sense of shuddering or shrinking.

HORSE, hor'se. s. A neighing quadruped, used in war, and draught and carriage; it is used in the plural sense, but with a singular termination, for horses, horsemen, or cavalry; something on which any thing is supported; a wooden machine which soldiers ride by way of punishment; joined to another substantive, it signifies something large or coarse, as a horse-face, a face of which the features are large and indelicate. . . .

HORSEMATCH, hor's-matsh. s. A bird.

HORSEMEAT, hor's-met. s. Provender.

HORSEMINT, hor's-mint. s. A large coarse mint.

HORSEMUSCLE, hor's-musl. s. A large muscle.

HORSEPLAY, hor's-pla. s. Coarse, rough, rugged play.

HORSEPOND, hor's-pond. s. A pond for horses.

HORSERACE, hor's-ras. s. A match of horses in running.

HORSERADISH, hor's-rad'-ish. s. A root acrid and biting, a species of scurvy-grass.

HORSESHOE, hor's-sho. s. A plate of iron nailed to the feet of horses; an herb.

HORSESTEALER, hor's-stel-ur. s. A thief who takes away horses.

HORSETAIL, hor's-tal. s. A plant.

HORSETONGUE, hor's-tung. s. An herb.

HORSEWAY, hor's-wa. s. A broad way by which horses may travel. . . .

HOSPITAL, a's-pi-tal. s. A place built for the reception of the sick, or support of the poor; a place for shelter or entertainment.

HOSPITALITY, hos-py-tal'-i-ty. s. The practice of entertaining strangers.

HOST, ho'st. s. One who gives entertainment to another; the landlord of an inn; an army, numbers assembled for war; any great number; the sacrifice of the mass in the Romish church.

To HOST, ho'st. v. n. To take up entertainment; to encounter in battle; to review a body of men, to muster. . . .

HURTLEBERRY, hur'tl-ber-ry. s. Bilberry.

HURTLESS, hurt'-lis. a. Innocent, harmless, innoxious, doing no harm, receiving no hurt.

HURTLESSLY, hurt'-lis-ly. ad. Without harm.

HURTLESSNESS, hurt'-les-nis. s. Freedom from any pernicious quality.

HUSBAND, huz'-bund. s. The correlative to wife, a man married to a woman; the male of animals; an oeconomist, a man that knows and practises the methods of frugality and profit; a farmer.

To HUSBAND, huz'-bund. v.a. To supply with an husband; to manage with frugality; to till, to cultivate the ground with proper management.

HUSBANDLESS, huz'-bund-lis. a. Without a husband.

HUSBANDLY, huz'-bund-ly. a. Frugal, thrifty.

HUSBANDMAN, huz'-bund-man. s. One who works in tillage.

HUSBANDRY, huz'-bun-dry. s. Tillage, manner of cultivating land; thrift, frugality, parsimony; care of domestick affairs.

HUSH, hush'. interj. Silence! be still! no noise!

37. NOAH WEBSTER

Dictionary Entries

Noah Webster's was the first genuinely American dictionary of significant scope; it is particularly distinguished for the clarity of its definitions as compared with those of many earlier dictionaries. The following are selected entries from the first edition of his *An American Dictionary of the English Language* (New York, 1828), 2 vols.

HOR′ROR, *n*. [L. from *horreo*, to shake or shiver, or to set up the bristles, to be rough.]
1. A shaking, shivering or shuddering, as in the cold fit which precedes a fever. This ague is usually accompanied with a contraction of the skin into small wrinkles, giving it a kind of roughness.
2. An excessive degree of fear, or a painful emotion which makes a person tremble; terror; a shuddering with fear; but appropriately, terror or a sensation approaching it, accompanied with hatred or detestation. *Horror* is often a passion compounded of fear and hatred or disgust. The recital of a bloody deed fills us with *horror.*

    A *horror* of great darkness fell on Abram. Gen. xv.

    Horror hath taken hold on me, because of the wicked that forsake thy law. Ps. cxix.

3. That which may excite horror or dread; gloom; dreariness.

And breathes a browner *horror* on the woods. *Pope.*

4. Dreadful thoughts.

5. Distressing scenes; as the *horrors* of war or famine.

HORSE, *n. hors.* [Sax. *hors;* G. *ross;* D. *ros.*]

1. A species of quadrupeds of the genus Equus, having six erect and parallel teeth in the upper jaw, and six somewhat prominent in the under jaw; the dog teeth are solitary, and the feet consist of an undivided hoof. The horse is a beautiful animal, and of great use for draught or convey-ance on his back. *Horse,* in English, is of common gender, and may com-prehend the male and the female.

2. A constellation.

3. Cavalry; a body of troops serving on horseback. In this sense, it has no general termination. We say, a thousand *horse;* a regiment of *horse.*

4. A machine by which something is supported; usually a wooden frame with legs. Various machines used in the arts are thus called. *Encyc.*

5. A wooden machine on which soldiers ride by way of punishment; some-times called a *timber-mare. Johnson.*

6. In *seamen's language,* a rope extending from the middle of a yard to its extremity, to support the sailors while they loose, reef or furl the sails; also, a thick rope extended near the mast for hoisting a yard or extending a sail on it. *Mar. Dict.*

To take horse, to set out to ride on horseback. *Addison.*

2. To be covered, as a mare.

HORSE, *v. t.* To mount on a horse.

2. To carry on the back.

The keeper, *horsing* a deer. *Butler.*

3. To ride astride; as, ridges *horsed. Shak.*

4. To cover a mare, as the male. *Mortimer.*

HORSEBACK, *n. hors' back.* The state of being on a horse; the posture of riding on a horse.

I saw them salute on *horseback. Shak. . . .*

HORSELAUGH, *n.* A loud, boisterous laugh.

HORSELEECH, *n.* A large leech. [See *Leech.*]

2. A farrier.

HORSELITTER, *n.* A carriage hung on poles which are borne by and between two horses. *Milton.*

HORSELOAD, *n.* A load for a horse.

HORSEMAN, *n.* A rider on horseback. *Addison.*

2. A man skilled in riding. *Dryden.*

3. A soldier who serves on horseback. *Hayward.*

HORSEMANSHIP, *n.* The art of riding, and of training and managing horses. *Pope.*

HORSEMARTEN, *n.* A kind of large bee. *Ainsworth.*

HORSEMATCH, *n.* A bird. *Ainsworth.*

HORSEMEAT, *n.* Food for horses; provender. *Bacon.*

HORSE-MILL, *n.* A mill turned by a horse.

HORSE-MUSCLE, *n.* A large muscle or shell-fish. *Bacon.*

HORSEPATH, *n.* A path for horses, as by canals.

HORSEPLAY, *n.* Rough, rugged play. *Dryden.*

HORSEPOND, *n.* A pond for watering horses.

HORSEPURSLANE, *n.* A plant of the genus Trianthema. . . .

HURT'LEBERRY, *n.* A whortleberry, which see.

HURT'LESS, *a.* Harmless; innocent; doing no injury; innoxious; as *hurtless* blows. *Dryden.*

2. Receiving no injury.

HURT'LESSLY, *adv.* Without harm. [*Little used.*] *Sidney.*

HURT'LESSNESS, *n.* Freedom from any harmful quality. (*Little used.*) *Johnson.*

HUS'BAND, *n. s.* as *z.* [Sax. *husbonda; hus,* house, and *buend,* a farmer or cultivator, or an inhabitant, from *byan,* to inhabit or till, contracted from *bugian;* Dan. *huusbonde;* Sw. *husbonde;* Sw. *byggia,* Dan. *bygger,* to build; D. *bouwen,* G. *bauen,* to build, to till, to plow or cultivate; G. *bauer,* a builder, a countryman, a clown, a rustic, a *boor;* D. *buur,* the last component part of *neighbor. Band, bond,* in this word, is the participle of *buan, byan,* that is, *buend,* occupying, tilling, and *husband* is the farmer or inhabitant of the house, in Scottish, a farmer; thence the sense of husbandry. It had no relation primarily to marriage; but among the common people, a woman calls her consort, my man, and the man calls his wife, my woman, as in Hebrew, and in this instance, the farmer or occupier of the house, or the builder, was called my farmer; or by some other means, *husband* came to denote the consort of the female head of the family.]

1. A man contracted or joined to a woman by marriage. A man to whom a woman is betrothed, as well as one actually united by marriage, is called a *husband.* Lev. xix. Deut. xxii.

2. In *seamen's language,* the owner of a ship who manages its concerns in person. *Mar. Dict.*

3. The male of animals of a lower order. *Dryden.*

4. An economist; a good manager; a man who knows and practices the methods of frugality and profit. In this sense, the word is modified by an epithet; as a good *husband;* a bad *husband.* [But in America, this application of the word is little or not at all used.] *Davies. Collier.*

5. A farmer; a cultivator; a tiller of the ground. [In this sense, it is not used in America. We always use *husbandman.*] *Bacon. Dryden.*

HUS'BAND, *v. t.* To direct and manage with frugality in expending any thing; to use or employ in the manner best suited to produce the greatest effect; to use with economy. We say, a man *husbands* his estate, his means or his time.

He is conscious how ill he has *husbanded* the great deposit of his Creator. *Rambler.*

2. To till; to cultivate with good management. *Bacon.*

3. To supply with a husband. [*Little used.*] *Shak.* . . .

HUSH, *a.* [G. *husch;* Dan. *hys, hyst.* In W. *hêz* is peace; *hêzu,* to make peace; *ews* is rest, sleep; and *hust* is a low, buzzing sound; Heb. חשה to be silent. Class Gs. No. 46.] Silent; still; quiet; as, they are *hush* as death. This adjective never precedes the noun which it qualifies, except in the compound, *hush-money.*

HUSH, *v. t.* To still; to silence; to calm; to make quiet; to repress noise; as, to *hush* the noisy crowd; the winds were *hushed.*

My tongue shall *hush* again this storm of war. *Shak.*

2. To appease; to allay; to calm, as commotion or agitation.

Wilt thou then

Hush my cares? *Otway.*

HUSH, *v. i.* To be still; to be silent. *Spenser.*

HUSH, imperative of the verb, used as an exclamation, be still; be silent or quiet; make no noise.

To hush up, to suppress; to keep concealed.

This matter is *hushed up. Pope.*

HUSH'MONEY, *n.* A bribe to secure silence; money paid to hinder information, or disclosure of facts. *Swift.* . . .

HUSS'ITE, *n.* A follower of John Huss, the Bohemian reformer.

HUSS'Y, *n.* [contracted from *huswife,* housewife.]

1. A bad or worthless woman. It is used also ludicrously in slight disapprobation or contempt. Go, *hussy,* go.

2. An economist; a thrifty woman. *Tusser.*

HUS'TINGS, *n.* [Sax. *hustinge;* supposed to be composed of *hus,* house, and *thing,* cause, suit; the house of trials.] . . .

WID'GEON, *n.* A fowl of the duck kind, or genus Anas, having a black bill, the head and upper part of the neck of a bright bay, the back and sides waved with black and white, and the belly white. *Dict. Nat. Hist.*

WID'OW, *n.* [Sax. *widew;* G. *wittwe;* D. *weduwe;* Dan. *vidue;* L. *vidua;* Fr. *veuve;* It. *vedova,* Sp. *viuda;* Sans. *widhava;* Russ. *vdova;* from the root of *wide, void.* See *Wide.*]

A woman who has lost her husband by death. *Luke ii.*

Widow's chamber, in London, the apparel and furniture of the bedchamber of the widow of a freeman, to which she is entitled. *Cyc.*

WID'OW, *v. t.* To bereave of a husband; but rarely used except in the participle. *Dryden.*

2. To endow with a widow's right. [*Unusual.*]

3. To strip of any thing good. *Shak.*

The *widow'd* isle in mourning — *Dryden.*

WID'OW-BENCH, *n.* [*widow* and *bench.*] In *Sussex,* that share which a widow is allowed of her husband's estate, besides her jointure. *Cyc.*

WID'OWED, *pp.* Bereaved of a husband by death.

2. Deprived of some good; stripped.

> Trees of their shrivel'd fruits
> Are *widow'd*. *Philips*.

WID'OWER, *n*. A man who has lost his wife by death.

WID'OWHOOD, *n*. The state of being a widow.

2. Estate settled on a widow. [*Not in use*.] *Shak*.

WID'OW-HUNTER, *n*. [*widow* and *hunter*.] One who seeks or courts widows for a jointure or fortune. *Addison*.

WID'OWING, *ppr*. Bereaving of a husband; depriving; stripping.

WID'OW-MAKER, *n*. [*widow* and *maker*.] One who makes widows by destroying lives. *Shak*. . . .

WI'ERY, *a*. [from *wire*.] Made of wire; having the properties of wire. It would be better written *wiry*.

2. [Sax. *waer*, a pool.] Wet; marshy. [*Not in use*.] *Shak*.

WIFE, *n*. plu. *wives*. [Sax. *wif*; D. *wyf*; G. *weib*, a woman.]

1. The lawful consort of a man; a woman who is united to a man in the lawful bonds of wedlock; the correlative of *husband*.

> The husband of one *wife*. 1 Tim. iii.

> Let everyone of you in particular, so love his *wife* even as himself, and let the *wife* see that she reverence her husband. Eph. v.

2. A woman of low employment; as, strawberry *wives*. [*Not in use*.] *Shak*.

WIG, in Saxon, signifies war. It is found in some names.

WIG, *n*. [G. *weck*, wig, and *weck-butter*, roll butter. It would seem that the sense is a roll or twist interwoven.]

1. A covering for the head, consisting of hair interwoven or united by a kind of network, formerly much worn by men.

2. A sort of cake. *Obs*. *Ainsworth*.

WIGEON. [See *Widgeon*.]

WIGHT, *n*. [Sax. *wiht*, G. *wicht*, a living being, Goth. *waiht*; L. *victum*, from *viva*, originally *vigo* or *vico*, and probably allied to *vigeo*. This, in the Celtic form, would be *quic* or *qwig*, Eng. quick, alive; and hence L. *qui, quae, quid, quod*, contracted from *quic, quiced, quoced*; Scot. *quhat*. The letter *h*, in the Gothic and Scottish, representing the *c* of the Latin, proves the word to be thus contracted.] A being; a person. It is obsolete, except in irony or burlesque. [See *Aught*.]

> The *wight* of all the world who lov'd thee best. *Dryden*.

WIGHT, *a*. [Sax. *hwæt*.] Swift; nimble. *Obs*. *Spenser*. [This seems to be a dialectical form of *quick*.]

WIGHTLY, *adv*. Swiftly; nimbly. *Obs*. *Spenser*.

WIG'WAM, *n*. An Indian cabin or hut, so called in America. It is sometimes written *weekwam*.

The following entries are from the second edition of Webster's *An American Dictionary of the English Language* (New York, 1848).

HOR'ROR, *n.* [L. from *horreo,* to shake, or shiver, or to set up the bristles, to be rough.]

1. A shaking, shivering, or shuddering, as in the cold fit which precedes a fever. This ague is usually accompanied with a contraction of the skin into small wrinkles, giving it a kind of roughness.

2. An excessive degree of fear, or a painful emotion which makes a person tremble; terror; a shuddering with fear; but appropriately, terror, or a sensation approaching it, accompanied with hatred or detestation. *Horror* is often a passion compounded of fear and hatred or disgust. The recital of a bloody deed fills us with *horror.*

   A *horror* of great darkness fell on Abram. — Gen. xv.

   Horror hath taken hold on me, because of the wicked that forsake thy law. — Ps. cxix.

3. That which may excite horror or dread; gloom; dreariness.

   And breathes a browner *horror* on the *woods. Pope.*

4. Dreadful thoughts.

5. Distressing scenes; as, the *horrors* of war or famine.

   The *horrors:* a result of habits of inebriation; a state of extreme bodily and mental agitation, occasioned by a withdrawment of the customary stimulus.

HOR'ROR-STRICK EN, *a.* Struck with horror.

HORS DE COM-BAT, [hor-de-kom-bá,] [Fr.]. Out of the combat; disabled to fight.

HORSE, *n.* [Sax. *hors;* G. *ros;* Fr. *rosse;* It. *rozzo.*]

1. A species of quadrupeds of the genus Equus, having six erect and parallel fore-teeth in the upper jaw, and six somewhat prominent in the under jaw; the dog-teeth are solitary, and the feet consist of an undivided hoof. The horse is a beautiful animal, and of great use for draught, or conveyance on his back. *Horse,* in English, is of common gender, and may comprehend the male and the female. . . .

HORSE'-MILL, *n.* A mill turned by a horse.

HORSE'MIL'LI-NER, *n.* [*horse* and *milliner.*] One who supplies ribbons and other decorations for horses. *Smart.*

HORSE'-MINT, *n.* A species of large mint.

HORSE'-MUS'-CLE, [-mus' 1,] *n.* A large muscle or shell-fish. *Bacon.*

HORSE'-PATH, *n.* A path for horses, as by canals.

HORSE'-PLAY, *n.* Rough, rugged play. *Dryden.*

HORSE'-POND, *n.* A pond for watering horses.

HORSE'-POW-ER, *n.* The power of a horse; or its equivalent, which has been estimated, by Mr. Watt, as a power which will raise 32,000 lbs. avoirdupois one foot high per minute.

HORSE'-PURS' LANE, *n.* A plant of the genus Trianthema. . . .

WID'GEON, [wij'un,] *n.* A water-fowl of the duck group, belonging to the genus Mareca of Stephens. The European species is the Mareca

Penelope, the American the M. Americana. The widgeons feed on grasses or vegetables, somewhat in the manner of geese. *Nuttall. Jardine.*

WID'OW, *n.* [Sax. *widew;* G. *wittwe;* D. *weduwe;* Dan. *vidue;* L. *vidua;* Fr. *veuve;* It. *vedova;* Sp. *viuda;* Sans. *widhava;* Russ. *vdova;* from the root of *wide, void.* See *Wide.*]

A woman who has lost her husband by death. *Luke* ii.

Widow's chamber, in London, the apparel and furniture of the bed-chamber of the widow of a freeman, to which she is entitled. *Cyc.*

WID'OW, *v. t.* To bereave of a husband; but rarely used, except in the participle. *Dryden.*

2. To endow with a widow's right. [*Unusual.*]

3. To strip of anything good. *Shak.*

The *widowed* isle in mourning. *Dryden.* . . .

WIGHT, [wite,] *n.* [Sax. *wiht,* G. *wicht,* a living being. Goth. *waiht;* L. *victum,* from *vivo,* to live, originally *vigo* or *vico,* and probably allied to *vigeo.* This, in the Celtic form, would be *quic* or *qwig,* Eng. *quick,* alive; and hence L. *qui, quae, quid, quod,* contracted from *quic, quiced, quoced;* Scot. *quhat.* The letter *h,* in the Gothic and Scottish, representing the *c* of the Latin, proves the word to be thus contracted.] A being; a person. It is obsolete, except in irony or burlesque. [See Aught.]

The *wight* of all the world who loved thee best. *Dryden.*

WIGHT, [wite,] *a.* [Sax. *hwaet.*] Swift, nimble. [*Obs.*] *Spenser.* [This seems to be a dialectical form of Quick.]

WIGHT'LY, *adv.* Swiftly; nimbly. [*Obs.*] *Spenser.*

WIG'WAM, *n.* An Indian cabin or hut, so called in America. It is sometimes written Weekwam. Mackenzie writes the Knisteneaux word *wigwaum,* and the Algonquin *wiguiwaum.* Query, is this the L. *vicus? Vic,* in Roman, was pronounced *wic* or *week.* These words may have been derived from one primitive root.

38.

Definitions of Horse

The following definitions of the word *horse* are taken from a number of modern dictionaries.

OXFORD ENGLISH DICTIONARY
A New English Dictionary on Historical Principles
(Oxford, 1888-1928)

Horse (hǭɪs), *sb.* Forms: *sing.* 1-6 hors, (3 *Orm.* horrs, 4 horce, ors, 5 orse, 6 horsse), 4- horse; *pl.* 1-6 hors, 4- horse, 3- horses. [Com. Teut.: OE *hors* = OFris. *hors, hars, hers* (Fris. *hoars*), OS. *hros* (MLG. *ros, ors,* MDu.

ors, LG. and Du. *ros*), OHG. *hros*, *ros*, MHG. *ros*, *ors*, G. *rosz*, all neuter, ON. *hross* masc.; not recorded in Goth. The affinities of the word outside Teutonic are uncertain: the conjecture that OTeut. **horso-*, pre-Teut. **kurso-* was from the root **kurs-* of L. *currere* 'to run' is favoured by many; but other derivations have also been suggested. Like several other names of animals (*sheep, swine, neat, deer*), this was originally neuter, applicable to the male and female alike; and like these words and other neuters in a long syllable, the nom. plural was the same as the singular. The plural *horses*, and the tendency to restrict the name to the male came in later: see 1 b, c.]

I. The animal, and senses immediately related.

1. A solid-hoofed perissodactyl quadruped (*Equus caballus*), having a flowing mane and tail, whose voice is a neigh. It is well known in the domestic state as a beast of burden and draught, and esp. as used for riding upon.

c 825 *Vesp. Psalter* xxi[i]. 9 Nyllað bion swe swe hors & mul in ðaem nis ondȝet. *c* 1205 LAY. 21354 þe king . . his hors he gon spurie. *c* 1290 *Beket* 1151 in *S. Eng. Leg.* I. 139 Hors ne hadde he non. *c* 1300 *Havelok* 126 Mi douhter . . Yif scho coupe on horse ride. *c* 1380 WYCLIF *Sel. Wks.* III. 231 A horce . . þat haves a sore back, wynses when he is oght touched. *c*. 1400 MAUNDEV. (1839) xxii. 237 [Thei] presenten the white Hors to the Emperour. 1567 *Gude & Godlie B.* (S. T. S.) 9 Nor wis His hors, his oxe, his maide nor page. 1584 POWEL *Lloyd's Cambria* 288 Falling off his horsse. 1594 SHAKS. *Rich. III*, v. iv. 7 A Horse, a Horse, my Kingdome for a Horse! 1654 WHITLOCK *Zootomia* 143, I believe Banks his Horse was taught in better language, then some would have Christians taught. 1782 COWPER *Gilpin* 45 John Gilpin at his horse's side Seized fast the flowing mane. 1848 W. H. BARTLETT *Egypt to Pal.* v. (1879) 116 Not a horse appears on the monuments prior to Thothmes III, who clearly in his conquests brought them from Asia.

b. *Plural.*

The plural was in OE. the same as the sing.; *horse* plural was in general use down to 17th c., and is still frequent dialectally; but *horses* appears as early as Layamon (*c* 1205), and its use increased till in 17th c. it became the usual plural in the literary language; sometimes *horse* appears as the collective and *horses* as the individual plural, which explains the retention of *horse* in military language as in 'a troop of horse.' The OE. dat. pl. *horsum* appears in early ME. as *horsen*, *horse*.

a. *a* 900 in *O. E. Texts* 177 Fiow(er) wildo hors. *Ibid.* 178 Ða cwom Godes engel . . and ȝestillde ðaem horssum. *c* 1200 *Trin. Coll. Hom.* 179 Hundes and hauekes, and hors and wepnes. *c* 1205 LAY. 1025 He sculde beon . . mid horsen [*c* 1275 horse] to-drawen. 1375 BARBOUR *Bruce* VIII. 446 Syne thame lay Apon their horss. 1387 TREVISA *Higden* (Rolls) VII. 121 Two gentil hors. 1422 tr. *Secreta Secret., Priv. Priv.* (E. E. T. S.) 219 We seen that knyghtis knowyth the goodnys of horsyn. 1480 CAXTON *Chron. Eng.* clxxxix. 167 Oftymes the poure peple . . ete also the houndes . . and eke hors and cattes. *a* 1533 LD. BERNERS *Huon* lxii. 215 Gerames . . bought horse and mules to ryde on. 1588 SHAKS. *Tit. A.* II. ii. 18 Come on then, horse and Chariots let vs haue. 1702 *Lond. Gaz.* No. 3783/3 We brought away . . above 500 Horse belonging to their Cavalry and Artillery. 1818 BYRON *Mazeppa* xvii, A thousand horse — and none to ride! 1832 LANDER *Adv. Niger* I. iv. 177 A few rough, ragged-looking ponies are the only 'horse' of which he has the superintendence.

β. *c* 1205 LAY. 3561 Hundes & hauekes & durewurðe horses [*c* 1275 hors]. 1297 R. GLOUC. (1724) 50 Here folc heo loren . . & heore horses [*MS. A* hors] ney echon. 1382 WYCLIF *Rev.* xix. 14 The hoostes . . sueden him in whijte horsis [*v.r.* hors]. 1434 *Priv. Purse Exp. Eliz. of York* (1830) 262/2 Three of her best horses. *c* 1511 1st *Eng. Bk. Amer.* (Arb.) Introd. 33/2 They haue horseys as great as a great dogge. 1584 POWEL *Lloyd's Cambria* 41 They were driuen to eat their own horsses. 1697 DRYDEN *Virg. Georg.* III. 178 Bold Ericthonius was the first, who join'd Four Horses for the rapid Race design'd. 1735 SOMERVILLE *Chase* III. 322 Intrepid Bands, Safe in their Horses Speed. 1859 F. A. GRIFFITHS *Artil. Man.* (1862) 156 The ride and spare horses will be on the left when picketed, the gun horses on the right.

c. *spec.* The adult male of the horse kind, as distinguished from a mare or colt: a stallion or gelding. *To take the horse:* (of the mare) to conceive.

c 1485 *Digby Myst.* (1882) II. 119. He was nother horse ne mare, nor yet yokyd sow. 1549 *Compl. Scot.* vi. 39 Baytht horse & meyris did fast nee, & the folis nechyr. 1577 B. GOOGE *Heresbach's Husb.* III. (1586) 117 What age doe you thinke best for the Mare to go to the horse? *Ibid.* 117 b, To put the Mare to the Horse. 1606 SHAKS. *Ant. & Cl.* III. vii. 7. 1617 MORYSON *Itin.* III. 56 They have goodly Mares to draw these Waggons, using Horses for the troops in their Army. 1697 DRYDEN *Virg. Georg.* III. 223. 1854 OWEN *Skel. & Teeth* in *Circ. Sc., Organ. Nat.* I. 285 Upon the rising of the third permanent incisor, or 'corner nipper' . . the 'colt' becomes a 'horse', and the 'filly', a 'mare'. 1870 BLAINE *Encycl. Rur. Sports* § 1013 Having taken the horse, i.e. being fecundated, is therefore a matter of uncertainty usually for three or four months, particularly in pastured mares.

d. In *Zool.* sometimes extended to all species of the genus *Equus*, or even of the family *Equidae*,

e. With qualifications denoting origin, variety, or use, as *Arabian, Barbary, Flemish, wild horse.* Cf. also CART-, DRAY-, SADDLE-, WAR-HORSE, etc.

c 1000 ÆLFRIC *Gloss.* in Wr.-Wülcker 119/33 Equifer, wilde cynnes hors. *a* 1400-50 *Alexander* 1250 þe multitude was sa mekill . . Of wees & of wild horsis [*v.r.* horse]. 1577 B. GOOGE *Heresbach's Husb.* I. (1586) 13, I have an other stable . . for my Horses of service and Hackneyes. 1607 TOP-SELL *Fouf-f. Beasts* (1658) 252 Single horses, which therefore they called Coursers, and now a days a Horse for Saddle. 1889 *Spectator* 21 Sept., As good, if not better, than the shire or cart-horse. 1890 BESANT *Demoniac* xv. 179 To have his flesh wrenched off with red-hot pincers and to be torn to pieces by wild horses.

THE CENTURY DICTIONARY AND CYCLOPEDIA
(New York, 1889-97), 10 vols.

horse[1] (hors), *n.* [<ME. *hors* (pl. *hors* and *horses*), <AS. *hors* (pl. *hors*) = OS. *hors, hros* (*hross-*) = OFries. *hors, hars* = D. *ros* = OHG. *hros, ros*, MHG. *ros* (*ross-*), G. *ross* (>It. *rozza* = Pr. *rossa* = F. *rosse*, a jade) = Icel. *hross, hors* = Sw. Dan. dial. *hors*, a horse. Root uncertain; some connect the word with AS. *horsc* = MHG. *rosch*, swift, referring both to a root shown in L. *currere* (for **cursere?*), run: see *current*[1]. The Indo-Eur. word for 'horse' is that represented by Skt. *açva* = Gr. ἵππος = L. *equus* = AS. *eoh*, etc.: see *Equus*. The ordinary Teut. terms outside of E. are D. *paard*, G. *pferd* (see *palfrey*); Sw. *häst*, Dan. *hest* (see *henchman*); the Rom. words are F. *cheval*, Sp. *caballo*, etc. (see *cheval, caple*[1], *cavalry*, etc.).] 1. A solidungulate perissodactyl mammal of the family *Equidae* and genus *Equus; E. caballus*. It has a flowing mane and tail, comparatively small erect ears, comparatively large rounded hoofs, shapely head, arched neck, a callosity on the inner side of the hind leg below the hock, in addition to one on the fore leg above the so-called "knee," and a peculiar voice called a "neigh." These are the principal distinctive characters of the existing horses, of whatever variety, in comparison with the asses and zebras, which are commonly placed in the same genus (*Equus*). The horse has no distinctive coloration, but is never conspicuously striped in any regular pattern, and seldom shows even the dorsal and shoulder stripe characteristic of the ass, though there is often an indication of this marking in horses which have reverted to a feral state and tend to assume a dun color. The horse is now known only as a domesticated and artificially bred animal, though in both North and South America, in Australia, and in some parts of Asia the descendants of domesticated ancestors run wild in troops. The native country of the horse and the period of its subjection to man are unknown. Animals congeneric with the present horse, if not conspecific, have left their remains with those of the mammoth and other extinct animals in the bonecaves of both the old and new worlds, but the genus *Equus* appears not to have been fully established before the close of the Pliocene. The evolution of the modern forms has been traced back through the whole Tertiary period, by the discovery of such genera as *Hipparion* and *Pliohippus* of the Pliocene, *Anchitherium, Miohippus*, and *Mesohippus* of the Miocene, and *Orohippus* and *Eohippus* of the Eocene. In the course of this evolutionary series is observed a very gradual and unbroken geologic pedigree, going back to a small animal, not larger than a fox, with several separate toes on each foot. The size has steadily increased, and other progressive modifications, especially of the limbs, have resulted in the existing horse in all its numberless artificial breeds, races, and strains, combining in various degrees the qualities of size, strength, speed, and bottom. Two breeds — namely, the large, powerful, black breed of Flanders, and the Arabian — have contributed more than all others to develop the present varieties. The former laid the foundation of size, strength, and vigor for draft-horses and for those formerly used in war; while, when mailed armor was laid aside, and the horse began to be used for the chase, the latter conferred the speed and endurance which distinguish the hunter. The ladies' palfrey is largely derived from the Spanish genet, a small, beautiful, fleet variety of the Moorish barb. The race-horse has less of Flemish and more of Arabian blood. Other leading varieties are the Suffolk Punch and Clydesdale, both chiefly of Flemish blood, and best for draft and agriculture; and several varieties of ponies, as Galloway, Shetland, etc. Carriage, riding, and other horses combine the above breeds in varying degrees, as speed, endurance, strength, or size, etc., may be required. Horses are said to have "blood" or "breeding" in proportion as they have a greater or less strain of Arab blood. The wild horse of Tatary is called a *tarpan*, that of northern Africa a *koomrah*, and that of America a *mustang*, the last being descended from imported Spanish parents. The male of the horse is a *stallion;* when gelded, a *gelding;* the female is a *mare;* the young, a *foal* — if a male, a *colt*, if a female, a *filly*. The colt and filly become "of age" when the "corner-nippers" (outer incisors) attain functional development. The age of the horse may be determined by the marks on the front teeth, which change with the wearing down of the crowns by use. When the mark disappears, as it generally does in the eighth or ninth year, the horse is "aged." The period of gestation is eleven months, and foals are generally dropped in the spring. Horses vary greatly in size, some standing more than twice as high as others. Very small horses are called *ponies*, as those bred in Shetland.

A-noon he made tweyne of his sones for to make hem redy and sette hem on two swifte *horse*. Merlin (E. E. T. S.), iii. 525.

Hast thou given the *horse* strength? hast thou clothed his neck with thunder? Job xxxix. 19.

> The *horse* that guide the golden eye of heaven,
> And blow the morning from their nostrils. *Marlowe*.

In the earliest period, the *Horse* seems to have been the favourite animal for sacrifice; there is no doubt that before the introduction of Christianity its flesh was universally eaten. *Grimm*, Teut. Mythol. (trans.), I. 47.

2. *pl.* In *zoöl.*, the horse family, or *Equidae;* the species of the genus *Equus* and related genera. These include all the existing asses of the restricted genus *Asinus*, and the quagga, dauw, and zebra, of the restricted genus *Hippotigris*, together with all the extinct forms of the Tertiary period which, however different from the modern horse, are connected closely by intermediate links. See *Equidae*.

3. The male of the horse kind, in distinction from the female or mare; a stallion or gelding.

> Lo, the unback'd breeder, full of fear,
> Jealous of catching, swiftly doth forsake him,
> With her the *horse*, and left Adonis there.
> *Shak.*, Venus and Adonis, 1. 322.

No cow-boy ever rides anything but *horses*, because mares give great trouble where all the animals have to be herded together. *T. Roosevelt*, The Century, XXXV. 656.

4. A body of troops serving on horseback; cavalry: in this sense a collective noun, used also as a plural: as, a regiment of *horse*.

> Our nineteen legions thou shalt hold by land,
> And our twelve thousand *horse*.
> *Shak.*, A. and C., iii. 7.

> The *horse* was the first that marched o'er,
> The foot soon followed a'ter.
> *The Boyne Water* (Child's Ballads, VII. 254).

> Back fly the scenes, and enter foot and *horse;*
> Pageants on pageants in long order drawn.
> *Pope*, Imit. of Horace, II. i. 315.

5. A frame, block, board, or the like, on which something is mounted or supported, or the use of which is in any way analogous to that of a horse. Compare etymology of *easel*.[1]

A kind of *horse*, as it is called with you, with two poles like those of chairmen, was the vehicle; on which is secured a sort of elbow-chair in which the traveller sits. *Richardson*, Sir Charles Grandison, IV, 299. Specifically — (*a*) A vaulting-block in a gymnasium. (*b*) A wooden frame on which soldiers are made to ride as a punishment: sometimes called a *timber mare*. (*c*) A saw-horse. (*d*) A clothes-horse. (*e*) A curriers' board, used in dressing hides. (*f*) In *printing*, a sloping board, with its support, placed on the bank close to the tympan of a hand-press, on which is laid the paper to be printed. (*g*) A support for the cables of a suspension-bridge. (*h*) A board on which the workman sits in grinding the bevels and edges of tools in their manufacture. Also *horsing*.

6. In *mining*, a mass of rock inclosed within a lode or vein, usually of the same material as the "country," or rock adjacent to the lode on each side.

The miner takes his chance of luck. He is generally content if he manages to pay his way along while the ores are poor; to lay by a little for the day when a *horse* or cut makes its appearance in the vein, confident that sooner or later he may strike a rich stretch of ore. Quoted in *Mowry's* Arizona and Sonora, p. 128.

[The entry totals fifteen long columns; the following will suggest the variety of compounds and phrases.]

horse-godmother (hôrs'god"muth-èr), *n.* A large masculine woman, coarsely fat. [Prov. Eng.]

> In woman, angel sweetness let me see;
> No galloping *horse-godmothers* for me.
> *Wolcot*, Peter Pindar's Ode upon Ode (In Continuation).

How do, my dear? Come to see the old man, hay? 'Gad — you've a pretty face, too. You ain't like that old *horse-godmother*, your mother. *Thackeray*, Vanity Fair, xxxix.

horse-gogs (hôrs'gogz), *n.* A kind of wild plum, a variety of *Prunus domestica.*

horse-gowan (hôrs'gou"an), *n.* One of several plants, as *Chrysanthemum Leucanthemum, Matricaria Chamomilla,* and *Taraxacum officinalis.*

horse-gram (hôrs'gram), *n.* A leguminous plant, *Dolichos biflorus,* a native of tropical and subtropical Africa and Asia, extensively cultivated in southern India as a food-plant.

horse-guards (hôrs'gärdz), *n. pl.* 1. A body of cavalry for guards. See *guard.* — 2. [*cap.*] The public office in Whitehall, London, appropriated to the departments under the commander-in-chief of the British army: so called from the two horsemen standing sentry at the gates. — 3. [*cap.*] The military authorities in charge of the war department of Great Britain, in distinction from the civil chief, the Secretary for War.

WEBSTER'S NEW WORLD DICTIONARY OF THE AMERICAN LANGUAGE
College Edition (*Cleveland and New York, 1953 and subsequently revised*)

horse (hôrs), *n.* [*pl.* HORSES (-iz), HORSE; see PLURAL, II, D, 1], [ME. *hors;* AS. *hors, hros;* akin to G. *ross* (OHG. *hros*); prob. IE. base *(s)ker-*, to leap, as also in L. *scurra,* buffoon, entertainer, joker (cf. SCURRILOUS)], 1. a large, strong animal with four legs, solid hoofs, and flowing mane and tail, long ago domesticated for drawing or carrying loads, carrying riders, etc. 2. the full-grown male of the horse; gelding or stallion, as distinguished from a mare. 3. anything like a horse in that a person sits, rides, or is carried on it. 4. a frame on legs to support something; specifically, *a*) a sawing frame. *b*) a clotheshorse. 5. a man: a joking, friendly, or insolent term. 6. [Colloq.], in *chess,* a knight. 7. [Slang], a translation used illegitimately by students in the preparation of their work: also called *trot, pony.* 8. in *gymnastics,* a padded block on legs, used for jumping or vaulting. 9. in *military usage,* mounted troops; cavalry. 10. in *mining,* a mass of earth or rock inside a vein. 11. in *zoology,* any of the horse species, as the zebra, tapir, etc. *v.t.* [HORSED (hôrst), HORSING], 1. to supply with a horse or horses; put on horseback. 2. to place on a man's back or a wooden horse for flogging; hence, 3. to flog. 4. [Slang], to subject (a person) to horseplay; make fun of. *v.i.* to mount or go on horseback. *adj.* 1. of a horse or horses. 2. mounted on horses. 3. large, strong, or coarse of its kind: as, *horse*radish.

[In addition there is a column of phrases and compounds.]

A DICTIONARY OF AMERICANISMS ON HISTORICAL PRINCIPLES
ed. Mitford H. Mathews (Chicago, 1951) 2 vols.

[The following entry is one taken from more than ten broad columns.]

3. b. In less frequent, often obs. or rare, combs.: (1) **horse ail,** some unidentifiable ailment or distemper of horses; (2) **bone limestone,** (see quot.); (3) **book,** a book of information about horses and their diseases; (4) **card,** a currycomb; (5) ***chestnut,** a color like that of a horse chestnut; (6) **dam,** (see quot.); (7) **dance,** an Indian dance in which, app., horses were imitated; (8) **duty,** ?signals or calls blown on a trumpet for a cavalry company; (9) **hunting,** (see quot.); (10) **jog,** designating something slow or old-fashioned; (11) **lawyer,** a lawyer without ability or standing; (12) **piano,** a calliope; (13) ***piece,** a horse drama; (14) **rail,** a horse rack; (15) **rattle,** prob. a bull-roarer; (16) **round-up,** *W.* the bringing together of horses on a ranch; (17) **shedder,** (see quot.), cf. 8. b. (2) below, and see **horse shedding** as a main entry; (18) **smoke,** (see quot.); (19) **trumpet,** ?a very large trumpet.

(1) **1872** HOLMES *poet* iii. 75 Something like horse-ail, very likely — horses get it, you know, when they are brought to city stables. — (2) **1870** *Rep. Comm. Agric.* 551 By leaching and concretion it sometimes forms a singularly irregular, perforated rock, known in Alabama as the 'bored,' and in Mississippi, where it also occurs, as the 'horse-bone,' limestone. — (3) **1643** *Essex Prob. Rec.* I. 30, I give to him my horse booke alsoe a pitchforke. — (4) **1832** *Louisville Pub. Advt.* 3 March, Whittemore's cotton and horse cards.

(5) **1897** MARK TWAIN *Following Equator* 622 (R.), There is every shade of complexion: ebony, old mahogany, horse-chestnut, sorrel. — (6) **1905** *Forestry Bureau Bul.* 61 B. Horse dam. A temporary dam made by placing large logs across a stream, in order to raise the water behind it, so as to float the rear. (N.F.) — (7) **1899** H. B. CUSHMAN *Hist. Indians* 499 Then followed the fun-making dances, such as chicken dance, horse dance. — (8) **1777** *N.J. Archives* 2 Ser. I. 327 A man well acquainted with blowing the trumpet, and capable of teaching the horse duty on that instrument. — (9) **1708** OLDMIXON *Brit. Empire in Amer.* I. (1708) 293 [The Virginians] also have other sorts of Hunting, as Vermine-hunting, and Horse-hunting; the latter is much delighted in by young People, who pursue wild Horses with Dogs, and sometimes without them.

(10) **1853** FOWLER *Home for All* 53, I leave you to either proceed in the old horse-jog mode of building, or adopt this new railroad style. — (11) **1890** *Cong. Rec.* I July 6900/2 If you speak of John McSweeney as a horse lawyer, God knows what will become of Missouri. — (12) **1920** C. R.

Cooper *Under Big Top* 202 The calliope player takes him along on parade and tells him the story of steam, to the accompaniment of the screaming notes of the howling, screeching 'horse piano.' — (13) **1856** *Chi. Democrat* 22 Oct., The stage is so constructed that it can be used to the best advantage for the exhibition of what are termed 'horse pieces.' — (14) **1861** Tallack *Friendly Sk.* 41 On arriving at the meeting-house, the horses are not usually taken out from their vehicles, but merely 'hitched up' to a tree, or 'horse-rail.'

(15) **1858** *Harper's Mag.* June 133/1 A 'horse-rattle' which he was whirling round and round to the disturbance of the town. — (16) **1927** Siringo *Riata & Spurs* 15, I had to attend the horse round-up . . . to brand up the W. B. G. colts. — (17) **1846** Cooper *Redskins* xiv, Your regular 'horse-shedder' is employed to frequent taverns where jurors stay, and drop hints before them touching the merits of causes known to be on the calendars. — (18) **1807** in Pike *Sources Miss.* ii. App. 22 The chief . . . filled a calumet, which several different Indians took from him, and handed the Osages to smoke. This was called the *horse-smoke*, as each person who took the pipe from the chief intended presenting the Osages a horse. — (19) **1850** H. C. Watson *Camp-Fires Revol.* 254 Bill Hurley had also brought with him an old horse-trumpet.

DICTIONARY OF AMERICAN SLANG
ed. Harold Wentworth and Stuart Berg Flexner
(New York, 1960).

horse *n.* 1 A joke, esp. a joke played on a person; a practical joke. *Some c1890 use. Obs. except in the stand.* "horseplay." 2 A literal translation or list of answers used while taking an examination; a pony. *Some c1900 student use.* →3 A diligent, able student; a grind. *Some c1900 student use; still some dial. use. Prob. from the expression* "to work as hard as a horse" *plus* "pony" *or* "horse" *(def. 2).* 4 Meat, specif. corned beef. *Sometimes modified as* "young horse," "red horse," "salt horse," *etc. Some student, USN, and Army use, mainly c1900-c1935.* 5 A thousand dollars; the sum of $1,000. *Some circus use. Perhaps from* "G" *and* "gee-gee." 6 Heroin. 1951: "Then he started on heroin, or 'horse.' " Kinkead, 16. 1952: "So Diane became a junkie, hooked by horse." P. Prescott in N. Y. *Times,* Apr. 29, 25. *Wide addict use. Fairly well known to the general public.* See H. 7 A stupid, rude, stubborn, or contemptible person. *Dial.* 8 A truck; a tractor. *Some farm and truck-driver use.* Cf. iron horse.

Subjects for Discussion

1. Try to discover in what ways Johnson's dictionary was superior to its predecessors; did Johnson have more knowledge, more intelligence, better judgment?

2. It has been said that Johnson learned from Bailey most of what he knew about making a dictionary. Can you find any important principle of making a dictionary illustrated in Johnson but not in Bailey?

3. How does Johnson's notion of usage differ from that of his predecessors? How does his notion of the nature, origin, and growth of language differ from that of earlier writers? From modern writers?

4. Martin thought he was providing a basis for the reform of pronunciation. Is his system of pronunciation clearer to you than earlier ones? Compare it with that of Sheridan and with modern systems of marking pronunciation.

5. How do Bailey, Johnson, and Martin differ in their reliances upon the forces which will determine usage and "refine" or "purify" the language?

6. Compare Noah Webster's etymologies with those of a good modern dictionary.

7. Some dictionaries make a specialty of phrases and compounds, that is, combinations like "tap the admiral" mentioned in the selection "The Way of a Man with a Word" (pp. 26-28), which means something that would not always be inferred from the individual words. Which lexicographers seem to have been alert to the need for phrases in dictionaries?

8. Obviously, one difference between modern and early dictionaries is that the modern dictionaries include more words, new words, and new meanings. Is it also true that many words have apparently died since the eighteenth century? For example, *horse-measure, horse-twitchers,* and *spoke* as a past participle in Bailey do not appear in most modern dictionaries. Why not? *Horsemeat* in Kenrick and Ash has a meaning not now current. Have other words in the early dictionaries disappeared or changed or lost their meanings? How accurately would a comparison of early and recent dictionaries reflect the history of the language?

9. Do the early lexicographers try to indicate the status of the words they enter? For example, Webster labels *widow, v.t.* sense 2 as *unusual.* What other such designations were used, and by which lexicographers?

10. You will find various spellings of the Old English word for *widow,* in some instances by various lexicographers, in some instances by the same lexicographer. Can you make any sense of this confusion? Are the lexicographers careless, indifferent to consistency, using variant forms, or what?

Suggestions for Investigation, Reports, or Brief Papers

1. In the selection from Goold Brown in Section VI, you will find Brown's comment on Webster and a sample of Webster's reformed spelling. How much of Webster's early theories about spelling seem to be reflected in his dictionary?

2. Compare Webster's dictionary in detail with Johnson's. Wherein does Webster seem to be imitating Johnson? Wherein is he violently and deliberately different?

3. Compare the selections from the 1828 and 1848 editions of Webster's dictionary. Are there changes? Can you guess at the reasons for the changes? One fact you may wish to consider is the date of Webster's death.

4. In Webster's time European scholars like Jacob Grimm, Rasmus Rask, and Franz Bopp were laying the foundation for modern understanding of language families and their growth. Is there any evidence that Webster was aware of this research, or does he seem mostly to repeat what Bailey had written a century before?

5. What does Webster say about the importance of following "rules"? Do you find that he follows his own rules?

6. What can you deduce from the spellings of *horror* in the various dictionaries?

7. Write an essay on the adequacy of early lexicographers as etymologists. Check their treatment of individual words — for example, Webster on *husband*.

8. Judging by the dictionary entries, what would you say has been learned about writing definitions since Johnson's day? Compare Johnson's definitions with Webster's and with those in several modern dictionaries.

9. Pick an individual lexicographer, say Kenrick or Sheridan, and try to find out from internal evidence whether he is copying Bailey or Johnson or both.

10. Using modern dictionaries, study the compounds and phrases for *horse*, expressions like *horseplay* and *horse lawyer*. Or better, choose another common word like *plow, road, fish, sea, man*.

11. Your library will probably have a copy of the first edition of the *New International Dictionary*. Compare it with the second edition for words added, words dropped, changes in pronunciation, spelling (*e.g., theatre* and *theater*), or meanings. You might try a number of words related to airplanes in both dictionaries, for example *supersonic*. Write a description of what the editors apparently tried to do in one phase of their revision.

12. A modern dictionary is likely to enter about thirty uses of *horse* in various parts of speech. Coles did not enter the word at all in the sense of a quadruped. Study the growth in usages for one word, at least insofar as the dictionaries reveal this growth. Can you distinguish between growth in the language and growth in the concepts of what a lexicographer should do?

13. On the basis of one of the dictionaries, what can you infer about changes in pronunciation since the eighteenth century?

14. Do the definitions for *horse* in the selection from the dictionary of slang suggest anything about how slang develops or how new meanings develop?

VI. PRESCRIPTIVE GRAMMAR AND USAGE PROBLEMS

While eighteenth-century lexicographers were compiling lists of words, other writers and scholars were working to describe or dictate the uses of language. This section includes discussions of grammar and usage, subjects that could disturb tempers in the eighteenth century as they still can. Much of the disagreement among students of language then, as now, grew from confusions about terms.

The word *grammar* has many uses, some of them now obsolete. It formerly referred to the whole body of writing, particularly the classical writing in Latin and Greek; this meaning survives in the phrase *grammar school*, a school where the curriculum includes elements of everything. From early times, also, it was the name for the way language works; in this sense it was used in the concept of Universal Grammar. The notion was that since grammar had come from God, it was everywhere the same, at least in its fundamental principles; of course some languages might have "bad" grammar, or very little grammar, but such grammar as there was would be God's grammar, and hence universal. This may seem a bit hard on the Chinese, who did not recognize the Christian deity, but at least some eighteenth-century grammatical thinkers took care of that dilemma by doubting that Chinese was a language anyhow. Modern linguists no longer believe in universal grammar in this sense, but they do use the word *grammar* to comprise the way a language works, the way the semantic units (which may or may not be words) are handled so that connected discourse becomes possible. Accordingly, a book which contains such a statement about a language is called a grammar — *Bennett's Latin Grammar, Wright's Old English Grammar.* Such a book is likely to attempt a description of the language and to provide paradigms of the forms to be learned in order to read, write, and speak the language.

Probably from these books grew another use of the word *grammar*, now the most common but not necessarily the most reputable. In the western European tradition, the grammar books were mainly grammars of Latin. Since they were intended as textbooks they informed the student how to use a foreign language correctly and warned him how to avoid using it incorrectly. Early English grammars were based upon these Latin grammars; they continued and even increased the tendency to tell the student how the language should and should not be used. Many were mainly concerned with policing the language, not with understanding it. Accordingly, *grammar* is often used to mean correct or elegant speech as against incorrect or crude speech. In this sense, *he doesn't* is grammatical, *he don't* is ungrammatical, or "bad grammar." This use of the word is so common just now that many people are unaware that there is any other meaning; but careful thinkers and writers about English do not usually use the word in this sense. To describe the problem of the rightness or wrongness of a locution they prefer the word *usage*.

Here we might distinguish between *use* and *usage*. The use of the language readily becomes the language itself. Language probably got started by use; certainly it grew by use. Whatever was said consistently was imitated by others, was learned by children, and was eventually elevated into the standard speech. Thus, at any one time any language will be the distillation of the use of that language during the previous generations. In Latin, one friend, used as the subject, is *amicus* and several friends are *amici;* this is true not because there is a rule or a paradigm for the masculine declension, but because these words, and other similar words, were long used in that way. In English we say *the missile* and not *missile the* because we use the definite article before the word to which it refers and not after it. True, the ancestor of our word *the* was not so used in Old English, but it has come to be, as all other facts of language have come to be, by use.

Thus all language and all languages grow by use and are determined, in the end, by use. But at any one time there may be locutions for which there is no such agreement in use as there is for the position of the definite article in English. Most of these variations pass unnoticed; for instance, a word like *mother* may be pronounced with or without the sound of *r* at the end. The differences, when they are observed at all, are thought of as dialectal, and few people would call either pronunciation "wrong." But about some locutions society has become self-conscious, and these may be branded either wrong or right, at least by purists. Currently, these policemen of the language are likely to say that it is wrong to say *it's me*, to confuse *like* and *as*, or to end a sentence with a preposition. That some of these locutions may have been attested by the best authorities is of course not the point. It so happens that words like *in* and *of* appeared at the ends of sentences in Old English and have ever since, but if anybody does not like them he certainly has the right to object to them and to try to get other people not to use them. If he does object, the preposition at the end of a sentence becomes a matter of usage; similarly the question of whether to say *ain't I, aren't I,* or *am I not* is a matter of usage. Thus *usage*, as a modern student of language employs the word, concerns the questions of right and wrong in language, or as the modern student probably prefers to say, of appropriateness or inappropriateness.

Thus *usage*, as the term is employed in this book and in most modern books on language, is a much more restricted term than *grammar* and refers only to the propriety of certain locutions, usually a rather limited body of locutions, which happen at any one time to be in dispute. Even so it is broader than might at first appear, since it concerns not only matters like the agreement of subject and verb and the use of words like *like*, but also disputed spellings and variant practices in punctuation. In spelling, most matters of usage have become matters of use, but as we have seen in earlier sections, this was not always so. If a student writes *to* for *too* he is using a variant which would have occasioned no comment a few centuries ago, but which has since become so fixed that not even the most liberal writer upon usage would defend him. A few differences remain; one may write *likeable* or *likable* without raising eyebrows, and in many contexts one may write *catalog*. In England one not only can but must write *labour*, but he no longer writes *errour*, which some eighteenth-century lexicographers considered the only correct usage.

Thus this section mainly concerns grammar in the sense of the principles and practices of language, and usage in the sense of correctness or propriety in language. The materials center in the eighteenth century when arguments about usage were many and violent — even more so than they are today — and the course of the argument may reveal much about what is still the most popular concern in language study. The section contains also characteristic observations on some other aspects of language, its history, for example, although most writers who were not concerned with universal grammar were concerned with local usage. In part they were so exclusively concerned because they believed that unless there were rules for language and these rules were enforced, the language would so decay that it would become unusable. If they had known how long language had been growing without such formal rules, they might have been led to wonder if it could not survive without them forever. But they knew little of the history of language and how self-reliant it can be. Their concern provides us with a splendid sample of the continuing battle between authority and currency in determining standards in language.

39. STERLING ANDRUS LEONARD

Correctness and Universal Grammar in the Eighteenth Century

Although scholars in the sixteenth and seventeenth centuries had a lively interest in language, they concentrated on questions of vocabulary and orthography. Grammar and "correct" usage emerged as major problems in the eighteenth century in a flood of pronouncements and rules. Sterling Andrus Leonard, in *The Doctrine of Correctness in English Usage 1700-1800*, University of Wisconsin Studies in Language and Literature, 25 (Madison, 1929), describes the questions and the arguments. He points out that two contrary principles were differentiated in the eighteenth century. "The one assumes the power of reason to remold language completely, and appeals to various principles of metaphysics or logic, or even makes pronouncements on mere individual preference posing as authority, in the endeavor to 'correct, improve, and fix' usage. The other, while admitting the usefulness of purism in recommending what may be regarded as improvements, recognizes language — even cultivated language — as a vastly complicated and often haphazard growth of habits stubbornly rooted . . . adherents of this second principle are primarily interested in studying the facts of usage. . . ." (p. 13.) Although, Leonard points out, eighteenth-century scholars had available sufficient basis for beginning a scientific study of English on this second principle, they generally preferred the first. "The prevailing view of language in the eighteenth century was that English could and must be subjected to a process of classical regularizing." (p. 14.) The following selections present some of Leonard's more specific observations. Footnotes have sometimes been altered to clarify them in their new context or to fit them to the forms of this book. The footnote numbers are those of the original text; because of omissions they are not always consecutive.

Reason building languages. The search for a universal grammar, based on universal reason and settling once for all every question of usage, was based on a different assumption about the origin of language from that of its divine creation. It had been proposed in the seventeenth century that languages were in certain cases made, to fit man's needs, by a popular assemblage for discussion and legislation.[1] Lord Monboddo, more than a century later, has a serious account of the Pelasgi at work modeling the Greek language out of their own speech with some admixture of native materials.[2] To be sure, Beattie contends seriously that the Greek language was not made complete before it was used.[3] But this view is quite reconcilable with the other, since there was always the grammarian, "the greatest of all artists, and next in rank and dignity to the philosophers," [4] to come in afterward, bring the language into form, and reconcile all anomalies.[5]

Robert Baker shows clearly how he conceived this ordering by reason or grammatical logic to have come about: "Why," /47/ he asks, "was Grammar invented, but that for want of it, Men were unable to convey their thought to each other in a clear and distinct Manner? . . . If we neglect those [few rules] we have already, we shall come in Time to understand

---

[1] This is naïvely put in Bishop Wilkins' *Essay toward a Real Character, and a Philosophical Language*, published by order of the Royal Society in 1668, concerning "the Malayan Tongue, the newest in the World": "It was invented or occasioned by a Concourse of Fishermen from Pegu, Siam, Bengala, and other nations at Malacca, where they built the Town of that Name, and agreed upon a distinct Language made up of the easiest Words belonging to each Nation." Bishop John Wilkins, *Works* (London, 1706), Part V, pp. 175-6.

[2] *Origin and Progress of Language* (London, 1774), II, pp. 498-500.

[3] James Beattie, *The Theory of Language* (London, 1787), I, p. 202.

[4] *Ibid.*, II, p. 510.

[5] A rational account of the relation of Greek grammar to the development of the language, as a mere business of codification after the fact, is given in Basil Gildersleeve, *Essays and Studies* (Baltimore, 1890), pp. 137ff.

one another no better than our Ancestors did before the Language was brought into any Form." [6] This is clearly a similar notion to the Parliament of Pegu which Bishop Wilkins conceived for legislating the Malay language into being.

Grammar universal. The idea of a universal grammar, following upon these notions, was of course shaped by them. Such a grammar was to be grounded in "Universal Reason," of which Harris speaks confidently:

> It may afford perhaps no unpleasing speculation, to see how the SAME REASON has at all times prevailed; how there is ONE TRUTH, like one Sun, that has enlightened human Intelligence through every age, and saved it from the darkness both of Sophistry and Error.

And so he defines "GRAMMAR UNIVERSAL; *that Grammar,* which without regarding the several Idioms of particular Languages, *only respects those principles, that are essential to them all.*" [7]

Thus, the article "Grammar" in the first edition of the *Encyclopaedia Britannica,* "supposing a language introduced by custom," defines "grammar as an art" as a just method of furnishing "certain observations called rules, to which the methods of speaking used in this language may be reduced." But there follows this enlightening definition of "grammar as a science": It "examines the analogy and relation between words and things; and thus furnishes a certain standard by which different languages may be compared, and their several excellencies and defects pointed out." This is "Philosophic or Universal Grammar." [8] In the pursuit of this chimera no pains were spared, and its domestication was considered accomplished when Bayly "printed in a larger letter . . . general rules, /48/ in which all languages agree, . . . to distinguish particulars, called idioms." [9] . . .

Reverence for the classical languages. . . . By the eighteenth century the Greek, from being merely one of the seventy-two languages which had sprung up at the dispersion of men from Babel, was given general pre-eminence. In Harris we read that "the *Greek* language . . . is of all the most elegant and complete," and even Latin, upon which Ben Jonson and other writers on grammars drew so heavily, "but a Species of *Greek* somewhat debased." [10] The Romance Languages are naturally held far below even that, being merely vulgar dialects or corruptions of Latin, and "the modern languages, particularly those of Gothic extraction, . . . not near so accurate, and . . . the sound of them . . . much more unpleasant than that of the Greek." On the contrary, a dead language "exists after it ceases to be a living language; and perhaps in greater purity, and with less hazard of corruption, than while it continued to be spoken." [11] Swift gave as one reason for the inferiority of

---

[6] *Reflections on the English Language* (London, 1770), p. 94.

[7] James Harris, *Hermes* (London, 1771), p. x.

[8] *Encyclopaedia Britannica* (London, 1775), p. 728.

[9] Anselm Bayly, *Plain and Complete Grammar* (London, 1772), pp. vi-vii.

[10] *Hermes*, pp. 147-8.

[11] Monboddo, *Origin and Progress* (1774), I, pp. 688-72 — rather a mixed figure. J. L. Moore gives interesting quotations, both praise and blame of English, in *Tudor-Stuart*

English that "the Latin tongue in its purity was never in /49/ the Island." [12] Dr. Johnson is quoted by the *Monthly Magazine,* 1800, as having said, in defence of his Latinisms, ". . . It is, seriously, my opinion, that every language must be servilely formed after the model of some one of the ancient, if we wish to give durability to our works." [13] In keeping with this is Walpole's vigorously expressed opinion of the utter barbarity of the Saxon tongue: ". . . never did exist a more barbarous jargon than the dialect, still venerated by antiquaries, and called *Saxon.* It was so uncouth, so inflexible to all composition, that the monks, retaining the idiom, were reduced to write in what they took or meant to be Latin." [14]

Analogy with Latin. As was inevitable with these views of the origin and nature of language prevailing in the eighteenth century, universal grammar was formed to a purely classical pattern. More than half of Harris' *Hermes* is filled with quotations from Latin and particularly from Greek grammars and rhetorics, and his examples are more frequently from the classics than from English. As a natural result, no English construction is accepted save as it represents, or departs only slightly from, a classical prototype; the only instances of such departure that were tolerated are the use in English of the indefinite article, absent from the Greek — admitted, but given no particular value — and the "natural genders" of English, which are praised by Harris and Lowth as offering scope for personification in noble poetry. Otherwise, only classic patterns and analogues prevail. Dryden's method of testing a doubtful passage in his own writing by turning it into Latin is frequently cited in the eighteenth century.[15] Of the argument that Swift, Addison, and Pope "had scarcely a single rule to direct them," Buchanan writes, "Had they not the Rules of Latin Syntax to direct them?" [16] Lowth requires that in the verb following subjects of various /50/ persons "the second Person takes place of the third, and the first of both"; [17] and this rule is repeated by grammarians down to the 1800 edition of Murray and later.

Bayly, inconsistent as usual, is scornful of Lowth's justification of a phrase "by having recourse to the Saxon; which I should apprehend there is no occasion to do any more than to the Hebrew . . . or to the Latin"; [18] yet he himself uses the analogy of the classics in defence of a point: He overrules Lowth's objection to "awaiting messengers, who if they come, I shall then be able to judge how to act" by saying that the expression is "purely Grecian and Roman" — he quotes Cicero — "And if the phrase is neat and

---

Views, Chapters I-III. [As it was printed the page reference contains an apparent typographical error; Leonard may have intended to write "pp. 668-72."]

[12] Jonathan Swift, *A Proposal for Correcting, Improving, and Ascertaining the English Tongue* (London, 1712), p. 9.

[13] *Monthly Magazine,* IX (1800), p. 150, cited by Fitzedward Hall, *Recent Exemplification of False Philology* (London, 1872), p. 111, n.2.

[14] Horace Walpole, *Historic Doubts on the Reign of King Richard the Third* (London, 1768), p. x.

[15] Dedication of *Troilus and Cressida,* Scott ed. (London, 1883), VI, p. 251.

[16] James Buchanan, *Regular English Syntax* (London, 1767), p. ix.

[17] Robert Lowth, *Short Introduction to English Grammar* (London, 1762), p. 105.

[18] *Plain and Complete Grammar,* 1772, p. 71.

correct in Greek and Latin without a pleonasm, certainly that figure cannot make it improper and mean in English." [19]

As late as 1793, John Shaw justified "John and I was . . ." on the Latin principle of "Zeugma," and applied the same rule for the "conjunction disjunctive" with singular subjects.[20] It is probable that the same principle, though not specifically invoked, lay behind defences of this structure by Greenwood and others earlier. Because it was more commonly known, Latin, not Greek, was alone appealed to in settling such problems as the proper expression of the negative.

As to the case of interrogative pronouns with a preposition following, Webster proposed an analogy with Latin that is inconsistent with his position on other questions: ". . . *'whom* do you speak *to?'* was never used in speaking, as [i.e., so far as?] I can find, and if so, is hardly English at all. There is no doubt, in my mind, that the English *who* and the Latin *qui* are the same word with mere variations of dialect. *Who* in the Gothic and Teutonic, has always answered to the Latin nominative, *qui;* and dative *cui,* which was pronounced like /51/ *qui,* and the ablative *quo;* in the same manner as *whose* has answered to *cujus,* in all genders; *whom* to *quem, quam,* and *what* to *quod.* So that *who* did he speak *to? Who* did you go *with?* were probably as good English, in ancient times, as *cui dixit? Cum quo ivisti?* in Latin. Nay, it is more than probable that *who* was once wholly used in asking questions, even in the objective case; *who* did he marry? until some Latin student began to suspect it bad English, because not agreeable to the Latin rules. At any rate, *whom* do you speak *to?* is a corruption, and all the grammars that can be formed will not extend the use of the phrase beyond the walls of a college." [23] . . . /52/

Differentiation of parts of speech. It was generally understood in the eighteenth-century grammars that the same word may appear as more than one part of speech, many of the authors giving lists of "derivations of substantives from verbs," and the like, often without change of form. But the feeling that there should be differences in terminations for the various parts of speech led to careful scrutiny of all cases that presented themselves to attention. Thus Lowth notes, "the Substantive becomes an Adjective or supplies its place; being pre- /66/ fixed to another Substantive and linked to it by a mark of conjunction: as, "sea-water . . ." [38] He notes no other possibilities. But Webster is clear that "adjectives frequently become nouns," and instances *evil, the good.*[39] Campbell noted a "want of correctness in using *everlasting* as a substantive" in a familiar passage from the Bible. "It

---

[19] *Ibid.,* pp. 82-3. He appears again inconsistent in marking *the same* redundant in "This Moses, whom they refused, the same God did send." (p. 84.)

[20] *Methodical English Grammar,* pp. 130-1.

[23] Noah Webster, *Dissertations on the English Language* (Boston, 1789), pp. 286-7.

[38] *Short Introduction* (Dublin, 1769), p. 158.

[39] Noah Webster, *Grammatical Institute of the English Language* (Hartford, 1784), p. 73. At the foot of the page in the New York Public Library (autograph) copy apparently Webster himself added in ink "the aged, the young, the wise, the foolish, the great."

should be eternity." [40] And *plenty* as an adjective, to be found in "works of considerable merit," he nevertheless brands as a gross vulgarism.[41]

J. Johnson's *Dictionary* says *"Notice* should not be used as a verb [since it is a noun]; the proper expression is *take notice.* Yet Lord Shaftesbury used *noticed,* the participle, and *unnoticed* is very common." [42]

The expressions *had rather, had better,* after being condemned heartily by Johnson, Lowth, Campbell, and others, and riddled through twenty-five pages of logic and analogy by Salisbury,[43] are gallantly rescued in eleven pages of rejoinder by Withers,[44] who concludes by crushing Dr. Johnson's objection under the weight of his own citation, in the *Dictionary,* of "I had rather be a doorkeeper . . ." We shall find Campbell rejecting the phrase, though admitting it is established in usage. Webster contests the usually accepted derivation of the construction, since he finds a weakness in Salisbury's parsing of *would rather,* and adds, "At any rate, the phrases have become good English." [46] Priestley noted as an anomaly, but without censure, *had as lief,* which Salisbury writes *had as lieve* and includes in his condemnation, and which Campbell cites as obsolete under his eighth canon.

Lindley Murray and others insisted always on *but* as a con- /67/ junction followed by the nominative case: "but thou and I," etc.[48] Tooke notes that Dr. Johnson "makes *without* a preposition, an adverb, and a conjunction, but under the head of a Conjunction says, . . . 'Not in use.' " What Johnson wrote in the 1785 edition was "Not in use except in conversation." [49] Tooke concurs, but notes, "It is however used as a *conjunction* by Lord Mansfield, in *Horne's Trial,* p. 56. 'It cannot be read, *without* the Attorney-General consents to it.' " [50] Webster demurs, "I do not see the propriety of discarding *without* [as a conjunction]. The best writers [he cites Chaucer, Congreve, etc.] use *without* in the sense of *unless.* . . . The best speakers use the word in this manner, in common discourse, and I must think with propriety." [51]

The problem of *like* as a conjunction is not discussed in the texts examined. George Harris, the Observer, says it "ought never to be used when it cannot be translated into Latin by the Word *Similis,*" but he is objecting to "had like to have perished." [52] . . . /68/

Differentiation of Shall and Will. As the notable points in the theory and practice of using *will* and *shall* have been adequately explored, it is sufficient

---

[40] George Campbell, *The Philosophy of Rhetoric* (London, 1776), I, pp. 463-4.
[41] *Ibid.,* pp. 473-4.
[42] *The New Royal and Universal Dictionary* (London, 1762), I, pp. 19-20.
[43] William Salisbury, *Two Grammatical Essays* (London, 1768).
[44] *Aristarchus* (London, 1788), pp. 194-204.
[46] *Dissertations* (1789), p. 266 n.
[48] *English Grammar* (York, 1800), p. 119.
[49] Samuel Johnson, *A Dictionary of the English Language* (London, 1785), art. *without.*
[50] John Horne, *A Letter to John Dunning, Esq.* (London, 1778). Included in vol. II of Horne Tooke, *Diversions of Purley* (London, 1829), p. 549 and n.
[51] *Dissertations* (1789), p. 387.
[52] *Observations upon the English Language* (London, 1752), pp. 20-21.

here to refer to Dr. Fries' study and that of Dr. Krapp.[74] These accounts are amply clear in proof that the rule stated by Wallis, elaborated by Lowth and Ward, and copied by almost everybody since, has at no time represented universal cultivated usage. Even Lowth did not, perhaps, observe the rule that "*Will* in the first Person singular or plural, promises or threatens," when he wrote in his introduction, "I will not take upon me to say, whether we have any Grammar, that sufficiently instructs us by use and example." [75] . . . /73/

The expression of the negative. Greenwood begins the battle on the double negative, a struggle prolonged even today on logical principles and in ignorance of the "genius of the language." Having derived *never* from *ne ever*, Greenwood adds: "I cannot here omit an Observation . . . relating to this Expression, *Never so much*, E.G. *A man gives so much as he never gave before.* By inadvertency this Phrase has been used for a Kind of Superlative: Nay, some have blundered on *ever so much*." [55]

The next reference to the question was discovered in Zachary Grey's *Free and Familiar Epistle to W. W.* Noting Mr. Upton's "sneering you upon using two *Negatives*, which he observes make one affirmative," [56] Grey quotes authority for "two *Negatives* don't always make an affirmative, but deny more strongly, as is well known from the *Greek* and *French* languages." [57] The tone of the rest of Grey's letter might suggest that he was rather "sneering" Warburton's scholarship than seriously proposing the foreign analogy. . . . /92/ The usual rule is dogmatically worded by Mennye, "Two negatives may make an affirmative but cannot express a denial," [65] and by Clarke, who says they "absolutely prove what you mean to deny." [66] Withers says the same in effect; but in concrete cases Withers' logic trips him badly: "NOR follows NEITHER and any *other* Negatives. E. G. *He is* NEITHER dead, NOR *indisposed. He is* NOT *dead,* NOR *indisposed. He is* UNwell, NOR *have we any hopes of his* Recovery." [67] He says emphatically that *neither* and *nor* are both negatives; yet he fails to note, as logical grammarians /93/ appear always to have done, that not alone his examples, but the conventionally required *neither* plus *nor*, contravene their principle of the effect of two negatives. . . .

Order of words in sentences. Priestley discovered quite a number of constructions which should not be "split," but most of them he condemned on

[74] Charles C. Fries, "The Periphrastic Future with *Shall* and *Will* in Modern English," *Publications of the Modern Language Association of America*, XL (1925), pp. 963-1024. G. P. Krapp, *The English Language in America* (New York, 1925), II, p. 266.

[75] *Short Introduction* (1762), p. x.

[55] James Greenwood, *An Essay Towards a Practical English Grammar* (London, 1711), p. 158.

[56] Warburton had written "he never asks but to abuse me, nor never talks but to misrepresent me." See John Upton, *Critical Observations on Shakespeare* (London, 1746), p. 316.

[57] Grey, *Free and Familiar Epistle to — W. Warburton* (London, 1750), pp. 28-9.

[65] J. Mennye, *An English Grammar* (New York, 1785), p. 18.

[66] John Clarke, *Rational Spelling Book* (London, 1796), p. 83.

[67] *Aristarchus* (1788), p. 416.

other grounds than logic — usually awkwardness. Two of his objections relating to the "split verb," however, he seems to make for logical reasons, though no grounds are assigned; and as these types of arrangement are still condemned by purists, their first proscription is worth noting: "Though the negative particles follow the auxiliary verb in an interrogative sentence, no other adverbs should be placed there along with them. *Would not then this art have been* . . . Harris's *Three Treatises*"*;* and "When there are more auxiliaries than one, the adverb should be placed after them, immediately before the participle. *Dissertations on the prophecies which have remarkedly been fulfilled* . . . Title page to Dr. Newton's treatise . . . This combination appears very irregular and harsh . . ." The "irregular" apparently implies a grammatical or logical objection. Some common adverbs he allows between /94/ the auxiliaries, as "He has always been reckoned . . ." [70] Webster had obviously no scruples about this kind of separation, as he wrote, " 'I *never* will be seen there,' seems not so elegant; as 'I will *never* be seen there,' " [71] and he cites with approbation, "nor can a selfish heart easily conceive. . . ." [72]

Baker discovered, if he did not invent, what he stigmatized as improper separation of the participle from the adverb modifying it: "So well a bred man, so poorly a painted picture." These might probably have been queried as effectively for awkwardness, without resort to grammatical logic.[72a] We apparently owe to Blair the nice distinction about "what is called splitting of particles, or separating a preposition from the noun which it governs — always to be avoided." [73] His instance is, "Though virtue borrows no assistance from, yet it may often be accompanied by, the advantages of fortune"; and he remarks, "In such instances, we feel a sort of pain, from the revulsion, or violent separation of two things, which by their nature, should be closely united. We are put to a stand in thought; being obliged to rest for a little on the preposition by itself, which, at the same time, carries no significancy, till it is joined to its proper substantive noun." [74]

But the most striking circumstance in this array of censured constructions is that no mention whatever of the "split infinitive" was discoverable, nor was the construction itself observed save once or twice in the authors read. Apparently, it was both a discovery and an aversion of nineteenth century grammarians. /95/

. . . *"Oblique cases of pronouns."* The case of pronouns after linking or copulative verbs, . . . was debated from various angles of Latin analogy, custom, euphony, and conflicting appeals of grammatical logic. Most of the

[70] Joseph Priestley, *The Rudiments of English Grammar* (London, 1769), pp. 180 and 182.

[71] *Grammatical Institute* (1784), p. 85.

[72] *Ibid.* (1804), p. 97.

[72a] *Reflections* (1770), pp. 19-20.

[73] Withers, concurring, attributes to the Bishop of London (Lowth) the counsel that "to split prepositions" is vulgar and inelegant, but I have not located either the phrase or the counsel in Lowth. See *Aristarchus* (1788), pp. 290-2.

[74] Hugh Blair, *Lectures on Rhetoric and Belles Lettres* (Philadelphia, 1793), I, p. 211. Here we have again "particles without meaning" and "nature" appealed to.

writers examined held inflexibly to the Latin rule, and gave considerable lists of "improprieties," from Shakespeare to their contemporaries. Lowth, holding this position, incidentally states that the verb in the infinitive requires always the accusative case of the pronoun after it,[13] and thus opens the brisk controversy on this point which still continues. Most prescriptive grammars insist on "it seems to be he," but the contrary ruling is also to be found.

The side of the observers of custom is, as usual, best stated by Priestley: "All our grammarians say, that the nominative case of pronouns ought to follow the verb substantive [*is* and the like] as well as precede it; yet many familiar forms of speech, and the example of some of our best writers, would lead us to make a contrary rule; or, at least, would leave us at liberty to adopt which we liked best: *Are these the houses? . . . Yes, they are* them. *Who is there? It is* me. *It is* him. *It is not* me *you are in love with.* Addison. *It cannot be* me. Swift. *To that which once was* thee. Prior. *There is but one man that she can have, and that is* me. Clarissa.

"When the word *if* begins a sentence, it seems pretty clear, that no person, whose attention to artificial rules did not put a sensible [i.e. *noticeable*] restraint upon his language, would ever use the nominative case after the verb *to be.* Who would not say, *If it be* me, rather than *If it be* I?

". . . I think no person, who reads the following sentence will question the propriety of the use of the oblique case. '. . . become in some measure *him* . . .' Smith's Moral Sentiments." But Dr. Bryan notes that Priestley himself wrote "It was *we*." [14] /186/

Robert Baker, while praising Congreve as superior to most writers "in Elegance of Stile," contends that to Petulant's "You were the quarrel," Millamant should have been made to answer "I!" "*Me* is wrong. . . . Yet it must be owned there are some Places where the Nominative is required, and where the Word *I*, as having too thin and unsubstantial a Sound, would not do." For "another me" in the same play he proposes another "my-self." A pencil note in the Harvard copy (1770 ed.) comments, "Self alone would do, & be better than myself." Though he admits that oblique cases are frequently used, "even by the better sort of people," Baker's condemnation is characteristically decided: "This is bad English." [15] Here appeals to euphony and to custom are overruled by grammatical logic built on the Latin analogy.

Baker speaks ironically of the "extraordinary correctness" of the use by "inferior Writers" of the forms "It was not *him* they attacked, *us* they slandered," where he erroneously supposed the government to be by the following rather than the preceding verb.[16] Campbell is hoist by precisely this false logic. He writes of this construction, citing one of Priestley's examples: "I shall observe in passing, that one of Priestley's quotations is defensible on a different principle, and therefore not to his purpose. 'It is not

<hr>

[13] *Short Introduction* (1762), pp. 105-6; (1769), p. 132.

[14] *Rudiments*, pp. 104-5; p. 191. W. F. Bryan, "Notes on the Founders of Prescriptive English Grammar," *Manly Anniversary Studies* (Chicago, 1923), p. 386 n.

[15] *Reflections* (1770), pp. 48-50.

[16] *Ibid.*

me you are in love with.' The *me* here is governed by the preposition *with*. 'It is not *with me* you are in love.' Such transpositions are frequent in our language." [17] One wishes Campbell had interpreted the construction of the "omitted relative" in this sentence. Lowth had already analyzed this construction with whatever logic applies, stating that the preposition governs the omitted relative, not the personal pronoun.[18]

A specific comment on "between you and I," in a footnote to Archibald Campbell's *Lexiphanes*, suggests that it was commonly censured: "In the first Edition of this work, I had used the phrase *between you and I*, which tho' it must be /187/ confessed to be ungrammatical, is yet almost universally used in familiar conversation, and sometimes by our best comick writers: see Wycherley's *Plain Dealer*. This very trivial slip, if it be one, has not escaped the diligence and sagacity of the learned and candid Reviewers. One of our worthy labourers in that periodical drudgery has declared this phrase, and a few others, which are only improper in his crazy imagination, to be more offensive to a judicious reader, than all the hard words I had attempted to expose. See Critical Review. His fellow drudge in the Monthly has used me with still less ceremony: 'The author of the Rambler, says he, is censured for writing ill by a person who cannot write at all.' To prove which, he instances this unlucky, *between you and I, old Veteran, I cannot for my heart*. Such are Reviewers, and such are their learned labors . . . I have observed in the Sale of Authors, and I repeat the observation, that our Reviewers, like Sir Roger de Coverly, who would suffer no body to sleep at church but himself, will not suffer an adventurer at the pen to be reprehended, tho' ever so justly, by any but themselves." [19]

In a letter written in 1774, Horace Walpole says, "You will be diverted to hear that a man who thought of nothing so much as the purity of his language, I mean Lord Chesterfield, says, 'you and *me* shall not be well together,' and this not once, but on every such occasion. A friend of mine says, it was certainly to avoid that female inaccuracy of *they don't mind you and I*, and yet the latter is the least bad of the two. He says too, Lord Chesterfield does, that for forty years of his life he never used a word without stopping a moment to think if he could not find a better. How agreeably he passed his time!" [19a]

Interrogative who or whom. Bayly, Priestley, and Webster dissent, in characteristic ways and with varying degrees of certainty, from the usual dictum that the interrogative *whom* must be used when it is governed by a following transitive verb or preposition — *whom is it for, did you see*, etc. Lowth is of course positive for the rule, citing in a footnote violations by /188/ Shakespeare, Dryden, Swift, and Addison.[20] Bayly writes that "in

---

[17] *Philosophy*, I, pp. 438-9 and n.

[18] *Short Introduction* (1762), p. 146, n.

[19] Archibald Campbell, *Lexiphanes* (London, 1767), p. 67 n.

[19a] Letter to Mason, April 17, 1774, Mrs. Paget Toynbee, ed., *Letters of Horace Walpole* (Oxford, 1903-5), VIII, p. 448.

[20] *Short Introduction* (1769), pp. 121-2.

these and the like phrases the ear is so accustomed to *who*, that it will not be reconciled to *whom*, till forced by the judgment" [that is, apparently, forced by Lowth's logic].[21] This "ear is accustomed" is the appeal to usage, stated in fuller form by Priestley: "When the pronoun precedes the verb, or par ticiple by which its case is determined [he does not mention the preposition, though his first example is of that government], it is very common, especially in conversation, to use the nominative case where the rules of grammar require the oblique. As Who *is this* for? Who *should* I meet *the other day but my old friend*. Spectator, No. 32. This form of speaking is so familiar, that I question whether grammarians should not admit it as an exception to the general rule. Dr. Lowth says, that grammar requires us to say, Whom *do you think me to be*. But in conversation we always hear, Who *do you think me to be*." [22]

Buchanan has a remarkable passage amending Touchstone's "who Time ambles withal" and so on. He makes it "with whom Time ambles withal," since *withal* should mean *likewise*, and its use for *with* is an "impropriety." [23] . . . /189/

John Hornsey fell into a curious trap of logical construction in this matter. His rule, common to several grammars, is: "When a relative pronoun comes immediately before a verb, it is in the nominative case." [27] As a result he wrote [28] "Who did you ride with?" This was not corrected on the first *errata* page following page 103, the last of his text; but in a later correction printed on the back of the title page it is squared with Lowth's rule; the dangerous clause "whom I learned with" [29] is made into "with whom I learned," and "The binder is requested to paste page 104 to the end leaf." He failed to do so at least in the Columbia University copy.

The case of the interrogative with a regimen logically determined by a following word was thus debated by all possible principles, but there was a preponderance among the liberal grammarians of satisfaction with the decision of Custom in the matter. The very difficult case of pronouns with a doubtful government roused still more unsettling discussion. . . .

An entertaining discussion was waged over the quotation "Whom do men say that I am?" from the Authorized Translation of the Bible. As might be expected, most of the grammarians who mention it censure it strongly. Bayly, however makes an attempt to justify it: /190/

"The ear, in this place, requires *whom*, and misseth it in a familiar passage, John 9:19, where the translators having gone contrary to the original, the ear is not satisfied: 'Is this your son, *who*, ye say, was born blind?' for, 'is this your son, *whom* ye say, *that* he was born blind?' " [31] Since, however, custom seems to Bayly an insufficient armor, there follows a defence of

[21] *Plain and Complete Grammar* (1772), p. 85.
[22] *Rudiments* (1769), pp. 107-8.
[23] *Regular English Syntax* (1767), pp. 138-9.
[27] *A Short English Grammar* (York, 1793), p. 49, **n.**
[28] *Ibid.*, p. 54, § 4, line 21.
[29] On p. 49, line 3.
[31] *Plain and Complete Grammar* (1772), p. 86.

whom by the analogy of the Greek, and a rather confused attempt to call the verb "an infinitive after the nominative case." [32]

Case of pronouns after as *and* than. This construction caused more uncertainty and controversy than any we have so far considered. Bayly commends Lowth for the rule, common later, that *the same case is required after these conjunctions as before them.*[33] This is repeated as late as Hornsey's grammar, with the examples *"he* writes better than *I; I* love *him* better than *her,* etc." [34] But apparently Bayly had read Lowth carelessly; for, except in the *than whom* construction, Lowth states the rule usually accepted by grammarians today, that the case is governed by whatever words are to be supplied or understood. With this Lowth confutes another of Bentley's emendations of *Paradise Lost* — "others to make such as I," which Bentley had altered to *me* "as the Syntax requires." [35]

Priestley attacked the problem with another theory: "Since it is allowed that the oblique case should follow prepositions; and since the comparative degree of an adjective, and the particle *than* have, certainly, between them, the force of a preposition, expressing the relation of one word to another, they ought to require the oblique case of the pronoun following: so that *greater than me,* will be more grammatical than *greater than I.*" He supposes the objection to the former to be based on the analogy to Latin, which he repudiates. He cites without objection three sentences from Smollett's *Voltaire,* one of /191/ which, "Tell the Cardinal that I understand poetry better than *him,*" is possibly ambiguous when taken out of context.[36]

William Ward, in a passage which gives a fair notion of his folio *Essay on Grammar,* presents both sides of the question and permits either construction: [37] "If the sentences [clauses] are supplied, the mode of expression is conceived to be of one kind; and if the oblique cases are used, the mode is conceived to be of another kind; and therefore the form of expression varies when the mode of estimation does so, although the result of either form amounts to the same thing." Buchanan seems to attempt explaining the same point Lowth has stated, but does not make it clear; he says that " 'You have given him more than *I*' is not good grammar because a Verb or Preposition understood comes between *than* or *as* and the pronoun." [38]

[George] Campbell is mildly astonished at Priestley's position on the case after *than* and *as.* Specifically averring his loyalty to usage, he grants Dr. Priestley the "colloquial dialect, as Johnson calls it," but insists that this proves no more than the prevalent *you was* and "there's the books." He then proceeds in the usual way to explain the ellipsis, using the same quotations

---

[32] *Loc. cit.*

[33] *Plain and Complete Grammar,* pp. 19-20 and n.

[34] *Short English Grammar,* p. 50, with reference to Harrison and Ash.

[35] Lowth, *Short Introduction* (1762), pp. 146-7, n.

[36] *Rudiments,* pp. 106-7.

[37] *Essay on Grammar* (London, 1765), pp. 483-4. In his *A Grammar of the English Language* (York, 1767), pp. 112-13, he lists *than* as sometimes a preposition governing the ablative.

[38] *Regular English Syntax,* p. 217. Cf. pp. 93-4 and 131, where he states that the nominative is always used "when the Verb is not repeated."

from Smollett which Priestley gave, and concludes, "But supposing good use were divided on the present question, I acknowledge that the first and second canons proposed on this subject, would determine me to prefer the opinion of those who consider the aforesaid particles as conjunctions." [40] The ingenious Withers was the only grammarian logical and subtle enough to discover that this whole procedure of supplying a construction after *than* harbors a hideous error: ". . . the Instance adduced by Lowth to corroborate this Hypothesis unfortunately subverts it – *thou are wiser than I am* WISER." [41] /192/

Lowth states that *than whom* alone is correct, since the relative has "reference to no Verb or Preposition understood, but only to its Antecedent, when it follows *than*." [42] . . .

Possessive cases. The remainder of the discussion of case is an account of wavering applications of analogy and logic in the attempt to fix the formation of the possessive or genitive of nouns and pronouns and to determine the uses of the structure. Ben Jonson's grammar states clearly that "the genitive plural . . . is all one with the plural absolute"; [46] and his paradigms give no apostrophe in either singular or plural. No doubt this represented preponderant usage during the seventeenth century. Morris notes that "the general use of the apostrophe in the singular is not often found before the end /193/ of the seventeenth century." [47] Greenwood follows Wallis [48] in stating that "the Genitive Case . . . ends, in Singular and Plural Number, in *s* or *es*." His examples are "Man's Nature, Men's Nature, the Churches Peace." [48a] He adds, "If the Substantive be of the Plural Number, the first *s* is cut off; as the Warriour's Arms . . . for the Warriours's Arms," and emphasizes in a note Wallis' argument that it is the *first s* which is "left out for better Sound's Sake. . . . We have really no distinct Genitive Plural." [49] He notes, as do most of the grammarians, the curious formation of group genitives like "the Queen of England's Crown." [50] We have seen that Wallis uses the apostrophe in this construction and before the *s* in the genitive plural.

The possessive singular form became fairly well established in the course

---

[40] *Philosophy of Rhetoric* (1776), I, pp. 437-9.

[41] *Aristarchus* (1788), p. 408.

[42] *Short Introduction* (1763), pp. 159-60; not in the first edition.

[46] *The English Grammar, The Oxford Jonson*, ed. Herford and Simpson (Oxford, 1925-51), VIII, p. 511.

[47] See Richard Morris, *Historical Outlines of English Accidence* (New York, 1880), p. 81.

[48] Wallis discusses the possessive or genitive of nouns under "*Adjectiva Possessiva*." His specific rule is "*Fit autem à quovis Substantivo (sive singulari sive plurali) addito s (aut es, si necessitas pronunciationis postulaverit)*"; his illustrations are *mans nature, Virgils poems*. Of the *substantivum aggregatum*, he notes the placement of *s* at the end of the phrase; his examples are *The Kings Court . . ., the King of Spain's Court*. This is the first appearance of an apostrophe in his discussion. Johannis Wallis, *Grammatica Linguae Anglicanae* (Oxford, 1674), pp. 69-71.

[48a] James Greenwood, *An Essay Towards a Practical English Grammar* (London, 1711), p. 52.

[49] *Ibid.*, pp. 52-3.

[50] *Ibid.*, p. 54.

of the eighteenth century, but the plural was unfixed from the beginning to the end of the period, as the following citations will illustrate. In the *Many Advantages of a Good Language to any Nation*, a proposal for an Academy (1724), we find *Mens Thoughts*, page 66, and *men's eyes*, page 68. Johnson's *Dictionary* (1755) has in the Grammar: "Genitive masters, plural masters" in the paradigm, "always written with a mark of elision *'s;* winter's severity." It is noted that "collective nouns" are similarly marked; the examples are "the multitude's folly" and "women's passions." But in the next column on the same page, he writes, "Plurals ending in *s* have no genitives; but we say Womens *excellencies,* and *Weigh the* Mens *wits, against the* ladies *hairs.* Pope." [51] /194/ If it were not for the quotation, we might suppose that this statement applied to speech only. Johnson adds, "Wallis proposes Lords' house for house of Lords . . . the mark of elision is improper, for in the Lords' house nothing is cut off," and noting that confusion [apparently in pronunciation] would result between this and "the Lord's house," insists that "house of Lords" is better.[52]

Lowth follows Johnson's account of the derivation of the possessive from the Saxon genitive — though he gives it incorrectly as *is,* a fourteenth-century form — and comes to the same conclusion: ". . . we now always shorten it with an Apostrophe; often very improperly, when we are obliged to pronounce it fully; as, *Thomas's* book." He refutes the derivation from *his,*[53] as does Greenwood. Finally, "When it is a Noun ending in *s,* the sign of the Possessive Case is sometimes not added; as, 'for *righteousness* sake'; nor ever to the Plural Number ending in *s;* as in 'on eagles wings.'" [54]

J. Johnson's *Royal and Standard English Dictionary* (1762) introduces a variation popular with school-children today; the genitive, he says, is formed "by adding *'s* to the nominative . . . generally distinguished by prefixing an apostrophe before or over the *s.*" If any critic had discovered this, he would have had "prefixing" to add to his lists of improprieties.

Priestley duplicates Lowth's account of the Saxon *is* genitive. "Sometimes the additional *s* is suppressed in writing," he says, "as in *Jesus feet,* more commonly by poets. Sometimes the apostrophe is wholly omitted, even after the plural number; tho' in that case, there is no other sign of the genitive case. *A collection of* writers *faults.* Swift's Tale of a Tub, p. 55. *After ten* years *wars.* Swift.

"When, in this and other cases, the terminations of words are such, that the sound makes no distinction between the genitive of the singular and of the plural number; as, *the prince's injuries,* and *princes' injuries.* Humes's Hist., vol. 5, p. 406. /195/ It should seem to be better to decline the use of the genitive in the plural number and say, *the injuries of princes.*[55] He coun-

---

[51] Samuel Johnson, *A Dictionary of the English Language* (London, 1755), *n.p.*
[52] *Ibid.*
[53] Advanced in *Spectator No. 135.*
[54] *Short Introduction* (1762), pp. 26-7.
[55] *Rudiments* (1769), pp. 68-9. I have carefully reproduced the exact punctuation, including the sentence separation and *Humes's,* elsewhere, and in the 1768 ed., p. 69, *Hume's.*

sels the same phrase construction in place of "the army's name, the Commons' vote," because of "harshness of the sound" with the genitive.

Buchanan gives a clear example of the difference between precept and practice. He states an explicit rule for the possessive singular, with many manufactured examples of "false syntax." [56] But these examples were unnecessary trouble, as he himself writes "childrens time" (p. xvii), "readers judgment" (apparently singular), "forms sake" (p. 171). Of the plural he says, "We certainly have a Genitive Plural, though there has been no Mark to distinguish it . . . *warriors arms — arms of the* warriors." He suggests an "apostrophe reversed, *warrior's arms*" as the sign for this. [57] /196/

40. THOMAS DYCHE AND WILLIAM PARDON

Grammar in the Dictionary

Although their dictionary was not among the most distinguished of the eighteenth century, Dyche and Pardon in 1735 established the custom of including a grammatical introduction to the vocabulary. The following excerpts are from this introduction to Thomas Dyche and William Pardon, *A New General English Dictionary; Peculiarly calculated for the Use and Improvement Of such as are unacquainted with the Learned Languages* (Dublin, 1744).

GRAMMAR is that Art or Science that teaches Persons the true and proper Use of *Letters, Syllables, Words* and *Sentences,* in any Language whatever. And though such particular Rules and Observations, as are immediately applicable to one Speech or Tongue, are different from those of another, according to the Mode or Idiom of Speech they are applied to; yet so far as they regard the general Relation, that Things have to their Modes, Qualities, Motions or Passions, all the Languages in the World are exactly the same; for whatever is a Substantive, Verb, &c. in one Language, is the same in any other, though expressed in different Terms or Words. From whence may easily be perceived the Falsity of that vulgar Error among the Generality of People, *viz.* that young Persons are necessitated to learn the *Latin,* or *Lilly's* Grammar, to understand *English,* that is, to spell according to the modern Manner of the best Orthographists, and write coherently and intelligently according to the Use and Phraseology of the most celebrated Authors: For all Grammars of the Latin Tongue are mostly employed to teach the various Terminations, &c. of the Flexions, Modes, Formations, and Words of that Language, a Matter the *English* is no Ways concerned in. But there are indeed some few general Rules and Definitions

[56] *Regular English Syntax* (1767), pp. 124ff., xvii, and 171.
[57] *Ibid.,* pp. 124-5.

in that, as there must be in all other Grammars, which may be universally applied to all Languages, as well *English* as any other. I shall not here enter into a critical Dissertation of each Letter, their Power, Formation, &c. nor divide them into Vowels, Consonants, Mutes, Liquids, &c. neither shall I divide the Language into eight Parts or Distinctions, as is generally done; but into four only, that being sufficient for my present Purpose, which is only to give a general Hint how Grammar may be as effectually applied to the *English* Tongue as to any others. Nor shall I enter into all the Niceties that may be started relating to these four Parts, intending here only a general Direction to know the Coherence between, and Dependence of one Part of a Discourse or Speech on another. And in [1] order to comply with common Custom, as far as possibly I can, I shall call these four Parts by the received Names of a *Noun Substantive*, a *Noun Adjective*, a *Verb*, and a *Particle*. By a Noun Substantive, I mean the plain simple Name of any material or ideal Substance or Thing, upon the Pronunciation whereof an Idea is excited in the Mind of the Hearer what Species of Beings or Things are then intended, without Regard to any inherent or accidental Qualities or Modes that may immediately result from, or belong to that particular Creature or Thing then signified; only observe, that those Names or Words that import the whole Species, are called Nouns Substantives Common, the other Proper: As, when I say *a Man*, the Hearer immediately knows I intend one of the human Species; but if I say *Peter, John*, &c. he knows that some particular Person is meant; but whether he be a tall, or a short Man, a black, or a white Man, a crooked, a straight, a learned, or an ignorant one, &c. he cannot by such bare Nomination possibly imagine; and therefore it is absolutely necessary some peculiar Characteristick should be specify'd, which is some distinguishing Mode or Quality. And this Mode or Quality is what is called a Noun Adjective under which Denomination all Manner of Modes or Qualities are expressed, such as tall, short, black, white, fair, foul, beautiful, ugly, learned, ignorant, sweet, stinking, rough, smooth, &c. The peculiar Property of these Sort of Words, which are called Adjectives, is, that till they are join'd to one or more Substantives, they leave the Sense imperfect and undetermined which, together with what is called the Degrees of Comparison, distinguish them from Substantives: For though there may be two or more Substantives that have the same general Nature, Mode or Quality, yet they differ and are distinguished by the one's being better or worse, &c. fairer or fouler, sweeter or sourer, &c. than the other; and by putting the Termination *er*, or *est*, to the Generality of Words, any *English* Person will immediately, by their Ear, determine whether it is agreeable to the Nature of the Language, to admit of such a Formation; and if it does, they may then assuredly know that Word is that Part of Speech called an Adjective and that some Quality or Mode of some Substance or Subject is designed by such Term or Word, and not the Substance or Subject itself; as for Example, fair, fairer, fairest; sweet, sweeter, sweetest; tall, taller, tallest; strong, stronger, strongest, &c. are Adjectives, by which the Mode or Quality of some Substance or Subject, and not the

Substance itself is intended. It is also to be noted, that Substantives are particular to one Thing or Species only; but Adjectives are universal, and may as well be applied to Beasts, Trees, Flowers, &c. as Men; as, one Horse, Dog, Tree, &c. may be swifter, taller, sweeter, &c. than another; as well as one Man may be taller, &c. than another. There are some few Variations from this general Rule of Formation and Distinction, of which [2] Notice shall be taken hereafter. The third general Head is the *Verb*, under which Term, the Existence, Action, or Passion of the Subject is affirmed, and which it is usual to call by different Appellations; such as, a Verb Substantive, a Verb Active, a Verb Passive; and, again, to subdivide these into Deponents, Neuters, &c. But I shall only inform the Reader, that where-ever, in the following Dictionary, he finds the Letter (V.) standing after any Word, it signifies the Word so mark'd to be a Verb; and then for the Truth of the Assertion, he has nothing more to do but to consider whether the Being, Action, or Passion of something is, or is not, signified by such Word; and if he is not sufficiently acquainted or accustomed with such Words or Reflexions, let him read the Definition adjoin'd, and he will immediately determine, whether the Mark of Signature is right or wrong. And this is the more requisite to be done, because that there are some Instances when the Word itself simply and unapply'd may mean any of the three Parts of Speech, that is, it may be a Substantive, an Adjective, or a Verb, as the word CALM sometimes signifies Substantively, and imports the Absence or Cessation of Storms, and sometimes the Want of a due Degree of Wind at Sea, &c. Sometimes, Adjectively, it signifies a serene or quiet Mind, State, or Condition; and sometimes, Verbally, to appease, settle, or quiet Rage, Passion, Storms, &c. But in general, the Words are as distinct as the Ideas intended; as, *The black Horse runs. The Common-Sewer stinks. The young Child cries*, &c. Here *black, common,* and *young* are *Adjectives,* as expressing some Mode or Quality of their Subjects or *Substantives, Horse, Sewer,* and *Child;* and the Words *runs, stinks,* and *cries,* are *Verbs,* denoting the several Actions of their Subjects or Substantives. The Fourth Class of Words, I call by the general Name of *Particles,* which are occasionally used to make the Sense of the Speaker more full, clear, and intelligible, by expressing the Manner or other Circumstances of the other Words, either by connecting or joining them together, or shewing the Manners or Qualities of them; as, *John and Mary strive earnestly;* here *and, earnestly,* are Particles; *and,* joining the two Substantives *John, Mary; earnestly,* shewing the Mode of their striving or endeavouring to accomplish their Intentions. And where you find these Words in the Dictionary, you will find them mark'd (Part.) to the others you will find (S.) for Substantive; (A.) for Adjective; and (V.) for Verb. . . . /a/

41. JAMES HARRIS

Universal Grammar

> The idea of a universal grammar, that back of all languages is a
> perfect grammar of which individual grammars are corruptions,
> provided the philosophy for much eighteenth-century discussion
> of usage. Harris's discussion of the theory appeared first in 1751;
> the following excerpts are from the third edition of James Harris,
> *Hermes, or A Philosophical Inquiry Concerning Universal Gram-*
> *mar* (London, 1771).

THUS in SPEECH for example — All men, even the lowest, can speak
their Mother-Tongue. Yet how many of this multitude can neither write,
nor even read? How many of those, who are thus far literate, know nothing
of that Grammar, which respects the Genius of their own Language? How
few then must be those, who know GRAMMAR UNIVERSAL; *that
Grammar*, which without regarding the several Idioms of particular Languages, *only respects those Principles, that are essential to them all?*

'Tis our present Design to inquire about this Grammar; in doing which
we shall /11/ follow the Order consonant to *human* Perception, as being
for that reason the more easy to be understood.

We shall begin therefore first from a *Period* or *Sentence*, that combination
in Speech, which is obvious to all, and thence pass, if possible, to those its
primary Parts, which, however essential, are only obvious to a few.

WITH respect therefore to the different Species of Sentences, who is
there so ignorant, as if we address him in his Mother-Tongue, not to know
when 'tis we *assert*, and when we *question*; when 'tis we *command*, and
when we *pray* or *wish?* . . . /12/

. . . WHAT then shall we say? Are Sentences to be quoted in this manner without ceasing, all differing from each other in /14/ their stamp and
character? Are they no way reducible to certain definite Classes? If not,
they can be no objects of *rational* comprehension. — Let us however try.

'Tis a phrase often apply'd to a man, when speaking, that *he speaks his*
MIND; as much as to say, that his Speech or Discourse is a *publishing of
some Energie or Motion of his Soul.* So it indeed is in everyone that speaks,
excepting alone the Dissembler or Hypocrite; and he too, as far as possible,
affects the appearance.

Now the POWERS OF THE SOUL (over and above the meer nutritive)
may be included all of them in those of PERCEPTION, and those of VOLI-
TION. By the Powers of PERCEPTION, I mean the *Senses* and the *Intellect;* by the Powers of VOLITION, I mean in an extended sense, not

only the *Will*, but the several *Passions* and *Appetites;* in short, *all that moves to Action, whether rational or irrational. /15/*

If then the leading Powers of the Soul be these two, 'tis plain that every Speech or Sentence, as far as it exhibits the Soul, must of course respect one or other of these.

If we *assert*, then is it a Sentence which respects the Powers of PER-CEPTION. For what indeed is to *assert*, if we consider the examples above alleged, but *to publish some Perception either of the Senses or the Intellect?*

AGAIN, if we *interrogate*, if we *command*, if we *pray*, or we *wish*, (which in terms of Art is to speak Sentences *interrogative, imperative, precative,* or *optative*) what do we but publish so many different VOLITIONS? – For who is it that *questions?* He that has *a Desire* to be informed. – Who is it that *commands?* He that has a *Will*, which he would have obey'd. – What are those Beings, who either *wish* or *pray?* Those, who feel /16/ certain wants either for themselves, or others.

If then *the Soul's leading Powers* be *the two* above mentioned, and it be true that *all Speech is a publication of these Powers*, it will follow that EVERY SENTENCE WILL BE EITHER A SENTENCE OF ASSER-TION, OR A SENTENCE OF VOLITION. And thus, by referring all of them to one of these two classes, have we found an expedient to reduce their infinitude. /17/

. . . The Extensions of Speech are quite indefinite, as may be seen if we compare /18/ the Eneid to an Epigram of *Martial*. But the *longest Extension*, with which Grammar has to do, is the Extension here consider'd, that is to say a SENTENCE. The great Extensions (such as Syllogisms, Paragraphs, Sections, and complete Works) belong not to Grammar, but to Arts of higher order; not to mention that all of them are but Sentences repeated.

NOW A SENTENCE may be sketch'd in the following description – *a compound /19/ Quantity of Sound significant, of which certain Parts are themselves also significant.*

THUS when I say [*the Sun shineth*] not only the *whole quantity* of sound has a meaning, but *certain Parts* also such as [*Sun*] and [*shineth.*]

BUT what shall we say? Have these Parts again other Parts, which are in like manner significant, and so may the progress be pursued to infinite? Can we suppose all Meaning, like Body, to be divisible, and to include within itself other Meanings without end? If this be absurd, then must we necessarily admit, that there is such a thing as *a Sound significant, of which no part is of itself significant.* And this is what we call the proper character of a WORD. For thus, though the /20/ Words [*Sun*] and [*shineth*] have each a Meaning, yet is there certainly no Meaning in any of their Parts, neither in the Syllables of the one, nor in the Letters of the other.

IF therefore ALL SPEECH whether in prose or verse, every Whole, every Section, every Paragraph, every Sentence, imply a certain *Meaning, divisible into other Meanings*, but WORDS imply a *Meaning, which is not so divisible:* it follows that WORDS *will be the smallest parts of speech,* in as much as nothing less has any Meaning at all. . . . /21/

Concerning the Species of Verbs, and their other remaining Properties.

ALL Verbs, that are strictly so called, denote (a) Energies. Now as all *Energies* are *Attributes,* they have reference of course to certain *energizing Substances.* Thus it is impossible there should be such Energies, as *To love, to fly, to wound,* &c. if there were not such beings as Men, Birds, Swords, &c. Farther, every Energy doth not only require an Energizer, but is necessarily conversant about some *Subject.* For example, if we say, *Brutus loves* — we must needs supply — loves *Cato,* /173/ *Cassius, Portia,* or some one. *The Sword wounds* — i.e. wounds *Hector, Sarpedon, Priam,* or some one. And thus is it, that every energy is necessarily situate between two Substantives, an Energizer which is *active,* and a Subject which is *passive.* Hence then, if the Energizer lead the sentence, the Energy follows its character, and becomes what we call VERB ACTIVE. — Thus we say *Brutus amat, Brutus loves.* On the contrary, if the passive Subject be principal, it follows the character of this too, and then becomes what we call a VERB PASSIVE. — Thus we say, *Portia amatur, Portia is loved.* It is in like manner that the *same Road* between the summit and foot of the same mountain, with respect to the summit is *Ascent,* with respect to the foot is *Descent.* Since then every Energy respects an Energizer or a passive Subject; hence the Reason why every Verb, whether active or passive has in language a necessary re /174/ ference to some *Noun* for its *Nominative Case* (b). /175/

42.

A Pocket Dictionary

The following excerpt is from the introduction to an anonymous dictionary which was mainly a compilation from its predecessors but which was interesting for its appeal to less sophisticated users, "Youth of both Sexes, the Ladies and Persons in Business": *A Pocket Dictionary or Complete English Expositor* (London, 1753).

Thus the English tongue, which was anciently pure British or Welsh, became a mixture of a little British, a great deal of Latin, a yet far greater part of Anglo-Saxon, some Danish, and abundance of Norman French: But since that time the revival of arts and sciences has added greatly to its imbellishment. These have introduced a vast variety of words from the Greek, Latin, Italian and modern French; our poets have added grace and harmony to their numbers, and our prose writers have strengthened and improved their periods, by selecting the most musical, expressive, and strongest terms from every known language; so that notwithstanding its being a compound of such heterogeneous ingredients, it is become the most copious and significant of any in Europe, adapted to all subjects, and expressive of every sentiment with elegance and propriety.

We come next to give a short account of what parts the English tongue consists, taken in a grammatical light: By which it will appear to be extremely simple in its composition, and free from the many rules which render others difficult to the learner: For though grammar is the same in all languages, except the Chinese, (if that may deservedly be call'd one) yet every grammar ought to be adapted to the genius of the language to which it gives precepts.

Without going into a critical dissertation on the letters of the alphabet, and the proper manner of dividing syllables, we shall immediately enter upon the parts of speech, which may be distinguished into these four. Nouns substantives, Nouns adjectives, Verbs, and Participles. /7/

43. JAMES BUCHANAN

On Verbs

> The following is from *The British Grammar, or an Essay in Four Parts on Speaking and Writing the English Language Grammatically and Inditing Elegantly*, 3rd ed. (London, 1779). Published originally in 1760, the work is generally attributed to James Buchanan.

A Verb is rightly defined a Part of Speech, which affirms some Attribute, with the Designation of Time, Number, and Person, expressing Being, Doing, or Suffering, or the Want of them, or the like. But it may be observed, that these supposed Affections of Verbs, namely, Number and Person, cannot be called a Part of their Essence, nor indeed of any other Attribute; being, in fact, the Properties not of Attributes, but of Substances. And as to Time, though joined to the Affirmation of the Verb, it is not the Verb's Signification, at least it can never become its principal Signification, because the same Time may be denoted by different Verbs; as in the Words, teacheth and learneth; and different Times by the same Verb, as in the Words, teacheth and taught; neither of which could happen, were Time any Thing more than a mere Concomitant. /104/

1. A Verb being the most necessary or essential Part, or, as it were, the very Soul of a Sentence, without which it cannot subsist; whatever Word with a Noun Substantive makes full Sense, or a Sentence, is a Verb; as, Man

exists, Trees grow, John laughs, Boys play, &c. But that Word which does not make full Sense, with a Substantive, is not a Verb.

2. Whatever Word has any of the Persons, *I, them, you, he, she, it, we, ye, they,* or that has *it shall* before it, and make Sense, is a Verb, otherwise not.

How many Voices has a Verb? A Verb has two Forms or Voices, the Active and Passive; the Active Voice expresses what is done or acted by the Nominative or Person, the Agent, before it; as, I burn, I hate.

The Passive Voice, which is made by the helping Verb *am,* expresses what is done to, or suffered by the Nominative or Person, the Patient, before it; as, I am burned, I am hated.

How many Numbers has a Verb? A Verb has two Numbers, the Singular and Plural.

How many Persons? A Verb has three Persons in each Number, viz. I, thou or you, and he, she, and it, for the Singular; we, ye or you, and they, for the Plural.

What is Mood? The Mood, Mode, or Manner of a Verb, denotes the several Volitions or Affections of the Mind.[17] */105/*

How many Moods are there? A Verb has four Moods, the Indicative, Subjunctive, Imperative, and Infinitive.

What do you mean by the Indicative Mood? The Indicative Mood, which is first both as to Dignity and Use, declares, affirms, or denies positively; as, I love, I do not love; or else doubts and asks a Question; as, Do I burn? Do I not burn? */106/*

[17] Most Writers of English Grammar implicitly follow one another in asserting, that our Tongue has no Moods, which, added to our supposed Want of Variety of Tenses or Times, is manifestly affirming, that the English Language is nothing superior to that of the Hottentots; and that the wisest and most respectable Body of People upon the Face of the Globe, own a Language which is incapable of ascertaining their Ideas, or of exhibiting the Soul, and its various Affections. They have been led to this Notion, from our Verbs having no Diversity of Termination, like those in the Latin. But as a great Variety of Terminations are not absolutely necessary to the Existence of Moods, why is our Grammar to be modelled by that of the Latin, especially in Cases where there is not the least Trace of Analogy?

All Languages share, in some Measure, one common Identity; but then each of them has its peculiar Diversity. For Instance, the Latins mark the Distinction of Tense and Mood by a great Variety of Terminations, which Trouble we being happily freed from, easily denote by a few auxiliary Verbs; and that too in a Manner so complete, that our Verb surpasses, for the Variety of its Conjugation, the Latin Verb, and is equal even to that of the Greek. The Truth is, no Language can exist without a proper Number of Moods and Tenses, else it must be so extremely equivocal and ambiguous as to become in a great Measure unintelligible. Our Language therefore, is no Way defective in Mood and Tense: But the Difference betwixt it and the Latin in that Particular, is clearly this, that we, as before observed, express perfectly by, as it were, a few additional Beginnings and some Endings, what the Latins do by a Diversity of Terminations; nay, by what (if it were to be accounted any Defect) the Greek, the most elegant Language that ever existed, has recourse to; I mean that of expressing the several Modes and Distinctions of Time by Variations in its Verb, some of which are at the Beginning as well as at the End.

44. ROBERT LOWTH

Forms for Past Time and the Participle

Robert Lowth (1710-87), famous in his day for his lectures on Hebrew poetry, composed in Latin, brought to his pronouncements upon grammar his authority as professor at Oxford University and later bishop of London. The following selection, including a long footnote, is from *A Short Introduction to English Grammar*, second edition (London, 1764); the first edition was 1762.

There are not in English so many as a Hundred Verbs, (being only the chief part, but not all, of the Irregulars of the Third Class,) which have a distinct and different form for the Past Time Active and the Participle Perfect or Passive. The general bent and turn of the language is towards the other form; which makes the Past Time and the Participle the same. This general /105/ inclination and tendency of the language seems to have given occasion to the introducing of a very great Corruption: by which the Form of the Past Time is confounded with that of the Participle in these Verbs, few in proportion, which have them quite different from one another. This confusion prevails greatly in common discourse, and is too much authorised by the example of some of our best Writers.[7] /106/ Thus it is said, *He*

[7] "He would *have spoke*." Milton, P. L. x. 517.
"Words *interwove* with sighs found out their way." P. L. i. 621.
"Those kings and potentates who *have strove*." Eiconoclast. xvii.
"And to his faithful servant *hath* in place
Bore witness gloriously." Samson Ag. ver. 1752.
"And envious darkness, ere they could return,
Had stole them from me." Comus, ver. 195.
Here it is observable, that the Author's MS. and the First Edition have it *stolne*.
"And in triumph *had rode*." P. R. iii. 36.
"I *have chose* / This perfect man." P. R. i. 165.
"The fragrant brier *was wove* between." Dryden, Fables. /106/
"I will scarce think you *have swam* in a Gondola." Shakespeare, As you like it.
"Then finish what you *have began*,
But scribble faster, if you can." Dryden, Poems, Vol. II. p. 172.
"And now the years a numerous train *have ran*;
The blooming boy is ripen'd into man." Pope's Odyss. xi. 555.
"*Have sprang*." Atterbury, Serm. I. 4.
"*Had spake — had began*" — Clarendon, Contin. Hist. p. 40 & 120.
"The men *begun* to embelish themselves." Addison, Spect. No. 434.
Rapt into future time the hard *begun*." Pope, Messiah.
And, without the necessity of rhyme:
"A second deluge learning thus *o'er-run*,
And the Monks finish'd what the Goths *begun*." Essay on Criticism.
"Repeats you verses *wrote* on glasses." Prior.
"Mr. Milton *has wrote*." Addison, Preface to his Travels. "He could only com-

begun, for *he began; he run,* for *he ran; he drunk* for *he /107/ drank:* the Participle being used instead of the Past Time. And much more frequently the Past Time instead of the Participle; as, *I had wrote, it was wrote,* for *I had written, it was written; I have drank,* for *I have drunk; bore,* for *born; chose* for *chosen; /108/ bid,* for *bidden; got,* for *gotten;* &c. This abuse has been long growing upon us, and is continually making further incroachments; as it may be observed in the example of those Irregular Verbs of the Third Class, which change *i* short into *a* and *u;* as, Cling, clang, clung; in which the original and analogical form of the Past Time in *a* is almost grown obsolete; and, the *u* prevailing instead of it, the Past Time is now in most of them confounded with the Participle. The Vulgar Translation of the Bible, which is the best standard of our language, is free from this corruption, except in a few instances; as *hid* is used for *hidden; held,* for *holden,* frequently; *bid,* for *bidden; begot,* for *begotten,* once or twice; in which, and a few other like words, it may perhaps be allowed as a Contraction. And in some of these, Custom has established it beyond recovery: in the rest it seems wholly inexcusable. The absurdity of it will be plainly perceived in the example of some of these Verbs, which Custom has */109/* not yet so perverted. We should be immediately shocked at *I have knew, I have saw, I have gave,* &c. but our ears are grown familiar with *I have wrote, I have drank, I have bore,* &c., which are altogether as barbarous. */110/*

mand his voice, which *was broke* with sighs and sobbings, so far as to bid her proceed." Addison, Spect. No. 164.

"No civil broils *have* since his death *arose*." Dryden, on O. Cromwell.

"Illustrious virtues, who by turns *have rose.*" Prior.

"*Had* not *arose.*" Swift, Battle of Books: and Bolingbroke, Letter to Wyndham, p. 233. /107/

"The Sun *has rose,* and gone to bed,
Just as if Partridge were not dead." Swift.

"This nimble operator will *have stole it.*" Tale of a Tub, Sect. ix.

"Some philosophers *have mistook.*" Ibid. Sect. ix.

"That Diodorus *has* not *mistook himself* in his account of the date of Phintia, we may be as sure as any history can make us." Bentley, Dissert. on Phalaris, p. 98.

"Why, all the souls that were, were forfeit once;
And He, that might the 'vantage best *have took,*
Found out the remedy." Shakespear, Meas. for Meas.
        "Silence

Was took ere she was ware." Milton, Comus.

"Into these common-places look,
Which from great authors I *have took.*" Prior, Alma.

"A free Constitution, when it has *been shook* by the iniquity of former administrations." Bolingbroke, Patriot King. p. III.

"Too strong to *be shook* by his enemies." Atterbury.

"Ev'n there he should *have fell.*" Prior, Solomon.

"Sure some disaster *has befell:*
Speak, Nurse; I hope the Boy is well." Gay, Fables.

45. LINDLEY MURRAY

Rules for Writing

> Lindley Murray, an American, produced in 1795 an authoritarian grammar which was to be the most popular textbook for many years. The following selections are from the thirty-first edition of his *English Grammar, Adapted to the Different Classes of Learners* (York, 1818).

OF VERBS

Section I. Of the nature of Verbs in general.

A VERB is a word which signifies to BE, to DO, or to SUFFER; as, "I am, I rule, I am ruled."

Verbs are of three kinds; ACTIVE, PASSIVE, and NEUTER. They are also divided into REGULAR, IRREGULAR, and DEFECTIVE.

A Verb Active expresses an action, and necessarily implies an agent, and an object acted upon: as, to love; "I love Penelope."

A Verb Passive expresses a passion or a suffering, or the receiving of an action; and necessarily implies an object acted upon, and an agent by which it is acted upon: as, to be loved; "Penelope is loved by me."

A Verb Neuter expresses neither action nor passion, but being, or a state of being: as, "I am, I sleep, I sit." /70/

OF PROPRIETY

1. Avoid *low expressions*: such as, "Topsy turvy, hurly burly, pellmell; having a month's mind for a thing; currying favour with a person; dancing attendance on the great," &c.

"Meantime the Britons, left to shift for themselves, were forced to call in the Saxons for their defence." The phrase *"left to shift for themselves,"* is rather a low phrase, and too much in the familiar style to be proper in a grave treatise. /276/

PERSPICUITY, &C.

The *fifth* rule for the strength of sentences is, *to avoid concluding them with an adverb, a preposition, or any inconsiderable word.*

Agreeably to this rule, we should not conclude with any of the particles, *of, to, from, with, by.* For instance, it is a /306/ great deal better to say, "avarice is a crime of which wise men are often guilty," than to say, "Avarice is a crime which wise men are often guilty of." This is a phraseology which all correct writers shun; and with reason. For as the mind cannot help resting a little, on the import of the word which closes the sentence, it must be disagreeable to be left pausing on a word, which does not, by itself, produce any idea.

For the same reason, verbs which are used in a compound sense, with some of these prepositions, are, though not so bad, yet still not proper conclusions of a period: such as, *bring about, lay hold of, come over to, clear up*, and many other of this kind; instead of which, if we can employ a simple verb, it always terminates the sentence with more strength. Even the pronoun *it*, should, if possible, be avoided in the conclusion: especially when it is joined with some of the prepositions; as, *with it, in it, to it*. We shall be sensible of this in the following sentence. "There is not, in my opinion, a more pleasing and triumphant consideration in religion, than this, of the perpetual progress which the soul makes towards the perfection of its nature, without ever arriving at a period *in it*." How much more agreeable the sentence, if it has been so constructed as to close with the word *period!*

Besides particles and pronouns, any phrase, which expresses a circumstance only, always appears badly in the rear of a sentence. We may judge of this by the following passage: "Let me therefore conclude by repeating, the division has caused all the mischief we lament; that union alone can retrieve it; and that a great advance towards this union, was the coalition of parties, so happily begun, so successfully carried on, and of late so unaccountably neglected, to say no worse." This last phrase, "to say no worse," occasions a falling off at the end. The proper disposition of such circumstances in a sentence, requires attention, in order to adjust them so as shall consist equally with the perspicuity and the strength of the period. . . . /307/ Though necessary parts, they are, however, like irregular stones in a building, which try the skill of an artist, where 50 place them with the least offence. But it must be remembered, that the close is always an unsuitable place for them. Notwithstanding what has been said against concluding a period with an adverb, &c. this must not be understood to refer to such words, when the stress and significancy of the sentence rest chiefly upon them. In this case they are not to be considered as circumstances, but as the principal objects; as in the following sentence: "In their prosperity, my friends shall never hear of me, in their adversity, always." Here, *"never"* and *"always"* being emphatical words, were to be so placed as to make a strong impression. /308/

46. NOAH WEBSTER

Spelling and Grammar

Noah Webster became bankrupt as a lawyer, fared but poorly as a teacher, and was never repaid for the time he spent preparing dictionaries. But through much of his life he lived comfortably on the proceeds of his "blue-backed speller," which appeared in 1789. By 1818 he boasted of sales of more than five million — approximately the population of the United States in 1800 — and that was only the beginning.

The following selections include samples from the speller and from other comments by Webster on grammar and language. The first is from "the revised impression" of *The American Spelling Book; Containing the Rudiments of the English Language, for the Use of the Schools in the United States* (Hartford, Conn., 1820). Webster marks some vowels by a system of his own; for clarity, the marks have been omitted, as has the first part of Table 38.

TABLE XXXVIII

Words in which *ch* have the sound of *k*.

char ac ter	pen ta teuch	sep ul cher	tech nic al
al chy my	an cho ret	brach i al	lach ry mal
mach in ate	sac char ine	syn chro nism	mich ael mas
chor is ter	chron i cle	or ches ter	och i my
chi me ra	pa ro chi al	cha mel ion	tri bec chus
chro mat ic	me chan ic	ca chex y	cha lib e ate
a nach ro nism	syn ec do che	pyr rhich i us	am phib ri chus
mel an chol y	chro nol o gy	chi rog ra phy	cho rog ra phy
chro nom e ter	the om a chy	an ti bac chus	cat e chet ic al
bac chan al ian	cat e chu men	ich thy ol o gy	*/95/* . . .

EXPLANATION

Of the PAUSES *and other* CHARACTERS *used in* Writing

A comma (,) is a pause of one syllable — A semicolon (;) two — A colon (:) four — A period (.) six — An interrogation point (?) shows when a question is asked; as, *What do you see?* An exclamation point (!) is a mark of wonder or surprise; as, *O the folly of sinners!* — This pause of these two points is the same as a colon or a period, and the sentences should usually be closed with a raised tone of voice.

( ) A parenthesis includes a part of a sentence, which is not necessary to make sense, and should be read quicker, and in a weaker tone of voice.

[ ] Brackets or Hooks, include words that serve to explain a foregoing word or sentence.

- A Hyphen joins words or syllables; as, *sea-water*.

' An Apostrophe shows when a letter is omitted, *us'd* for used. */150/*

Less successful than the "blue-backed spellers" were some of Webster's attempts to reform spelling — although many of the spelling changes he advocated have since been accepted. The following is from his *An Essay on the Necessity, Advantages and*

Practicability of Reforming the Mode of Spelling . . . (Boston, 1789), taken from *Dissertations on the English Language,* Scholars' Facsimiles and Reprints (Gainesville, Florida, 1951).

. . . Several attempts were formerly made in England to rectify the orthography of the language.* But I apprehend their schemes failed of success, rather on account of their intrinsic difficulties, than on account of any necessary impracticability of a reform. It was proposed, in most of these schemes, not merely to throw out superfluous and silent letters, but to introduce a number of new characters. Any attempt on such a plan must undoubtedly prove unsuccessful. It is not to be expected that an orthography, perfectly regular and simple, such as would be formed by a "Synod of Grammarians on principles of science," will ever be substituted for that confused mode of spelling which is not established. But it is apprehended that great improvements may be made, and an orthography almost regular, or such as shall obviate most of the present difficulties which occur in learning our language, may be introduced and established with little trouble and opposition.

The principal alterations, necessary to render our orthography sufficiently regular and easy, are these:

1. The omission of all superfluous or silent letters; as *a* in *bread.* Thus *bread, head, give, breast, built, meant, realm, friend,* would be spelt, *bred, hed, giv, brest, bilt, ment, relm, frend.* Would this alteration produce any inconvenience, any embarrassment or expense? By no /394/ means. On the other hand, it would lessen the trouble of writing, and much more, of learning the language; it would reduce the true pronunciation to a certainty; and while it would assist foreigners and our own children in acquiring the language, it would render the pronunciation uniform, in different parts of the country, and almost prevent the possibility of changes.

2. A substitution of a character that has a certain definite sound, for one that is more vague and indeterminate. Thus by putting *ee* instead of *ea* or *ie,* the words *mean, near, speak, grieve, zeal,* would become *meen, neer, speek, greev, zeel.* This alteration could not occasion a moments trouble; at the same time it would prevent a doubt respecting the pronunciation; whereas the *ea* and *ie* having different sounds, may give a learner much difficulty. Thus *greef* should be substituted for *grief; kee* for *key; beleev* for *believe; laf* for *laugh; dawter* for *daughter; plow* for *plough; tuf* for *tough; proov* for *prove; blud* for *blood;* and *draft* for *draught.* In this manner *ch* in Greek derivatives, should be changed into *k;* for the English *ch* has a soft sound, as in *cherish;* but *k* always a hard sound. Therefore *character, chorus, cholic, architecture,* should be written *karacter, korus, kolic, arkitecture;* and were they thus written, no person could mistake their true pronunciation.

* The first by Sir Thomas Smith, secretary of state to Queen Elizabeth: Another by Dr. Gill, a celebrated master of St. Paul's School in London: Another by Mr. Charles Butler, who went so far as to print his book in his proposed orthography: Several in the time of Charles the first; and in the present age, Mr. Elphinstone has published a treatise in a very ridiculous orthography.

Thus *ch* in French derivatives should be changed into *sh; machine, chaise, chevalier*, should be written *masheen, shaze, shevaleer;* and *pique, tour, oblique*, should be written *peek, toor, obleek.*

3. A trifling alteration in a character, or the addition of a point would distinguish different sounds, without the substitution of a new character. Thus a very small stroke across *th* would distinguish its two sounds. A point over a vowel, in this manner, *à*, or *ò*, or *ī*, might answer all the purposes of different letters. And for the dipthong [sic] *ow*, let the two letters be /395/ united by a small stroke, or both engraven on the same piece of metal, with the left hand line of the *w* united to the *o*.

These, with a few other inconsiderable alterations, would answer every purpose, and render the orthography sufficiently correct and regular. . . . /396/

It will perhaps surprize my readers to be told that, in many particular words, the modern spelling is less correct than the ancient. Yet this is a truth that reflects dishonor on our modern refiners of the language. Chaucer, four hundred years ago, wrote *bilder* for *builder; dedly* for *deadly; ernest* for *earnest; erly* for *early; brest* for *breast; hed* for *head;* and certainly his spelling was the most agreeable to the pronunciation.* Sidney wrote *bin, examin, sutable*, with perfect propriety. Dr. Middleton wrote *explane, genuin, revele*, which is the most easy and correct orthography of such words; and also *luster, theater*, for *lustre, theatre.* In these and many other instances, the modern spelling is a corruption; so that allowing many improvements to have been made in orthography, within a century or two, we must acknowledge also that many corruptions have been introduced. /400/

> By the time of his dictionary in 1828, Webster had modified some of his views on spelling, but he advocated spellings customary in America over British spellings. The following is from the introduction to *An American Dictionary of the English Language* (New York, 1828), 2 vols.

From the period of the first Saxon writings, our language has been suffering changes in orthography. The first writers, having no guide but the ear, followed each his own judgment or fancy; and hence a great portion of Saxon words are written with different letters, by different authors; most of them are written two or three different ways, and some of them, fifteen or twenty. To this day, the orthography of some classes of words is not entirely settled; and in others, it is settled in a manner to confound the learner and mislead him into a false pronunciation. Nothing can be more disreputable to the literary character of a nation, than the history of English orthography, unless it is that of orthoepy.

1. The Saxon diphthong *æ*, which probably had a specific and uniform sound or combination of sounds, has been discarded and *ea* generally sub-

---

* In Chaucer's life, prefixed to the edition of his works 1602, I find *move* and *prove* spelt almost correctly, *moove* and *proove*.

stituted in its place, as *bræth*, breath. Now *ea* thus united have not a uniform sound, and of course they are no certain guide to pronunciation. In some instances, where the Saxon spelling was not uniform, the modern orthography follows the most anomalous and difficult, instead of that which is regular. Thus the Saxons wrote *fæther* and *fether*, more generally the latter, and the moderns write *feather*.

2. The letter *g* in Saxon words, has, in many English words, been sunk in pronunciation, and either wholly lost, or it is now represented by *y* or *w*. Thus *dæg*, or *dag*, has become *day; gear* is *year, bugan* is *bow*, and *fæger* is *fair*. . . . /10/

5. In a vast number of words, the vowel *e* has been discarded as useless; as in *eggs* for *egges; certain* for *certaine; empress* for *empresse; goodness* for *goodnesse*. This is an improvement, as the *e* has no sound in modern pronunciation. But here again we meet with a surprising inconsistency; for the same reason which justifies this omission, would justify and require the omission of *e* final in *motive, pensive, juvenile, genuine, sanguine, doctrine, examine, determine*, and a multitude of others. The introduction of *e*, in most words of these classes, was at first wrong, as it could not plead any authority in the originals; but the retaining of it is unjustifiable, as the letter is not merely useless, but in very numerous classes of words, it leads to a false pronunciation. Many of the most respectable English authors, a century ago or more, omitted *e* in such words as *examin, determin, famin, ductil, fertil, definit*, &c. but these improvements were afterwards rejected to the great injury of orthography. In like manner, a final *e* is inserted in words of modern coinage, as in *alumine, chlorine, chloride, oxyde*, &c. without the least necessity or propriety. . . .

7. Soon after the revival of letters in Europe, English writers began to borrow words from the French and Italian; and usually with some little alteration of the orthography. Thus they wrote *authour, embassadour, predecessour, ancestour, successour;* using *our* for the Latin termination *or*, and the French *eur*, and writing similar words, in like manner, though not of Latin or French original. What motive could induce them to write these words, and *errour, honour, favour, inferiour*, &c. in this manner, following neither the Latin nor the French, I cannot conceive. But this orthography continued down to the seventeenth century, when the *u* began to be rejected from certain words of this class, and at the beginning of the last century, many of these words were written, *ancestor, author, error*, &c. as they are now written. But *favor, honor, labor, candor, ardor, terror, vigor, inferior, superior*, and a few others, were written with *u*, and Johnson introduced this orthography into his dictionary. Nothing in language is more mischievous than the mistakes of a great man. It is not easy to understand why a man, whose professed object was to reduce the language to some regularity, should write *author* without *u* and *errour* and *honour* with it! That he should write *labour* with *u* and *laborious* without it! *Vigour*, with *u*, and *vigorous, invigorate*, without it! *Inferiour, superiour*, with *u*, but *inferiority*, and *superiority*, without it! Strange as it is, this inconsistency

runs through his work, and his authority has been the means of continuing it, among his admirers, to this day.

In this country, many of our best writers have rejected the *u* from all words of this class, and reduced the whole to uniformity. This is a desirable event; every rejection of an anomaly being a valuable improvement, which sound judgment approves, and the love of regularity will vindicate and maintain. I have therefore followed the orthography of General Washington, and the Congress of the United States, of Ash in his Dictionary, of Mitford in his History of Greece, &c.

. . . 10. Johnson introduced *instructer*, in the place of *instructor*, in opposition to every authority which he has himself adduced to exemplify his definitions; Denham, Milton, Roscommon, Locke, Addison, Rogers, and the common version of the Scriptures. But what is more singular, this orthography, *instructer*, is contrary to his own practice; at least, in *four* editions of his Rambler which I have examined, the word is uniformly written *instructor.* The fact is the same with *visitor*.

This is a point of little importance in itself, but when *instructor* had been from time immemorial, the established orthography, why unsettle the practice? I have in this word and in *visitor* adhered to the old orthography. There is not a particle of reason for altering *instructor* and *visitor* which would not apply to *collector, cultivator, objector, projector*, and a hundred other words of similar termination.

11. Most of these and some other inconsistencies have been of long continuance. But there are others of more recent date, which admit of no apology, as they are changes from right to wrong. Such is the change of the old and correct orthography of *defense, expense, offense, pretense*, and *recompense*, by substituting *c* for *s* as in defence. This change was probably made or encouraged by printers, for the sake of avoiding the use of the old long *s;* but since this has been discarded, that reason no longer exists. The old orthography, *defense*, &c. is justified, not only by the Latin originals, but by the rule of uniformity; for the derivatives are always written with *s, defensive, extensive, offensive, pretension, recompensing.* . . .

13. In like manner, *dispatch*, which had, from time immemorial, been written with *i*, was changed into *despatch*, on the wonderful discovery, that the word is derived from the French *depêcher*. But why change one vowel and not the other? If we must follow the French, why not write *despech*, or *depech?* And why was this innovation limited to a single word? Why not carry the change through this whole class of words, and give us the benefit of uniformity? Is not *disaster* from the French *desastre?* Is not *discharge* from *decharger?* Is not *disarm* from *desarmer?* Is not *disobey* from *desobeir?* Is not *disoblige* from *desobliger?* Is not *disorder* from *desordre?* The prefix *dis* is more properly English than *de*, though both are used with propriety. But *dispatch* was the established orthography; why then disturb the practice? Why select a single word from the whole class, and introduce a change which creates uncertainty where none had existed for ages, with-

out the smallest benefit to indemnify us for the perplexity and discordance occasioned by the innovation?

It is gratifying to observe the stern good sense of the English nation, presenting a firm resistance to such innovations. Blackstone, Paley, Coxe, Milner, Scott and Mitford, uniformly use the old and genuine orthography of *instructor, visitor, sceptic* and *dispatch*. /11/

> The following examples of Webster's views on grammar and usage are taken from his *Rudiments of English Grammar: Being an Introduction to the Second Part of the Grammatical Institute of the English Language* (Hartford, Conn., 1790).

What is English Grammar? The art of speaking and writing the English language correctly, according to rules and general practice.

Where are the rules of the language to be found? In the language itself.

Give an instance of a rule in the English language. If we speak of more things than one, we add an *s* or *es* to the name of the thing; as *two books, four boxes*, where *s* is added to *book*, and *es* to *box*. . . . /5/

Why do we not always follow rules?

Because language is made by practice and when practice differs from rule, it is better to follow practice than attempt to alter it, which is difficult and often impossible.

What is meant by practice?

The general custom or manner of speaking in a nation.

When people differ in practice, how shall we know which is right?

By examining the language itself to find some rule or reason in one practice, to give it the preference.

Give an example.

Some people say *housen* instead of *houses*. To find which is right, look to the general rule, which is, to speak of many things by adding *s* or *es* to the name, as *tree, trees; pen, pens; horse, horses; church, churches;* therefore it is the best practice to add *s* to *house*, and say *houses*. /6/

. . . There are some nouns in English, that have a plural termination, which are really in the singular, and are followed by verbs in the singular. Such are *news, pains, odds, victuals, alms, bellows, gallows,* and sometimes *wages. Means* is used in both numbers, and sometime *pains*. /35/

EXAMPLES

"What *is* the *news*," General Practice.

"Much *pains was* taken." General Practice.

"Great *pains was* taken." Pope.

"It *is odds;* what *is* the *odds?*" General Practice.

"The *victuals is* good." General Practice.

"We had such very fine *victuals* that I could not eat *it*." Swift.

"He gave *much alms*." Bible. . . .

"This *is* a *means*," General Practice, and almost all good writers. . . .

"In one hour *is* so great *riches* come to nought." Bible. /36/

. . . A Collection of Improper and vulgar expressions, found in various authors or heard in conversation.

Improper Expressions	*Corrected*
I had as goods go.	I may as well go.
He lives *opposite* the Coffee house.	Opposite to.
I am done.	I have done.
He has got to learn.	He has to learn or *must* learn.
You will *write* him often.	Write to him.

But when an object follows the pronoun, the preposition may be omitted; as, you will write him word. —

His wives fortune.	His wife's fortune.
There are many persons *acquire* to themselves. (Shenstone.) /44/	Who acquire.
It is a year *ago since* he left town.	It is a year since.
I will lay down.	Lie down.

Perhaps we must give way to practice in the use of this word.

His master *learns* him.

Teaches him is better; but *learns* is used in the same sense by Spenser and Shakespear; it is so used by most people in England and America, and Johnson admits it as good English.

Thee *is*, thee *does*, thee *thinks*.	Thou *art, dost, thinkest*.
He *dares not go*.	He dare not go.
He *needs not learn*.	He need not learn.

Dare and *need*, when helping verbs, have not *s* in the 3d person. He *dares* or *needs* not go, is as bad English as he *cans not* or *wills not go*. But when they are transitive verbs, they are regular in the 3d person, as *he dares me, he needs courage*.

I should *have went*.	Have gone.
Different *to*.	From.

Ingenious and *ingenuous* are often confounded. The first signifies *able, skilful*; the last, *frank, candid*.

If, in case he should.	*If* alone, or *in case*.

this is tautology.

Arrive *to*.	*As* is generally better. /45/
Come *here* and go *there*, and *where*, are you going? are too well established to be amended in practice. . . .	Strictly, come hither, go thither, whither are you going.
Where did he come from — I came from *there* — he went from *here*, will never be corrected.	Strictly, *whence* came he — He came from *thence*, he went from *hence*.
It was *of* a Friday.	On Friday.
These kind, *these* sort.	*This* kind, *this* sort.
"You must know, says Will, the *reason is because*, they consider every animal as a brother or sister in disguise." (Spect.)	The reason is that.

Improper Expressions	*Corrected*
To *account for the reason.*	To give the reason.

"The reason of this may be *accountable* from the decline of social affections." (Shenstone.) Barbarous English.

| He *enjoys* a bad state of health — *enjoy* is used in a good sense. | Suffers. /46/ |
| *Equally the same.* tautology. | *Equally, or the same;* |

Either separately, but not both.

| She is *of all others,* the most beautiful. | The most beautiful of all. |

"The largest cities are the most vicious *of all others.*" (Shenstone.)

I *expect* it *was.*	I *believe* it was. Expect refers to futurity, I expect it *will be.*
He thinks *like* you do.	As you do.
A *pair* of bars or stairs.	A set of bars, a flight of stairs.
Considerable of a sum.	A considerable sum.
He went *on* board.	Aboard.
I admire to ride.	I am pleased or delighted.
He is going *past.*	Going by.

Perhaps *gone past,* may be correct; but *going past* is barbarous.

Better than half.	*More* than half.
Bred and born.	Born and bred.
The ship will fail *in all* next week.	*Some time* next week.
To abide the decision.	Abide *by* the decision.
An hour by sun.	The sun an *hour high.* /47/
If I mistake not, I think so and so.	

Mistake and *think* should not be used together. A man may doubt of the *thing* thought of, but not of his *thinking* of it.

He will *set* down.	Sit down.
He *sat* himself down.	He *seated* himself, or sat down.
He *is* home.	He is at home.
In *eminent* danger.	Imminent.
One shilling *per* yard, *per* pound, *per* day, &c.	One shilling *a* yard, *a* pound, *a* day (more correct and concise.)
I *propose* to go.	Purpose to go.

A great fault and very common. *Propose* a plan is good — but *purpose* is the word to express *intention.*

Him and me went.	He and I went.
'Tis them, or him, or her.	'Tis they, or he, or she.
Their *pulse* beat together.	*Pulses* — This word has a plural.
He can neither *read* nor *write.*	Neither *write* nor *read.*

It is needless to use *write* after *read,* for if a man cannot *read,* he cannot *write.*

Great *quantities* of horses and cattle.

Numbers; for *quantity* expresses bulk — *number* should be applied to seperate [sic] articles.

Improper Expressions	*Corrected*
To profit *of*.	By. /48/
The *manner* is *thus*.	The manner is *this* — for *thus* implies the manner.
Computed *to*.	At.
To *wreck* malice.	To wreak malice.
They *both* met.	They met — *both* is superfluous.
In comparison *of*.	With.

The verb compare may be followed by *with* or *to*.

Such persons *whose* names are under-written.	*Those* persons *whose* — *Such* requires *as*.
Every *one* of them *are*.	Is.
I *never* expect to receive the profits.	I do *not* expect *ever* to receive —
With *that* zeal *as* he wished.	With *such* zeal *as*; or *that* zeal *which*.

This was common in Sir Willian [sic] Temple's time; but is not the modern practice.

He wrung off the bird's neck.	Bird's head.
The *attempt* is *impracticable*.	The *thing intended* may be *impracticable*; but not the *attempt*.
A strange sort of *a* man.	Omit *a*.
Whenever he sees me, he *always* enquires after your welfare.	*Whenever* means at *all* times *when*; *always* is therefore superfluous.
Independent *on*.	Independent *of*.
Situated *to* the east side.	On. /49/
There is *nothing* scarce.	*Scarcely* any thing.
There is *almost* nothing.	*Scarcely*, or *hardly* any thing.
Never so much.	*Ever so* much.
Time immemorial.	*From* time immemorial.
These folk.	These folks.
This is the last time I *shall* write.	This is the last time of my writing — or the last time I purpose to write.
Such another person.	Another such person.
The preference *of*.	*To* — and sometimes *before*.
What you mention is *impossible to do*.	What you mention is *impossible*.
The *design* is *in order to* explain — (Tautology.)	The design is to explain, or it is in order to explain.
To be revenged *of* a man.	On.

On is generally to be preferred, except when speaking of the *crime* or *fault* to be revenged, when *of* or *for* may be employed.

It is very true *what* you say — (very ungrammatical.)	What you say is very true.
Agreeably to his orders.	*Agreeable* to his orders.
Previously to this.	*Previous* to this. /50/
Consistently with his promise.	*Consistent* with his promise.
I heard of the *law being* passed.	I heard of the *law's being* passed.
It occasioned the *book being* read.	It occasioned the *book's being* read.
Had it been now existing.	Were it now, or if it were now.
I *intended* to *have* written.	I intended to write.

Improper Expressions	*Corrected*
He was so ill that every one imagined he *would have died*.	Imagined he would die.
Need *for* assistance.	Need *of*.
Averse *from*.	To. "My aversion *to* popery (Middleton.) /51/

47. CHARLES M. INGERSOLL

Punctuation: The Colon

By the nineteenth century many writers considered grammar and usage in considerable detail. The following is from Charles M. Ingersoll, *Conversations on English Grammar* (New York, 1821).

OF THE COLON

The Colon is used to divide a sentence into two or more parts, less connected than those which are separated by a semicolon; but not so independent as separate distinct sentences.

The Colon may be properly applied in the three following cases.

1. When a member of a sentence is complete in itself, but followed by some supplemental remark, or further illustration of the subject: as, "Nature felt her inability to extricate herself from the consequences of guilt: the gospel reveals the plan of Divine interposition and aid." "Nature confesseth some atonement to be necessary: the gospel discovers that the necessary atonement is made."

"Great works are performed, not by strength, but perseverance: yonder palace was raised by single stones; yet you see its height and spaciousness."

"In faith and hope the world will disagree;
"But all mankind's concern is charity:
"All must be false that thwart this one great end;
"And, all of God, that bless mankind or mend."

2. When a semicolon, or more than one, have preceded, and a still greater pause is necessary, in order to mark the connecting or concluding sentiment: as, "As we perceive the shadow to have moved along the dial, but did not perceive it moving; and it appears that the grass has grown, though nobody ever saw it grow: so the advances we make in knowledge, as they consist of such insensible steps, are only perceivable by the distance." /346/

"A Divine Legislator, uttering his voice from heaven; an almighty governor, stretching forth his arm to punish or reward; informing us of perpetual rest prepared hereafter for the righteous, and of indignation and wrath awaiting the wicked: these are the considerations which overawe the world, which support integrity and check guilt."

3. The Colon is commonly used when an example, a quotation, or a speech, is introduced: as, "The Scriptures give us an amiable representation of the Deity, in these words: 'God is love.'" "He was often heard to say: 'I have done with the world, and I am willing to leave it.'"

The propriety of using a colon, or semicolon, is sometimes determined by a conjunction's being expressed, or not expressed: as, "Do not flatter yourselves with the hope of perfect happiness; for there is no such thing in the world."

"Where grows? — where grows it not? If vain our toil,
"We ought to blame the culture, not the soil:
"Fix'd to no spot is happiness sincere;
"'Tis no where to be found, or ev'ry where." /347/

48. JOSEPH E. WORCESTER

Orthography

> Webster's assistant, and later his great rival, was Joseph E. Worcester (1784-1865) from whose *A Comprehensive and Explanatory Dictionary of the English Language . . .* (Boston, 1831), the following is taken. Webster's and Worcester's dictionaries became the basis of the "War of the Dictionaries," which echoed down through much of the nineteenth century, although the war was promoted by the publishers, more than the lexicographers.

Much care has been taken with regard to Orthography, a subject which presents considerable difficulty; and, in order to adjust the spelling of many words which are written differently, an examination has been made of several of the best English dictionaries, and regard has also been had to usage and to analogy. With respect to several classes of words hereafter noticed, the orthography of this book has been nearly conformed to that of Dr. Webster's Dictionary; but there are various words to which Dr. Webster has given a new orthography, that will be found here in their usual form.

"Dr. Johnson's Dictionary," says Mr. Nares, "has nearly fixed the external form of our language." Before the publication of that Dictionary, the orthography of the English language was very unsettled; and notwithstanding the influence which that great work had in producing uniformity, the diversities, even now, are numerous; more so, doubtless, than is supposed by those who have not turned their attention particularly to the subject. Two of the most noted diversities are found in the two classes of words which end in the syllables *ic* or *ick*, and *or* or *our*; as in the words *musick, publick, favour, honour*. Dr. Johnson, in accordance with the general usage of his predecessors, spelled these classes of words with the *k* and *u*.

With respect to the *k*, though it is still retained, in the class of words referred to, in the recent editions of Johnson's Dictionary, and also in those of Sheridan, Walker, Jones, and Jameson, yet in most of the other English dictionaries which have been published since that of Johnson, it is omitted; as it is, also, by Dr. Rees and Mr. Fulton in their miniature abridgements of /*xv*/ Johnson. Walker, although he retains it in his Dictionary, yet, in his remarks upon it, decides against it, and observes, that "the omission of it is too general to be counteracted, even by the authority of Johnson." But general usage, both in England and America, is now so strongly in favor of its omission, that it is high time it was excluded from the dictionaries. It is, however, retained in monosyllables; as, *stick, brick;* and in words ending in *ock;* as, *hemlock, hillock.* The verbs *frolic, mimic,* and *traffic,* which Dr. Webster exempts from his general rule, and writes with the *k*, stand, in this Dictionary, without it, as they do in those of Dyche (17th edition, 1794), Perry, Rees, Maunder, &c.; but in forming the past tenses and participles, the *k* must be used; as *trafficked, trafficking,* &c.

The question respecting the letter *u*, in words ending in *or* or *our*, is attended with more difficulty. Though the tendency to its exclusion has long been gaining strength, yet its omission is far from having become so general as that of the *k*. Dr. Johnson himself does not retain it in all the words in which consistency with this rule would require it; for though he writes *anterior* and *interior* with the *u*, he writes *posterior* and *exterior* without it. Some of the English dictionaries, which have been published since that of Johnson, scrupulously follow him in generally retaining the *u*, yet they omit it in the words in which he omitted it; but the greater part of the more recent English dictionaries carry the omission much further than Johnson did, and restrict the use of it to a small number of words, chiefly of two syllables. Entick excludes it from all words of the class in question which are derived directly from the Latin, but retains it in the following words, which have a different origin, namely, *behaviour, demeanour, enamour, endeavour, harbour, neighbour, parlour, saviour, succour, tabour;* also *arbour* (which is derived remotely from the Latin); and *armor* and *savor* he gives in both forms. Dr. Ash gives many of the words derived from the Latin both ways, but seems to prefer the omission of the *u*, according to the system of Entick. Dyche, Barclay, Fulton and Knight, Enfield, and Maunder, also Rees and Fulton in their respective abridgements of Johnson, retain the *u* in the words above enumerated, and also in the following twenty words of two syllables (except that Dyche and Barclay omit it in *ardour*, and Barclay and Fulton and Knight, in *tremour*), which are of Latin origin, namely *ardour, candour, clamour, clangour, dolour, favour, fervour, flavour, fulgour, honour, humour, labour, adour, rigour, rumour, splendour, tremour, valour, vapour,* and *vigour;* also in words derived from these, as *disfavour, dishonour, favourable, honourable:* but the dissyllables *error, horror,* and *terror,* as well as all the original and uncompounded words of more than two syllables, they write without the *u;* as, *inferior, emperor,* &c. Dr. Webster extends the omission not only to those words which are of Latin origin but also to all the others above enumerated. If we turn from the diction-/xvi/ aries, in order to inquire what is the general usage of those who write the language, we shall find it in a very unsettled state. Many exclude the *u* altogether from the final syllable of the whole class of words in question; yet a greater number, doubtless, retain it in a part of them; but few of these, however, have probably settled very definitely, in their own minds, to what words they would limit it.

Such diversities being found in the dictionaries and in usage, it becomes a question of some difficulty to be determined, what course it is most advisable to adopt; for there is no one against which respectable authorities may not be cited. But as the omission of the *u*, in many words in which it was retained by Johnson, has now become the established usage; as a tendency to further omission has long been gaining strength; as an entire exclusion is now supported by some good authorities; and as a partial omission is attended with inconvenience, on account of the difficulty of fixing the limit, the Compiler of this Dictionary has, after considerable hesitation, decided on an entire exclusion of the *u* from the whole class of words in question. If any, however, are dissatisfied with this course, they can supply the deficiency with respect to the words which are not of Latin origin, according to the system of Entick; or, together with these, they can include also the words of two syllables above enumerated, which are derived from the Latin, according to the manner of Dyche, Barclay, and others. . . . /xvii/

In some cases, words are so variously affected by etymology, analogy, authority, and general usage, that it is difficult to determine what orthography is best supported. This is the fact with respect to the words *abridgment* or *abridgement*, *aught* or *ought*, *base* or *bass* (in music), *connection* or *connexion*, *controller* or *comptroller*, *contemporary* or *cotemporary*, *despatch* or *dispatch*, *diocese* or *diocess*, *divest* or *devest*, *duchy* or *dutchy*, *holyday* or *holiday*, *gaol* or *jail*, *instructer* or *instructor*, *judgment* or *judgement*, *marquis* or *marquess*, *loadstone* or *lodestone*, *loadstar* or *lodestar*, *meagre* or *meager*, *naught* or *nought*, *pumpkin* or *pompion*, *sceptic* or *skeptic*, *strew* or *strow*, *thresh* or *thrash*, *wave* or *waive* (to put off), *woe* or *wo*, *yelk* or *yolk*, and various others.

There is a class of words which have, in their derivation, a two-fold origin, from the Latin and the French languages, and are indifferently written with the first /345/ syllable *en* or *in*, the former being derived from the French, and the latter from the Latin. With respect to some of these, it is difficult to determine which form is best supported by usage. This is the fact in relation to the words *enclose* or *inclose*, *enquire* or *inquire*, and *ensure* or *insure*. A few of these words, respecting which the two forms are about equally authorized, are placed in the left hand column in each mode, and stand in a corresponding manner in the Dictionary; but those which are not repeated under the two initial letters *E* and *I*, stand with the orthography which is most approved, placed in the left hand column.

There are some words, of which the present established orthography is at variance with the most approved dictionaries. This is true with respect to the words *chemistry*, *chemist*, *chemical*, *reindeer*, and *scythe*. The orthography of these words which is here countenanced, though different from that best supported by the dictionaries, is the one which is now established by general usage.

Notwithstanding the orthography of the word *show* is uniformly supported as here exhibited by the best dictionaries, and also best corresponds to its pronunciation; yet the other form, *shew*, maintains its ground by a usage quite as common with the best authors.

The two different modes of spelling a few of the words in the Vocabulary, are in established usage, and one is to be preferred to the other according to the sense in which the word is used; as, for example, the orthography of *flour* instead of *flower*, though not recognised by Johnson, is now well established, when the word is used to denote *the edible part of corn*; also the orthography of *dye* instead of *die*, in the sense of *color* or *to tinge with color*, is in common and good use; yet the forms *flower* and *die* are unquestioned, when the words are used in other senses.

With respect to the word *mosquito* or *musquetoe*, which appears in such a variety of forms, the spelling here preferred, though little supported by the dictionaries, is used in works of science. The form of *mosquito* is the orthography of the Spanish and Portuguese languages, from which the word is derived, and the one made use of with respect to various geographical places, to which the term is applied. */346/*

49. GOOLD BROWN

Nineteenth-Century Controversy about Grammar

> Goold Brown (1791-1857), a Massachusetts pedagogue and a writer of moderately popular textbooks, composed *The Grammar of English Grammars* (Boston, 1850-1851), which probably runs to more than a million words; the selections below are taken from the fifth edition, "revised and improved," 1860. Brown was one of the last of the older grammarians — learned, critical, voluble, picayune, and vitriolic. To parody his own style one might say that his monumental industry was exceeded only by his monumental conceit. He warred especially with Samuel Kirkham, perhaps because Kirkham's textbooks greatly outsold Brown's.

Lily says, "Grammatica est recte scribendi atque loquendi ars;" that is, "Grammar is the art of writing and speaking correctly." . . . [He] not improperly placed writing first, as being that with which grammar is primarily concerned. For it ought to be remembered, that over any fugitive colloquial dialect, which has never been fixed by visible signs, grammar has no control;

and that the speaking which the art or science of grammar teaches, is exclusively that which has reference to a knowledge of letters. It is the certain tendency of writing, to improve speech. And in proportion as books are multiplied, and the knowledge of written language is diffused, local dialects, which are beneath the dignity of grammar, will always be found to grow fewer, and their differences less. There are, in the various parts of the world, many languages to which the art of grammar has never yet been applied; and to /22/ which, therefore, the definition or true idea of grammar, however general, does not properly extend. And even where it has been applied, and is now honoured as a popular branch of study, there is yet great room for improvement: barbarisms and solecisms have not been rebuked as they deserve to be. . . . /23/

All languages, however different, have many things in common. There are points of a philosophical character, which result alike from the analysis of any language, and are founded on the very nature of human thought, and that of the sounds or other signs which are used to express it. When such principles alone are taken as the subject of inquiry, and are treated, as they sometimes have been, without regard to any of the idioms of particular languages, they constitute what is called General, Philosophical, or Universal Grammar. But to teach, with Lindley Murray and some others, that "Grammar may be considered as *consisting of two species*, Universal and Particular," and that the latter merely "applies those general principles to a particular language," is to adopt a twofold absurdity at the outset.* For every cultivated language has its particular grammar, in which whatsoever is universal, is necessarily included; but of which, universal or general principles form only a part, and that comparatively small. . . . /25/

. . . Hence the need that an able and discreet grammarian should now and then /29/ appear, who with skillful hand can effect those corrections which a change of fashion or the ignorance of authors may have made necessary; but if he is properly qualified for his task, he will do all this without a departure from any of the great principles of Universal Grammar. He will surely be very far from thinking, with a certain modern author, whom I shall notice in an other chapter, that, "He is bound to take words and explain them as he finds them in his day, *without any regard to their ancient* construction and application." — Kirkham's Gram., p. 28. [Pre-

---

* Horne Tooke eagerly seized upon a part of this absurdity, to prove that Dr. Lowth, from whom Murray derived the idea, was utterly unprepared for what he undertook in the character of a grammarian: "Dr. Lowth . . . with the best intention in the world, most assuredly sinned against his better judgment. For he begins most judiciously, thus — 'Universal grammar explains the principles which are common to *all* languages. The grammar of any particular language *applies* those common principles to that particular language.' And yet, with *this clear truth* before his eyes, he boldly proceeds to give a *particular* grammar; without being himself possessed of one single principle of *universal* grammar. — *Diversions of Purley*, Vol. 1, p. 224. [Brown was presumably quoting from John Horne Tooke, *Epea Pteroenta; or, The Diversions of Purley* (Philadelphia, 1806.)] If Dr. Lowth discredited his better judgement in attempting to write an English grammar, perhaps Murray, and his weaker copyists, have little honoured theirs, in supposing they were adequate to such a work . . ."

sumably Samuel Kirkham, *English Grammar in Familiar Lectures*, 2nd ed. (New York, 1829).] The whole history of every word, so far as he can ascertain it, will be the view under which he will judge of what is right or wrong in the language which he teaches. Etymology is neither the whole view nor yet to be excluded from it. I concur not, therefore with Dr. Campbell, who, to make out a strong case, extravagantly says, "It is *never from an attention to etymology*, which would frequently mislead us, but from custom, the only infallible guide in this matter, that the meanings of words in present use must be learnt." *—Philosophy of Rhetoric*, p. 188. [Presumably the American edition of George Campbell (Philadelphia, 1818).] Jamieson, too, with an implicitness little to be commended, takes this passage from Campbell; and, with no other change than that of "learnt" to "learned," publishes it as a corrollary of his own. *— Grammar of Rhetoric*, p. 42. [Alexander Jamieson, *A Grammar of Rhetoric and Polite Literature*, presumably from the American edition (New Haven, 1820).] It is folly to state for truth what is so obviously wrong. Etymology and custom are seldom at odds; and when they are, the latter can hardly be deemed infallible . . . /30/

[Lindley] Murray was an intelligent and very worthy man, to whose various labours in the compilation of books our schools are under many obligations. But in original thought and critical skill he fell far below most of "the authors to whom," he confesses, "the grammatical part of this compilation is *principally indebted for its materials;* namely Harris, Johnson, Lowth, Priestley, Beattie, Sheridan, Walker, Coote, Blair, and Campbell." *—Introd. to Lindley Murray's Gram.*, p. 7. [Presumably the fourth American edition of *An English Grammar* (New York, 1819)] . . . From the very first sentence of his book, it appears that he entertained but a low and most erroneous idea of the duties of that sort of character in which he was about to come before the public.† He improperly imagined, as many others have done, that "little can be expected" from a modern grammarian, or (as he chose to express it) "from a *new compilation*, besides a careful selection of the most useful matter, and some degree of improvement in the mode of adapting it to the understanding, and the gradual progress of learners." *— (op. cit.*, p. 5.) As if, to be a master of his own art — to think and write well himself, were no part of a grammarian's business! . . . /41/

. . . It will be found on examination, that what this author [Kirkham] regarded as *"all the most important subject-matter of the whole science"* of *grammar*, included nothing more than the most common elements of the orthography, etymology, and syntax, of the English tongue — beyond which his scholarship appears not to have extended. Whatsoever relates to deriva-

---

† For this there is an obvious reason, or apology, in what his biographer states, as "the humble origin of his Grammar"; and it is such a reason as will go to confirm what I allege. This famous compilation was produced at the request of *two or three young teachers,* who had charge of a *small female school* in the neighbourhood of the author's residence; and nothing could have been more unexpected to their friend and instructor, than that he, in consequence of this service, should become known the world over, as *Murray the Grammarian.* . . .

tion, to the sounds of the letters, to prosody (as punctuation, utterance, figures, versification, and poetic diction,) found no place in his "comprehensive
system of grammar;" nor do his later editions treat any of these things amply
or well. In short, he treats nothing well; for he is a bad writer. Commencing
his career of authorship under circumstances the most forbidding, yet receiving encouragement from commendations bestowed in pity, he proceeded,
like a man of business, to profit mainly by the chance; and without acquiring either the feelings or the habits of a scholar, soon learned by experience
that, "It is much better to write than (to) starve." — (*op. cit.*, p. 89). It is
cruel in any man, to look narrowly into the faults of an author who peddles
a school-book for bread. The starveling wretch whose defence and plea
are poverty and sickness, demands, and must have, in the name of humanity,
an immunity from criticism, if not the patronage of the public. Far be it
from me, to notice any such character, except with kindness and charity.
Nor need I be told, that tenderness is due to the "*young*;" or that noble results sometimes follow unhopeful beginnings. These things are understood
and duly appreciated. The gentleman was young once, even as he says; and
I, his equal in years, was then, in authorship, as young — though it were to
be hoped, not quite so immature. But, as circumstances alter cases, so time
and chance alter circumstances. Under no circumstances, however, can the
artifices of quackery be thought excusable in him who claims to be the
very greatest of modern grammarians. The niche that in the temple of
learning belongs to any individual, can be no other than that which his own
labours have purchased: here, his own merit alone must be his pedestal. If
this critical sketch be unimpeachably *just*, its publication requires no further
warrant. The correction has been forborne, till the subject has become rich,
and popular, and proud; proud enough at least to have published his utter
contempt for me and all my works. /47/

. . . The grand boast of this author is, that he *has succeeded* in "pleasing
himself and the public." He trusts to have "gained the latter point," to so
great an extent, and with such security of tenure, that henceforth no man
can safely question the *merit of* his performance. Happy mortal! to whom
that success which is the ground of pride, is also the glittering aegis of his
sure defence! To this he points with exultation and self-applause, as if the
prosperity of the wicked, or the popularity of an imposture, had never yet
been heard of in this clever world!† . . .

. . . The history of *Dr. Webster* [Noah Webster], as a grammarian, is
singular. He is remarkable for his changeableness, yet always positive; for
his inconsistency, yet very learned; for his zeal "to correct popular errors,"
yet often himself erroneous; for his fertility in resources, yet sometimes
meagre; for his success as an author, yet never satisfied; for his boldness of

† "What! a book have *no merit*, and yet to be called for at the rate of *sixty thousand
copies a year!* What a slander is this upon the public taste! What an insult to the
understanding of the good people /49/ of these United States! According to this reasoning, all the inhabitants of our land must be fools, except one man and that man is
GOOLD BROWN!" Kirkham, *in the Knickerbocker*, Oct., 1837, p. 361. /50/

innovation, yet fond of appealing to antiquity. His grammars are the least, and at present the least popular, of his works. They consist of four or five different treatises, which for their mutual credit should never be compared: it is impossible to place any firm reliance upon the authority of a man who contradicts himself so much. . . . I do not say that he has not exhibited ingenuity as well as learning, or that he is always wrong when he contradicts a majority of the English grammarians; but I may venture to say, he was wrong when he undertook to disturb the common scheme of the parts of speech, as well as when he resolved to spell all words exactly as they are pronounced.

It is not commonly known with how rash a hand this celebrated author has sometimes touched the most settled usages of our language. . . . /133/ I copy literally, leaving all my readers to guess for themselves why he spelled "*writers*" with a *w* and "*riting*" without.

"During the course of ten or twelv yeers, I hav been laboring to correct popular errors, and to assist my yung brethren in the road to truth and virtue; my publications for theze purposes hav been numerous; much time haz been spent, which I do not regret, and much censure incurred, which my hart tells me I do not deserv." * * * "The reeder wil observ that the *orthography* of the volum iz not uniform. The reezon iz, that many of the essays hav been published before, in the common orthography, and it would hav been a laborious task to copy the whole, for the sake of changing the spelling. In the essays, ritten within the last yeer, a considerable change of spelling iz introduced by way of experiment. This liberty waz taken by the writers before the age of queen Elizabeth, and to this we are indeted for the preference of modern spelling over that of Gower and Chaucer. The man who admits that the change of *housebonde, mynde, ygone, moneth* into *husband, mind, gone, month,* iz an improovment, must acknowlege also the riting of *helth, breth, rong, tung, munth,* to be an improovment. There iz no alternativ. Every possible reezon that could ever be offered for altering the spelling of wurds, stil exists in full force; and if a gradual reform should not be made in our language, it wil proov that we are less under the influence of reezon than our ancestors." — *Noah Webster's Essays, Preface,* p. xi. [Published in Boston, 1790, the collection carries the title *A Collection of Essays and Fugitiv Writings, on Moral, Historical, Political and Literary Subjects.*] /134/

Subjects for Discussion

1. Compare what Leonard has to say about universal grammar with Harris, and with the statements in modern dictionaries. How do these statements differ, if at all?

2. Most modern grammarians would deny that there is a "universal grammar" in Harris's sense. Which of the eighteenth-century writers you have encountered assume the truth of universal grammar, whether or not they mention it? Cite specific instances.

3. Consider the comments on the spoken language which precede Kenrick's dictionary entries in Section V. Try to epitomize Kenrick's attitude toward language. How much of it rests upon the notion of universal grammar; what in it is a denial of universal grammar? For instance, how does his reliance upon the oral form of the language relate to universal grammar?

4. Leonard indicates that most eighteenth-century grammarians were inclined to make arbitrary and ill-founded pronouncements upon usage. Support or refute his statements on the basis of the selections you have read.

5. Consider the questions raised in Section III concerning sixteenth-century pronouncements and practices in such subjects as spelling, punctuation, capitalization, and grammatical usage. Have these changed by the eighteenth century? Do the pronouncements fit or differ from the apparent practice?

6. Goold Brown was certainly one of the more learned grammarians of his day in this country, but too late to be included in Leonard's study. In what respects, if at all, does he represent an improvement over Webster? Over Mulcaster?

7. Which of the locutions condemned by eighteenth-century writers on usage are still condemned? Which are now in common use?

Suggestions for Investigation, Reports, or Brief Papers

1. Try to make a fair statement of Harris's exposition of universal grammar. What would be wrong with this statement from the point of view of a modern student of language? Explain how this belief would have gained support from a history of the language like that provided by Webster.

2. Take the pronouncements of any one writer on usage, for example, Lowth or Murray, and show which of his declarations presume the importance of something like universal grammar.

3. What does Murray seem to mean by "low expressions"? What expressions today would be probably considered "low"?

4. Write a critical estimate of Goold Brown as a grammarian who did original thinking as against one who applied rules which he supposed to be already established.

5. Contrast Webster and Worcester, both of whom commented on usage. How did they differ on questions like spelling? Or try this: Knowing what you do by now about language and the study of language, and about the products of the two men, how did Webster and Worcester differ temperamentally?

6. Goold Brown was obviously intelligent; quite as obviously, he was sometimes intemperate. Write a critical essay on him considering any of the following questions: How just was he in his judgments upon Webster? Upon Murray? Upon Kirkham? Can he on the whole be trusted? In what sorts of statements is he likely to be reliable and in what unreliable? What languages does he seem to know at first hand, and for which languages does he probably lean on others? Is there any evidence that he had firsthand knowledge of Old and Middle English?

7. Consider an individual writer on usage, summarizing what he said that is still valid today and what is now outmoded. For example, what has happened to our concept of the verb since the time of Buchanan? Since Lowth? Or compare the concept of the colon in Ingersoll and in your composition handbook.

8. Try to make a fair statement of what Brown would seem to suppose a grammarian should be. Would this be an adequate statement today?

9. Webster's recommendations for spelling reform contain some errors of fact, but many people consider his statement generally sensible in spite of them. Endeavor to defend or refute this estimate. You might, for instance, defend or discredit his attack upon Samuel Johnson's spelling, or you might consider in detail his recommendations for one letter.

10. Webster is concerned with the reform of spelling; does he seem much concerned with the further confusion of spelling through borrowing? Many words like *klystron* and *quisling* had not been borrowed in his day, and he probably did not imagine from what diverse sources English would borrow. Meanwhile, Spanish, which also borrows widely, is becoming more rather than less regular in its spelling. Can you devise any procedure to regularize words as they are borrowed into English?

VII. THE MODERN PROBLEM OF USAGE

New thinking, new tools to work with, new materials to work on — this trinity accounts in part for the undeniable fact that language study is livelier today than it has ever been, and it shows no signs of diminishing. We are becoming more and more aware of the importance of language for personal success and happiness, for the advance of modern technology and understanding, and for the promotion of peace in the world; with this heightened sense of the importance of language come new and exciting ways of working with it.

Take the dictionary, for example; it grew from a fresh idea, from a new way of working, and new materials to work with. The dictionary as we know it stems from the eighteenth century, when the notion that a scholar could describe the language word by word was a fresh idea. The idea alone was not worth much unless the lexicographers had a means of describing words; this they found in what is called the historical method. Earlier lexicographers mainly wrote down what they themselves thought the word meant; now the idea was growing that a lexicographer should not compile a personal book, but should read widely and base his description of a word upon the use of the word. From this theory and practice modern dictionaries have grown. But theory and practice alone were not enough; if a learned and industrious fourteenth-century Englishman — say John Gower, a lesser contemporary of Chaucer — had known how to make a good dictionary he could not have made one. Writing existed only in manuscripts in his day, and manuscripts were scarce and hard to come by. In Shakespeare's day, although printing was then more than a century old in western Europe, books were scarce. Even by the eighteenth century, books were scarce by our standards, but they had now become common enough so that a Bailey or a Johnson could hope to get his hands on large numbers of them — with the results we have studied in Section V.

The dictionary is now a highly developed tool, and all educated people know something of how to use one. This is not true of all the new techniques. Consider, for example, *glottochronology*. The approach is so new at this writing that few people but experts have heard of it, and the experts do not as yet know how reliable it may be. The idea is that over long periods of time all languages change at a constant rate; this may or may not be true, but there is evidence for it, if not conclusive evidence. Of course change may accelerate in a language, as it apparently did in English for a time after 1100, or it may decelerate, as the change in Icelandic apparently did after the migration to Iceland, but presumably these periods of notable growth or stability cancel out over the millennia. Now, certain ideas and objects are so common to the human race that all peoples must have had them; all languages must have had equivalents for words like *head*, *eat*, *mother*, and the like. If all this is true, and we have records — or can reconstruct them — from various stages of a language, we can guess roughly at the time that must have elapsed from one stage to another. For example, let us assume that from four modern Algonquin languages we can reconstruct two earlier forms of the language, as follows:

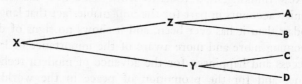

With glottochronology, by studying the loss of essential elements from one stage of the language to another, the linguist could presumably tell roughly how many years elapsed from the parent language X to the daughter languages Y and Z and the modern languages ABCD. This knowledge, if it is reliable, should be very useful in studying the past, since it will provide a check upon archaeology and history and may supply information which those disciplines cannot discover. Unlike lexicography, glottochronology is in its infancy, but it is like the older discipline in that it required new thinking, new techniques for working, and new evidence, the latter being the very extensive materials that have now been built up in the study of primitive languages.

Glottochronology is no plaything for beginners, and lexicography has been pretty well worked out, but between them in time and development are a number of approaches to language which even a beginner can enjoy. The essential thinking has been done; reliable techniques are well established, and extensive materials are available. For instance, consider etymology. Johnson's etymologies were unreliable and inadequate, and Webster's were sometimes nothing short of ridiculous. Neither man had the advantage of modern thinking and investigation; Johnson could not know and Webster did not know about language families. And without knowledge of descent from Indo-European and the differences between descent within a language and borrowing from another language, reliable etymology was impossible. Now dictionaries that are available almost everywhere contain so much etymological information that anyone who has a fundamentally sound notion of the way language works can trace a word from Indo-European to current slang.

Quite as intriguing as etymology, perhaps more so, is usage. Here is a body of material about which almost everybody will argue and some will fight. Here, also, the essential thinking has been done, new techniques are being developed, and material is plentiful. We have outgrown our eighteenth-century blunders — we no longer suppose that the language will decay and become gibberish if we do not succeed in keeping everybody from saying *ain't* or ending sentences with prepositions — but we have not solved our problems. We are now agreed that in the end usage depends upon use, but how much? How soon? How? We do not as yet know with any accuracy how we talk or who talks that way. We know that one speaker uses the language differently than does another speaker. We know that the same speaker does not use the language in the same manner under all circumstances. But we do not know in much detail how we use the language, nor have we decided how we should use it.

Fortunately, this is not a difficult subject with which to begin. Anybody can start listening to the language in his own family or at the college dining hall. He can notice the difference between the way a professor speaks when he is lecturing and when a student asks him a question in the hall. Similarly, anyone can compare the pronouncements in dictionaries and in books of usage, and discover that they differ. He can do some reading on linguistic geography, one of the newer tools for studying language (see the readings from Kurath, Marckwardt, and Allen in Section II). Accordingly, this section is devoted mainly to modern studies in and discussions of usage. The various writers do not always agree. That is as it should be; *usage* may not be a fighting word, but it is a fighting subject.

50. CHARLES V. HARTUNG

Doctrines of English Usage

The following summary of attitudes toward usage is from Charles V. Hartung, "Doctrines of English Usage," *The English Journal*, 45 (1956), 517-25.

Generally speaking, the four main doctrines current among those concerned with judging the propriety of language usage are: (1) the doctrine of rules; (2) the doctrine of general usage; (3) the doctrine of appropriate usage; (4) the doctrine of the linguistic norm. Rarely do those interested in language adhere consistently to any one of those doctrines. Instead there is the usual divergence between theory and practice; some linguists profess one doctrine and practice another. Also there is the usual eclectic compromise. Nevertheless, it is possible to make roughly approximate groupings of schools of opinion according to the degrees of emphasis given to these various doctrines.

The Doctrine of Rules

From the point of view of the modern school of linguistics the doctrine of rules is, or at least should be, moribund. But even a cursory glance at handbooks and grammars of recent date reveals what a tenacious hold it has on life. And even when the doctrine is dis /518/ claimed in theory, we find grammarians following it in spirit and practice. For example, in the preface to R. W. Pence's *A Grammar of Present-Day English,* we find the following statement: "Grammar is not a set of rules thought up by and imposed by some invisible godlike creature." [4] Yet the text itself consists of a set of prescriptions in the spirit of the eighteenth century grammarians and having the effect if not the form of the old rules. Here is an example:

> . . . inasmuch as an interrogative pronoun normally introduces a clause and so may not have the position that a noun of like function would have, the function of an interrogative pronoun may be easily mistaken. Care needs to be exercised to meet the demands of subjective complements of finite verbs and of infinitives. But especial care needs to be taken that the proper objective form is used when an interrogative pronoun coming first functions as the object of a preposition that is delayed.
>
> 1. Subjective complement
>   *Whom* do you mean? (*Whom* is the object of *do mean.*)
> 2. Object of a preposition
>   *Whom* were you with last night? (*Whom* is the object of the preposition *with. Not:* Who were you with last night?) [5]

In a note some concession is made to the demands of spoken discourse: "Who are you looking for? (Accepted by some in spoken discourse.)" But in the same note we find this comment: "This use of the nominative in informal spoken discourse is regarded by a few as acceptable, although the fastidious person will probably look upon it as sloppy speech." It is noteworthy that the text in which this judgment is to be found reached its seventh printing in 1953. Yet the sentence *Who are you looking for* is listed as *Accepted* in the Leonard survey printed in 1932.

It would be possible, of course, to multiply examples of the continuing hold that the doctrine of rules still has on a large proportion of present day students of language, but it is more to the point to examine the reasons for this hold. Probably the most important reason is that the doctrine has behind it the weight of over a century and a half of almost undisputed dominance. This is the result of two main sources of authority: the assumed correspondence of the rules of grammar with basic principles of reason and the supposed correspondence of the rules with the usage of the best writers. Some grammarians have assumed that reason has the prior claim and determines usage: others have placed usage first and have claimed that rules are inductively derived from the best usage. The eighteenth century grammarian William Ward gives typical expression to the view of the first group:

> Use and Custom are considered as the only Rules by which to judge of what is right or wrong in Process. But is the Custom which is observed in the Application of any Language the Effect of Chance? Is not such a Custom a consistent Plan of communicating the Conceptions and rational discursive Operations of one Man to another? And who will maintain, that this is, or

[4] New York: The Macmillan Co., 1947, p. v.
[5] *Ibid.*, pp. 204-205.

can be, the Effect of unmeaning Accident? If then it be not so, it must be the Effect of the Reason of Man, adjusting certain means to a certain End: And it is the Business of Speculative or Rational Grammar to explain the Nature of the Means, and to show how they are applied to accomplish the End proposed. If this can be done with sufficient Evidence, the most simple of the Elements of Logic will become familiar to those who engage in a Course /519/ of Grammar, and Reason will go Hand in Hand with Practice.[6]

Ward's linking of grammar and logic was a common eighteenth century practice and carried over into the nineteenth century, receiving the approval of even such a great philosopher as John Stuart Mill. Mill says that "the principles and rules of grammar are the means by which forms of language are made to correspond with the universal forms of thought." [7] The weakness of this thesis was, of course, evident to the language experts of Mill's own time. Henry Sweet and A. H. Sayce brought to bear their great knowledge of comparative philology to show how little actual correspondence there is between logic and grammar, and modern linguists and semanticists have agreed with them. Probably the most judicious summation of the problem is that of Otto Jespersen:

> Most linguists are against any attempt to apply a logical standard to language. Language, they say, is psychology, not logic; or "language is neither logical nor illogical, but alogical." That is to say, language has nothing to do with logic. To many philologists the very word, logic, is like a red rag to a bull. . . . It would be surprising however if language which serves to express thoughts should be quite independent of the laws of correct thinking.[8]

As Jespersen demonstrates, however, what often has pretended to be logic is no more than Latin grammar disguised, and arguments declaring the correspondence of grammar with logic have often been little more than the forcing of English into Latin syntactical patterns. For example, the rule that the predicative must stand in the same case as the subject is not, as has been claimed, an incontrovertible law of thought but merely a rule of Latin grammar. Many languages of different types violate this so-called incontrovertible law.

The authority that the rules have derived from deductive logic has never been equal to the support given them by the belief that rules are inductively derived from examination of the best usage. George Campbell's dictum that reputable, national, and present usage determines correctness has been cited with approval from the days of Lindley Murray, probably the most popular of eighteenth century grammarians, to the present day. Many writers on language have, in fact, cited Campbell's doctrine as liberalizing in effect, but it is difficult to see how such a belief can be accepted. Campbell so restricted the field of acceptable usage that the doctrine of rules lost little

---

[6] William Ward, *English Grammar* (1765). Quoted by C. C. Fries, *The Teaching of English* (Ann Arbor: The George Wahr Publishing Co., 1949), p. 13.

[7] See I. A. Richards, *Interpretation in Teaching* (London: Routledge & Kegan Paul, 1938), p. 280.

[8] *Mankind, Nation and the Individual* (London: Geo. Allen, 1946), p. 114.

of the force it had held in the writings of such prescriptive grammarians as Bishop Lowth and William Ward. Lowth had, of course, declared the independence of grammar from the usage of even the best writers, whereas Campbell paid lip service to the doctrine of usage. But in practice Campbell, as S. A. Leonard has shown, repudiated the very theory he had set up as a guide. We can see what the doctrine of usage actually became when we examine the following statement from a latter day follower of Campbell:

> By good usage is meant the usage generally observed in the writings of the best English authors and in the speech /520/ of well-educated people. Dictionaries, grammars, and books on rhetoric and composition record this usage, on the basis of wide observation and study.[9]

This definition follows a pattern dating from the eighteenth century and repeated in scores of nineteenth century handbooks and grammars. The doctrine of usage in the hands of the grammarians has been practically identical with the doctrine of rules.

The Doctrine of General Usage

Joseph Priestley, the eighteenth century scientist and grammarian, was probably the first writer in English to show a consistent regard for the doctrine of general usage. But his views were neglected, and it was not until the rise of scientific linguistics in the late nineteenth century that the doctrine began to make headway against the doctrine of rules. Among the pioneers were W. D. Whitney, Fitzedward Hall, and Alexander Bain. The first full-fledged popular exposition and exemplification of the doctrine, J. Lesslie Hall's *English Usage* (1917), was not published until well into the twentieth century. In contrast with most of his predecessors, who only paid lip service to the doctrine of usage, Hall is consistent and documents his opinion with particular examples. In his article, "Who for Whom," for instance, Hall cites the opinions of contemporary liberal grammarians in favor of *who* as the objective form in questions, and he gives a number of examples from usage, citing Shakespeare, Marlowe, Defoe, Kingsley, and Froude, as well as less well-known writers.

Comprehensive as it is, Hall's work is limited primarily to an examination of written documents, and it was not until Leonard's *Current English Usage* that there was a systematic survey of spoken usage to support Hall's findings. Strictly speaking, the Leonard report is not a survey of the facts of English usage but of opinion about the relative standing of various debatable items. The guiding principle of the survey is indicated succinctly in the statement that "allowable usage is based on the actual practice of cultivated people rather than on rules of syntax or logic." [10] In keeping with this principle, Leonard submitted a number of items of debatable usage to a jury

[9] Edwin C. Woolley, *Handbook of Composition*, Revised Edition (Boston: D. C. Heath, 1920), p. 1.

[10] Sterling Andrus Leonard, *Current English Usage* (Chicago: The National Council of Teachers of English, 1932), p. 95.

consisting of linguistic specialists, editors, authors, business men, and teachers of English and speech. These judges were to decide the standing of the items according to what they thought the actual usage to be. Four levels of acceptability were indicated: "literary English," "standard, cultivated, colloquial English," "trade or technical English," and "naif, popular, or uncultivated English." The findings of the report provided evidence to demonstrate the discrepancy between actual usage and the rules of common school grammar. Among the items indicated as *established*, or acceptable on the cultivated colloquial level by more than seventy-five percent of the judges, were *it is me, who are you looking for, I feel badly*, and many other locutions that had long been proscribed by the handbooks and grammars.

The Leonard report was not a survey of "general" usage but of "cultivated" usage. It is not until the research studies of C. C. Fries that we find a truly inclusive and adequately /521/ documented study of general usage. Eschewing the guidance of the grammars and even of polls of "educated" usage, Fries stated that "it is probably much more sound to decide that the spontaneous usage of that large group who are carrying on the affairs of English speaking people is the usage to be observed and to set the standard." [11] To provide evidence of actual usage, Fries has used letters and transcripts of telephone conversations. Like other modern advocates of the doctrine of usage, Fries has not held to the theory that the standard of general usage should apply in all language situations. In concession to the demands of effective communication and to the practical problems of the teacher in the classroom he has given assent to the doctrine of appropriateness. The problem of the teacher, according to Fries, is to develop in the student the habits that will enable him to use freely the language appropriate to his ideas, the occasion of their expression, and the needs of his hearers. To bring about this end, the teacher needs to become sensitive to the different levels and functional varieties of usage and to develop a program of study designed to meet the particular needs of each class. Although the teacher must take into account the prevailing demand that he equip his pupils with the language habits that have attained the most social acceptability, he needs to develop also an intelligently liberal attitude toward the particular language habits of any group of students.

The Doctrine of Appropriateness

In its essentials the doctrine of appropriateness has not changed since the full exposition by George Philip Krapp in his *Modern English* (1909). Krapp introduces his exposition by making a distinction between "good" English and "conventional" or "standard" English. Good English, according to Krapp, is any language which "hits the mark." Since the purpose of language is the satisfactory communication of thought and feeling, any language which satisfactorily performs this function is good English. Standard English is that usage which is recognized and accepted as customary in

[11] *The Teaching of English*, p. 35.

any particular community. Such locutions as *he don't* or *these kind of people* or *I will* may be standard in one community and not standard in another. Custom is the only relevant determinant of the standard. Krapp's relativism is evident in the following statement:

> What is defended as customary use by a community, or even by a single speaker, to carry the matter to its final analysis, is standard, or conventional, or "right," or "correct," in that community or for that speaker.[12]

In analyzing the concept of "good" English, Krapp arrives at the doctrine of appropriateness. He describes three tendencies in English speech — "popular English," "colloquial English," and "formal or literary English" — and declares that each of these has its appropriate uses. They are three kinds of arrows by which the speaker attempts to hit the mark of good English. Whether the speaker hits the mark or not depends upon his skill and upon his acumen in sizing up the particular speech situation:

> . . . the degree of colloquialism which one permits, in one's self or in others depends on the subject of conversation, on the intimacy of the acquaintance-ship of the persons speaking, and in general on all the attendant circumstances . . . language which may be adequately expressive, and therefore good, under one /522/ set of circumstances, under a different set of circumstances becomes inadequately expressive, because it says more or less than the speaker intended, and so becomes bad English. One learns thus the lesson of complete relativity of the value of language, that there is no such thing as an absolute English, but that language is valuable only as it effects the purpose one wishes to attain, that what is good at one time may be bad at another, and what is bad at one time may be good at another.[13]

This doctrine has been somewhat qualified by some of its recent exponents, particularly by Pooley and Perrin, but it has not been changed in its essentials. And it is still subject to the same sort of objection that J. Lesslie Hall made to Krapp's statement of it. Hall pointed out that Krapp's conception of "good" English was unprecedented and varied from the commonly accepted meaning of the term. He also deprecated Krapp's advocacy of "a sort of isolated, neighborhood English" and declared that the consistent carrying out of Krapp's ideas would mean the decline of a *general* and reputable usage for which students of language had been struggling. Consistent application of the doctrine of appropriateness would mean that every newcomer to a community would need to learn a new set of speech habits and that every traveler would need to be sensitive to innumerable local dialects and to cater to the personal language habits of his listeners. This would finally result in the decline of a general standard of cultivated speech understood everywhere and acceptable everywhere. In answer to Hall's objections Krapp might very well have repeated what he had said in *Modern English:* that the completely consistent adherence to the idea of general usage would mean finally a fixed language inadmissive of improve-

[12] New York: Charles Scribner's Sons, 1909, p. 332.
[13] *Ibid.,* pp. 327, 329-330.

ment and that the interplay of standard English and good English makes for a language constantly improving in expressiveness and effectiveness of communication.

The Doctrine of the Linguistic Norm

Under the heading of the linguistic norm may be grouped those concepts which emphasize that language is above all responsible to an expressive ideal. Some advocates of the normative approach hold that language should not be subservient to usage and should be judged by consciously derived criteria. I. A. Richards, for instance, has characterized the doctrine of usage as "the most pernicious influence in current English teaching." [14] In attacking the doctrine of usage, Richards does not recommend a return to the doctrine of rules and of what he calls the illegitimate application of logic and philosophy to language. Instead he recommends a self-critical reflection about the conduct of thought in language. Richards' evaluation of modern linguistic theories and his own program are explicitly stated in his latest book:

> There are vast areas of so-called "purely descriptive" linguistics which are a grim danger at present to the conduct of language, to education, to standards of intelligence, to the reserves in theory and in sensibility of the mental tester. . . . The appeal to mere *usage:* "If it's widely in use, it's O.K.," is a case in point. Every useful feature of language was *not in use* once upon a time. Every degradation of language too starts somewhere. Behind usage is the question of efficiency. Inefficient language features are not O.K., however widespread their use. Of course, to the linguistic botanist it is important to preserve all varieties until they have been collected and described. But that is not the point of view of the over-all study of language, its services and its powers. /523/ That over-all view is, I am insisting, inescapably NORMATIVE. It is concerned (as every speaker and every listener is always concerned) with the maintenance and improvement of the use of language.[15]

As instances of degradation in language Richards cites the current practice of using *uninterested* and *disinterested* and *imply* and *infer* as synonyms. In each instance the confusion has brought about a loss in precision without a corresponding gain.

Not all adherents to the concept of a linguistic norm have held as strongly as Richards to the principle of consciously critical evaluation of language. Instead such linguistic scholars as Otto Jespersen and Edward Sapir have held that linguistic efficiency is often the result of the spontaneous and intuitive expression of the folk. Probably the best known statement of the belief that language tends constantly toward a norm of maximum expressiveness with least effort is Otto Jespersen's theory of energetics, most recently restated in his *Efficiency in Linguistic Change* (1941).[16] According

[14] *Op. cit.,* p. 174.
[15] *Speculative Instruments* (Chicago: University of Chicago Press, 1955), pp. 123-124.
[16] Copenhaven: Ejnar Munksgaard, 1941, pp. 15-16.

to Jespersen's theory, linguistic changes involve a constant interplay of opposing demands, one by the individual seeking ease of expression and the other of a social character calling for distinctness of communication. The first tendency is subversive of traditional forms of expression; the second is conservative and tends to keep alive the traditional norm. The interaction between these two demands brings about language changes designed to conserve the energy of the speaker and at the same time to retain the power of exact communication.

Edward Sapir's *Language* contains a discussion of the expression *Who did you see* that may serve to illustrate Jespersen's theory.[17] Sapir declares that the syntax of "whom" in *whom did you see* is logically and historically sound but psychologically shaky. The construction is kept alive by social snobbery but will eventually succumb to the pressure put on it by the uncontrolled speech of the folk. Meanwhile, users of *whom* are torn between an unconscious desire to say *who* and a fear of social penalty. The correctness of *whom* is fundamentally false and within a couple of hundred years the "whom" will probably be as delightfully archaic as the Elizabethan "his" [f]or "its." In his analysis, Sapir cites four reasons for the linguistic shakiness of *whom*. First, *who* is becoming invariable because of its linguistic similarity to such invariable forms as the interrogative and relative pronouns, *which, what,* and *that* and the interrogative adverbs *where, when* and *how*. Second, interrogative pronouns normally play an emphatic part in the sentence, and emphatic elements are typically invariable. The third powerful reason for the interrogative use of *who* rather than *whom* is its position in the sentence. Normal word order in English places the subject at the beginning of the sentence, before the verb. And the word in the subject position normally takes the subjective form. A fourth difficulty in *whom did you see* is that the *m* sound slows down the movement of the sentence and calls for a deliberate mental and physical effort at odds with the spontaneous speech situations in which the expression is normally used. For these reasons then *whom* is on psychologically shaky /524/ grounds and will eventually be replaced by the more natural and expressive *who*. As another instance of the prevalence of psychology over logic in language usage we may cite the rule about the placement of adverbial modifiers. The latest version of Woolley's handbook still carries the following precept and example: "Place such adverbs as *only, merely, just, almost, ever, hardly, scarcely, quite, nearly* next to the words they modify. COLLOQUIAL: *I only want three.* BETTER: *I want only three;* (or) *I want three only.*"[18] It may be that the constructions labeled BETTER are more logically sound, but rhetorically and psychologically they may not be as effective as the COLLOQUIAL version. The intention of the speaker may be to emphasize the reasonableness of his request, not the request itself or the exact amount being requested. If such is his intention, the sooner he introduces the idea of reasonableness into his expression the truer he is to his actual meaning and

---

[17] New York: Harcourt, Brace, 1921, pp. 156-162.
[18] *College Handbook of Composition* (Boston: D. C. Heath, 1951), p. 89.

the more likely he is to get a favorable response. The placement of a modifier depends therefore not on an invariable rule of logic or grammar but on the speaker's full meaning. It is this insistence on precision and fullness of meaning which gives force to the doctrine of the linguistic norm. In its expressive aims it is similar to the doctrine of appropriateness, but whereas the doctrine of appropriateness emphasizes the social situation, particularly the effect on an audience, the doctrine of the linguistic norm holds in balance the intention of the speaker, the nature of the language itself, and the probable effect on the audience.

Because of its over-all point of view the doctrine of the linguistic norm is probably the best vantage ground for the teacher. It provides criteria by which to evaluate both the conservative and the liberalizing forces in language. It does not, to be sure, provide the sense of psychological security and social approval so long associated with the doctrine of rules. But submission to dogmatic authority merely out of a desire to gain security hardly seems a constructive attitude. Nor does it seem desirable to compromise personal conviction in the way so often demanded by consistent adherence to either the doctrine of general usage or the doctrine of appropriateness. The most suitable philosophy of language for the teacher would seem to be one calling for a maximum expression. And this is the point of view of the doctrine of the linguistic norm. /525/

51. BERTRAND EVANS

Who Is Subverting Whom? — Grammar and Writing

This selection and the following one should be read as a pair; taken together they suggest how far apart two respected professors of English teaching in the same community can find themselves. Professor Bertrand Evans is associated with the College English Association of the San Francisco Bay Area, and Professor James Sledd, who is at this writing with Northwestern University, was at the University of California in Berkeley when he wrote his reply. Professor Evans has long been a student of the teaching of English; Sledd is associated with a number of important works, including the standard study of Johnson as a lexicographer and *A Short Introduction to English Grammar*, an attempt to reconcile structuralist and more conventional approaches. The following is from Evans's "Grammar and Writing," *Educational Forum*, 23 (1959), 215-28.

As everyone knows, the study of English grammar in the public schools has had a precarious existence for at least twenty-five years. It has been suspect from contrary directions, on quite opposite grounds.

On the one hand, college English professors who have had anything to do with freshman composition have charged, often and hotly, that the study of grammar has simply been neglected or omitted entirely for otherwise how could high school graduates possibly write with such utter disregard for discipline? All over the nation the problems of dealing with the grammatical incompetence of freshmen entering college have been numerous and severe. Along with those of the colleges, voices of the public have been raised in anger and dismay also — voices of parents who remembered the drilling *they* had in school, which surely *must* have been good for them because it was so exacting and so tedious, and voices of businessmen whose office workers did not prove notably grammatical. From this side, then, the din has been loud and continuous. The voices have often been confused, but the general sense has always been unmistakable: the study of grammar has been neglected and should be restored.

On the other hand, especially during the late 1920's and 1930's, professional educationalists challenged the basic assumptions of the study of grammar, partly because their tests proved to them — if not to everyone else — that grammatical knowledge had no appreciable value and partly because the arduous kind of study that has always been associated with grammar did not fit the pattern of the new child-centered, activity conscious, experimental "progressive" school. And, in fact, in some high schools — where there prevailed a coalition of avid educationistic administrators, self-expressionistic young English teachers fresh from teachers' colleges whose English departments had surrendered responsibility for teacher training to departments of Education, and core-curriculum-minded young social studies teachers, early embracers of Educationism — the study of grammar was put aside, along with whatever else carried a taint of the "traditional." Then, more recently, taking up where the most enthusiastic educationists left off, the professional linguists — perhaps more aptly called "linguisticists," that eager band of anti-traditionalists in language studies whose zeal to prevail sorts so oddly with their claim of disinterested, scientific observation — have been carrying the battle against the old-fashioned study and teaching of old-fashioned grammar.

Thus, between charges that it was *not* being taught and *should* be taught and charges that it *was* being taught and should *not* be, grammar has had a very /215/ bad time of it for more than a quarter of a century. And, frankly, its troubles are likely to get worse before they get better.

During this unstable, often chaotic, always trying period, however, in nearly all of the English classrooms with which I have had direct or indirect acquaintance, the teaching of the same old grammar has continued in essentially the same old way. English teachers trained before the mid-1930's, and therefore taught to believe in the values of traditional grammar and in traditional methods of teaching it, have remained dominant forces. They have stood off the educationists; though waves of "progressive" theory lapped high on their classroom walls, the doors held firm. And of late they have been standing off the linguisticists, whom someone has called "kissing-

cousins of educationists." These, replacing the gross-sounding jargon of educationism with the high-sounding jargon of linguisticism, flushed with victories over old-fashioned philologists in colleges and universities, and affecting the dispassion that more conspicuously marks true scientism than
true science, are urgently, even fanatically, storming the classroom in order
to persuade the old-fashioned grammar teacher that she, too, should be dis-
passionate in her attitude toward language so that the attitude of linguisticism
can prevail: let her just accept the view that there are merely "different"
levels of usage — *not* "good" and "bad," "acceptable" and "unacceptable" —
and all will be well.

The reader will possibly have guessed by now, correctly, that I am
neither educationist nor linguisticist, and he may have assumed that the
present essay is to be an attack on the attackers of the beleaguered teacher
of grammar and a defense of the matter and methods that she has continued
to use. But although my sympathies are wholly with grammar and the grammar teacher, my purpose just now is not to dissipate my own energies or
to suggest that she dissipate hers by swatting at her swarming assailants, but
to urge her to take a long and uncompromisingly honest look at what she
has been and is doing in her teaching. For what is even more disturbing
than the fact that such highly mobile forces are allied against her is the
fact that though she has been teaching grammar faithfully throughout the
years, the results, observed by college professors and employers, have given
rise to the belief that she has *not* been teaching it. I shall certainly not go
so far as to suggest that unless she mends some of her ways she will deserve
to become extinct, but I have no choice other than to predict that unless she
does so, she *may*.

But how to mend them? And, harder than that question, will mending
them really do any good? The implications of many charges made in the
past quarter of a century are that grammar would not do any appreciable
good no matter how it might be taught. I have taught grammar in high
school and junior college and to future English teachers undergoing their
final years of preparation, have observed many teachers and student teachers
in action, and, by means of freshman classes in college composition, have
had a dozen years of steady necessity to examine the results of the teaching
of grammar in high school. My /216/ variety of experiences has tempted
me to a number of conclusions, which I will try to boil down to a single
one. Let me say, first, that it seems to me there can be only one of two
possible reasons why students who have been exposed to a great deal of
grammar nevertheless continue to write so ungrammatically that even
friendly critics of the schools have concluded that they surely must have
been exposed to none at all: either grammatical knowledge really has little
connection with problems of writing, or it has latent bearings which our
methods of teaching have failed to exploit and which our students have
therefore failed to translate into practice. I take the latter view. My conclusion is that *grammar has failed to do what, at best, it can do because our
methods have not been designed to establish and maintain a sufficient con-*

nection between grammatical knowledge and the practice of writing. I make this statement in full awareness, I believe, of the efforts of the so-called "functionalists" of the past twenty years.

My use of "sufficient" implies, inevitably, a conviction that if such a degree of connection *were* maintained by our methods, the study of grammar would produce appreciable results. . . . . /217/

. . . As a matter of fact, I shall not argue that the study of grammar will enable students to write interestingly, effectively, elegantly, eloquently, logically, persuasively, or even clearly and intelligently. My claim is only that the study of grammar *can* enable students to solve certain problems of form and order that inevitably occur whenever they write: in short, that grammatical knowledge, applied, enables students to write — grammatically. Moreover, I believe that the study of grammar is much more likely to equip students to write grammatically if the teacher holds only to this lower expectation and manages her teaching accordingly. I believe that our first and greatest mistake in the past has been our assumption that if we could just force students to "learn" it, all of it, a knowledge of grammar would somehow, miraculously, transform them — "dignify human nature, and meliorate the condition of man." I believe that if grammar is taught with that high but obscure purpose, it may not even help anyone to write more correctly. /218/

. . . The present essay is obviously not the place in which to outline or to describe in detail the connections between particular grammatical elements and particular problems that occur in the course of writing sentences, paragraphs, and essays. The full analysis requires an elaborate representation that should be tedious and unsightly here. But there is a better reason for omitting a full analysis here. I do not believe that my analysis would help another teacher very much. I believe that the individual teacher of grammar and writing needs to work out these relationships of grammatical knowledge and writing for herself, by herself in her own way. I do not believe that it is a job to be left to writers of textbooks and workbooks. My purpose in the remainder of this essay, therefore, is only to suggest ways of proceeding that the teacher may want to try — and, of course, to reject when she finds sounder ones.

The immediate aim of the investigation, then, is to find, not excuses for teaching a vast amount of grammar that tradition or blind faith tells the teacher she must teach, but precisely what grammatical knowledge is necessary and at what points it is applicable. The ultimate aim, of course, is to make oneself ready to explain and demonstrate to students, *while they are learning the elements themselves,* just how the knowledge of these elements enables them to solve problems that occur in the course of writing.

There are two possible approaches to the investigation. First, one can take the parts of speech, the word-group elements, and the "uses," such as subject, direct object, and so forth, and put the same direct question to each in turn: "Just what problems of writing are solved by knowledge of this element?" (Or, of course, one can put the same question in a blunter way:

"What grammatical blunder may the student make if he lacks knowledge of this element?") Second, one can start from the other end, with the major characteristic ways in which writing does in fact go wrong grammatically, and can put this question to each in turn: "Just what knowledge of what element or elements is needed to solve this problem?" (Or, more baldly: "Just what grammatical knowledge is needed to avoid this gross blunder?")

The first approach is slower, less certain, involves far more repetition and duplication of data. Let me illustrate briefly by using one part of speech, one word-group, and one "use." How, for lack of knowledge of the *adjective*, may one blunder in writing? The possibilities are not numerous: one can get the wrong degree ("It is the best of the two"), and one can use adjective where /223/ he should use adverb ("This car runs real good"). I would not set children to underlining the adjectives on a workbook page unless they understood that these are the immediately demonstrable reasons for their learning to identify adjectives. For the word-group, let us take the *participial phrase* and ask the same basic question of it. So far as I can ascertain, the major demonstrable "faults" that can be directly associated with lack of knowledge of participial phrases are only three: dangling modifier, fault in parallelism, and fault in comma punctuation. Finally, for the "use," let us consider the *subject* of a sentence or clause. The major grammatical faults that result from failure to identify a subject are only two: improper case of a pronoun as subject ("Give the book to *whomever* wants it") and faulty agreement of the verb with the subject ("A pile of books *were* on the table"). It would seem to me that if students have underlined ten workbook pages of subjects without realization that these are the main reasons for recognizing subjects, they have wasted their time.

The second approach to the analysis means starting from the "surface spots" in writing at which lack of grammatical knowledge betrays itself and working back to discover precisely what knowledge of what elements is applicable at these points. One of the most obvious of these focal centers is that at which it becomes necessary to choose between the case forms of pronouns, and the teacher may wish to begin her research by examining some sentences in which the problem occurs. Her immediate purpose will be to find just what must be known — and, therefore, taught — before one can choose knowingly between, for example, *whoever* and *whomever*. Let her take an ordinary sentence: "Give the book to (whoever-whomever) you believe will like it." The bare outline of grammatical knowledge that must be called into play in solving this problem includes recognition (1) that "whoever" is the subjective and "whomever" the objective form; (2) that "whoever you believe will like it" is a dependent clause; (3) that a dependent clause can perform offices of the noun — and in this instance serves as object of the preposition; (4) that "whoever" serves as subject of its clause. If the teacher will go on to examine a dozen such sentences in which it is necessary to choose between forms of pronouns, she will discover that at one time or another a writer needs to use knowledge of a considerable body of that grammar which some have scrapped too hastily and which others have "taught" without advising either themselves or their pupils in what precise ways it will be useful. She will discover also how to make connections in the minds of students between their knowledge of particular elements and these particular problems. And, finally, she may glimpse, in the act of doing this research, profound implications for her method of teaching grammar.

The necessity to choose between case forms of pronouns, then, is one of the villains that make knowledge of numerous grammatical elements, facts, and principles indispensable. Clearly, if distinctions of this kind "did not matter," /224/ as some linguisticists assert, it would be possible for us to put aside a good deal of grammar that we must otherwise teach; but I assume that the reader who has read thus far into the present essay agrees with me that these distinctions do matter, and that equipping students to make them is a part of the responsibility of the English teacher. If that supposition is accurate, the reader will agree that we must ferret out the particular portions of total grammatical knowledge that bear on the problem.

But even though we could be freed from the necessity of choosing between case forms of pronouns, we should still have to deal with problems of a structural kind whenever we write, and a second "surface spot" from which the teacher can work backward, or inward, to discover what grammatical knowledge she should give her students is the complex, but fairly well defined, assortment of places in the sentence at which these problems arise. Wrongly solved, or slipped over naively, as though no problem were present, these problems manifest themselves as structural faults, in the forms of sentences run together, fragments set down as whole sentences, modifiers that dangle or are misplaced, pronouns that refer to the wrong noun or to two nouns or to none, subjects and verbs that do not agree in number, nonparallel elements that should be parallel, and so forth. Let us take only two examples from this assortment of characteristic ways in which students go wrong structurally when they either lack the right knowledge to solve the problem or fail to apply the right knowledge at the right time.

First, what knowledge of what elements do students need to have in order to solve correctly the problem that, incorrectly solved, expresses itself in the form of a dangling modifier? Three rather similar elements lend themselves most readily to the vice of dangling: the participial phrase, the prepositional phrase containing a gerund, and the elliptical clause; once in a great while a student contrives to dangle an infinitive phrase also. Danglers persist in the styles of students who have been taught a great deal of grammar, including recognition of participial and prepositional phrases and elliptical clauses; indeed, it is a fair guess that they persist in the styles of such students every bit as much as in the styles of those who have been taught little or no grammar. Mere ability to recognize these elements, then, is next to useless: *it is necessary to teach students at the time they are learning to recognize them that a major reason for learning to recognize them is the problem of proper modification.* I believe that the student who has learned only to identify a participial phrase has learned only the half of his lesson that, alone, will not do him any good; he must learn also *why* he has learned to identify it.

Second, what knowledge of what elements do students need to know in order to solve correctly the problem that, incorrectly solved, shows up as a fault in parallelism? Of all the major structural blunders, the fault in parallelism is the most tenacious. It hangs on even in rather sophisticated styles, long after the /225/ writer has ceased to commit such barbarities as dangling modifiers, agreement errors, reference errors, and case-form errors. The reason it is most tenacious is not hard to find: the problem of maintaining grammatical parallelism requires knowledge of a greater number of elements of the sentence than does any other single problem of sentence construction. In fact, equipping students to solve problems of parallelism necessitates the teaching of *all* elements of the sentence, for all elements of the sentence are capable of being compounded with their likes, and every problem of compounding elements is a problem of parallelism. Conversely, if we have "taught" all the elements of the sentence and failed to relate the students' knowledge of them to the problem of parallelism, we have failed to focus on one of the very largest single reasons for teaching grammar. Grammatical parallelism is of course a matter of balance, of coordinating like elements that perform like functions. We compound two nouns, two verbs, two adjectives, two adverbs — indeed, even two prepositions, two interjections, and two conjunctions. The problem of compounding all these simple parts of speech is easy enough: only the true dullard needs any instruction in compounding these properly and in avoiding coordinating, say, a noun and a verb, an adverb and an adjective. But we also compound prepositional phrases, participial phrases, gerund phrases, infinitive phrases, absolute phrases, noun clauses, adjective clauses, adverb clauses, independent clauses — and in order to be sure of compounding these likes with one another, one must be capable of distinguishing them. So long as a writer is unable to distinguish one from another, he is certain occasionally, if not frequently, to cross them up. The possibilities of "going wrong" in solving the problem of parallelism are as numerous as the elements of the sentence, and the only sure way of enabling students always to solve the problem correctly is to teach them to recognize every element of the sentence and to distinguish it from every other. But, again, the ability to do so will have no significant effect on the way in which students solve the problem of parallelism unless they have also been taught the application of their knowledge. I do not believe that a student should ever be set to underlining prepositional phrases, infinitive phrases, participial phrases, or any of the other phrases or clauses, unless he is made aware, and ideally kept constantly aware while he is doing so, that the greatest single application for his knowledge of these elements is in solving the problem of parallelism that occurs every time he compounds two elements.

Finally, the teacher who is searching out the precise connections between grammatical knowledge and the practice of writing may want to look at the "surface spot" of punctuation, particularly comma punctuation. During the past twenty-five years much strange advice has been given students about comma punctuation: "Use commas where they are needed to make your sentence clear" — a certain way to invite students to write miserably sprawled sentences and then attempt to make them "clear" by /226/ punctuation; "Use commas where there is a natural pause" — but the most masterful oral readers of prose pause before, on, and after single words and phrases according to nuances of meaning and special emphases of personal interpretation, and to use commas at all these places would simply be a lunatic practice. The "clarity" and "natural pause" directives are possibly useful for sophisticated writers who have already mastered the art of writing, including punctuation; given to the unsophisticated, they merely become a license for indulgence in a foolish sort of stylistic anarchy. The fact is that sufficiently exact directives for punctuation can be given to students only in the terms of the grammar of the sentence: "Use a comma after an introductory participial phrase," and so on. If these directives are to have any meaning, the student must obviously be able to identify the sentence elements that are employed in them: there is no way, really, of circumventing that necessity.

Possibly I have now sufficiently illustrated the two approaches by means of which the individual English teacher can work out for her own use the specific connection between grammatical knowledge and the practice of writing. I do not know which is better — to start from a list of the parts of speech and the several forms and functions of sentence elements and to attempt to state the precise applicabilities of each to problems of writing, or to start with the major problems of grammatical writing as these show in the "surface spots" at which sentences most often "go wrong" in the hands of the inept and to work back from these points to the particular grammatical knowledge that is useful in solving them. I suspect that both approaches are needed, each complementing the other; in working out this huge problem, the teacher will probably find herself playing one against the other.

The finished analysis is not likely to be very tidy; it is likely to be sprawling and gigantic, if not monstrous. It is likely to be filled with repetitious detail. It may not be perfectly complete or perfectly accurate. In the midst of her undertaking, surrounded by sheets of paper bearing portions of uncertain outlines, the teacher may sometimes fear that she is caught in a messy bad dream. She may very likely find herself wishing that she had never started, and she is almost certain to despair of ever finishing. But in the end, if she persists, she will emerge from her experience much wiser about the teaching of grammar than before. She will have a healthier respect for grammatical knowledge than before. In place of what may have been a growing uneasiness about it in the pit of her stomach — "What if, after all, the educationists and the linguisticists *were* right, and there *was* no really honest value in the study of grammar?" — she will have gained an insight into the indispensability of grammatical knowledge for solving certain problems that occur in writing.

Her study will probably make instant, drastic differences in her method of /227/ teaching grammar. She will probably want fewer workbook sentences in which students endlessly underline elements without knowing why. She will certainly not spend weeks getting students to underline subjects and verbs without making sure they understand, every step of the way, that one of the very greatest reasons for being able to identify subjects and verbs is that when we write or speak we have to make these agree in number. She will probably want to replace most of her old drill sentences with others in which it is possible actually to demonstrate to students the usefulness of the knowledge that they are being made to acquire: for example, she may want to eliminate drill on objects of prepositions in sentences like "Give it to *John*," in which there is no immediately demonstrable reason for recognizing the object of the preposition, since it is a noun, and to do all or most of her teaching of objects of prepositions through sentences like "Give it to *him*," in which there *is* demonstrable reason for recognizing them. She may no longer be content with having students underline gerund phrases in the usual workbook sentences in which it is impossible to demonstrate that a knowledge of gerund phrases has any earthly use; she may want sentences in which gerund phrases are involved in a problem of parallelism, in a problem of punctuation, and in a pronoun which "possesses" the gerund. These are random samples only: she will unquestionably want to reconsider her means of teaching every element.

If the student needs more than merely to "know" grammar in order to make use of his knowledge in his practice of writing, clearly it is even more important that the teacher who directs his learning be prepared not only with knowledge of grammar but with knowledge of the specific uses of grammar: to make that point has been the main purpose of my discussion here. If my notion of the usefulness of grammar looks small and mean beside the grand conception advertised by the nineteenth-century grammarian whom I quoted earlier — a conception which sets grammar second only to religion as a proper influence on young lives — perhaps teachers can believe more honestly in my claim than in his, and if their methods are devised to implement the lesser purpose for which I have argued, grammar may be made to do more good in more immediate and obvious ways than it has been doing hitherto in our time. If it can be made just to help students write more grammatically, I, at least, will settle for that objective. /228/

52. JAMES SLEDD

Who Is Subverting Whom? — Grammar or Gramarye?

The following selection should be read in connection with the preceding one by Bertrand Evans; it is from James Sledd, "Grammar or Gramarye?" *The English Journal*, 49 (1960), 293-303.

Grammarians are accustomed to humiliation. It is their heritage. They are dry, they are plodding, they are mere: at their funerals no one weeps. Grammarians make, indeed, no loud pretenses to high status. In the great chain of academic being there is a place for regents, a place for coaches; there are places for vice-chancellors, publicity directors, maintenance engineers, careerists, critics, hollow men, and teachers of teaching; there is even a place, though an inferior one, for grammarians. That station, with its duties, is all they claim.

Yet not even a grammarian should always be meek. Like a rat-catcher, a word-catcher has worked hard to master the secrets of his trade. Not every man can catch a rat or define a noun, and if the grammarian has abandoned all foolish hopes of a place at the top of the totem pole, at its foot he wants no amateurs shouldering him aside. He is a professional. It took a long time to separate grammar from astrology and magic, grammar from gramarye; and an honest grammarian cannot keep his peace when he sees knowledge and superstition once again confused.

That confusion was exemplified in an article in the *Educational Forum* for January 1959. Under the title "Grammar and Writing," Professor Bertrand Evans offered a defense of English grammar which was more damaging to that ancient study than any attack he could have made. And Evans' theory, it now appears, is not the solitary aberration of an isolated individual. He is a leading member of a small group within the College English Association of the San Francisco Bay Area which has recently sold a remarkable bill of goods to that association and to the English departments /293/ of California's colleges and universities. According to this group, education is by its very nature dictatorial, and there is just one way by which the high school teacher of English can achieve "real integration" in his "total work with language" (James J. Lynch in *College English*, November 1959). Evans' statement may therefore be taken as a kind of semi-official appendix to the communal manifesto of California's educators for unfreedom; and since these would-be dictators have gained powerful support for their doctrine, the potential influence of the statements makes it imperative that it receive an answer which its quality would not deserve.

The theory is not abstruse; it may be stated in a single paragraph. In order to help students avoid "grammatical blunders" in their writing, Evans would have teachers in the schools teach the old-fashioned grammar of the schoolroom to its full extent. He would have them teach students "to recognize every element of the sentence and to distinguish it from every other," but he would have them insist always on practical applications. Each bit of grammar should be presented as a means to correct a specific blunder. The result would be that students would write more grammatically.

So simple an argument is appealing to a simple conservative mind, particularly when it is accompanied by stern denunciation of a mythical academic monster branded "linguisticist": the old-fashioned teacher can go on teaching the same old grammar in much the same old way, and she can take pride in her ignorance of everything that she might otherwise feel bound to learn. But the argument really will not do. Evans has systematically begged every important question which his subject raises, and his fourteen pages succeed only in revealing him (if I, too, may rudely neologize) as a sophisticist. The meekest grammarian must defend himself against such defenders.

Linguists and Standards

Let me begin my self-defense by disposing of Evans' mythical monster, the "linguisticist." To amateurs, the monster must be fearsome, since he is characterized, at his introduction, as a professional, one of "the professional linguists." Moreover, he is eager, he is convinced he is right, he believes in "disinterested, scientific observation," and he strongly attacks "the old-fashioned study and teaching of old-fashioned grammar." So far, the description applies quite well to a substantial number of the most learned, able, and responsible professional students of the English language in the United States and elsewhere in the English-speaking world; many grammarians might be proud to answer "present" to such a roll-call. The description even remains accurate (though no longer a matter of pride) when Evans complains of the jargon of the linguist. Technical terms are necessary, and inevitably distressing to those who cannot understand them; but the linguist has certainly gone too far, as his colleague the literary critic has gone too far, in coining awkward phrases: the linguist has only the advantage that *morphophonemics* has a precise meaning, while *dissociation of sensibility* is vague. When Evans goes on, however, to repeat the old slander that linguists have no standards, he has turned his back on reality. A livelier respect for fact would have /294/ constrained him to say rather that many linguists have standards different from his own and that this difference places upon each party the responsibility for a reasoned statement of its views.

Both Evans' own standards and the precise nature of his charges against the linguist should therefore be examined. In general, he says, the linguist takes "the view that there are merely 'different' levels of usage — *not* 'good' and 'bad,' 'acceptable' and 'unacceptable' "; as a particular example of this heresy, Evans alleges an assertion by "some linguisticists" that distinctions among the case forms of English pronouns "do not matter." He rounds out his indictment with the surprising assertion that linguists believe there is "no really honest value in the study of grammar."

A harsh answer to these charges could very easily be given: the man who makes them is either culpably ignorant or maliciously deceitful. I have studied linguistics off and on for twenty years and have taught it for ten, my acquaintance with linguists studying English is wide and representative, and I do not know a single linguist who holds the views which Evans attributes to his unnamed bogeyman. Is it not suspicious that the bogey *is* unnamed? Linguists would not write grammars if they saw no value in the study of grammar; they would not describe pronominal forms and their uses if such distinctions did not matter; and they do not believe that in language anything goes. To say they do is to say that which is not.

What charitable explanation might be given of the origin of Evans' gross misstatement? I can think of only one. It is true that many linguists see no way of judging the system that is a language, or an element in that system, as in itself either good or bad. I say *bucket* where my Northern friends say *pail;* I pronounce *mother* without a final *r;* I use *you all* as a plural pronoun; and in humorous conversation I revert to my childhood ways and *I used to could.* I have no means of deciding, in absolute terms, whether these expressions, simply as expressions, are good, bad, or indifferent. They are just some possible ways of saying certain things in one variety of English, and I would not waste time in fruitless discussion of the absolute merits or demerits of postvocalic *r.* This is not to say, however (and here may be the source of Evans' blunder), that the *use* of these expressions may not be good or bad. On the contrary, outside the South I deliberately drop a number of my Southernisms, since they are not always understood; and I distinguish sharply between those forms which are appropriate for serious exposition and those which are fit for laughing talk. The writer's or speaker's task is precisely such choice among the available resources of his language, and he will best accomplish that task if he defines good English as that English which will best do, in the given situation, what a good man would want his English to do there. To deny the necessity of linguistic choice, or to make that choice mechanically, is the part of fools.

What Evans' own standards are is not quite clear. He wants students to write "grammatically"; he wants stenographers to write in a way that will please their employers; but he never clarifies his measure of grammaticality. /295/ One may be pardoned for suspecting that to write "grammatically" is to follow the unreasoned and perhaps unreasonable rules of some outmoded handbook, to surrender one more small part of that responsibility for rational choice which makes us human. I say this for two reasons. First, Evans himself perpetrates bad sentences with obvious pride in their "correctness": "The full analysis requires an elaborate representation that should be tedious and unsightly here"; "I have never asked these questions but that I have not been assured . . ."; etc. [Quoted from a portion of Evans' article omitted here.] No one could write so badly without working at it. Second, Evans condemns as grossly ungrammatical at least one sentence which outstanding grammarians for the past seventy years (Curme, Jespersen,

Kruisinga, Palmer, Sweet, Zandvoort) would have accepted: "A pile of books *were* on the table." Often and properly, a collective noun may stand as the subject of a plural verb, especially when it is followed by a prepositional phrase whose object is plural; but presumably, for Evans, the chastity of the singular subject is violated if it lies down with a plural verb. Such scrupulosity is vice, not virtue, and the linguist who derides it is no enemy of standards but of *low* standards. Man, if not reasonable, at least is capable of reason.

Purpose of Grammatical Instruction

So much for the "linguisticist" and his sins against the dark light of schoolroom grammar. It is confessed that his jargon is ugly, but nothing else is proved against him by Bertrand Evans. It must also be admitted, however, that the insulting attack on linguists is only one part, and that a minor part, of Evans' argument. His principal contentions must still be examined. As I have said, they are very simple. The teacher in the schools, he argues, should reconsider her teaching of grammar (I do not know why Evans' teacher is always feminine). The main purpose of her teaching should be to improve her students' writing, to make them write "grammatically"; and to this end she should teach only those elements of grammar whose relevance to specific writing problems she is prepared to demonstrate. At best, "she should set about a patient, thorough, systematic, and painfully honest examination of each separate grammatical element in the entire battery of parts, forms, and functions. Her question of each should be the same: 'What problems that occur in writing will knowledge of this one element solve or help to solve?' Her purpose should not be to find excuses to 'justify' the teaching of all the elements listed in the index of a textbook on grammar; on the contrary, her purpose should be to seek the indispensables of grammatical knowledge." Yet this "painfully honest examination," it happily turns out, will not place the teacher in the ranks of the technologically unemployed. She has only to think of the problem of parallelism, and her job is saved. "The possibilities of 'going wrong' in solving the problem of parallelism are as numerous as the elements of the sentence, and the only sure way of enabling students always to solve the problem correctly is to teach them to recognize every element of the sentence and to distinguish it from every other." The upshot is that the teacher may begin — or continue — to /296/ teach the whole of some traditional description of English but that she will teach her traditional description with just one narrow purpose in her mind: "to help students write more grammatically." She will present all the familiar paraphernalia of rules and analysis, but she will make her teaching effective by reminding the students that the purpose of the analysis is to enable them to follow the rules.

To avoid misunderstanding, let me say at once that I am as eager as anyone else to improve the quality of student writing, that I share the conviction that more grammar than is usually taught today should be taught not only in our schools but in our colleges and universities, that I believe the teaching of more grammar *might* make for better writing, and that at the very least I do not see how a teacher can discuss a student's use of language without some set of grammatical terms and distinctions. To these aims and propositions, so stated, I believe I can guarantee the assent of a large number of Evans' despised linguisticists. But when all these things have been said, the big questions are still unanswered. What is the purpose of grammatical instruction? Is it only the narrowly practical purpose of enabling students, in their writing, to conform to some arbitrary set of rules, or is it also the humanistic purpose of advancing the study of man as proper to mankind? There are many grammars of English, not just one; which grammar, or which grammars, should prospective teachers learn, and which grammar or grammars should practicing teachers teach? It is quite impossible, in one year, or two, or twelve, to teach students to "recognize every element of the sentence and to distinguish it from every other" (Jespersen's grammar runs to seven volumes, and Curme's to some thousand pages); since there is no such thing as a "complete grammar" of English and since we have neither time nor teachers to teach one if there were, how shall we determine and how shall we teach the real "indispensables of grammatical knowledge"? What real evidence is there that extensive and intensive grammatical training is a necessary condition of better writing or even the best means to achieve it? These are some of the questions which articles on "grammar and writing" should attempt to answer, but Evans' only answer is to pretend the questions are not there.

I can finish my self-defense, and turn it to some constructive purpose, by offering my own answers. Admittedly they are incomplete, and they may be worse than incomplete: they may be wrong; at least they are answers, my best efforts to face some of the issues which Evans has evaded; and argument, not bluster, will be needed to refute them. *Linguisticist* is only a sophisticistic word.

In stating the purpose of grammatical instruction, I shall take, with some circumspection, the highest ground I can. The teaching of writing is a mysterious process. For myself, I often doubt that I can teach a student to write better; I sometimes hope that I can help him learn. But my uncertainty does not extend to the teaching of English grammar. I know I can teach grammar, and I teach it for a good reason. The proper study of mankind *is* man, and there is nothing so basic to our humanity as our language. That, and the fact that people will pay me for innocently /297/ amusing myself by studying and teaching English, are my reasons for doing what I do. I could not prove, and I know no one else who could prove, that the vast sums devoted to the teaching of English grammar pay off in terms of better student writing. I know expert linguists who write badly, and I know students who write well but could no more define an auxiliary verb than they could lay an egg. Maybe the best way to make a student write well is to get him born into an educated family where good books are cherished, but neither linguisticist nor classroom teacher can play God. Given a man, they *can* help him to understand what he is and what makes him so, and if in the process they may help him to become a writing man, they should be thankful for an added blessing.

What Grammar to Teach

My statement of the reason for grammatical instruction thus differs widely from Evans' statement, and my choice of grammars to be taught differs yet more widely. Evans writes as if English grammar were a fixed and unalterable body of knowledge which he controls but is willing to share with the uninitiate. In his questioning of teachers, he says, he has "sampled the full range of descriptive grammar" and has been assured "that most English teachers do in fact cover the forms and functions of all but the most obscure elements." What can he mean? The claim seems preposterous on the face of it, and concrete evidence seems to refute it. "The full range" of a fairly traditional descriptive grammar of English includes phonology, morphology, and syntax. An adequate phonological statement involves, among other things, the distinction between phonetics and phonemics and the description of the English vowels, consonants, stresses, pitches, and junctures. The morphology can be separated from the syntax only by some kind of definition of the word as distinct from larger forms, and within the morphology one must deal with such thorny questions as the distinctions between inflection and derivation and between the native and foreign derivational patterns. In the syntax, one must establish a number of "parts of speech," some of them large open classes like nouns, others small closed classes like prepositions; one must somehow relate these syntactic classes to morphological classes defined in terms of inflection or derivation or both; one must establish a concept of modification or expansion and state the positions of modifiers of noun heads and verb heads; one must describe the favorite sentence patterns for statements, questions, and requests; etc., etc. The barest outline of such a description is a lesson in modesty, and the rash amateur who lightheartedly begins to fill up the outline is quickly overwhelmed. To cite a few problems quite at random: How can one change the meaning of an alternative question by changing its intonation? How shall a compound word be defined? What subclasses of nouns and of determiners need be recognized, and how are they related? What distinguishes the *keep* of *to keep going* from the *be* of *to be going?* What subclasses of adverbs are necessary in order to deal with such various forms as *then, there, thus, not, never, very, so?* What order-classes are represented in a monstrous phrase like *not quite all those same two extremely bad ar-* /298/ *chitects' own first four very markedly inferior brown French stone houses over there on Main Street that are being remodeled?* Are all the objects of *take* alike in the old sentence *He took umbrage, alarm, his hat, his departure, no notice of his pursuers, a pistol from his pocket, and finally his life?* Why will every reader happily accept Bertrand Evans' phrase *the very best kind of answer* although many will reject as un-English or effeminate his similar phrase *the very most pragmatic sense?* It is easy to talk about "sampling the full range of descriptive grammar" or about "teaching students to recognize every element of the sentence"; I have yet to meet the teacher who has accomplished such wonderful things.

Some of the teachers, indeed, whom I have met in the last twenty years could not even understand a statement of the problems of describing English. I know one noisy teacher of teachers who conducts advanced classes in English grammar yet boasts that he knows no linguistics and means to learn none, and when I examine teacher candidates on traditional grammatical problems I get astounding answers. . . .

I can only conclude, after analyzing Evans' claim and some of the evidence bearing on it, that his concept of descriptive grammar must be pathetically limited. I suppose he hopes and thinks that most teachers know and teach some traditional handbook of grammar and that such a handbook treats "the forms and functions" of all the important grammatical elements in English. I can share neither these hopes nor these beliefs. The biggest of all the questions which Evans begs is just the question of which grammar shall be taught, and until it is answered the plea for grammar in the /299/ schools is almost meaningless. Does grammar mean Lowth in Victorian dress or Jespersen's *Essentials* or Paul Roberts' *Patterns?* My own experience with traditional grammars (they are not all alike) was so bad that I should not like to repeat it or to inflict it on other students. Precisely because the conventional handbooks that I know are mainly intended for the correction of errors in student writing, they overemphasize those elements of English structure where usage is divided, and underemphasize those elements where divided usage is impossible for native speakers and writers. For instance, some good speakers and writers may prefer Evans' *was* in "A pile of books *was* on the table," others "A pile of books *were* on the table"; some use the forms interchangeably; others use now one and now the other, with a difference in meaning. Certainly a student should be aware of the different practices and should have some principles to guide his own choices in such matters: presumably to use *were* in a paper for Bertrand Evans would be bad English, since it would produce an unfortunate effect. But who would build a teaching program on a foundation of pedantry? If Evans would, then indeed he is upholding standards, but bad standards. By way of contrast to the disagreement about the pile of books, one might point out that no native speaker or writer would have the least hesitation in determining the proper order of the six forms *dogs, big, the, black, ten, same;* but the statement of that order is a much more important part of a descriptive grammar than the rules for the agreement of verbs with collective nouns. It is much more important, that is, if the purpose of grammatical instruction is primarily the humanistic purpose of inculcating a conscious and organized knowledge of the mother tongue. Naturally the technologist who is concerned to make secretaries acceptable to tired executives will pass a contrary judgment, for he is neither humanist nor scientist but a social manipulator. . . . /300/

53. JOHN S. KENYON

The Meaning of Colloquial

The following summary is the conclusion of John S. Kenyon, "Cultural Levels and Functional Varieties of English," *College English*, 10 (1948), 31-36.

The term *colloquial* cannot properly designate a substantial cultural level of English. It designates a functional variety — that used chiefly in conversation — and it itself says nothing as to its cultural level, though this discussion, and the dictionary definitions, are chiefly concerned with cultivated colloquial, a functional variety of standard English. When writers of such standing as those I have mentioned slip into expressions that imply lower cultural status of colloquial English, it is not surprising that colloquialisms should not be represented as standard American speech. But the context of the statement indicated that its author was using *colloquialism* in the sense of 'localism.' I could hardly believe how freqeunt this gross error is, until I heard it from a well-known American broadcaster.

The best dictionaries, at least in their definitions, give no warrant for the various misuses of *colloquial, colloquially, colloquialism, colloquiality*. I urge the reader to study carefully the definitions in the *Oxford English Dictionary* with its many apt examples from standard writers, and in *Webster's New International Dictionary, Second Edition*, with its quotations from George Lyman Kittredge. Kittredge's views on the standing of colloquial English are well known. It is said that somebody once asked him about the meaning of the label "Colloq." in dictionaries. He is reported to have replied, "I myself speak 'colloke' and often write it." I cannot verify the story, but it sounds authentic.

It seems to me inevitable that the frequent grouping of so-called "levels" such as "Literary, Colloquial, Illiterate," and the like, will lead the reader to suppose that just as Illiterate is culturally below Colloquial, so Colloquial is culturally below Literary. While I can scarcely hope that my humble remonstrance will reform all future writing on "levels of English," I believe that writers who confuse the meaning of the term *level* must accept some part of the responsibility for the popular misunderstanding of the true status of colloquial English; for I cannot avoid the belief that the popular idea of colloquial English as something to be looked down upon with disfavor is due in part to the failure of writers on the subject to distinguish between *cultural levels of English* and *functional varieties of standard English*. /36/

54.

Modern Dialect and Cant; Word Lists

The following selection is from Herbert L. Hughes, "A Word-list from Louisiana," *Publications of the American Dialect Society*, No. 15 (1951), 69-71.

appreciate: *v.t.* To enjoy. "I want to *appreciate* myself at the party."

bat 'em in: *phr.* To move very fast. "That fellow in the yellow car is *battin' 'em in.*"

believe: *v.t.* To exhibit traits of character or the sort of person one is. "What does he *believe?*"

bow up to (baʊ): *phr.* To assert oneself. "*Bow up to* him. Don't let him bluff you."

build: *v.t.* Of clothing; to make. "Mother *is building* a dress."

chawed up: *adj.* Embarrassed; confused. "Mary was all *chawed up* because she didn't have no new dress."

cope: *v.t.* Kept; past tense of *keep.*

cowbuncle: *n.* A carbuncle; a boil.

dog my cats: *interj.* A mild oath, such as "doggone it."

down on: *phr.* To dislike anyone. "He is *down on* Tom." /69/

ficety (faɪstɪ): *adj.* Frisky, affected. "That girl is too *ficety* to suit me."

foxy: *adj.* Frisky.

forewritten: *adj.* The above, the above-written.

frog-strangler: *n.* A flood rain.

gaited: *adj.* Tired, weary. "I've worked so hard today I am *gaited.*"

get with it: *phr.* To attempt to hurry up someone. "You know what you are to do, so *get with it.*"

g'land (g'lant): *v.t.* To woo or court or "wait on" a girl. Said of a man who "dates" a girl. "I see that Harry has ben *g'lanting* Louise lately."

go to do: *phr.* To intend. "I am sorry I hit your nose. I did not *go to do* it."

hair: *adj.* Expert. "He is *hair* on catching fish."

hoped I had: *cl.* For "I wish I had."

lay out with the dry cattle: *phr.* To stay out late at night; said of young single men. "You *have been laying out with the dry cattle,* haven't you, boys?"

limb, on a low: *phr.* In poor health or spirits. "I've been *on a low limb* lately."

nainy (nenɪ): *adj.* None.

ooze up to: *phr.* To make advances to a girl. "He just *oozed up to* Sally any old time."

paddyrole: *n.* Police; a patrol. "Run, nigger, run; the *paddyrole* will catch you." — Old Song.

pass by for: *phr.* To call for someone. "Just *pass by for* me and I'll be ready to go."

pet: *n.* A small sore or boil. "I have a *pet* on my chin."

pull: *v.t.* To straighten. "Negroes have their hair *pulled.*"

rib: *v.t.* To ask a favor. "Bill has a new car. Let's *rib* him for a ride."

snide: *adj.* Aristocratic, proud. Said of the wealthy or "big shots." "The people on north Main street are pretty *snide.*"

stay at: *v.i.* To reside. "Elwin *is staying at* the Laney Hotel."

take out: *v.i.* To quit work. Said of plow hands or other laborers. "My hands *took out* at half past eleven today."

wamperjawed: *adj.* Crooked, twisted. "That box looks kinder *wamperjawed* to me." /70/

The following is from David W. Maurer, "The Argot of the Racetrack," *Publications of the American Dialect Society*, No. 16 (1951), 3-70.

hand ride: *v.t.* 1. To lift a horse's head at the beginning of his stride, thereby lengthening his stride. Such tactics call for strong hands and expert timing. 2. To ride a horse "by hand" rather than by spurs and whip; bringing out the best in a horse by crossing the reins up on his neck and literally riding him by hand. An experienced jockey who has perfected this technique can do remarkable things with a horse in the stretch without recourse to punishment. . . . /34/

heavy headed horse: *n.* A horse which is difficult to hand ride, especially one with strong neck muscles or one that runs with its head low. See *hand ride*, . . .

heavy shoes: *n.* Heavy training plates for a horse's hooves.

heavy steel trailer: *n.* A type of racehorse shoe. . . .

heavy track: *n.* A track which has passed beyond the sloppy stage; the worst possible track condition for most horses. . . .

herder: *n.* 1. A jockey who maneuvers his horse is front of the pack. 2. A horse that crosses to the inside at the start, forcing the pack to bunch.

hide: *n.* See *bang tail.* [Entry under bang tail, p. 12, reads: "A racehorse, originating from the obsolete practice of tail-bobbing. Also *beagle, beetle, dog, gee gee, goat, hide, jobbie, lob, meat eater, oat burner, oat muncher, oil burner, plater, plodder, stiff,* and many other terms not included."]

high on a horse: *phr.* To back a horse heavily; to be confident that he will run in the money. . . .

high school horse: *n.* A horse which often wins when the price is high on him; the implication is that he is able to read the approximate odds on the board.

hold him back: *phr.* To prevent a horse from winning. Usually this is done when the owner is waiting until the odds are better.

hold him in: *phr.* 1. Of a jockey: to force his horse to run behind at the beginning of a race so as to reserve speed for the finish. See *Garrison finish*. Of a jockey: to force his horse to stay near the inside rail at the turns. . . . /35/ [The entry under *Garrison finish*, p. 30, reads, "A fast driving finish named after a jockey who was famed for holding his horse back until the last minute and then letting him out to win, thus preserving all his strength for the final drive. 2. Any close finish."]

55.   NORMAN D. HINTON

Language of Jazz Musicians: Glossary

Among the most interesting of contemporary special vocabularies is that of jazz musicians, some examples of which are listed in the following glossary from Norman D. Hinton, "The Language of Jazz Musicians," *Publications of the American Dialect Society*, No. 30 (1958), 38-48. Abbreviations in the glossary are for the designations "old fashioned," "recent" (within the last eight or nine years), "older" (before the bop period), "common," and "occasional."

This glossary makes no pretensions to completeness. It is simply a list of words used by jazz musicians in their everyday speech with equals. Some of the etymologies may seem fanciful; these men do not worry themselves about the origins of their words. I believe, however, that the etymologies are correct, and I can vouch for the use of the words.

Apple, the, *n.* New York City. Derivation obscure, but dates from the late '30's, when New York was the center of jazz in America. Occ., o.f.

ax, *n.* Any of the solo reed or (less commonly) brass instruments. Orig. a saxophone. Fr. fancied resemblance in shape plus the abbr. *sax*. Occ.

bad, *adj.* & *adv.* Good. However, at times, it may mean "bad," and the listener must determine meaning fr. context, tone of voice, facial expression, etc. Occ., older.

beat, *n.* & *v.* (*p.p.*) (1) As *n.*, musical rhythm, "the beat" (fr. *beat time*). (2) As *v.*, tired, exhausted (preservation of old p.p.; comm. us- /43/ age particularly adopted by jazzmen. *OED* citations from 1830 on). Both comm. (Actually 1 & 2 *altogether* separate terms.)

blow, *v.* Orig. to play a wind instrument. Generalized to performing upon any instrument (thus, one can "blow guitar"). Probably fr. fact that all solo instruments in traditional jazz are wind instr. Comm.

box, *n.* A piano (undoubtedly fr. shape of upright piano and spinet, usually found in jazz night clubs). Comm., rec.

bread, *n.* Money. A double pun — (1) "dough," (2) bread, the necessity. Occ., rec. (Invented by Dizzy Gillespie.)

bring down, *v.* To make one feel low. See *put down.* Occ., rec. in this sense. (Obs. — to make one feel good — out of use since the '30's.)

bug, *v.* To bother, especially to get one in such a state that he cannot play well. Extended to mean getting annoyed at anything.

cat, *n.* Orig., one who was "hep." Obs. in this sense; now, any person. (Thus, a musician can now speak of a "square cat" — a contradiction in terms in the '30's.) Comm.

changes, *n.* The chords for whatever melody is being used as a basis for improvisation. Comm., older.

chase, *n.* A 32-bar chorus divided so that two men (usually) take alternate four- or eight-bar sections. Occ.

chick, *n.* A girl. Not specifically a jazzman's term, but very common.

clinker, *n.* A missed note, or other error in playing. Largely replaced by *goof* (q.v.). Occ., o.f.

combo, *n.* A small band, a "combination" of from three to ten pieces. Basic, comm.

come on, *v.* Strictly, to begin a chorus, but almost always used with an approving or disparaging phrase — "Man, you came on like the end." Older (one of the oldest words still in use), comm.

cool, *n. & adj.* Agreeing with the generally received aesthetic standards of the modern jazzman. Basic, comm.

corny, *adj.* Non-jazz, extremely commercial music. Origin doubtful, but since it is often expanded to "corn-fed" and "corn-ball" (or may actually have been a clipped form of one of these words), I think it once meant "country" music: polkas, square dance music, etc. Comm., basic, older.

crazy, *adj.* Like *cool* and almost interchangeable with it. Fr. description of bop as "crazy music." Has to do most basically with harmonies used in playing, but generalized like *cool.* Comm., basic. /44/

cut, *v.i. & t.* (1) (intr.) To leave. Usually to "cut out" (cut = leave out, leave). "Man, nothin's happening, let's cut out!" Occ., rec. (2) (tr.) To play an instrument better than another musician, or to produce better jazz than another. Also said of whole orchestras. The winner in a musical contest is said to have "cut" the other. Comm., older (even pre-'30's).

cute, *adv.* (Playing) in an ingenious, intriguing manner. Occ., in an amusing manner. Occ., rec.

dig, *v.* To understand and agree with: not limited to music alone. (Perhaps fr. a sense of "getting to the bottom" of things.) Comm., older, basic.

end, the, *n.* The best, the most pleasing. Like *most* (q.v.), but better. *Absolute end, n.,* intensified form. Comm., basic.

eyes, *n.* An expression denoting approval. "I've got eyes for that" means "I like it." Extreme approval is expressed by the qualifying words "big" or "bulging." Invented by Lester Young. Comm.

fake, *v.* To improvise. Sometimes also means to pretend to know a tune, but usually has meaning above. Comm., older.

flip, *v.* To approve wildly. Orig. to "flip one's wig" (akin to "blow one's top," but never denotes anger for jazzmen). Usually indicates response to another's solo. Comm.

funky, *n.* An old word, orig. meaning earthy or odorous. Now, a piece or player imbued with the basic spirit of the blues, although in a modern idiom. Occ. (The *original* meaning is obs.; the newer meaning is rec.)

gas, *v. & n.* To please, or, as noun, spoken of a situation which pleases — "It's a gas!" gasser, *n.* Something which pleases extremely. Origin unknown, at least to me. Occ.

go, *expl.* Really a fan's word, to express excitement at a particularly "swingin'" solo. Often used derisively, sometimes approvingly, by musicians. (The fan's full phrase is "Go, man, go!") Occ.

gone, *adj.* In the ultimate state of happiness, usually inspired by music. *Real gone, adj.,* intensified form. (Perhaps from dope addiction, but it is equally possible that the borrowing went the other way.) Occ., older. the gonest, *n. The most, etc.*

goof, *n. & v.* A mistake in playing, and to make that mistake. Extended to all errors. Comm., basic.

greatest, *n.* See *most, end.* Comm. /45/

head arrangement. A musical arrangement which is not written down and never has been, but is known by all the members of the ensemble. Usually the product of group effort. Comm.

hep, *v.* See *hip.* O.f.

hip, *v.* "In the know," or one of the elite. Occ. means simply to understand. Comm., basic.

horn, *n.* Any musical instrument, but especially (and originally *only*) the wind instruments. (See *blow* for a similar extension.) Comm.

jazz, *n.* Nonsense, completely worthless information or attitude. "Don't hand me that jazz" = "quit kidding." Comm., rec.

jive, *n.* Same as *jazz.* Occ., o.f.

lead, *n.* The top, or melody part in an arrangement: therefore, the melodic line. lead man, *n.* One who plays the "lead" in his section of the ensemble. Comm., basic.

least, the, *n.* Opposite of *the most.* Occ.

like, *interj.* Means little or nothing. Used to fill up gaps in the sentence. Comm., rec.

Man, *interj.* Used in direct address. Comm., basic.

Mickey, *adj.* "Corny," old-fashioned, "ricky-tick" music. Short for "Mickey Mouse music," but usually abbreviated. Originally referred to the sort of pseudo-jazz that accompanied animated cartoons. Sometimes referred to as "businessman's bounce." Occ., o.f.

moldy fig. One who likes or plays "traditional" jazz exclusively. Comm. (Refers mostly to fans, not musicians.) Often abbr. *fig.*

most, *n.* The best, the most in line with jazzmen's aesthetic standards; see *cool, crazy.* Comm.

number, *n.* A tune. Perhaps from the fact that bands give their arrangements numbers rather than names, to make filing easier. Comm., basic.

pad, *n.* A bed. Extended to mean bedroom, or even apartment. Occ.

put down, *v.* To belittle, criticize adversely, another man's playing. Perhaps related to *bring down* (q.v.). Occ., rec.

ride-out, *n.* The final chorus of an arrangement. (In dixieland, the clarinet "rides" above the ensemble.) Occ., o.f.

riff, *n.* & *v.* A short musical phrase (usually 4 or 8 bars), whose chords, repeated the length of a chorus, become the basis for improvisation. To play a riff. Origin doubtful. Comm., older, basic. /46/

see, *v.* To read music. Occ., rec.

session, *n.* Shortened form of obs. *jam session;* an informal gathering of musicians playing for their own amusement. Occ., older.

square, *n.* Not in accordance with the jazzman's aesthetic standards. Probably comes from steady 1-2-3-4 rhythm without variation. Many musicians, while saying the word, will make a motion similar to the band director's indication for 4/4 time — the hand moves in a square for the four beats. Comm., older, basic.

swing, *v.* To play well in all senses, technically and otherwise, but especially to have the basic feel for jazz rhythms. A man can play well harmonically and rhythmically, but he will not swing without a feel for "the beat." Comm., older, basic.

swingin', *adj.* Actually, the participle of *swing,* but used for many nonmusical things. The highest term of approval. May be applied to anything a jazzman likes, or any person. (Although the verb is of long standing, the use of the participle is relatively recent.) Comm., basic.

too much, *adj.* Same as *the most, the greatest.* Comm.

way out, *adj.* Departing greatly from the norm; especially said of unusual (or unusually good) treatment of melody or harmony; now of anything that seems especially good — though still used in the original sense too. Occ., older (found on records in the '30's).

wig, *v.* To think; to play extremely intellectual music. Occ., rec.

wild, *adj.* Same as *crazy, cool.* Occ.

worst, the, *n.* Opposite of *most, end,* etc. See *least.* Occ.

write, *v.* To make an arrangement. writer, *n.* Arranger. Comm.

you know, *inter. phr.* Means nothing (see *like*), but used as a question at the end of a statement. /47/

56. STUART ROBERTSON

It Is I, It Is Me

One of the most frequently disputed questions of English usage is the subject of the following passage from Stuart Robertson, *The Development of Modern English*, revised by Frederic G. Cassidy (Englewood Cliffs, N. J., 1954).

. . . Let us observe the history of the phrase that is now either *It is I* or *It is me* (usually in the form *It's me*) — a differentiation to which we shall return. In old English, the corresponding idiom (like the Modern German "Ich bin es" except for the order) was *Ic hit eom.* In Middle English, this alters to *Hit am I;* but it proves impossible, eventually, to maintain *I* as Subject when it follows the Verb, for the Verb seems to belong to the word preceding it — that is, the word in "Subject position." The Verb is therefore altered to *is*, and the phrase becomes *It is I.* But in this new phrase, as early as the sixteenth century, *me* is competing with *I*, obviously because the Object form is expected in the position following the predicate. The point that we would emphasize here is the thorough-going way in which the syntax of the phrase has been shifted.

The rival phrases that have just been alluded to form one of the battle-grounds in current discussions of "correct English." It seems worth while, therefore, to go somewhat more deeply into the implications of divided usage in *It is I (me)* and kindred phrases. First, just how is usage divided? There can be no doubt that the frequent condemnation of *It is me* as "ungrammatical" is absurd in view of the actual facts of the case. Even a better-informed view, such as that of Professor Curme [18] — "the predicate pronoun should be in the nominative and in choice language usually is, but in popular and loose colloquial speech there has persisted . . . a tendency to employ here the accusative of personal pronouns as the predicate complement after the copula" — overstates the case for *It is I (he, they,* and so on). It seems more accurate to distinguish, not between "choice" and "loose colloquial" speaking or writing, but between more and less formal occasions for both speaking and writing. Here, as always, the spoken language sets the pace; and in the spoken language, especially of the less formal (but not necessarily the "loose") type, only *It is me* is in natural, idiomatic use. [19] Writers

[18] *Syntax,* Boston (Heath), 1931 [Vol. III of Curme and Kurath, *A Grammar of the English Language*], page 41.

[19] This includes, of course, the spoken language realistically rendered in literature. See the many examples, chiefly from contemporary British practice, of the literary use of "It is me" cited by G. H. McKnight in *Modern English in the Making*, New York (Appleton) 1928, pages 532 and 533.

employing dialog in the printed page sometimes hesitate to use this phrase, out of deference to a tradition that condemns it; or if they use it, they do so either apologetically or defiantly, in such a way as /293/ to indicate that they recognize that they are violating a generally accepted grammatical rule. The quotations which follow illustrate these attitudes.

> His eye was so dim,
> So wasted each limb,
> That, heedless of grammar, they all cried *That's Him.*
> (Ingoldsby, *The Jackdaw of Rheims*) [20]

"That's *him* [italics]," said Ann Veronica, in sound idiomatic English. (H. G. Wells, *Ann Veronica*, Chap. VI) [21]

"He may be any of the passengers who sit with me at table."

"He may be me," said Father Brown, with cheerful contempt for grammar. (G. K. Chesterton, *The Incredulity of Father Brown*, p. 145)

The true status of the two expressions actually seems such that *It is I* rather than *It is me* is now on the defensive. This reversal of attitudes that have obtained in the past is illustrated in a characterization of *It is I* as "suburban English." [22] The implication is of course that the phrase is over-correct, artificial, and stilted. A contemporary American novelist, Robert Nathan, touches this distinction very neatly when he has a character, speaking naturally, say, ". . . it's me she's married to, not him, and I won't stand for it" (*There Is Another Heaven*,[23] p. 124); a little later (p. 128), the same character, in a formal, almost a bombastic tone, gives utterance to these words: "It was I with whom she lay in bed; it was I she consoled." The difference in the atmosphere of the two speeches, be it noted further, is suggested also by the stilted "with whom she lay in bed," as contrasted with the colloquial "she's married to." Contemporary English, in other words, discriminates between *It is I* and *It's me* by employing the one phrase in formal, literary style and the other in informal, colloquial expression; and it may well be argued that the language is the richer for the distinction.

How can we account for the drift to *It's me?* The chief reason is, quite certainly, that the sense of case has become so weakened in Modern English, and the force of word order so dominant, that the latter overrides the former. Furthermore, the objectives of the per- /294/ sonal pronouns have been gaining at the expense of the nominatives, which tend more and more to be used only when they are immediately followed by a predicate. We feel, in some obscure fashion, that the objectives are both the more normal and the more emphatic words. The classical illustration of this emphatic use of *me* is in the passage from Shelley's *Ode to the West Wind,*

[20] Boston (Houghton Mifflin), 1919.

[21] Quoted by McKnight, *supra.*

[22] By William Ellery Leonard in "Concerning the Leonard Study," *American Speech*, Vol. VIII, No. 3 (October 1933), p. 58. See also Wallace Rice's article "Who's There? — Me," *ibid.*, pages 58-63.

[23] New York (Bobbs-Merrill), 1929.

> Be thou, spirit fierce,
> My spirit! Be thou me, impetuous one!

This is indeed the triumph of poetry over grammar. And how feeble, how grotesque would *I* have been! Another illustration of the greater force of the objective pronominal forms is thus cited by Havelock Ellis: [24] "The Frenchman, when asked who is there, does not reply, 'Je!' But the would-be purist in English is supposed to be reduced to replying, 'I!' Royal Cleopatra asks the Messenger: 'Is she as tall as me?' The would-be purist no doubt transmutes this as he reads into: 'Is she as tall as I?' We need not envy him." Shakespeare of course lived before the establishment of the "rules" by grammarians of the eighteenth and nineteenth centuries; the freer syntax that his works display — where not "corrected" in modern school editions — often anticipates developments that are only now being given academic sanction. As to the "corrections," the First Folio reading of a familiar passage in *Macbeth* is

> lay on, Macduff,
> And damned be him that first cries, "Hold, enough!"

It's me is undoubtedly in a stronger position than *It's them, It's him,* or *It's her.* Many of us, without being able to give very sound reasons for doing so, would agree with Professor Weekley's practice: "Personally I say 'That's me,' hesitate at 'That's him (*or* her)' . . ." [25] *Current English Usage* likewise lists *It is me* as "established," but finds that *If it had been us* . . . is on the border-line, while *I'll swear that was him, I suppose that's him, I am older than /295/ him,* and *It seems to be them* are all "disputable." [26] Nevertheless, good contemporary speech and writing often employs the objective forms of other pronouns than the first personal (singular) in analogous ways. A former Prime Minister, Ramsay MacDonald, used these words in his speech opening the naval conference of January, 1930: "The way of Great Britain is on the sea, for it is a small island . . . Its defence and its highroad have been the sea . . . Our navy is no mere superfluity to us: it *is* us." Though the *us* was widely criticized, would not *we* have been both flat and absurd? Aldous Huxley uses a similar *us* in this phrase: "A movement whose consummation is *us* [italicized] must be progressive." [27]

A few years ago,[28] Winston Churchill, visiting the United States and making a special recording of his voice, addressed the workers of the Soundscriber Corporation factory as follows, "This is me, Winston Churchill,

[24] *The Dance of Life*, Boston (Houghton Mifflin), 1929, Chapter IV. The whole argument for the "psychological necessity" of ". . . a double use of 'me' in English" is worthy of consideration.

[25] *Cruelty to Words*, New York (Dutton), 1931, p. 79. And of course others who condone "It is me" will condemn "It's him" or "It's them" more emphatically. C. T. Onions (*An Advanced English Syntax*, London (Kegan Paul, Trench, Trubner), 4th ed., 1927, p. 34) takes this stand: the one is "used even by educated speakers," the others are "generally regarded as vulgar or dialectal."

[26] It should, perhaps, be added that "You are older than me" is also "disputable." . . .

[27] "One God or Many," *Harper's*, No. 952 (September 1929), p. 401.

[28] Cf. *Time*, Vol. 47, No. 13 (April 1, 1946), p. 66.

speaking himself to you. . . ." This seemingly innocent remark created a considerable flutter for some weeks. An editor of the *New York Times* commented with obvious disapproval that this was a "remarkable sentence," and when *Time* reported the incident, letters from readers berated the Prime Minister for his "bad grammar," the most extreme of all seeing in such language a general reflection of the decay of the British Empire, and a consequent threat to the United States if we ally ourselves to Britain. Least stirred by the incident were those who were best informed, the professors at Columbia University whom *Time* consulted. They agreed unanimously that Churchill was using perfectly acceptable informal English.

In the light of usages like these, it would seem that the traditional textbook statements on the use of the personal pronouns need revision. (Some revisions there have been, it is true, but by no means enough.) What is really happening to pronouns in general has been summed up thus by Jespersen: "On the whole, the natural tendency in English has been towards a state in which the nominative of pronouns is used only where it is clearly the subject, and where this is shown by close proximity to (generally position immediately before) /296/ a verb, while the objective is used everywhere else." [29] This tendency, more marked as we have shown it to be in colloquial than in literary style, has as yet won but little recognition in the grammars and handbooks of writing and in our schools. When it is admitted that there is a drift in current English that takes more account of the position of pronouns in the sentence than of the traditional meaning of their case forms, the drift is all too likely to be noted as resulting in "incorrect" syntax. . . . /297/

57. ALBERT H. MARCKWARDT AND FRED G. WALCOTT

Facts About Usage

> In the late 1920's Professor Sterling A. Leonard attempted to survey opinions about English usage by questioning a group of 229 "judges" about the appropriateness of 230 expressions "of whose standing there might be some question." The judges included linguistic specialists, editors, authors, businessmen, and teachers, and they were asked to classify the expressions — according to their observation of what usage is, not what it ought to be — as formally correct, acceptable for informal conversation, or illiterate. Some years later, Professors Albert H. Marckwardt and Fred G. Walcott, *Facts about Current English Usage* (New York, 1938), reconsidered Leonard's findings, partly to ascertain the reliability of such information as that provided by the judges.

[29] *Essentials of English Grammar*, New York (Holt), 1933, p. 136. This statement applies better to personal pronouns than it does to relatives and interrogatives.

They compared Leonard's opinions with the facts of usage recorded, mainly as recorded in such extensive dictionaries as the *Oxford English Dictionary*. They found that the opinions of the group of judges were not always consistent with recorded data. For example, of Leonard's "disputable" usages, the 121 items about which the judges could not agree, they found sixty-three recorded as belonging to literary usage and forty-three recorded as colloquial. The Leonard study, now rare, is reprinted in the Marckwardt-Walcott volume. In the passages below, selected items are brought together from both the Leonard and the Marckwardt-Walcott sections of the book; this reorganization accounts for the apparent irregularity in the pagination. To avoid confusion, abbreviations have been expanded without notification.

They invited my friends and *myself*.   (91: established)

One linguist says: "It occurs to me that I am willing to make an exception of Omar's 'Myself when young,' because of its sheer charm. But I would shut it out everywhere else save for emphasis."

The editors rated this highest, linguists second, business men last. 62 per cent of all the judges approved it, thus placing it low among established usages. This would suggest that, while perhaps people /71/ who are especially careful of their speech would avoid this expression, nevertheless it would hardly be safe to condemn it as incorrect. /72/

New English Dictionary, third usage, 1205-1856, "in an enumeration, when not occupying first place . . . commonly preferred to me." /38/

It is *me*.   (73: established)

This is a construction which has been made the subject of newspaper editorials beyond counting; and every purist who has felt the sanctity of grammatical English threatened has gone forth to do battle against those who would permit the verb *to be* thus to be followed by an objective pronoun. The fact seems to be that schematic grammar has little to do with usage.

Many of the comments recorded were flatly contradictory. Here are some of them:

"Unpardonable grammar."

"Incorrect — *bad* — but used often by discriminating people who rebel against the formalism of 'it is I.' I prefer 'it is I.' "

"Many purists approve it, but it seems not to have gained respectability."

"This expression is used so commonly that, among certain classes of people, it is considered quite correct. Others, however, never use it."

"Emerging into [literary English]." /77/

"*I* sounds quite mad in certain cases: e.g., point to a photo: 'Which is I?' ! ! ! 'Oh, I see, that's I' ! ! ! Absolutely non-English, hang all the grammarians on earth."

This expression is listed here among the established usages on the basis of the way the linguists voted — only three of twenty-eight condemning it as illiterate. If all the judges' estimates had been taken into consideration, without weighting on the basis of the greater expertness of one group as against another, this sentence would have been placed among the disputable usages — only the business men, of whom eighteen condemned and five approved, would place it among expressions clearly illiterate. One hundred thirty judges altogether approved this; ninety-one condemned. This can hardly constitute sufficient reason for taking time to teach "it is I" in school. As a matter of fact, both forms are at present avoided by careful speakers. /78/

New English Dictionary, sixth usage, 1591-1758, Shakespeare and Goldsmith cited. New International Dictionary (1934), "colloquial and dialect." /35/

I am older than *him*.   (181: disputable)

Linguists say:

"Personally I generally say 'I am older than *he is*.' But never 'older than *he*.' Sometimes, no doubt, 'older than him.'"

"We all know that these expressions are taboo. Also that most people (educated or otherwise) use them to the exclusion of the alternate form." . . .

Speech teachers and business men place this expression at the bottom of the list of expressions on the first ballot; the other groups of judges place it higher, but there is a decided majority against its inclusion among allowable expressions. /79/

New English Dictionary, third usage, 1759-1764, but the predicative *him* citations range from 1381-1840. "Common in colloquial language from the end of the sixteenth century." /48/

If John *had of* come, I needn't have.   (224: illiterate)

This expression has no standing in current usage. /116/

Do it *like* he tells you.   (186: disputable)

A British linguist says: "I rate this as good colloquial English — good literary English where clause-verb is suppressed; e.g. 'Roared like a bull.' Where *like* means definitely 'in the very manner' I should rather say, 'Do it the way he tells you,' or even 'Do it how he tells you,' though I feel the latter (not the former) to be doubtful — children's English.

"When I use *like* it is rather, so to speak, apposition. 'I ran away of course, like you did' (the same thing which you did).

"When the clause-verb is omitted, everyone uses *like* (even the blithering purists — not realizing, with their usual ignorance, what they are doing). 'He drank like a fish.' ('He drank as a fish' would mean, of course, when he was a fish.) So that one is forced, of course, to say, 'He danced like a child' since 'as a child' would mean 'when he was.' Meredith says, 'threading it with color, like yewberries the yew.'" . . .

The various groups of judges agreed rather closely on this expression.

Their vote gives little support to those who consider use of *like* permissible. /114/

New English Dictionary, 1530-1886, "Now generally condemned as vulgar or slovenly, *though examples may be found in many recent writers of standing.*" Citations include Shakespeare, Southey, and William Morris. /48/

58. ELLSWORTH BARNARD

A Teacher Declines to Turn the Other Cheek

The following exchange appeared in two issues of *The Reporter*, 15 (December 27, 1956); 16 (January 24, 1957). The first comment is from a regular column entitled *"The Reporter's Notes"*; the second part is the teacher's reply.

FOR WHO THE BELL TOLLS

It is sad enough when standards slip; it is horrifying when they are officially encouraged to slip. We refer to some remarks made by an English Professor at Bowdoin College, who said among other things that "People should not worry so much about their grammar," and that it made no difference whether a person used "who" when he should have said "whom," or "will" when "shall" was correct. "Any large group of people sets its own standards," he said.

If ever there were incitement to mob rule, this is it.

LETTER TO THE EDITOR

I am the "English professor at Bowdoin College" (actually "Visiting Lecturer") so vehemently reprehended in *"The Reporter's* Notes" in your December 27 issue, and I hope you will let me be heard in my own defense. This kind of comment one expects, and can laugh at, in the Chicago *Tribune*. But in *The Reporter*, which I have been praising for years as the best magazine of news and opinions, it is not funny.

In the first place, your quarrel is only partly with me. It ought to be mainly with the ethical standards of newspaper editors. The original story was based on a telephone interview between me and a United Press reporter following a talk that I gave to a group of English teachers; and although I never saw it, I judge that, though oversimplified and misleading in some passages, it was an honest story. But the editors of the country's newspapers evidently had no scruples about cutting and revising it to suit their own notions of what is "news." In particular, I have heard of but one version (I believe in the Providence *Journal*) that included the two most important paragraphs, which read as follows:

"Dr. Barnard said teachers should teach Johnny a few fundamental grammar rules — that is all. This will leave all concerned more time for more important matters.

"He said four points should be hammered into students in high schools. They are: sentences ('knowing the difference between a complete and an incomplete sentence'); making sure that subjects and verbs agree; direct, straightforward language instead of flowery poetic words; and organization of material."

You will agree that the omission of these paragraphs totally falsifies the point that I was trying to make. Perhaps you will also forgive me, as a mere English teacher who tries to teach his freshmen not to quote inaccurately or out of context, and to have respect for facts, for not anticipating that the nation's news editors and editorial writers would be quite so contemptuous of the truth.

There *is* a quarrel between us, however, even on the basis of the mangled versions of the story whose authenticity you did not bother to check. You seem not to have heard of certain principles accepted by all competent students of linguistic science. The first is that a living language is organic and ever-changing, that therefore usage is the only ultimate determinant of correctness, and that lexicographers and grammarians record and do not legislate. The second is that there are "levels of usage," generally held to be three: formal written English; the informal spoken English of educated people ("colloquial" English); and the normal spoken English of nonprofessional people (called, with no implied disparagement, "vulgate"). Language is like dress: The question is one of manners and not morals, of what is appropriate and not what is legal. "Ain't," for instance, has a long and honorable etymological pedigree, and it is a useful word, which I envy ordinary folk the right to use with propriety, as I cannot — simply because professional people do not use it.

But, further, many of the textbook "rules" bear no relation to actual practice, even on the level of formal English. The multifarious textbook distinctions between "shall" and "will" are cheerfully ignored by practically everybody — as any honest observer will have to agree — and no harm is done to anyone or to the language. As for "who" and "whom," even educated people get hopelessly confused. And so on through a lengthy list.

My appeal is simply to honesty and common sense — is simply that we do not force students to join us in the pretense that certain verbal expressions are taboo, although they and we meet these expressions every day of our lives in the most respectable newspapers and magazines and in the most highbrow radio and television programs. We can then concentrate on the *real* problems of communication — some of which I mentioned in the paragraph that most editors did not see fit to print.

59.   H. W. FOWLER

Modern Pronouncements on Usage

H. W. Fowler's *A Dictionary of Modern English Usage* has been, since its appearance in 1926, one of the most popular guides to usage in both England and America. The following excerpts, which concern problems considered in other selections in this book, are from a later edition (Oxford, 1937).

because.   After such openings as *The reason is, The reason why . . . is,* the clause containing the reason must not begin with *because,* but with *that. . . .*

dare.   . . . 1. *Dare* as 3rd pers. sing. pres. indic. is the idiomatic form instead of *dares* when the infinitive depending on it either has no *to* or is understood; this occurs chiefly, but not only, in interrogative & negative sentences. Thus *dares,* though sometimes used in mistaken striving after correctness, would be contrary to idiom in *Dare he do it?; He dare not! — Yes, he dare; He dare do anything; No-one dare oppose him. . . .*

expect.   Exception is often taken to the sense *suppose, be inclined to think, consider probable.* This extension of meaning is, however, so natural that it seems needless PURISM to resist it. *E.* by itself is used as short for *e. to find, e. that it will turn out that,* that is all: *— I e. he will be in time; I e. he is there by this time; I e. he was there; I e. you have all heard all this before; Mr——'s study is scholarly & thorough, & has had a good deal of expansion, we e., since it took the —— Essay Prize,* i.e., if the facts ever happen to come to our knowledge, we shall be surprised if they are not to that effect. The OED remarks that the idiom is 'now rare in literary use'; that is owing to the dead set that has been made at it; but it is so firmly established in colloquial use that if, as is suggested above, there is no sound objection to it, the period of exile is not likely to be long.

me   is technically wrong in *It wasn't me* &c: but, the phrase being of its very nature colloquial, such a lapse is of no importance; & this is perhaps the only temptation to use *me* instead of *I.* There is more danger of using *I* for *me,* especially when *& me* is required after another noun or pronoun that has taken responsibility for the grammar & has not a separate objective case; *between you & I, let you & I try,* are not uncommon. . . .

whence, whither.   The value of these subordinates of *where* for lucidity & conciseness seems so obvious that no-one who appreciates those qualities can see such help being discarded without a pang of regret. Why is it that substitutes apparently so clumsy as *where . . . from, & where . . . to,* can be preferred? It is surely because the genius of the language actually likes the PREPOSITION AT END that wiseacres have conspired to discourage, & thinks 'Where are you coming to?' more quickly comprehensible in moments of threatened collision than 'Whither are you coming?'. We who incline to weep over *whence* & *whither* must console ourselves by reflecting that in the less literal or secondary senses the words are still with us for a time; 'Whither are we tending?', & 'Whence comes it that . . . ?', are as yet safe against *where . . . to* & *where . . . from;* & the poets may be trusted to provide our old friends with a dignified retirement in which they may even exercise all their ancient rights. But we shall do well to shun all attempts at restoration, & in particular to eschew the notion (see FORMAL WORDS) that the writer's duty is to translate the *where . . . from* or *where . . . to* of speech into *whence* & *whither* in print. On the other hand, let us not be ultra-modernists & assume that *whence* & *whither*, even in their primary senses, are dead & buried; that must be the view of the journalist who writes: *The Irregulars have been compelled to withdraw their line from Clonmel,* to where *it is believed they transferred their headquarters when they had to flee from Limerick.* If *whither* was too antiquated, the alternative was 'to which place', but occasions arise now & then, as in this sentence, to which *whence* & *whither* are, even for the practical purposes of plain speech, more appropriate than any equivalent.

write. . . . 1. *W.* with personal object. In *I will write you the result,* there are two objects, (direct object) *the result,* & (indirect object) *you.* In literary English, an indirect object is used after *write* only if there is also a direct object, but the direct object may be used without an indirect; that is, *I will write the result,* & *I will write you the result,* are idiomatic, but *I will write you soon,* or *about it,* is not; if a direct object is wanting, the person written to must be introduced by *to: I will write to you about it.* . . .

60. HUGH SYKES DAVIES

A Word to End a Sentence With

> The following discussion of an old schoolroom "rule" is a chapter of Hugh Sykes Davies, *Grammar Without Tears* (New York, 1953).

It is not surprising to find that the fuss about prepositions at the end of sentences was started by Dryden. Brought up on the grammatical principles of Mulcaster, Greaves, and Hewes, which based English usage on Latin, and himself addicted to the method of translating English into Latin when he wanted to find out what he was saying, it was natural enough that he should have made at least one outstanding contribution to the confusion of real English grammar.

Dryden had already spent some twelve years in the energetic pursuit of letters when he suddenly announced that the preposition at the end of a sen-ence was a 'fault': one which 'he had but lately observed in his own writings,' and which was very common in Ben Jonson. He might well have added that it was very common in the great masters of English contemporary with Ben Jonson. Shakespeare, for example, in *As You Like It,* feels no qualm in making a very courtly and polished gentleman say: 'I would have told you of good wrestling, which you have lost the sight of.' And Macbeth thus addresses Banquo's Ghost: 'Thou hast no speculation in those eyes Which thou dost glare with.' The Authorised Version, generally (and perhaps wrongly) thought to be a very good example of English, has at /114/ Genesis 28: 'for I will not leave thee, until I have done that which I have spoken to thee of.' And Lord Bacon has: 'Houses are built to live in, and not to look on.'

So far as 'Custom, the most certain Mistresse of language,' is concerned, there can be no doubt that the placing of the preposition at the end of a sentence was fully authorised. Dryden himself, in the earlier part of his career, had given it further authorisation of the same kind, by writing freely such phrases as 'the age I live in.' But having come to his great decision, he resolutely changed his own custom for the future, and when he got the chance of re-editing his older writings, he amended them, so that the phrase just quoted became 'the age in which I live.'

Unfortunately, he never explicitly stated the principle which thus led him to interfere with the custom of the best English writers, and with his own earlier practice. But it is not difficult to see how he arrived at it. Whenever he wrote Latin to stabilise his English grammar, he would find the prepositions always removed from the end of the sentence. He could not conceivably have written 'aetas qua vivo in'; the Latin order was always 'aetas in qua vivo.' But to follow the example of Latin here was to ignore a great difference between Latin and English in their manner of connecting verbs and prepositions. In Latin, following the generally synthetic method of grammar, the prepositions tended to become prefixes, and to be fused with the verbs. For example, the preposition *in* was fused with the verbal root *pos* /115/ to make the word which we have in English as *impose*, meaning literally 'to put upon.' But when the English version is used, the preposition remains a separate word, and it follows the verb. The same is true of the nouns derived from these two verbs; the Latin noun is the synthetic 'imposter,' the English is the analytic phrase 'a person you are put upon by.'

It follows naturally from this difference in the handling and placing of the preposition that in English it very often comes after the verb, and may well work its way to the end of the sentence. The attempt to place it somewhere else can produce effects of great awkwardness, such as Dr. Johnson's 'wonders of which he proposed to solace himself with the contemplation.'

On the other hand, it must be admitted that sometimes the end preposition may produce, if not quite the same awkwardness, an impression of untidiness and weakness, as it does in these examples from Fielding:

> *Many stories of the lady, which he swore to the truth of.*
> *His Sophia, whom he now resolved never more to abandon the pursuit of.*
> *He expressed so much devotion to serve me, which at least I was not certain of the falsehood of.*

It would seem, therefore, that any simple grammatical rule for the placing of the preposition is liable to lead to trouble. It is wrong to say that it never ought to appear at the end of a sentence; but /116/ it would be just as wrong to say that it ought always to be placed there.

It may well be that no rule at all is needed, that the common linguistic instinct of the English is well able to look after placing prepositions, now, as it did before Dryden set the unhappy example of meddling with them in the Latin manner. But if a rule should be needed, it must be sought by means of a consideration of English grammar, and its special, non-Latin use of meaning and word-order. A rule of this kind might perhaps be derived from the fact that in the average English sentence, one of the positions of greatest emphasis is the ending. The reasons for this are not quite clear; perhaps the ending remains especially clear in the reader's mind because he has heard it more recently than the rest of the sentence; or it may be that the usual intonation of English speech, which affects the 'inner voice' of the reader, gives a kind of climax at the end of the sentence. But whatever the reason may be, the fact itself is clear enough. And it would suggest this much guidance for the placing of prepositions: when the meaning of the sentence demands that weight and emphasis should fall upon them, they are well placed at the end, but when the meaning demands no such weight, they are best placed elsewhere, in a less conspicuous position that befits their less emphatic role.

On this principle, all the examples just quoted from Fielding would be bad, because the prepositions are doing merely grammatical hack-work, and no important stress of meaning is intended to fall on them. /117/ On the other hand, the sentence quoted from Bacon is good: 'Houses are built to live in, and not to look on.' It is entirely in harmony with the meaning, and adds greatly to the force of the expression, to give the greatest emphasis to 'in' and 'on.' To a lesser extent, the same might be said of this sentence from Pope: 'In the most regular gardens, art can only reduce the beauties of nature to more regularity, and such a figure, which the common eye may better take in, and is therefore more entertained with.'

This principle, which no doubt has many limitations, would at any rate be superior to the dismal little piece of pedantry so unhappily introduced by Dryden. It would avoid latinisation and formalism, and it would serve the purpose of directing attention to what is really important in the use of English: to the attainment of an effective harmony between the meaning and the natural properties of emphasis in the different parts of the sentence. /118/

Subjects for Discussion

1. Which of Hartung's doctrines seems to you the best explanation of usage standards? Explain.

2. Analyze your college English text. With which of Hartung's doctrines does it seem to agree?

3. Try to assign the attitudes of each of the writers on usage in this section to one of the classifications given in Hartung's essay. In which class would you place most of the writers in Sections IV and VI?

4. What are the major points of disagreement between Evans and Sledd as indicated in their essays?

5. Mention other writers whose selections in this book seem to represent an attitude like that of Evans or that of Sledd.

6. Could any of the writers in this section be considered one of those whom Kenyon accuses of failing "to distinguish between *cultural levels of English* and *functional varieties of standard English?*" Give examples.

7. Compare the dialect and slang terms collected by Hughes, Maurer, and Hinton with the lists of Elizabethan slang. Are there similarities in specific terms, or in the subjects about which slang terms develop?

8. Compare Fowler's statements about specific usages with Webster's comments on the same problems a century earlier. Compare his comments on *me* with those of Robertson and Cassidy and the findings of the Leonard study.

Suggestions for Investigations, Reports, or Brief Papers

1. Attempt a study of a debatable locution, similar to the Robertson and Cassidy article, *It Is I, It Is Me.* Likely candidates might include the following: It tastes good *like* a cigarette should. Everybody took *their* hats. I didn't *calculate* to go. I'm right, *ain't* I? I shall go, *providing* the bus is not late. I *will* be there if I can. I hate *those* kind of people. My father was one of those men who *hates* to pay taxes. They invited my wife and *I*. He *don't* understand.

2. Make a list of slang or dialect terms you know which might make up a glossary like those of Hughes, Maurer, or Hinton. Write a paper discussing the list, making any observations you can about characteristics of the terms. You might, for example, collect teen-age terms, hot-rod terms, restaurant slang, or slang connected with athletics, fraternities, the classroom, or a summer job you have had.

3. Using a method like that of Leonard, as described by Marckwardt and Walcott, take a poll among friends and acquaintances on some disputed usages. You might begin with those used by Leonard and compare your results with his. Check various dictionaries and handbooks of usage to see if they agree or disagree with your findings. Then you might try other usages. Following are some of the other sentences Leonard used: None of them *are* here. You *had better* stop that foolishness. I *can't help but* eat it. It's *real* cold today. *Most* anybody can do that. He did *noble*. I must go and *lay* down. *Who* are you looking for?

4. See if you can find other comments in early discussions of grammar to supplement Davies' observations on the final preposition.

5. Attempt to write an analysis of your own views of usage and your own habits, mentioning agreements or disagreements with articles in this section.

SUGGESTIONS FOR LONGER PAPERS

The selections in this book provide source and secondary materials for a variety of documented studies concerning language. On the whole, subjects for these studies may be inferred from the suggestions at the end of each section, but by now the student should be prepared to embark on projects that can be either broader or more intensive than were appropriate earlier. For example, at the close of Section III, one question implied that the second-person personal pronoun forms were used to distinguish the ruler from his subjects, friends from acquaintances, formal conditions from informal, servants from the served, and the like. Evidence was provided from one scene from *King Lear*, but naturally the social situation was too complicated to be completely revealed in one scene. If the student cares to read more widely in Shakespeare's other plays, he can collect material for a much more elaborate study. He can also transfer his activities to the library; this peculiarity of the second-person pronoun has not gone unobserved; the student will find it mentioned in editions of Shakespeare, in articles on Shakespeare's usage, and in books on language.

In some similar way almost any of the subjects previously proposed can be clarified by enlarging the evidence the writer considers. On the other hand, a student may now wish to enlarge his subject. For example, several of the suggestions hinge upon the idea that language has changed, is changing, and probably always will change. We have observed that *horse-twitcher*, entered in Bailey, has vanished from modern dictionaries, while usages which Lowth called barbarous are now commonly accepted. The whole problem of language change is obviously big enough for a book and too big for a long paper, but the student might treat some aspect of it more broadly now than he could after he had studied only the various versions of the Sermon on the Mount. He might consider the history and growth of the idea that language changes. Many writers made egregious blunders, and many people still do, because they do not understand the nature of language, how resilient it is, how self-reliant it is, how it goes its own shifting way despite the wrath of purists or the drudgery of pedagogues. The student might try to write the history of our growing understanding of language, or a part of the history. Or he might observe into what absurdities intelligent and honest men have been brought because they supposed that they or anyone could control language, or that anybody could philosophize successfully about language without first studying it objectively.

The student who will look back through the queries and topics at the ends of main sections of the book should have little trouble finding a subject, but for convenience, some specific suggestions follow. The subjects can be developed into topics for papers based on the selections of the book or, for longer papers, can be amplified with library investigation.

The Nature and Philosophy of Language

What is the Nature of Language?
Obviously much of it rests on oral speech; what clearly does? What may not?

Speakers of a Language Make the Language
   What specific evidence can you bring forward that they do?
Are There Any Good Guesses as to the Origin of Language?
   Webster's guess was obviously bad; have there been good recent ones?
A Short History of the Belief that Language is Fluid
   See above.
A Short History of the Belief in the Oral Basis of Language
   How early can you discover the idea? Who had it? Who made amusing
   blunders because he did not have it?
Language and Society
   What evidence can you deduce that one influences the other?
Language and the Human Mind
   If men made language, how are mental processes reflected in language and lan-
   guage change?

Words, Their Etymologies and Histories

Biography of a Word
   By now you have elaborate materials for the study of *horse*, less extensive materials for *curmudgeon, curfew, host, horror, housewife, husband, wife,* and
   widow. You might use Laird's article on *tap* as a rough model, and add material
   from other dictionaries, for example from those cited in No. 27. Or take an
   entirely new word, preferably a common word like *ball, drive, road, plane*.
Descendants of Indo-European in Modern English
   For this you will need to consult a dictionary which includes Indo-European
   bases; the most readily available is *Webster's New World Dictionary of the
   American Language* (Cleveland and New York, 1953, with subsequent minor
   revisions.)

Some Changes in Vocabulary Since Chaucer's Day
   You can start with selections above; any library will contain an edition of
   Chaucer with glossary; and there is always the *NED*.
Some Changes in English Vocabulary Since the Eighteenth Century

Words, Their Forms and Meanings

Meaning and Meanings
   How do words get and change their meanings? For more evidence than that
   included above and for modern theory, look up *Semantics* in your library
   catalogue.
Some Changes in Meaning Since Old English
   Or Chaucer, or Johnson; you might notice that *horse-meat* appears in Bailey,
   but does not mean what *horse-meat* means now.
Forms of English Words
   You have extensive evidence in the selections in this book; if you need more,
   use the *NED*. There is good material in several books by H. C. Wyld, if you
   can cope with them.
The Proliferation of Usages
   Take several key words and study the way they have sprouted new usages in
   the last two centuries

Words and Dialects

Early Dialect Differences
Make a more careful study of differences between Chaucer and Mandeville, Malory and Henryson, Shakespeare and Awdeley.

Some Slang through the Ages
Try to trace some bodies of slang from early times to today — the slang of thieves, actors, musicians, or whomever.

A Dialect I Know
Perhaps you have lived among the Cajuns of Louisiana, the Amish in the Middle West, the Pennsylvania Germans (called Dutch) in Pennsylvania, the mountaineers of eastern Kentucky. Collect expressions that seem to you local and significant and study them in the light of what you can find in dictionaries.

College Slang of My Day
Study current slang expressions in relation to slang and dialect dictionaries; you may find that some slang expressions are older than you think.

Linguistic Geography: A Coming Study
Kurath's *Word Geography of the Eastern United States* is likely to be in your library.

Dictionaries

Johnson and His Successors
In what, if anything, did Johnson's successors outdo the master?

Bailey and Johnson
Johnson certainly developed the dictionary; did he discover anything not in Bailey?

An American Lexicographer
Webster defended his dictionary by saying that it was American as no British dictionary could be. Was it distinctive, and if so, how?

What Makes a Dictionary Modern?
Take two good modern desk dictionaries, say *Webster's New Collegiate* and *Webster's New World Dictionary of the American Language;* compare them in detail, entry by entry, picking sample entries, for selection of entries in word list, etymologies, meanings, phrases, spelling, pronunciation, and whatever else makes a good dictionary; then write a report of your findings.

Is There a Best Dictionary?
Compare different sorts of dictionaries — a pocket dictionary, a cheap reprint of an old dictionary, a desk dictionary, an "unabridged," the *Century,* the *NED* — and note the virtues and the limitations of each.

Grammar

The Role of Universal Grammar
Look up the questions on universal grammar, Section V, and enlarge upon them.

The Decline of Inflection in English
Notice inflection from Old English to Middle English to Modern English. What kinds of words have lost all inflections? Which have retained some? When did these changes take place?

Word Order in English

Obviously word order was important in late Old English and has become more so. Can you write some of the history of this change?

What is Grammar?

Does Sapir's concept differ from that of Goold Brown and Webster? Do other writers differ in their assumptions about grammar?

Development of Function Words

Compare selections from different periods to see what use is made of words that show relationships or grammatical functions but carry little meaning in the usual sense. Can you observe words in the language today which are developing new and different uses — *pretty, better, keep, go, dig,* and *man,* for example?

Usage

Usage: A Modern Conflict

What seem to be the differences among those who argue about usage? Can you resolve any of these differences?

A Disputed Point of Usage

Choose a disputed usage not discussed above, or discussed only briefly: *They invited Mary and I, He is stupider than me, Can I go now,* or something of the sort. Consult reference works, listen to your friends, to broadcasts, and notice written usage. Try to make a statement on the currency of the locution. In this connection, you might recall that Leonard's investigation was made more than a quarter of a century ago; a similar survey today would inevitably reflect some changes — for example in the use of the word *like,* or *good* as an adverb.

Consistency and Inconsistency in Usage

Make a list of disputed items in usage, or select a list from the glossary of your handbook of composition. Look up these locutions in a number of commonly used dictionaries. Do the dictionaries agree? Report your findings.

On Usage: A Reply

Consider one of the controversial writers in Section VII and endeavor to answer him, gleaning support wherever you can find it.

A Short History of the Development of the Usage Theory

Where do you first find expressions of views like those held by modern writers?

Mechanics

Introduction to a History of Spelling

Or punctuation, or capitalization, or italics, or whatever.

A Modest History of the Comma

Or the colon, or any other mark of punctuation, or any letter. Do not hesitate to cut this down: "A Modest History of the Comma before 1660" might be better.

Early Printers and Spelling

Or punctuation, or capitalization, or italics. Clearly, printers had much to do with standardizing mechanics. Can you find out what?

Eighteenth-Century Purists in Light of Their Own Rules

Leonard should provide a start; go on from there.

The Letter *E* since Mulcaster and Hodges
The Spellings *or* and *our* in Modern English
Pronunciation and Spelling
   Account for some of the consistencies or inconsistencies; for example, trace the doubling of consonants from Orm.